Pashtun Identity and Geopolitics in Southwest Asia

ANTHEM MIDDLE EAST STUDIES

The Anthem Middle East Studies series is committed to offering to our global audience the finest scholarship on the Middle East across the spectrum of academic disciplines. The twin goals of our rigorous editorial and production standards will be to bring original scholarship to the shelves and digital collections of academic libraries worldwide, and to cultivate accessible studies for university students and other sophisticated readers.

Series Editor
Camron Michael Amin – University of Michigan – Dearborn (USA)

Editorial Board
Benjamin Fortna – School of Oriental and African Studies, University of London (UK)
John Meloy – American University of Beirut (Lebanon)
Lisa Pollard – University of North Carolina Wilmington (USA)
Mark L. Stein – Muhlenberg College (USA)
Renée Worringer – University of Guelph (Canada)

Pashtun Identity and Geopolitics in Southwest Asia

Pakistan and Afghanistan since 9/11

Iftikhar H. Malik

Anthem Press
An imprint of Wimbledon Publishing Company
www.anthempress.com

This edition first published in UK and USA 2020
by ANTHEM PRESS
75–76 Blackfriars Road, London SE1 8HA, UK
or PO Box 9779, London SW19 7ZG, UK
and
244 Madison Ave #116, New York, NY 10016, USA

First published in the UK and USA by Anthem Press 2016

Copyright © Iftikhar H. Malik 2020

The moral right of the authors has been asserted.

All rights reserved. Without limiting the rights under copyright reserved above,
no part of this publication may be reproduced, stored or introduced into
a retrieval system, or transmitted, in any form or by any means
(electronic, mechanical, photocopying, recording or otherwise),
without the prior written permission of both the copyright
owner and the above publisher of this book.

British Library Cataloguing-in-Publication Data
A catalogue record for this book is available from the British Library.

Library of Congress Cataloging-in-Publication Data
Library of Congress Control Number: 2020930705

ISBN-13: 978-1-78527-245-5 (Pbk)
ISBN-10: 1-78527-245-4 (Pbk)

This title is also available as an e-book.

CONTENTS

Preface vii
Acronyms xi
Glossary xiii
Maps xv

Introduction 1
Chapter One   Gandhara Lands: Wrestling with Pashtun Identity and History 13
Chapter Two   Imperial Hubris: The Afghan Taliban in Ascendance 33
Chapter Three   Masculinities in Conflict: Western Pedagogy and the Return of the Afghan Taliban 53
Chapter Four   Understanding Pakistan: Geopolitical Legacies and Perspectives on Violence 67
Chapter Five   Understanding Civic Sentiments and Movements in Pakistan: Stalemated Cycle, or a Way Forward? 83
Chapter Six   The United States and Pakistan: Friends or Foes! 103
Chapter Seven   The European Union and Southwest Asia: Perceptions, Policies and Permutations 115
Conclusion: Pashtun Troubled Lands, Uncertain Southwest Asia or a New Beginning! 133

Notes 151
Bibliography 195
Index 205

PREFACE

Momentous and painful developments in both Afghanistan and Pakistan, and especially in their Pashtun regions, over the past two decades make it pertinent to analyse their respective and often conflictive quest for a consensus-based identity within the parameters of ethnic and religious pluralism. While the Pashtuns on both sides of the Durand Line – seen through the Orientalist or neo-Orientalist prisms – have been in the throes of these vital historical, ideological and geopolitical events, studies have often tended to focus only on the high politics of the two Southwest Asian states, the North Atlantic Treaty Organization (NATO) and the Afghan Taliban. Other than a pronounced and no less grievous reality of various forms of violence, these countries and especially their Pashtun regions are hastily caricatured as the epicentre of world terror and an exclusive and inherently militant political Islam. In the process, the securitization of scholarly investigation ends up overshadowing the historical and sociological aspects of life in the Gandhara lands, or upper Indus Valley. Ironically, it may appear convenient to hastily lump a historical (Gandhara) region like Southwest Asia – or western territories of the Indus Valley – only as an area of perpetual conflicts, porous borders, volatile ethnicity and a militant Islamism, and even its reconstruction as the romanticized graveyard of the old and new empires is not too unfamiliar. These factors may operate as significant determinants, but one needs to go beyond them. While recapping history, sociological hypotheses and security analysis, this volume seeks out more recent and ongoing thematic issues such as state formation, civil society clusters, multiple forms and postulations of violence and postulations from the outside. Southwest Asia, especially after the Western invasion of 2001, has encapsulated varying but no less problematic relations with NATO, the European Union (EU) and regional neighbours, along with intermittent tensions between Kabul and Islamabad, further complicated and influenced by ground realities, grass-roots defiance and various forms of competitive *modernist* and *traditional* trajectories.

Whereas since the withdrawal of most NATO and International Security Assistance Force (ISAF) troops from Afghanistan in 2014 politicians and strategists have talked of 'minimal deterrence' and 'zero option', Afghans and Pakistanis are faced with fresher challenges and opportunities with varying regional and global ramifications. With the new political dispensation already ensconced in Islamabad and Pakistani generals settling for a less obtrusive role, the Kabul regime is cautiously eager towards building bridges across deeper ethnic and ideological chasms despite apparent hesitation, ambivalence and uncertainty. However, both these countries still need to move towards substantive regionalization and consensual politics, and the hitherto traditions of distrust, scapegoating and dependence on external support have yet to give way to pragmatic and systemic alternatives. Mutual accusations and mistrust, or falling prey to a new great game between India and Pakistan (and possibly involving China, Iran and Central Asian Republics), can only exacerbate the ongoing human predicament on all sides, as is sadly being experienced in Iraq, Syria, Libya and Somalia. Both Afghanistan and Pakistan have been the casualties of multiple forms of militarist enterprise and, without succumbing to a debilitating victimhood or seeking scapegoats in each other's state structures, they can move towards more cohesive and gradualist consensus without falling for any ethnic discretion in the sense of taking pluralism aboard instead of forming a government by selecting some ethnic groups and ignoring others. While Pakistan needs to augur a fresher and co-optive approach towards Afghanistan's various ethno-regional particularities, Kabul is equally required to reciprocate in similar terms, while India, China and Iran can certainly follow a 'hands-off' policy towards trans-Indus communities. If it acts more responsibly and in a collective spirit, Afghanistan in the post-2015 era can still engender a long-awaited phase of regional peace, as it may also bleakly fall victim to increased militancy in the name of religion, vendetta and ethnicity in which numerous factions might accentuate their jockeying for political power. In that case, Pakistan and, for that matter, India will be gravely impacted from the fallout, which could further aggravate their respective discretionary interventionism. In other words, the next few years are crucial for this heart of Asia and that is where civil societies as well as the respective political elite can exhibit a greater sense of responsibility and regional ethos instead of pushing South Asia into another abysmal phase of moroseness, violence and instability. As has been the case so far, insurgency, militancy, midnight raids and drone warfare have rendered the Pashtun regions on both sides of the Durand Line into a simmering cauldron, and here instead humane imperatives deserve fresher dynamics auguring a new era of Pak-Afghan interdependence. Or, conversely, their free fall into a new chaos could also mean unbridled and extensive violence at various levels. In the same vein, increased Indo-Pakistani discord can lead all the three states to a bleeding balkanization with the horrid spectre of a new nuclear showdown.

My sincere thanks to a number of individuals and institutions who come from a wide variety of disciplines and regions and who are too numerous to be acknowledged in a paragraph, but whose words and time have duly benefitted this sociopolitical commentary. My colleagues and students at Bath Spa University kept me going with their queries and nods, while the family as always stood in good stead as I tended to disappear for extended spells at the Old Bodleian, Oriental Institute, Wolfson and the British Library. I am thankful to James Hollifield, Yunas Samad, Pritam Singh, Meena Dhanda, Farzana Shaikh, Ian Talbot, Gurharpal Singh, Alan Marshall, Elaine Chalus, Brian Griffin and several other colleagues whose works and words never allowed me to slow down. My deeper appreciation is due to Anthem Press and its team, especially Brian Stone, Kiran Bolla, Tej Sood and the production group for their persistent faith in my commitment to this research. In addition, I duly acknowledge the feedback and criticism from two anonymous reviewers, whose comments led me to newer angles and better presentation of this complex terrain. My Pakistani, Afghan, Iranian, Indian, Turkish, Arab, European and American friends – too numerous to be identified here – deserve my gratitude for keeping me on course. Of course, the situation on the ground remains quite fluid, but there is nothing wrong in talking about regional interdependence and the yearning for peace in the old Gandhara lands.

I dedicate this book to the dignity of countless innocent lives lost over the last several years with the hope that we will finally see light at the end of this bleak night.

Oxford
8 June 2016

ACRONYMS

AL	Awami League
ANP	Awami National Party
ASEAN	Association of Southeast Asian Nations
ASSP	Anjuman-i-Sipah-i-Sahabah, Pakistan
BJP	Bharatiya Janata Party
CTBT	Comprehensive Test Ban Treaty
ETIM	East Turkestan Islamic Movement (of Xinjiang)
EU	European Union
FATA	Federally Administered Tribal Agencies
GCC	Gulf Cooperation Council
HRCP	Human Rights Commission of Pakistan
HuM	Hizb-ul-Mujahideen
HuT	Hizbul Tehrir
INC	Indian National Congress
IS	Islamic State or ISIS (Islamic State of Iraq and Syria, often known as Daesh)
ISAF	International Security Assistance Force
ISI	Inter-Services Intelligence
JA	Jamaat-ul-Ahrar
JuA	Jundullah/Jundallah
JeD	Jamaat-e-Daawa
JeM	Jaysh-e-Muhammad
JI	Jamaat-i-Islami
JUI (F)	Jamiat-i-Ulama-i-Islam (Fazlur Rahman Group)
JUI (S)	Jamiat-i-Ulama-i-Islam (Sami-ul Haq Group)
JUP	Jamiat-i-Ulama-i-Pakistan
KP/KPK	Khyber Pakhtunkhwa (NWFP)
LFO	Legal Framework Order
LeJ	Lashkar-e-Jhangvi
LeT	Lashkar-e-Tayyaba
MI	Military Intelligence
ML	Muslim League (founded in 1906 in Dhaka, but now divided)
MMA	Muttahida Majlis-i-Amal
MNA	Member, Pakistan's National Assembly
MPA	Member, Provincial Assembly

MQM	Muhajir/Muttahida Qaumi Movement
NAP	National Awami Party (now ANP)
NATO	North Atlantic Treaty Organization
NGO	nongovernmental organization
NPT	Nuclear Non-Proliferation Treaty
NWFP	North-West Frontier Province
PATA	Provincially Administered Tribal Areas
PML(N)	Pakistan Muslim League's section led by Mian Nawaz Sharif.
PPP	Pakistan People's Party
PTI	Pakistan Tehrik-i-Insaaf
RSS	Rashtriya Swayamsevak Sangh
SAARC	South Asian Association for Regional Cooperation
SM	Sipah-i-Muhammad
TNFJ	Tehrik-i-Nifaz-i-Fiqah-i-Jaafria
TNSM	Tehrik-i-Nifaz-i-Shariat-i-Muhammadi
TTP	Tehrik-i-Taliban, Pakistan

GLOSSARY

Ahl-i-Kitab	People of the Book
Alim	a Muslim religious scholar
Ayatollah	preeminent Shia jurist/imam
Chador	a loose wraparound for women
Chardiwari	within four walls of the home
Da'awa/Dawah	Invitation to Islam
Fatwa	a religious decree
Fiqh/Fiqah	jurisprudence
Ijtiha'ad	innovation
Imam	a religious leader
Jihad	holy struggle
Jihadi	holy warrior
Khan	a respectable clan chief (often a landlord)
Madrasa/Madrassa	a Muslim seminary
Maulvi/Mullah	Muslim religious leader
Millet	a transnational community
Mofussil	outlying, rural areas
Mujahid	one who undertakes *Jihad*
Mujahideen	pl. of *Mujahid*
Muhajir	Muslim migrant
Muhajireen	pl. of *Muhajir*
Pir	Sufi saint
Salafiya	back-to-roots
Sharia/Shariat	Islamic law; jurisprudence
Shia/shi'ite	Follower of Caliph Ali, a doctrinal Muslim sect
Shura/Shoora	consultative body
Silsilah	a Sufi order
Sufi	a mystic
Sunni	lit. a follower of the Prophetic traditions, a majority doctrinal sect
Taleban/Taliban	pl. of *Taleb/Talib*: students
Ulama	Muslim religious scholars (pl. of *alim*)
Umma	transnational Muslimhood

MAPS

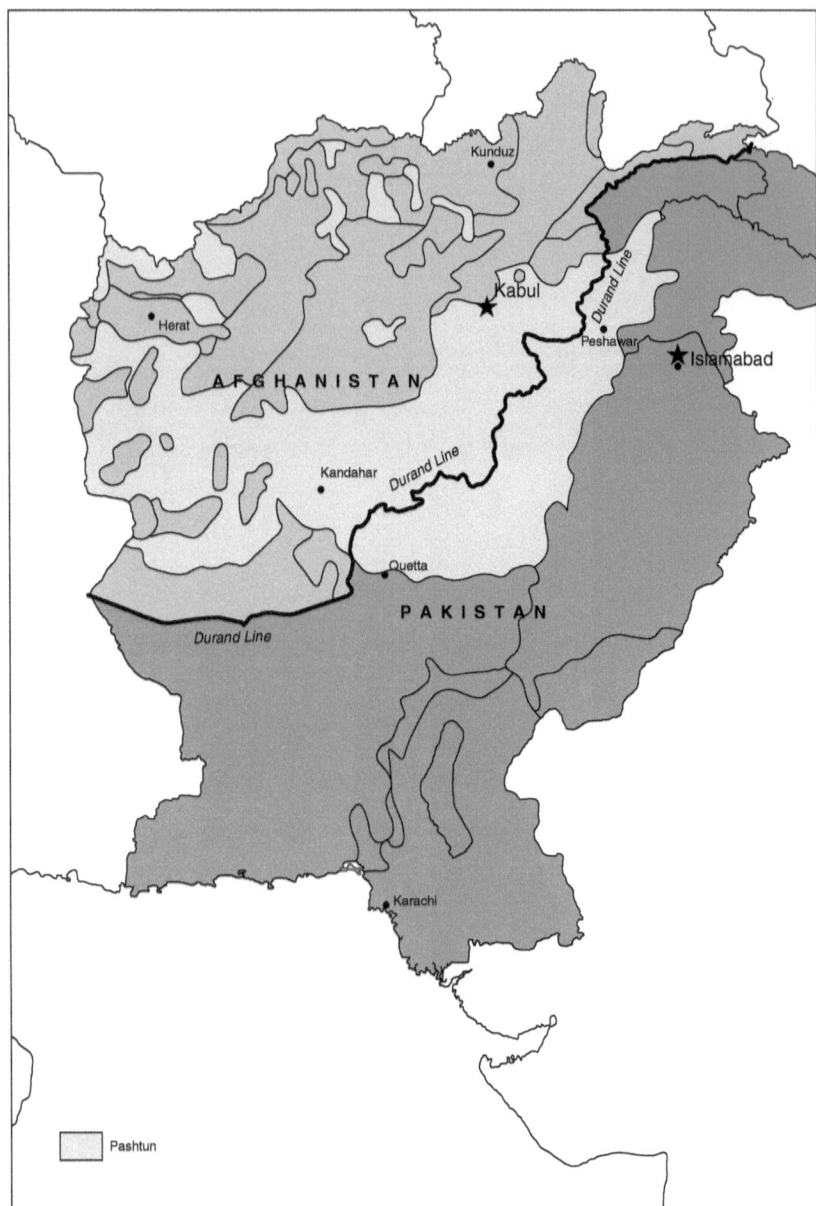

Map 1 Pashtuns in Afghanistan and Pakistan

This map shows the Pashtun concentration on both sides of Pak-Afghan borders; there is a sizeable presence of Pashtuns in Karachi, Islamabad, Quetta, Herat and Kunduz.

Source: http://education.nationalgeographic.co.uk/education/maps/afghanistan-and-pakistan-ethnic-groups/?ar_a=1

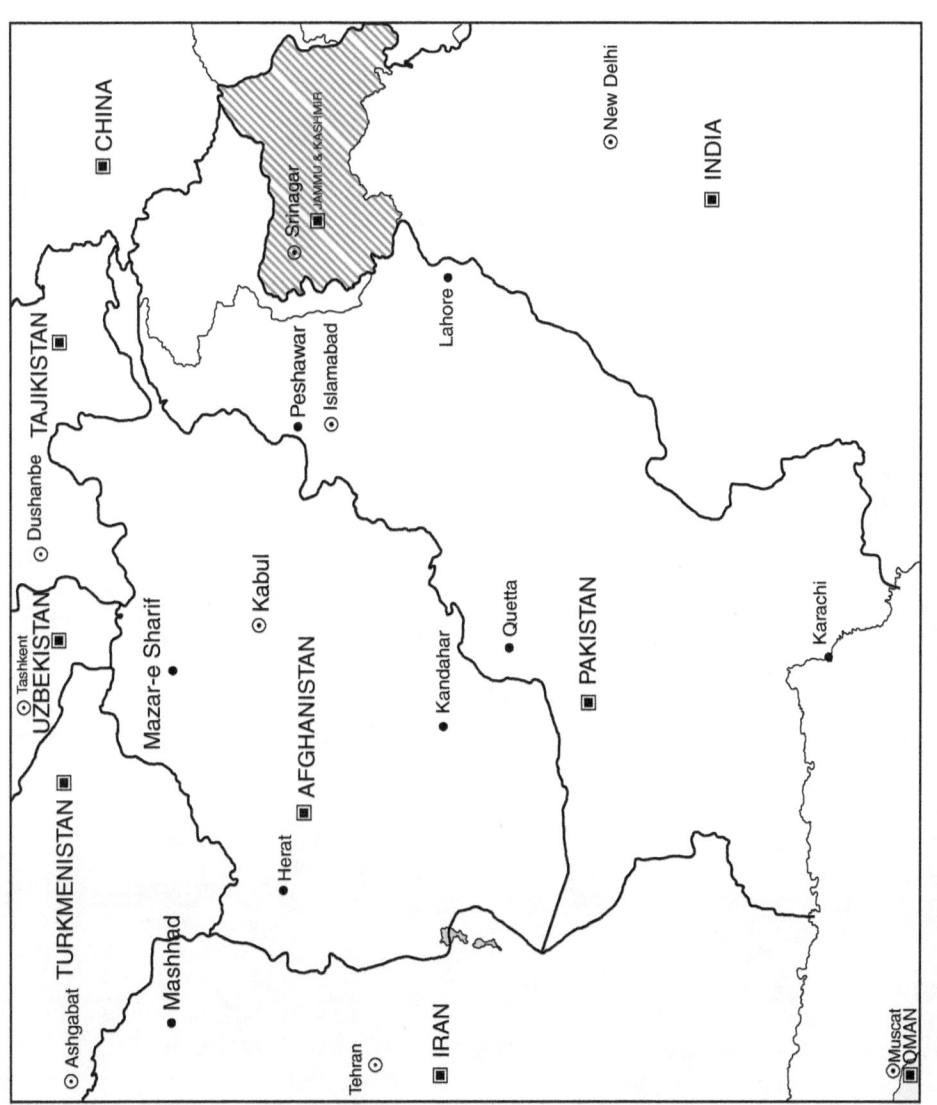

Map 2 Pakistan and Afghanistan in Southwest Asia
Source: http://www.sitesatlas.com/Maps/Maps/801.htm

INTRODUCTION

'Tribe wars with tribe. Every man's hand is against the other and all are against the stranger [...] the state of continual tumult has produced a habit of mind which holds life cheap and embarks on war with careless levity.'
Winston Churchill on Pakhtuns[1]

'For the poor, bloodied Afghans, Peace Be Upon Them.'
Book's Dedication[2]

'We should evacuate the entire civilian population from FATA and let the U.S. air force raise [sic] the entire region to the ground. No more extremists, no more foreign militants.'
A reader's comment, *Dawn*[3]

Historically, and more so since the Soviet invasion of Afghanistan in 1979 and following the transforming events of September 11, Pakistan and Afghanistan, the two neighbouring Southwest Asian nations became the centrepiece of sustained global geopolitical, military and intelligence pursuits.[4] Amidst military campaigns and militant attacks daily claiming numerous lives, along with the destruction of infrastructure and the environment, a comparatively less developed region in South Asia was catapulted into a cause célèbre of some of the longest and most expensive wars[5] that the North Atlantic Treaty Organization (NATO) and its allies have ever fought, costing them in the trillions besides providing substantial justification for the militants to act upon their own agendas.[6] Southwestern Asia – sometimes simplified as Af–Pak – not a core area in the erstwhile cold war yet home to the historic and ancient Indus Valley civilization characterized by diversity and cultural fertility, has been transformed into a core region in what President George W. Bush, Prime Minister Tony Blair and scores of their allies rushed to call the 'war on terror', or what some saw as the ultimate clash of cultures or even of fundamentalisms.[7] Both Afghanistan and Pakistan turned into the proverbial bull's eye for a whole generation of military planners, strategists, scholars, think tanks, spies, journalists and certainly the warriors, all imbued with professional or moral righteousness to pursue the new millennium's sustained and taxing confrontation in the valleys of the Hindu-Kush and the upper reaches of the Indus.[8] Here, modern cave busters, 'dumb bombs', midnight search operations, the whisking of the bearded fellows to Bagram and Guantanamo, ever-escalating, round-the-clock predator drone (UAVs) flights unleashing Hellfire missiles, and a whole generation of suicide bombers wearing crudely made vests or planting improvised explosive devices (IEDs) kept filling the cemeteries. Beside profiling millions of people, especially Muslims even totally unrelated with the conflict or September 11, intermittent scholarly treatises and specialist reports have been preoccupied with the familiar subjects including Islam as a faith, diverse Muslim political groups often lumped together as Al-Qaeda or jihadists, the ideology of jihad itself, gender issues and the students and syllabi at seminaries (*madrasas*).

This heightened multidisciplinary investigation often featuring objectification – akin to military orientalism –, or even the sheer denigration of Muslim communities and traditions in general, has uniquely focused on the Pashtuns/Pushtuns/Pakhtuns, and a juxtaposition of Al-Qaeda, the Taliban and the Pashtuns has turned Waziristan, Helmand, Kandahar, Khost, Kunar and Ghazni into 'badlands'. Hasty security assessments and scholarly works on Southwest Asia have, to a great extent, reawakened orientalism [neo-orientalism] in which military ventures such as invasions, the internment of thousands of people in addition to massive profiling, midnight raids by special forces, transcontinental renditions, and the drone-led round-the-clock surveillance and attacks became justifiable or even acceptable aspects of a war against an enemy perceived as savage, uncouth, sexist and inherently violent, embodying wider regional and global intentions. In a historical sense, the denigration as well as the exaggeration of the prowess of these Muslim communities underlay this double jeopardy, in which the Pashtuns – in a presumptuous bipolar characterization of 'good Muslims, bad Muslims' – were posited as both the perpetrators and victims of violence. In the panoply of neo-orientalism, militant Islam, a revengeful Pashtun culture, an anachronistic Taliban ideology shorn of decency and respect for life, and turf wars spawned over narcotics have been aggregated to posit the Pashtuns as medieval tribals – the antithesis of modernity and its endowments – whose redemption lies in some awaited reincarnation under the aegis of khaki and civil do-gooders from across the Bosphorus. According to such discourse, the Taliban masculinity is to be thwarted or even quashed by a more assertive and self-righteous masculinity that has been somehow divinely ennobled to rescue the lesser children of gods, especially minorities and women.[9] Except for more diversity and an intensity of media now available to these contemporary visionaries, their self-righteousness is not dissimilar to that of their Victorian and tsarist predecessors flagging the white man's burden.[10] In the same vein, Islamism, or what Paul Berman defined as Islamofascism – more sinister than Europe's fascist totalitarianism – has to be confronted through military onslaught, democracy and modernization by using willing partners as surrogates in this rescue and restoration mission.[11] While Islamism is a global problem of the umma per se, in a Southwest Asian context, it is seen as an inherently *Pashtun* problem, which has been overdue for transformation from its tribal origins into modern postulations. According to this premise, the Pashtuns in general – especially of the border regions – are viewed as perverse repositories of whatever is wrong with Islam since its inception in Arabia almost 15 centuries back. Here, the proverbial million mutinies pervade at the expense of weaker elements, non-Muslims and women, whose emancipatory redemption becomes the moral imperative for the West and the rest. In a way, re-orientalized Pashtuns became the poster boys of whatever is wrong with Muslims everywhere. And that is partly the reason for one more book on these western parts of South Asia.

The Pak–Afghan border, also known as the Durand Line, since its demarcation in 1893 has earned unparalleled global attention, which vacillates between curiosity and notoriety. To the west of the 1,600-mile-long Durand Line, the provinces of Paktia, Nangarhar, Paktika, Khost, along with regions such as Helmand and Kandahar are predominantly inhabited by the Pashtuns with their sizeable presence in Kabul, Herat and around Kunduz, though it is the southern and eastern areas which, in total, account for Afghanistan's largest ethnic community. On the Pakistani side of the trans-Indus regions, the Pashtuns are likewise divided into tribal and settled categories and are governed by diverse forms of traditions and laws. Divided into seven autonomous tribal agencies and inhabited by about four million inhabitants, they are collectively called the Federally Administered Tribal Areas (FATA) and have been governed under a duopoly of customary tribal laws with some recourse to Pakistan's own legal traditions, which are rooted in the ignominious and rather discretionary Frontier Crimes Regulation (FCR). The FCR dates from the colonial era and has been faithfully preserved by Pakistani authorities since 1947, despite some recent changes such as positive discrimination – the quota system – for tribal youths and a universal right to vote.[12] The governor of the Khyber Pakhtunkhwa (formerly the North-West Frontier Province, or the Frontier [KP]) operates as the main instrument of the country's policies in the FATA over and above the provincial legislature in Peshawar. Other than the settled districts of Swat, Changla and Dir, the Malakand administrative division has its own *tribal* regions, defined as Provincially Administered Tribal Areas (PATA), but they fall within the administrative writ of the KP. Quite clearly, a substantial change in the status of the tribal regions, especially the FATA is overdue, which must go beyond mere administrative or security-based measures and instead should augur their full, equal and participatory integration within the rest of the country. Rather than being seen as a no-man's-land, demands for their proper redefinition as a separate and fully empowered province gained further momentum in the wake of military operations in North Waziristan during 2014–15 and in view of the gradual withdrawal/drawdown of foreign troops from Afghanistan.[13]

Further north, the Pak–Afghan border straddles the non-Pashtun Nuristan-Chitral districts, while deeper in the south – closer to Iran– they appropriate Baloch areas on both sides. Thus, whereas the Pashtuns remain divided into two neighbouring states, the Baloch are divided into three respective states, though in terms of demography, Pakistan accounts for the largest number of Pashtuns and Baloch on its territory. Altogether there are over 31 million Pashtuns in Pakistan, with Afghanistan accounting for near about 15 million, and given the eastward and southward migrations from across the Indus and the Durand Line, the Pakistani port city of Karachi has become the largest Pashtun city in the world – superseding other metropolitan cities such as Peshawar, Kabul, Jalalabad, Kandahar, Mardan, Mingora, Dir, Quetta, Bannu or Kohat.[14] Spawned by significant economic, ethnic and geopolitical factors, these regions remain restive and so do the border areas on both sides of the Line of Control (LOC) passing through the disputed region of Jammu and Kashmir, part of which is also claimed by China.[15] During the 1980s, a jihadi culture purported to fight the Soviets and, holistically supported and even romanticized by the United States and other Western and Muslim nations, evolved in these areas until the Soviets withdrew in 1989.[16] Following a period of warlordism and a taxing civil war, militancy in Afghanistan turned into a predominantly Pashtun Taliban metamorphosis at a time when their former non-Afghan colleagues in Al-Qaeda determined to initiate a holy war against the United States. Whereas the Taliban, erstwhile mujahideen and their supporters from across the world might have been basking in self-glorification for having caused the rollback of a superpower and the dissolution of the Cold War, their former allies in the West were now confronted with newer challenges.[17]

From a theoretical perspective, an increased global accent on a more exclusive [majoritarian!] form of nationalism with religion(s) refusing to assume a marginal role and the weakening of a liberal ethos only helped the solidification of religio-political organizations such as the Taliban, the Bharatiya Janata Party (BJP), Hamas, Likud and several others across the world. While some pundits in the early 1990s might have heralded the end of history amidst some triumphal march towards global sameness, others saw a new paradigm of cultural clash taking its roots across *civilizational* fault lines.[18] In the wake of a bleeding Afghanistan, Kashmir, Bosnia and Chechnya and a pervasive disillusionment with the postcolonial modernist elite at the helm in the Muslim world, Islamists sought to redraw the ideological contours of their own nations in addition to taking the war to the very soil of the remaining superpower. Within the South Asian context, ethnic movements seemed to follow a similar model of militancy, anchored on political grievances and mostly justified through religious and cultural distinctness. The Baloch, Sindhis, Tamils, Kashmiris and such *minority* groups did not take that long to adjust to the changed global political patterns, and even without erstwhile backers such as the Soviet Union, their separatism now rationalized itself, among other trajectories, on ethno-religious exclusivity, which they justified under the rubric of the universal creed of self-determination.[19] In India, Hindu nationalism turned more muscular and following several weaker governments in New Delhi often at the behest of the Indian National Congress, it began to juxtapose both India and Hinduism with a new daredevil vigour. Eventually, under Narendra Modi it obtained a nationwide salience in 2014. A restive Kashmir Valley often supported from across the LOC by Pakistani intelligence agencies and several jihadi groups risked a new partition, and Delhi opted for coercion just like in Punjab in the earlier era. Moreover, the New Hindu movement certainly demanded its greater pound of flesh from other sizeable minorities such as Muslims and Christians, often argued in the name of majoritarianism. Similar to the Arab world in 2011–15, demography, ideology and geopolitics all came together to reconfigure South Asia, and despite economic liberalization and such other measures, the accent remained on this so-called majoritarianism that has often metamorphosed into fragmentation.

In February 1999, Atal Behari Vajpayee and Mian Nawaz Sharif, the prime ministers of India and Pakistan, respectively – and the proponents as well as the beneficiaries of this new majoritarianism – met in Lahore to augur a peaceful South Asia. Following their nuclear tests of May 1998, for a time a new realism seemed to be seeping in, but the traditionally powerful khaki establishment in Rawalpindi pursued its own whims and secretly planned on occupying Kargil Heights in the disputed Kashmir region. They wanted to repeat what the Indians had done to them in the mid-1980s when, finding Pakistan's forward positions on the Siachen Glacier unoccupied, the former had quietly encroached on them. Since then, both of them have engaged in sporadic fighting in a high-altitude war in an undemarcated, glacial region where more troops die of frostbite than from gunshots.[20] However, this Kargil advance by Pakistani troops and their Kashmiri allies and masterminded by General Pervez Musharraf, took a dangerous turn, bringing South Asia closer to a nuclear showdown. Arbitration by the Clinton administration only precluded that horrendous scenario, though the BJP was able to cash in on a rising tide of patriotism and returned with an absolute majority. In Pakistan, the Sharif regime itself became the casualty of increased chasm between an elected prime minister and an impetuous, commando general.[21]

While India and Pakistan pursued their respective political paths in the late 1990s, the Taliban persisted with their consolidation in 90 per cent of the country, besides imposing a strict, puritanical form of Islamic ethos on an otherwise plural and diverse Afghanistan, which had grievously suffered under factionalist warlordism.[22] However, the Taliban were able to eradicate poppy production from the country, and instead of the traditional khans, now the mullahs assumed primacy within the country's sociopolitical fabric. Trained in madrasas on the Frontier – presently called the KP – they had been hardened by the jihad of the 1980s and deeply inspired by like-minded purist, Salafi groups elsewhere. Some of their former non-Afghan colleagues went back to their ancestral lands across Asia and Africa to establish similar polities, though the Afghan model of a very strict, male-dominated and anti-Western Islam did not sit well with modernist Muslims elsewhere. People viewed the Taliban as the product of warfare, primitive tribalism, extreme poverty and an austere Islam that had mixed with politics and was nourished by petrodollars. The emergence of the Central Asian Republics (CARs) and the major energy needs of the developing economies of India and China were baffled by the events in Afghanistan, though some international oil companies, fronted by Afghan intermediaries such as Hamid Karzai and Zalmay Khalilzad, tried to negotiate with the Taliban. The attacks on the US embassies in East Africa in 1998 along with exhortations by Osama bin Laden to fight the next jihad against the American troops and interests in the Muslim world soon put Afghanistan in the proverbial bull's eye.[23] Intermittent American retaliation proved unsuccessful in countering the Al-Qaeda leadership, whereas the induction of the latest information technology (IT) facilities added to a kind of romantic and defiant mystique about the ragtag radicals sheltering at places like Khost – not far from the Durand Line. The Taliban, ambiguously beholden to Osama bin Laden and his cohorts and true to their tribal hospitality, were soon to face the brunt of Western outrage when in the closing months of 2001 Afghanistan, once again, became the battleground of the longest warfare in recent history.[24] One of the poorest countries on earth, with a very low per capita and life expectancy just around 40 was now the recipient of cluster bombs, precise bombings, midnight raids and protracted guerrilla warfare. Bagram, Kunduz, Tora Bora and Guantanamo soon earned global notoriety featuring renditions, waterboarding and such other practices to eliminate both Al-Qaeda and the Taliban. With more than a trillion dollars spent on this belligerence by 2014 and ever since the weekly expense of one billion dollars incurred by the United States alone, intermittent drone attacks both by the United Kingdom and the United States, and Taliban-led suicide missions had turned Afghanistan into a complex and taxing battleground. Soon, Pakistan[25] was to overtake Afghanistan and Iraq in this new spate of violence and bloodshed, and the FATA came to be designated as the epicentre of the Pakistani Taliban, no less ruthless in their campaign against their compatriots whom they accused of surrogacy.[26]

In Pakistan, Musharraf, following his coup on 12 October 1999, had stopped short of assuming the title of the chief martial law administrator – erstwhile popular among his predecessors in uniform – yet ensured a perpetual exile for Benazir Bhutto and Nawaz Sharif. Both these politicians and former prime ministers had been leading two nationwide parties, the Pakistan People's Party (PPP) and the Pakistan Muslims League (PML), which posed political opposition to Musharraf at a time when the world in general had greatly lost its enthusiasm for military dictators. With the military and judiciary fully behind him, Musharraf like any other dictator assuming political overlordship, sought some discretionary constitutional and political props, which were facilitated through an obliging civil service and a constellation of countrywide loyal and self-seeking politicians. But Musharraf, like his erstwhile Taliban allies across the Durand Line, was largely being shunned by the democratic regimes in the North Atlantic regions, who viewed him as a pariah leader of a plural and nuclearized nation that faced its enduring problems of governance. Located in a testing region with fluid and often-volatile borders all around, Pakistan was then being viewed with intense concern. Despite its often impressive economic growth, the sixth most populous nation in the world was a hotchpotch of age-old ethnicities and sectarian fault lines, which kept Karachi and other parts of the country often in turmoil. In spite of a vocal civil society and the majority of its stakeholders living in the Indus Valley, Indo-Pakistani relations were frozen if not explosive for a long period of time and had been interspersed with a history of conflicts and controversies. The grievous events of 1947 and the subsequent wars of 1948, 1965 and 1971 never allowed cordiality between these two neighbours. Pakistan's border with Afghanistan was meant only for the people from settled areas; otherwise, a 20-mile-wide territory was almost autonomous and was divided into seven tribal agencies in which an amalgam of anomalous imperial and tribal laws governed. Here, more like the rest of the country, the emphasis was on administration and not on governance. This territory and its fiercely independent people had continued to pose serious problems for the British as well as for dynasts in Kabul, until in 1947, Muhammad Ali Jinnah (1876–1948), the founding father of Pakistan, decided to withdraw troops from their forward positions. It was only in 2001 that Pakistan sent in troops to quell the Taliban and Al-Qaeda stragglers heading towards the FATA, and that it eventually, like NATO, found itself in a deepening quagmire. The policy of hammer and anvil applied in this region from both sides only added to the local hardships, in addition to expanding the 'war on terror' to the entire region, exacerbating anti-American sentiments and the revulsion against Islamabad's kowtowing to external interests.

Following September 11, Southwest Asia turned out to be an epicentre of global engagements, warfare, violence and espionage, ushering in a new era of complex, unresolved and taxing challenges with their direct impact on neighbouring states and communities. Given their geographical proximity and ethnic commonalities, Afghanistan and Pakistan, often called Af-Pak in official jargon, became the centrepiece of a unique geopolitical jigsaw puzzle in which ideological, interstate and international determinants converged to spawn new configurations.[27] The Afghan Taliban, since their inception as a largely Sunni, Pashtun movement in 1994, had received moral and material support from Pakistan and a few other states for their own respective self-interests. Even several extra-regional powers such as the United States cautiously saw in them the guarantors of country's stability and regional security. However, for non-Pashtun Afghans such as the Northern Alliance, and the other regional states including India, Iran and the CARs, the Taliban's form of Islam and militancy raised some dire challenges. The presence of Osama bin Laden at the helm of Al-Qaeda, mostly consisting of Arab and Central Asian fighters often known as the 'Afghani Arabs', equally posed newer security dilemmas for their respective states and the West.[28] These fugitive radicals, freshly inspired by their rolling back of a superpower, had now embarked upon defying the United States and its allied elite across the Muslim world, who, in most cases, happened to be coercive and non-democratic. Islam, being a political religion and with a strong tradition of anti-colonialism and anti-Westernism, now turned against these two forces, unleashing a turbulent, taxing and volatile phase in Muslim-Muslim and Muslim-Western relationships. Other than the bombings of the US embassies in East Africa in 1998, these Islamist radicals opted to take their warfare onto the mainland United States and caused September 11. In a backlash, their hosts – the Taliban – and dozens of groups of Islamists across the world now faced the Western and even global fury, with some interpreting it as the new Crusades, or 'a clash of civilizations'.

Instead of receding into the back pages of history and geopolitics, the border regions on both sides of the Durand Line now became the focal point of this new conflict, with the Pashtuns, regional states and global forces (NATO and the International Security Assistance Force [ISAF]) zeroing in with diverse, gigantic and sometimes even conflicting trajectories. Unlike their Afghan counterparts, the Pakistani Taliban evolved during the Musharraf-led military regime, when his political allies, the Combined Council of Action, or Muttahidda Majlis-i-Ammal (MMA), assumed ministries in the Frontier and Balochistan following the elections of 2002. However, their formal launch took place later in 2007. Musharraf had annoyed Pakistani tribal clerics by sending in troops in pursuance of a Washington-led military invasion in which NATO from the west and Pakistani armed forces from the east operated in the FATA apprehending militants of all kinds, who, in some cases, had sought refuge in this belt to escape the American wrath. When Musharraf persisted with further military campaigns including the assault on the Red Mosque in Islamabad in 2007, all kinds of Pakistani disgruntled groups took up arms against the army and security agencies and soon organized themselves into the Tehreek-i-Taliban, Pakistan (TTP). They were able to recruit aggrieved tribals as well as the members of Pakistani militant groups such as the Lashkar-e-Jhangvi (LeJ) and Lashkar-e-Tayyaba (LeT), and began a taxing series of suicide and truck-laden bomb attacks across the country. Following an understanding between the Pakistani military establishment and the CIA, the first drone attack in June 2004 targeted Nek Muhammad, a rebel leader in Waziristan, with more to follow including the killing of Baitullah Mehsud on 8 August 2009, Waliur Rehman on 29 May 2013 and Hakimullah Mehsud on 1 November.[29] All four had been founding members of the TTP but, in general, the ratio of deaths of such militants compared to that of ordinary Pashtun tribals has been almost one to seven or even fewer. Over the past several years, amidst claims and counterclaims the predator flights became a round-the-clock fixture across the FATA, much to the resentment of the local population and vocal groups across Pakistan, though President Barack Obama and other senior officials in Washington often defended drone missions in the name of eliminating terrorists and their network in the border regions.

Imran Khan and other Pakistani critics saw drones behind the steady rise in militancy in Pakistan, and these two positions have remained mutually antagonistic, causing serious popular resentment on both sides. By 2011–13 and ever since, their almost constant flights over the FATA accounting for millions of hours and the frequent usage of missiles on people and places had cost more than 4,000 human lives, causing nationwide resentment in Pakistan and elsewhere.[30] Even some American analysts such as Vali Reza Nasr, who had been involved with the policy planners such as Hillary Clinton and Richard Holbrooke, found serious issues with a total dependence on drones. Here containment seemed to override engagement with the realities on the ground within the context of a policy that tended to exaggerate terrorist threats while staying shy of firming up participatory institutions in Southwest Asia, North Africa and the Middle East. By using austerity and efficiency as the main arguments behind the wider usage of drones, the Obama administration definitely offered a new leash to the very challenge that it was otherwise aiming to resolve.[31] Critical views about contrasting attitudes and policies attributed to Obama's presidency were highlighted in works such as *The Stranger*, underlining a lack of consistency and resolution in dealing with the Muslim regions and regimes.[32] Even during the height of military and related operations in Southwest Asia, NATO and ISAF military commanders had developed serious differences over their respective national policies and strategies, though at the time such contentions were stringently hushed up.[33] This criticism gained more ascendancy following the dissolution of state infrastructures in Iraq and Libya, with Yemen and Syria already in the doldrums. Other than human rights issues, legal and moral questions arising due to sizeable and even indiscriminate human costs on the receiving end, the core issue of the territorial and legal sovereignty of those nations and their regimes proved problematic, underpinning intense anti-Americanism as well as posing serious challenges to the nascent civic institutions in those countries.[34] Certainly, some American strategists, other than the Central Intelligence Agency (CIA), the Pentagon, the State Department and National Security staff, have justified drones by dismissing the local and global critique owing to their low cost and the desire to take the war to the militants themselves. To such apologists for aerial attacks on otherwise civil targets, drones and not democracy have saved American lives from Al-Qaeda and its franchises in Muslim regions.[35] Of course, most of these American analysts, irrespective of their affiliations with specific think tanks or some universities, have routinely blamed Muslim West Asians for all the travesties without every undertaking any critique of their own powerful institutions.

Osama bin Laden's killing on 2 May 2011 in Abbottabad – no less disputatious even after the passage of several years – happened at a time when the United States and its several allies were engaged in waging the longest warfare in their respective histories with no end in view, and the Obama administration needed a major achievement in view of its fledgling popularity.[36] Serious issues of misgovernance, instability, and economic and ethnic schisms concurrently continued to bedevil regional states such as Afghanistan and Pakistan, which were faced with 'a million mutinies', while the Indo-Pakistani relationship remained deadlocked since the Mumbai attacks of November 2008. Instead, both India and Pakistan morphed into a regional great game with both countries trying to outdo each other's influence in Afghanistan, almost proving a 'deadly triangle'.[37] In the meantime, the Pakistani Taliban and their Al-Qaeda associates wreaked havoc on Pakistanis in the KP and Karachi, mounting revenge sprees for the dead Saudi militant. Concurrently, Iran as well as the CARs kept striving hard to maintain the status quo amidst an enormity of challenges from within and outside. To the north, the Pakistani-Afghan border remained porous and turbulent due to increased [tribal] Pashtun activism at the beck and call of the Taliban in both the countries, while towards the south, Iran often battled with Jundullah – a Sunni, Baloch group – allegedly based in Pakistani Balochistan.

Pakistan's Baloch separatists have been mounting attacks on Pakistani security forces amidst stories of kidnaps and 'deaths in armed encounters'. The non-Baloch residents of this province that itself accounts for 43 per cent of the country's territory and is presumably endowed with an unexplored, stupendous wealth in natural and mineral resources, have frequently faced a kind of selective ethnic cleansing at the hands of Baloch militants. Not only the divisions of the Baloch territories across the three adjoining states are an eyesore for the nationalists but also their internal changing demographics equally frighten them, as in the case of Pakistan, the Pashtuns – both Pakistani and Afghani – appear to have already outnumbered the former. More like the Pashtuns in Afghanistan and their counterparts in the FATA, the Baloch in all three countries remain restive, posing serious challenges for their respective nation states. Interestingly, Karachi, Pakistan's main port and the economic hub – the world's largest Pashtun and Baloch city – has become a reflection of Pakistan's uneven and conflictive demography in which Urdu speakers, Pashtuns and Baloch, in their jockeying for political and economic power, have often reposed loyalty in their respective ethnic firebrands.[38] Other than divisive ethnic loyalties, sectarian and ideological chasms further fragment Pakistani nationhood. To the east, Indo-Pakistani and Sino-Indian dichotomies have remained subterranean given their enduring disputes and counterclaims over Kashmir and the lower Himalayas, while a pervasive defiance in the predominantly Muslim Valley has kept half a million Indian troops tied down in a security cul-de-sac.[39] Of course, political Islam poses worries for the People's Republic of China in Sinjiang, which happens to be its largest western territory with a predominantly Muslim population, in addition to being quite vital in linking this emerging global power with the CARs, Southwest Asia, and the Near East. The Chinese understand this ethno-religious irredentism in the border regions which is vitally connected with the Muslim heartland, and which, unlike Tibet, is avidly resistant to an increasingly regimented Sinification. Beijing, as seen in high-profile exchange visits and investment projects of 2015, is eager to contain dissent in its own western territories by using a carrot-and-stick policy. Simultaneously, it has been seeking trade routes and energy corridors through neighbours such as Pakistan and may be willing to play a major role in softening the internal and regional grievances in Southwestern Asia.[40]

Complex and ever-shifting geopolitical configurations with their regional and global security ramifications can be understood, to a large extent, within the security perspective of post–September 11 developments, with ideologues, ethnic leaders, ulama and the respective ruling elite appropriating most of our space. Concurrently, a wider matrix of varying demographics, economic interests, a desire for political power in the name of political Islam or sheer geopolitical interests need to be taken aboard, yet this premise may signal two major deficiencies. First, there have been several such studies on the Taliban, Al-Qaeda, Pakistan, Afghanistan, Iran, Kashmir, India and even Sinjiang in more recent times, and adding another volume, even though quite ambitious and interdisciplinary, may not break any new scholarly ground. Secondly, narrowing it down to more recent times and only to security issues may deprive readers of the knowledge of the early modern era when empires calibrated their strategies on contemporary diplomatic and militarist chessboards, until this familiar political map evolved in recent times. This imperial foreground is vital in understanding the evolution of the colonial borders, which over the successive decades have become national boundaries by assuming their own sacrosanctity even if they may appear to be arbitrary and hasty, especially by causing tribal, ethnic and territorial divisions. Some recent studies on the British period with a focus on boundary demarcations, military campaigns, ethnic reconfigurations and the emergence of the ideology of jihad have certainly added to our knowledge about Pashtun societies and their relationship with metropolitan powers as well as their interface with local stakeholders such as khans and clerics. Studies by Akbar Ahmed, Mukalika Bannerjee, Robert Nichols and William Dalrymple have attempted to focus on societies and their politico-social contours by avoiding an unneeded romanticization of the Frontier, imbued with too familiar imperial nostalgia.[41] Essentialization of these borders, contestations over them by the regional states as well as by the respective ethnicities and even by transnational actors ranging from Al-Qaeda to the Taliban to NATO, all are curial in understanding the 'porous' nature of the borders in Southwest Asia besides a complex but virulent 'retribalization' in which Pashtun identity issues transcend every other thematic aspect. Here, Islam, Pashtun ethnicity, resistance against external influences and their surrogates amidst a greater contest for local power and honour (*Izzat*) necessitate an investigation which benefits from studies of history, anthropology and politics, with special reference to the Pashtun territories straddling the Hindu Kush and Suleiman Mountains.

While there are numerous works on Pakistan and Afghanistan by scholars, policy makers and journalists, there is still an urgency to research Southwest Asia in an integrated way by focusing a bit more on their divisive yet undefined ethnic and territorial borders. Most studies either focus on the imperial past in which the Great Game becomes a romanticized theme or deal with the Raj and then dilate on the security issues of new South Asian states. Like earlier works falling within domains such as history and anthropology, books on these countries often happen to be political commentaries, usually with a large section devoted to international relations and security matters. Works by Fredrik Barth and Akbar Ahmed have focused on anthropological areas, largely ignoring ideological and geopolitical drivers, while Robert Kaplan, Barnett Rubin, Ahmed Rashid, Peter Marsden and Kamal Matinuddin have commented on strategies, geopolitics and external threat perceptions.[42] Other than the Orientalist writings of the colonial period, penned by civil and military officials such as Lord Roberts, Rudyard Kipling, Captain Slessor, Olaf Caroe and others, one needs to consult gazetteers, personal reportages and media coverage of border communities. Recent works by Peter Hopkirk, John Keay, Victoria Schofield, James Spain, Alice Albinia and William Dalrymple reflect the contrasting elements of nostalgia and bewilderment about sociopolitical challenges faced by communities living on both ends of the Indus Valley.[43] And, certainly the post–September 11 writers of Raj-related themes such as Charles Allen only see continuity in jihadist traditions first flagged in the 1820s from the seminaries in northern India. Mullah Zaeef's study is perhaps the only riposte by the Taliban, while tracts and visual archives of the Jamaat-i-Islami (JI), Jamiat-i-Ulama-i-Islam (JUI), LeJ and other organizations espouse a transborder communitarianism, which is a kind of pan-Islamism from below.[44] Zaeef's work has been recently added by a laudatory work on the Afghan Taliban by Maulana Samiul Haq, the principal of a well-known Deobandi madrasa in Akora Khattak, where many Taliban leaders including Mullah Omar were students at one time or the other.[45] Needless to say, jihadi binary thinking equally marginalizes the *ijtihaadi* thinkers such as Muhammad Iqbal, Fazlur Rahman, Khalid Masud, Javed Ghamdi and certainly a whole generation of progressive Muslims. Studies by Ayesha Jalal, Husain Haqqani, Hasan Abbas, Zahid Hussain and Amin Saikal raise historical and ideological issues, though Robert Wirsing, Bob Woodward, Stephen Cohen, Peter Bergen, Antonio Giustozzi and several other Western scholars remain more focused on security-related themes wherein military and militants both emerge as decisive forces behind vital developments.[46] These and similar other works may offer modernist views on regional and statist politics, yet one needs to locate media outpourings and public opinion surveys along with some fieldwork-based deliberations on subjects including ideology, class, demography, mobility and state formation.

There has been a need for a volume which is interdisciplinary and puts Southwest Asia within its historical and contemporary contexts without orientalizing its people or exceptionalizing their creed(s).[47] The global or Western preoccupation with this region since an early period can provide a constructive engagement in understanding its foibles and complexities. One may also acquire a better understanding of the human predicament of the Pashtuns and neighbouring peoples who, despite their distant and even landlocked situation, became the centre of global attention, which undoubtedly will stay negative. Though our study, going beyond the usual writ of reports on the Af-Pak region, purports to locate macro issues involving Southwest Asia, and several external forces, our initial focus will be on the Pashtuns, who straddle a challenging geography besides retaining some of the world's oldest surviving tribal systems. The interaction between modernity and tradition has never been so apparent and equally complex as it is here, nor is there any other place on earth where ethnicity, religion and resistance all combine to sustain an enduring defiance in human history and that too against some of the most developed and powerful nations. Subsequently, we shall look at the issues of civil society in Pakistan, major mutualities characterizing Pakistani–US relations including some discussion on drone attacks, to be followed by a summation giving the multiple challenges lying ahead for Southwestern Asia. The book is not meant to be just another tirade against external interventions in Muslim Southwest Asia – though no less serious and traumatic they have been – it equally acknowledges the ideological and institutional polarization and its malafide role in misgovernance, sectarian conflicts and violent pulls towards an exclusive majoritarianism. While being sensitive to the human spatial rights of tribal and ethnic communities, the book disallows their romanticization in the name of tradition or faith, in the way it avoids an uncritiqued adulation of modernizing forces and processes. Other than ethnic dissensions, it is alert to gender- and class-based chasms, which often exacerbate inequalities, and thus vigorously subscribes to the idea of civic reformism without pursuing too familiar courses of apologia or aggression.[48] Muslim pluralism has to be taken aboard by Muslims first for their own imperatives, and substantive reforms anchored on universal empowerment and equal citizenship have to be prioritized both by the state and civic forces along with educational and economic uplift of the masses. Here internal peace and development are contingent upon regional cooperation, soft borders, resolution of territorial and water-related disputes as well as sharing knowledge and experience without sundering the larger commonalities that these people have inherited from the Indus civilization. While the Pashtuns and for that matter millions of Pakistanis and Afghans have experienced the pangs and pains let loose by some discretionary forces and their toll remains unmitigated, still it is a vanguard challenge in which South Asia and beyond can be the ultimate beneficiaries of a shared peace. Given the cultural, historical, geopolitical and even academic location of Southwest Asia as perhaps the most testing and unnerving region in recent times, it can also herald a more promising future for all. Like the Middle East and North Africa (MENA), this region's sociopolitical destiny is certainly contingent upon the interplay of numerous yet interdependent domestic, regional and global trajectories.

Chapter One

GANDHARA LANDS: WRESTLING WITH PASHTUN IDENTITY AND HISTORY

'The Afghans were known to be a "race of Tigers" who had already shown their teeth in 1838–42, a hard, warlike people toughed by a harsh, dry, mountainous country, passionately nursing their independence, family loyalty, courage, and a highly developed sense of personal honour and hospitality, but conversely regarded by unwelcome visitors as "robbers and cutthroats."'

Rodney Atwood[1]

'The most notable traits in their character are unbounded superstition, pride, cupidity and a most vengeful spirit [...] They despise all other races [...] They cannot deny the reputation they have acquired for faithlessness.'

Henry Bellew[2]

'The Indian subcontinent – and the Frontier in particular – is littered with half-forgotten graveyards filled with the bones of unlucky lives extinguished before they had a chance to shine.'

Charles Allen[3]

Gandhara, the ancient name of the upper Indus Valley – which makes up most of present-day Pakistan and Afghanistan – is the historic gateway to the subcontinent where cultures, creeds, communities and languages mingle, although not often without violence. Over the past two decades, we have witnessed here numerous trajectories of violence, owing to external and internal forces, which have claimed countless lives and resources of the Af-Pak region and beyond. The violence has often been nihilistic, and continues to be perpetrated and retribution carried out mainly by Pashtuns across the Durand Line in addition to its larger remit in these two countries. Without singling out Pashtuns as perpetually violence-prone tribes and as resistant to modern nation building, more recent and enduring developments such as the North Atlantic Treaty Organization's (NATO's) struggle against the Afghan Taliban and Pakistan military operations in Swat and the Federally Administered Tribal Areas (FATA) certainly necessitate a broad understanding of questions about Pashtun identity, highlighted in the later portion of this study.

In the Eye of the Storm

Following the torching of more than 400 girls' schools, the closing down of numerous video and music shops and the public executions of men and women incriminated under all kinds of charges without any recourse to public review or accountability, Swat had by 2009 turned into a Taliban-controlled state within Pakistan. The area had been one of the most scenic, glacial and forested valleys in Southwest Asia. Teachers were forbidden to run their modern schools; young men were ordered to grow beards of a specific size; women were strictly ordered to stay indoors and the police and other civil officials were either compelled to obey the orders of the superior committee (*shura*) or be prepared for public wrath. The committee comprised some senior clerics who were led by Maulvi Fazlullah, the son-in-law of Maulana Soofi Muhammad, who is the leader of Tehreek-i-Nifaz-i-Shariat-i-Muhammadi (TNSM) and a senior religious-political leader who had descended on Swat from the neighbouring Dir in the 1990s and spearheaded demands for the implementation of sharia. During the 1990s Pakistani political authorities such as Mian Nawaz Sharif, in order to avoid any new confrontation in the Pashtun region, entered into an agreement with Soofi Muhammad, but after September 11, the latter took it upon himself to send in thousands of volunteers to fight the Americans across the Durand Line. Many of them were killed or ended up in Afghan and American jails, or were never heard from again until, in several cases, their local captors began demanding ransom. But following Musharraf's hasty decision to use force against the Islamists taking shelter in Islamabad's Red Mosque in 2007, Soofi's son-in-law and the future TTP leader began exploiting local grudges against the administration and landlords, and came up with the idea of creating an emirate through iron-cast policies, justified in the name of sharia. Stragglers from other Pashtun areas and returnees from Afghan jihad joined Fazlullah, who began issuing edicts through an FM radio station in addition to coercing and even executing local clerics and civil servants. These hasty punishments, often recorded on camera and posted online for wider impact, soon created a state of terror in an area always known for better schools, a comparatively prosperous economy and a more cosmopolitan outlook due to the annual influx of tourists from across the Indus land. Swat was not an isolated downtrodden tribal agency in the backwaters of tribal territory and was quite a distance from the Durand Line, where the displacement of official writ caused serious apprehension, especially when Fazlullah's followers, by now closely aligned with the TTP, took control of Dir, Buner and Changla districts, with the entire Malakand Division under their control.

The questionable examples of the Taliban-style of government, based on unilateralism and the prompt execution of accused individuals, especially women, became a major issue for the Pakistan People's Party (PPP) administration in Islamabad as well as for the provincial regime led by the Awami National Party (ANP), the secular nationalist Pashtun organization. Following the elections in February 2008, the PPP had eased out Pervez Musharraf, and with Asif Ali Zardari as the president and Yousaf Raza Gilani as prime minister, re-establishing official writ in Swat was a new and even more daring challenge. The Taliban had begun to summarily execute ANP activists along with engaging in daredevil attacks on girls attending schools in Mingora and Saidu Sharif, minutely recorded in a BBC blog by Malala Yousafzai, whose father, Ziaud Din, ran an English-medium school.[4] Pakistani civil society and the military stood by the political authorities in undertaking a prompt military operation in 2009 which temporarily displaced about two million inhabitants of Swat, yet met with local approval. Militants were either arrested or pushed out of the region, with Fazlullah seeking refuge among Afghan tribals in Kunhar, while Soofi was put under house arrest in Peshawar. The operation rolled back the rapid encroachment by Pakistani Taliban and re-energized the critique of this version of political Islam, which fiercely opposed modern education and women's empowerment and even conducted witch hunts against the medical staff administering polio drops to children. Most Pakistanis, including a vast majority of Pashtuns, abhorred this form of exclusive and even repressive Islamization of their lands, which to them was essentially criminalization in the name of religion and politics.[5] It is true that the local complaints against a tardy administration in Swat coalesced with anti-Westernism and zeroed in on Pakistani political and civil echelons but appeared to have been hijacked by a militant rhetoric, as had been seen in the FATA. Pashtuns in and around Swat who supported or worked for the regime in Islamabad sought modern education for their daughters and had voted for a Pashtun nationalist party that ran the provincial administration in Khyber Pakhtunkhwa (KP). However, they were now viewed as worthy of a severe reprimand including sheer elimination by the Taliban, who themselves overwhelmingly happened to be Pashtun. Such fratricide neither reflected the familiar parameters of tribal- or clan-based rivalries nor could it be interpreted solely on the basis of a new class formation in which the have-nots, especially the landless peasants, could have taken up arms against local influential persons and intermediaries. The *othering* of Pashtuns centring on arms, revenge and violence is certainly not an indigenous discourse and has its own complex geopolitical origins.[6] This violence cannot be explained as Pakistan's Islamist utopia, the counterpart of India's Naxalbari defiance, nor can it be understood through traditional Orientalist views of Pashtuns being inherently violent and revenge-seeking medieval groups who had been unnerved by the onslaught of modernity. Crucial developments spewing violence of various types in Malakand and the FATA are similar largely because local inhabitants happen to be predominantly Pashtun, and Pakistani Taliban leadership itself comes from Pashtun cadres. However, concurrently there have been significant differences as well in which crucial denominators such as external intervention and local chasms have underwritten mass dislocations and intermittent military operations.[7]

While Malakand showed a spectre of militant encroachment on the civil population and institutions in the name of sharia in predominantly Pashtun districts, otherwise known as 'the settled zones', the turbulent situation in all the seven agencies of the FATA has been even more complex. Here, other than the issues of local power contestations between the 'old' (landlords/*khans*) and 'new', post-1979 (jihadi rhetoricians/mullahs) stakeholders, the intra-jihadi strife and resistance against the ISAF and NATO presence across the Durand Line and Pakistan's perceived surrogacy to the West underpinned militancy. At one level, this was the traditional form of jihad, which, as against British colonialism, would stipulate support for the Afghan Taliban fighting NATO and the Kabul regime.[8] At another level, various clusters within the TTP pursued their own agendas against authorities in Islamabad and Peshawar for undertaking military operations in the FATA, besides facilitating the 80 per cent of NATO supplies through Pakistan. The TTP and their supporters believed that both Pakistan and the Kabul regime were working as surrogates for non-Muslim forces. The former blame Islamabad for undertaking military operations in the FATA. They have also accused Pakistani authorities of facilitating most of NATO's supplies into Afghanistan by leasing out country's road and railways infrastructure. Pakistan's tacit support for drones, although often denied; arrests of all types of jihadi and resistance groups by the authorities; and the perception of the Pakistani state system as being non-Islamic also underpinned this TTP-led defiance. At the third level, some groups like the Lashkar-e-Jhangvi (LeJ), fired up by anti-Shia sentiments and not entirely Pashtun by ethnicity, sought training and shelter in the FATA to carry out attacks in Kurram, Hangu, Peshawar, Chilas, Quetta, Karachi and across the country. At the fourth level, the TTP supported specific groups of non-Pakistani stragglers from across the Muslim world and China by sheltering them so as to make the struggle umma wide.[9] At another level, the TTP provided help to some of its own favourite groups fighting against pro-regime khans and clerics forming forces (*Lashkar*) in their respective agencies. Sustained warfare and defiance in Afghanistan and the attendant escalating costs, along with grudges against Kabul and Islamabad in a kind of exceedingly taxing status quo on both sides of the Durand Line without any major political breakthrough over the years guaranteed a ready supply of recruits and fighters for all the above strands of violence. The NATO troops undertaking multiple land-based and aerial campaigns, and similar operations by the Afghan army and Pakistani troops certainly turned the Pashtun regions into hotbeds of several forms of enduring warfare and escalating violence. Following war fatigue and confronted by other regional and global issues, the eventual decision by the United States and other NATO nations to withdraw most troops from Afghanistan, as affirmed through a treaty between the Obama administration and the recently elected Kabul regime led by President Ashraf Ghani, did not lessen the militarist defiance by the Afghan Taliban. Instead, they appeared to intensify their attacks on military and civil installations to convey their kind of triumphalism against the various odds since October 2001. Since assuming the presidency, Ghani chose China for his first official visit given Beijing's growing influence in the region along with a steady interest in the minerals and gas reserves in Afghanistan.[10] In the same vein, despite efforts for peace parleys by Islamabad initiated by the newly installed Nawaz Sharif, the TTP refused to relent in its campaign across the Indus Valley until Islamabad decided to pursue a long-awaited military operation in North Waziristan in 2014, which certainly fragmented the Pakistani Taliban and their allies but fell short of their total elimination. The most dramatic proof of this was conveyed through a spectacular suicide bombing on 2 November 2014 at the Indo-Pakistani border, just outside Lahore, killing around 60 Pakistani spectators at a military parade.[11] More assaults were yet to come, such as when the TTP attacked the Army Public School in Peshawar on 16 December 2014, killing 145 schoolchildren and their teachers. Jundullah, a TTP associate spearheading a campaign against the Shias, perpetrated three major attacks in early 2015. On 30 January, TTP militants attacked a Shia mosque in Shikarpur, killing 61 worshippers, followed by a similar attack on 13 February in Peshawar, which claimed 21 fatalities and several casualties. On 13 May, six Jundullah militants – university graduates and members of Karachi's burgeoning middle class – boarded a bus and killed 47 Ismaili Shias en route to their schools and jobs.

The post–September 11 entanglement of the Musharraf regime on several fronts in a closer alliance with Washington, operations by Pakistani army units and the Frontier Constabulary, the fiasco of the Red Mosque in 2007 and the congregation of foreign and Pakistani Jihadi groups in North Waziristan collectively led to the evolution of the TTP.[12] Numerous punitive operations in the FATA by Pakistani troops in the post-Musharraf era in South Waziristan, Bajaur and Mohmand – like the large-scale campaign in Swat in 2009 – had apparently weakened the TTP and its affiliates, yet failed to eliminate them. Instead, these groups filtered into North Waziristan – the most populous of all the seven agencies forming the FATA – and even after the intermittent deaths of their top leadership in drone attacks, they persisted with their suicide missions and other such attacks across Pakistan. The Pakistani army, as often reported in the Western media, was hesitant to undertake a comprehensive military operation in North Waziristan because of the presence of the pro-Islamabad Haqqani group in the agency, in addition to being apprehensive about the displacement of 800,000 local inhabitants. In addition, General Pervez Kayani's own vacillations in mounting another major onslaught also allowed North Waziristan to become the de facto TTP emirate until the blatant attacks on Karachi's airport in June 2014, when the Pakistani civilian and military leadership lost their patience and hesitancy. Consequently, Pakistani troops led by General Raheel Sharif, Kayani's successor, initiated a holistic aerial and land-based operation – 'Zarb-e-Azb' – in the agency, which was commented upon positively both in Pakistan and abroad, while the TTP bided its time in seeking its own revenge to mark its resilience.

Although the Pakistani Taliban and even Osama bin Laden always acknowledged the ideological leadership of the late Mullah Muhammad Omar of the Afghani Taliban as the ultimate emir or mentor, the TTP since its inception in 2007 has been mainly focused on Pakistani security and civic targets with some occasional ventures across the Durand Line. Its past and present leaders such as Baitullah Mehsud, Hakimullah Mehsud and Fazlullah often operated autonomously from the remit of their Afghan counterparts, who avoided getting embroiled in Pakistani issues. Midnight missions by Western special forces and drone operations by the US Central Intelligence Agency (CIA) in these Pashtun areas escalated resentment against the West, Kabul and Islamabad, the latter two viewed as mercenaries of the former 'non-Muslim' 'crusading' occupier. Although most of the initial suicide bombers happened to be Pashtun, and especially young and poor, subsequently, younger, slightly educated volunteers from Punjab and Karachi – called Punjabi Taliban – began to provide the TTP with a steady stream of militants. Predominantly Pashtun mentors and experts on preparing suicide vests and improvised explosive devices conducted training programmes in the FATA and Kunhar, while comparatively most of their early targets happened to be in the KP as well. Thus the Pashtun factor seemed to be operative in different forms in various geopolitical developments in which local, regional and global congruities and proclivities began to converge. The Pashtun dimension of this imbroglio has been quite equally evident in bickering between the United States and Pakistan, especially with several high-profile border attacks costing the lives of numerous Pakistani citizens and troops in the FATA. In addition, violence in Karachi in its recent incarnation has involved the Urdu-speaking Muhajireen and Pashtun groups based in localities like Sohrab Goth. The emergence of the Islamic State of Iraq and Syria (ISIS) in 2014 and its declaration of a Sunni caliphate proved quite attractive to some TTP leaders, who already under pressure and hotly pursued by

Pakistani troops and the CIA-operated drones, were in a state of disarray. Their leaders, seeking new hideouts in the Tirah Valley or in Afghanistan, faced desertions and disillusionment since some of them began to support ISIS, while the rest still followed Fazlullah. Unlike the earlier groups, which collectively followed Mullah Omar as the ultimate emir, the ideological cracks became more acute during 2014, often leading to intra-TTP escalations.[13]

Certainly, the KP and Pashtun areas on the other side of the Durand Line became the focal point of multiple forms of violence, causing thousands of deaths and undermining law and order, along with dislocating countless people. In addition to the communities that were affected, interstate relations were seriously impacted by the multiplicity and enormity of this violence. For instance, on 26 November 2011, 26 Pakistani soldiers guarding two posts at Salala in Mohmand Agency on the Pak-Afghan border were killed by US aircraft and helicopter gunships, and an already fragile bilateralism characterized by mutual accusations and distrust nosedived. The operation by US Navy SEALs targeting Osama bin Laden in the garrison town of Abbottabad on 2 May 2011 acutely strained a murky bilateralism.[14] The secret operation not only put Pakistan under a global negative spotlight but also, equally, raised several issues on both sides.[15] The Pakistani security and intelligence agencies were found inefficient, tardy and even culpable in not locating such a high-profile militant who was hiding right next to their top-notch military academy.[16] The publication of the 322-page report of the special commission headed by a senior Pakistani judge and based on detailed interviews with more than 200 witnesses found the entire Pakistani security system wanting in several areas, and was not sparing in regard to its political authority as well. In the same vein, the report censored the United States for a 'gross violation' of Pakistan's sovereignty.[17] Earlier, in February, Raymond Davis, a CIA agent, had shot down two Pakistanis in a busy area of Lahore, and despite public demands for a proper trial, he was allowed to leave the country after he paid blood money to the bereaved families.[18] On 5 June 2012, several Pakistani Taliban, joined by their Afghan allies, attacked Salala border post in Mohmand Agency and claimed to have killed more than six Pakistani soldiers since they viewed Pakistani security forces as collaborating with the non-Muslim invaders and thus acting as accomplices in an intra-Muslim fratricide. The latest killing of Pakistani troops by their compatriots occurred at a time when the US predators – drones – had intensified their operations in North Waziristan. Washington had already accelerated drone operations since the inauguration of the Obama presidency in 2009, but there was a renewed intensity following the NATO conference in Chicago in May 2012. Amidst an ascendant American rebuke of Pakistan, the warring nations threatened to speed up their operations against suspected militants inside the FATA irrespective of Pakistani criticism and a general Muslim discomfort with unaccounted for and underreported killings of people in Southwest Asia.[19] Despite a familiar Pakistani official protest in Islamabad conveyed to the American ambassador, Leon Panetta, the US defence secretary, reiterated Washington's resolve to persist with drone attacks in addition to other such military operations. His reiteration was expressed in Delhi during his visit and was characterized as a strong critique of Pakistan, along with seeking a greater Indian role in Afghanistan.[20]

Panetta's message to Pakistan was in line with the usual American exhortations which unleashed multiple cross-currents of violence and anger on both sides and might have been partially addressed to China, Russia and such other neighbours to the north, who had been discussing Afghanistan following the postulated NATO withdrawal in 2014. On 29 May 2013, three weeks after elections for the new political government in the country, an aerial missile killed Waliur Rahman, one of the senior members of the TTP since its formal existence in 2007 and based in the FATA. A day after Nawaz Sharif took the oath as prime minister before the newly elected National Assembly, a drone attack fired missiles at a house in North Waziristan killing seven residents, all characterized as militants. Sharif, in his inaugural speech, had demanded the halting of drone flights and attacks, a subject that had become a major public demand since Imran Khan led a major protest into South Waziristan in November 2012, and for a time, there was a lull in attacks, although predatory flights never stopped. However, such public denunciations did not seem to register any response from Washington since the aerial attacks continued, including one on 3 July 2013 on a market area in Miran Shah in North Waziristan which claimed 18 lives.[21] On 1 November 2013, a day after Sharif's US visit, a missile struck Hakimullah Mehsud, obviating the possibility of any peace negotiations between Islamabad and the TTP. Imran Khan's Tehreek-i-Insaaf (PTI) viewed it as another affront to Pakistan's sovereignty and began to block NATO's supply convoys plying across the Khyber Pass. The drone attacks certainly became infrequent in 2014, and a few sorties coincided with the above-mentioned Zarb-e-Azb operation in North Waziristan and curiously did not register any large-scale public reproach, largely because of the support for this long-awaited military campaign.

While drones had continued to zero in on Pashtun tribal hamlets, the TTP persisted with its multiple campaigns across Pakistan, with the larger share again destined for KP. True to its claims of thwarting the elections in the country and by specifically targeting the PPP, ANP and Karachi-based Muttahida Qaumi Movement (MQM), TTP affiliates killed scores of Pakistanis, with the ANP paying the biggest price.[22] The TTP had defined these political parties as secular organizations, and thus, they appeared to follow an un-Islamic agenda and needed to be targeted in particular. The ANP could not hold its public rallies out in the open, and Asfandyar Wali Khan, the grandson of Khan Abdul Ghaffar Khan (d. 1984), strictly confined himself to television interviews and messages through social media. The PPP and certainly the MQM could not convene any electoral rallies in KP as well, although Imran Khan's PTI and Jamiat-Ulama-i-Islam (JUI-F) initially escaped such wrath.[23] However, it is equally significant to note that a vast majority of Pakistanis participated in these elections, including two pioneering women candidates from the FATA itself.[24] In a restive Balochistan, when six bombs planted by the LeJ blew up Jinnah's last abode in Ziarat, outside Quetta, on 15 June 2013, the TTP connection was not missed by anyone. The LeJ confessed their culpability in a phone message to the BBC, simply because Jinnah was presumably Shia, or had been at least a secular Muslim and still an 'apostate'.[25] It is not crucial that Ziarat, the summer resort, lies in a relatively peaceful Pashtun areas of Balochistan, but simply because the LeJ and the TTP had been operating in tandem, and tribal valleys provided both munitions and training for such otherwise ruthless and unnecessary ventures against historical monuments. A puritanical version of Sunni Islam, imbued with a strong anti-Shia component, and refurbished by guerrilla training imparted by Pakistani Taliban mentors to Punjabi militants such as LeJ reveal diverse ethnic and sectarian strands converging to cause an organized spectre of spectacular destruction, with the result that the global media allocated coverage to both these groups. On the same day, a female bomber blew herself up in a bus carrying female students from Bahadur Khan University, the only women's university in Balochistan, causing several deaths and injuries. When the casualties were taken to Bolan Medical Hospital in Quetta, another suicide bomber blew himself up, while some other militants took patients and medical staff in the Emergency Ward as hostages. It was only following a military operation and extended firefight that the building was freed of the hostage takers. The blast on the bus and the subsequent siege of the hospital, presumably by the Baloch Liberation Army (BLA), resulted in 28 deaths and several casualties. Both the above events, which occurred on the same day, were carried out meticulously by two separate organizations, followed by self-confession, which shows that Pakistan was facing multiple forms of violence, the paths of which intersected one another and often went through the rough and tumble of the FATA, widening the distance between these Pashtun regions and the rest of the world.[26] Even when the Sharif regime was holding peace parleys with the TTP in March–April 2014, Pakistani soldiers and civilians were being killed in targeted attacks in Karachi, Sibi, Islamabad and Rawalpindi. Following these assaults on trains, courts and markets, the TTP would deny any role and instead blame other 'splinter groups', determined to derail those negotiations.

One may say that the Shia-Sunni volatility might have roots in Punjab or in pre-1947 United Provinces (UP) during the colonial era, but no region in Southwest Asia is free of such violence.[27] Although, traditionally, the Hazaras of central Afghanistan had been persistently discriminated against due to their denominational and ethnic identities, even fellow Shia Pashtuns have not been spared by the so-called Sunni majoritarianism, which intensified following the Iranian revolution and resistance in Afghanistan. Most Turis in Kurram Agency and some Bangash from the neighbouring Hangu's settled areas have been traditionally Shia, although they remain surrounded by overwhelming Sunni majorities on all sides. While traditional tribal mores, despite some flare-ups during Muharram, disallowed any persistent campaign against the Turi and Bangash Shias, the Hazara ethnicity proved more problematic until many of them decided to move into colonial India. Their migrations to Quetta allowed them better educational and economic opportunities, in addition to more breathing space in an immensely plural subcontinent. However, as mentioned above, the emergence of LeJ in recent times and its connivance with the TTP have resulted in an unremitting campaign against Hazaras in Quetta. A highly literate and comparatively well-placed community has been encountering an even more insidious campaign against their religious and commercial places, besides attacks on buses carrying Hazara Shia pilgrims travelling between holy places in Iraq, Iran and Pakistan. In January 2013, an attack on a Hazara snooker hall killed 90 people and grievously injured many more, while two well-organized attacks in February on Shia mosques claimed over 100 lives owing to coordinated suicide bombings carried out and vocally admitted to by LeJ.[28] Such large-scale and even spectacular attacks on Shias in 2014–15 happened along with target killings of Shia professionals across the country, and it appears that a parallel system of networking, recruiting and training of guerrilla-like militants went on unhindered. All these groups seem to have been co-opted by the TTP, which never seemed to run out of fronts, cadres and perpetrators, although some of them might have been pursuing their own agendas without any recourse to the latter.[29]

Taliban: The Pashtun Dimensions

Undoubtedly, these multiple forms of violence have claimed thousands of lives, mostly from amongst the ordinary people, a major portion of them being Pashtun, and they have been perpetrated by private outfits such as Al-Qaeda and the TTP, and were also visibly linked to the more than 30 NATO nations fighting the longest war in their histories in one of the poorest regions of the world. The killing of Osama bin Laden in May 2011 in Abbottabad, with its fallout for the country and its external allies, and a chain of violence in the FATA and across the border in Afghanistan turned this predominantly Pashtun region into the most talked-about and feared territory, with its traditional Pashtun inhabitants perhaps the most stigmatized people on earth. The way in which political Islam has often been construed only in its virulent and violent manifestations, ignoring a vast terrain of complex and parallel political strands and strategies, the *Taliban* as such have become the fulcrum of a Southwest Asia–based Pashtun militancy that confronts local and extra-regional political actors in a nihilistic way. Political Islam, Taliban and Pashtun ethnicity tend to get juxtaposed to augment simplistic and alarmist views on Muslim militancy, which seems to be rooted in the forces of ethnicity and ideology – both anchored in some atavistic, anachronistic, totalitarian and false consciousness. Certainly, NATO has been fighting the Afghan Taliban for more than 13 years, and their defiance has refused to wither away, and since they are based in Southwest Asia around the Durand Line, both Afghanistan and Pakistan have become the hotbed of this global encounter.

Pakistan, given its size, location, population, plurality and diverse forms of militancy has occasionally been called a failed state or even 'a tinderbox' – perceptions which may also have roots in regional discord such as with India.[30] The Indo-Pakistani dissension over Siachin, water resources and accusations of interference in each other's internal affairs, and certainly the human rights violations in Kashmir Valley by Indian troops and the massacre of 2,000 Muslims in Gujarat, followed by organized attacks on a Samjhota train and on Mumbai only helped extremists on both sides. In addition, the Saudi-Iranian conflict and growing chasms between Sunnis and Shias across West Asia have coalesced with the ethnic and sectarian conflicts within Pakistan and Afghanistan. Not only are these two countries defined as the epicentre of terror but they also equally and insidiously have graduated into the Muslim *other*, often seen as anti-Western, violent and anti-modern, falling closer to North Korea and Somalia in popular Western consciousness. Since the border regions of these neighbours are predominantly populated by the Pashtuns – both in urban settings and tribal hinterlands – their ethnicity routinely gets even more problematized, which misimages and perceptions rooted in Orientalism and post–September 11 vengeful geopolitics tend to supersede. It is certainly true that the pro-West Northern Alliance in Afghanistan was anchored in anti-Taliban trajectories, and predominantly consisted of Tajik, Uzbek and Hazara ethnic groups, and was often seen as an anti-Pashtun coalition in which local interests spawned collaboration against a perceived common foe that traditionally held power in Kabul. The demographic figures – somehow legitimizing the traditional Pashtun hegemony over Afghanistan since 1747 – spawned this alliance at a time when the external support during the Cold War often ended up shoring Pashtun groups. Iran and some other neighbours might have assisted those clusters – forming the Northern Alliance – but not to the extent that it could have displaced Pashtun supremacy over the rest. Most groups within the Northern Alliance, including the mythical and even controversial leaders such as Ahmad Shah Masud, Muhammad Fahim, Rashid Dostam, Karim Khalili, Abdul Ali Mazari or Ismael Khan, did not gain any nationwide, cross-ethnic profile, and were seen within the confines of their own ethno-regional specificities.[31]

Ethnically and demographically, the Taliban in Afghanistan are overwhelmingly Pashtun, while in Pakistan, despite a strong and even a dominant Pashtun ethnic configuration, they reflect a more cross-ethnic mix. There are groups of people from Punjab, Karachi and Azad Kashmir who are collectively known as Punjabi Taliban, and are often motivated by a discretionary jihadist spirit which is rooted in specific anti-Western, anti-Indian and even anti-Shia sentiments.[32] Speaking Urdu, but having been influenced by a more purist and austere version of faith called Deobandi Islam, these younger elements are the end result of geopolitical, demographic and local trajectories imbibed through madrasas, or they could have been ideologically influenced by social media. Pakistan's Jamaat-i-Islami (JI) and Jamiat-i-Ulama-i-Islam (JUI) played vital role in the early indoctrination of these people among whom anti-Western sentiments abounded, though shorn of militarist defiance. These were purist and visibly masculine trajectories, which were inherently political and bonded with fellow Islamists in Afghanistan, especially following the Soviet invasion. The displacement of millions, especially the Pashtuns and their concentration in KP and Balochistan, along with the emergence of madrasas offered the groundwork, while volatile politics in Southwest Asia and then the post–September 11 developments turned these purist views into a full-fledged warfare. Not all Taliban sympathizers are the firebrand graduates from madrasas, though some leaders, foot soldiers and followers, including Mullah Omar, his colleagues and their counterparts in the KP have been graduates of seminaries such as Darul Uloom Haqqania, Akora Khattak, run by Maulana Samiul Haq (who also heads a faction of the JUI). Additionally, there is another recent strand of activists and militants manifesting a cross-ethic mix of university graduates, who subscribe to a divine mission of defending fellow Muslims and are willing to involve themselves in militarist acts at varying places.[33]

In the case of Pashtun tribals on both sides of the Durand Line, other than strong religious, denominational and ethnic solidarity, the class dimension has been quite crucial since most of these people come from rural and agrarian networks. In contrast, the Punjabi Taliban, despite an overwhelming rural and agrarian presence, can be from middle-class urban clusters and were either brought up in seminaries in towns and cities, or might have grown up inside a well-knit mohalla culture. There are certainly *external* Taliban as well, who either belong to Diaspora Muslim groups or come from Central Asia, embodying their own experiences of Islamist activism in which local dislocation as well as the global romanticism of jihad became the ultimate definers. NATO, Kabul, Islamabad and a number of Muslim capitals have traditionally opined about their indigenous jihadis, but it is mainly the Afghans and the Taliban, whose training and ideological orientation across Afghanistan and on the Frontier lie behind this trans-ethnic activism. Still, it would be ahistorical to underemphasize the predominantly Pashtun background of the Taliban in both the adjacent countries since their relations with Al-Qaeda have often been viewed as either too close, or, at least, functional. While the US government and its other allies mostly saw the Afghan Taliban and Al-Qaeda as mutually interdependent and intertwined, several other observers found their interface rather casual as both are mainly interested in humbling the occupying forces.[34] Certainly given that the Afghan Taliban, the TTP, Al-Qaeda and other groups share a wider convergence in distrusting and resisting Western powers and their Muslim allies, any possibility of their working together and sharing information, space or strategies is comprehensible. However, unlike Al-Qaeda, the Taliban in both Afghanistan and Pakistan have informal networks and lack a kind of sophistication and global outreach that the groups like Al-Qaeda may have.

As mentioned above, the Pakistani Taliban are far from being a monolithic group, but share a wider concurrence on ideological fronts and certainly display diverse manifestations of political Islam. However, both of them are the foci of global military, political, media and academic attention and, owing to this a number of countries, other than Afghanistan and Pakistan have been on the receiving end of Western scrutiny and ire. Since Obama's assumption to the White House, the purview of 'the war on terror' has expanded to several other regions – nearly all of them Muslim. Whereas in 2005 the United States had around 70 drone predators in its arsenals, by 2013 their number had increased to several thousand, with their operations extended to many other Muslim countries.[35] During the George W. Bush presidency, there were 16 drone attacks on Pakistani soil, while since Obama assumed power there have been over 350. There has been a similar multiplication in Afghanistan, Yemen, Syria and Somalia. Meanwhile, the continuation of Guantanamo Bay, the elimination of individuals through military means without recourse to prior legal or judicial processes and the unaccounted and underreported deaths of civilians in predatory and midnight attacks have registered a major increase under the Obama administration. Moreover, following the Chicago NATO conference in May 2012, drone attacks on the FATA became even more frequent. In fact, President Obama

> [has] embraced a disputed method for counting civilian casualties that did little to box him in. It in effect counts all military-age males in a strike zone as combatants, according to several administration officials, unless there is explicit intelligence posthumously proving them innocent [...] It is the strangest of bureaucratic rituals: every week or so, more than 100 members of the government's sprawling national security apparatus gather, by secure video teleconference, to pore over terrorist suspects' biographies and recommend to the president who should be the next to die.[36]

While in late 2011 senior officials, including Hillary Clinton, supported negotiations with the Taliban, by the summer of 2012, the priority had shifted to ensuring a safer and quicker withdrawal of troops from Afghanistan. Negotiations were mostly discontinued either because they did not make any headway, or simply because the Obama administration did not want to look weak during a re-election year. The latter kind of realpolitik had certainly resulted in the Democratic administration being perceived as a regime on steroids.[37] A year later, Washington, in view of a major military withdrawal from Afghanistan, again sent mixed and blurry messages about the Taliban, vacillating between rejection and reconciliation, and often left negotiations to the discretion of Kabul and Islamabad. Ashraf Ghani's regime in 2015 was making some headway in seeking regional consensus by reaching out to China, Pakistan, India and Iran, though suspicions and even violent confrontation between Kabul and the Taliban continued. Ghani's own partners, such as the Northern Alliance's Abdullah Abdullah, often procrastinated on pursuing closer collaboration with Islamabad, partly to avoid antagonizing India and also due to age-old reservations against Pakistan.

Pashtuns: Ethnicity, Nationalism and Resistance

The Taliban, as mentioned above, are essentially or at least in their earliest incarnation, were mainly a Pashtun trajectory, though they subsequently gained supporters and allies from a wide variety of other Islamist groups. Their accent on jihad by virtue of fighting the non-Muslim occupying forces of a Muslim country and their accomplices, added to an aura of Muslim 'Che Guevaras', who belonged to some of the most traditional societies on earth, yet had the temerity to take on the most powerful nations of the world. Despite their outdated weaponry and outmoded wherewithal, they continued their defiance for more than 13 years, which, to them and many other observers, had caused the retreat, if not a total defeat, of the most formidable alliance in human history.[38] Their capacity to mount diverse and deadly attacks, and still survive serious human losses over a long period of time with several hostile factors and forces arrayed against them added to a kind of mystique about them. This adulation was more evident especially among many younger Muslims, who might have even overlooked their idiosyncrasies or other violent outbursts largely because of their resistance against the commonly irreverent West and its surrogates. For some observers, including former Soviet soldiers, the Taliban, like erstwhile mujahideen, added a new dimension to guerrilla warfare, which the Western forces, despite their resources and outreach, could not eliminate.[39] On the Pakistani side, despite a strong Punjabi element the TTP has been led by the Pashtuns; is based in Pashtun regions, especially the FATA; and most of its attacks on security forces, politicians, polio workers and schools occurred largely in Pashtun-inhabited regions, though they were subsequently extended to other metropolitan centres as well.

Often called Pashtuns/Pushtuns or Pakhtun/Pukhtuns, the well-knit communities of trans-Indus regions may have different genealogies and hypotheses on their origins, but it is the common language – Pushto – and a greater sense of shared history and culture that configure them into a larger ethnic identity. Despite belonging to several tribes or *khels*, the Pashtuns straddle the territories on both sides of the Pak-Afghan border, all the way from the lower reaches of Chitral/Nuristan, for 1,600 miles to the south where three regions of Balochistan cohere across the three states of Pakistan, Afghanistan and Iran.

Accounting for 42–45 per cent of Afghanistan's population, they number around 16 million, though a significant proportion has been living in exile especially following the Soviet invasion of 1979. On its own, Pakistan accounts for around 31 million Pashtuns, divided between 'settled areas' of the KP and about 20-mile wide tribal territory adjacent to the Durand Line. The latter accounts for around four million Pashtuns, whose tribal demarcations roughly fall in sync with the names of the agencies they come from. Other than their tribal and rural configurations in Pakistan, urban Pashtuns account for a growing proportion of their total population, and no wonder Karachi – neither Peshawar nor Kabul – is the largest Pashtun city in Southwest Asia. This Pashtun urban diaspora has expanded to cities such as Islamabad, Lahore, Quetta and Karachi due to economic, geopolitical and demographic mobility, but language and greater sense of kinship keep defining their primordial identities.[40] Unlike the usual view of the FATA Pashtuns being inherently and rather statically archaic and less mobile, many Pashtun merchants, lorry drivers and blue-collar workers across the Indus Valley and in the Gulf happen to be from those tribal agencies. There is no denying that they are rapidly changing societies due to the factors mentioned here, and the Taliban on both sides equally manifest the same causal factors in their evolution. In a generalist sense, the Pashtun Taliban are certainly the offshoot of, as well as the retort to the transformative forces of modernity and geopolitics where socio-spatial mobility appears both vexing and unavoidable.

There are numerous hypotheses about the origins of the Pashtuns which vary from their Semitic beginnings to an Indo-Aryan inception. Given their long, aquiline noses and physical resemblance with the Biblical prophets, the Pashtuns have been seen as the Twelfth Tribe of Israel, which sought refuge in the mountainous lands during the ancient dispersals.[41] However, a predominant view posits them as an Indo-Aryan ethnicity called Ashvaka in Sanskrit, while Herodotus, the ancient Greek historian, mentioned them as the tribe of Pactyans in the Hindu Kush. Some people link their ancestry with the ancient Greeks, long before Alexander invaded these lands in the fourth century BCE, as he certainly encountered some Greek people across the Oxus River in present-day Uzbekistan. The Pashtuns provided the vanguard troops for Central Asian invaders of India and also established a few dynasties in Delhi until an Uzbek prince, Babur, founded the Mughal Empire in India in 1526 following his conquest of present-day Afghanistan. Babur, the grandson of Tamerlane and Genghis Khan, was an eminent literary figure in classical Turkish (spoken in Central Asia among the Turkic tribes) and ensured the grandeur of Kabul as his favourite city, where he even willed to be buried. Later, the Persians captured southern regions around Kandahar from the Mughals, until in the early eighteenth century, the Hotakis, a Ghilzai Pashtun tribe (led by Ahmed Shah Abdali), formed their own government, and by 1747 established the territorial, multi-ethnic state, now known as Afghanistan but traditionally called the Kingdom of Kabul until 1919. Thus, since the eighteenth century, the Pashtuns have been the dominant and ruling configuration in Afghanistan, whereas the Dari (Persian)-speaking Tajiks account for 27 per cent of the total population and the Hazaras of the central regions, who make up around 9 per cent, did not have that privilege until the US-led invasion in October 2001, which catapulted them into power. Joined by the Uzbeks from Mazar-i-Sharif and surrounding areas, the Tajiks and Hazaras comprise the Northern Alliance, which gained ascendancy in Kabul following the Taliban ouster on the heels of the NATO attack. Though Kabul has been the traditional centre and magnet for capturing power in the country – despite a wider tradition of several local power centres – the Pashtuns have usually comprised only one-third of the capital's demography, with the Tajiks from the north accounting for more than half of its inhabitants. Afghanistan's smaller ethnic communities consist of the Nuristanis and Balochis, and except for the Hazaras of Bamiyan and the central regions, the rest of the country has been traditionally and overwhelmingly Sunni by denominational persuasion. The Hazaras, often seen as the descendants of Genghis Khan and the thirteenth-century Mongol invaders, were occasionally discriminated against on the basis of their presumed ethnic origins and Shia denomination.[42]

Despite diverse views about their ethnic origins, Pushto and a shared social code called Pashtunwali have solidified common cultural and religious bonds among the Pashtuns. Pushto is an Indo-Aryan language that is quite similar to Persian and Punjabi and that applies Arabic script. Over the centuries its literary traditions have allowed the Pashtuns a shared historical bond with their past, depicting liberationist, romantic and nostalgic strands – both oral and written – and Sufis and poets such as Rahman Baba, Khushal Khan Khattak, Abdul Ghani Khan, Ajmal Khattak and Israel Ashna, along with folk minstrels have developed it into an extensive literary corpus. Pashtunwali, or the Pashtun code, is a well-researched area among Western anthropologists and sociologists, which centres on individual and tribal honour (*malmastia*) and is rooted in the triangle of *Zan*, *Zar* and *Zameen*. *Zan* (woman) is used here in a wider sense of ethnic purity and family honour in which she is both to be respected and protected. As a young woman, she is romantically yearned for, but has to be approached physically only through marriage; otherwise, any extramarital liaison will result in a societal backlash in the name of *izza/(izzat)* (honour). Thus, woman becomes the repository of ethnic, tribal and familial traditions disallowing any marriages outside these boundaries, especially when most Pashtuns remain rural and tribal. Even among the urban Pashtuns, marrying outside one's clan and tribe may be taboo. The Pashtuns are divided into 60 tribes, which are further subdivided into 400 clans, and such exclusive marital preferences have certainly, to a great extent, allowed the continuity of the world's oldest tribal system.

Zar, in a rudimentary sense, may mean wealth but in fact encapsulates a wider terrain of material and spiritual domains. It may mean family jewellery that links the family with its ancestors and also ensures a financial guarantee during hardship, while concurrently, any other material assets such as house and belongings may mean greater respect within the clan. Prosperity may be translated as divine pleasure requiring charity, contributions to the local mosque and helping the needy and the poor in the locality. A genuinely earned wealth becomes a barometer of success and common respect, and not an enigma, which opens up opportunities for the family and dependents besides helping them gain influence with the local functionaries. *Zameen* means land per se but also assimilates a stronger sense of rootedness both in the native land, the relevant clan and a larger Pashtun *qaum* (community). Land is definitely inherited from parents, and thus is not merely a means of livelihood but also is essentially the identity marker and cause célèbre that has to be defended from exogenous encroachments. Quite significantly, *zameen* is feminine in gender and like the country and *zan*, it is the 'motherland', whose sanctity remains sacrosanct. Like other agricultural societies, selling or losing land for any reason whatsoever becomes a blot and stigma, which again is linked with the concept of *izzat*, and here it is understandably quite local, since honour, by protecting women and wealth, ensures respect among the local clan. Both family and the clan thus become interdependent and anchor as well as benefit from this traditional attribute.

Before political scientists and consultants began to write on Southwest Asian politics and societies, especially the Pashtuns, it had been largely a purview of colonial historians, diplomats and travellers, who were both fascinated as well as intrigued by some of the oldest tribal societies on earth which seemed to have intermittently thwarted external onslaughts.[43] The colonial interest coincided with the contemporary imperial British and tsarist policies when spies such as Alexander Burnes, Mountstuart Elphinstone, Charles Masson and others penetrated these regions, until the military commanders came in with their narratives of campaigns on the Frontier, as fighting the Pashtuns in one of the toughest and almost inaccessible terrains became a prideworthy pursuit.[44] Fortune seekers followed earlier literary figures such as Rudyard Kipling and colonial-anthropologists, and with the influx of tourists and journalists in more recent times a 'mystique' developed around these people.[45] The Cold War certainly combined exotica with strategic imperatives, and other than fiction, political studies began to focus on Afghanistan and Pashtun tribals, which certainly received a major impetus after 1979. Laudatory works on jihad reflected a form of romanticization of traditional Pashtun lands where the West and East met in rugged mountains to thwart some common rivals. Whereas anthropologists and sociologists had continued to define the Indus as the cultural border between Hindustan and West Asia/Turkistan, political scientists in general reflected pervasive macro geopolitical premises. The Indus demarcated clan-based, land-dependent, honour-bound and often change-resistant Pashtun tribal clusters along with smaller communities of Kalashas, whereas Punjabis, inclusive of Hindko, Pothowari and Saraiki speakers, epitomized land-based and caste-ridden yet transforming agrarian communities. The latter, according to this anthropological classification, were seen as the prototypes of their other South Asian counterparts all the way to the forested reaches of the Arakans in Myanmar. One wonders how far this kind of intellectual formulation underlay or was even spawned by the imperial and administrative rearrangements of the nineteenth century, since Sir George Campbell, on the eve of the Second Anglo-Afghan War and a few years before the delineation of the Durand Line, had characterized the inhabitants of the trans-Indus regions as Afghans and noted, 'The Indus, in fact, is a true ethnological boundary, the population on one side being Indian, and on the other side Afghan'.[46] In fact, as early as 1808, Elphinstone Mountstuart had recommended that Indus be a feasible boundary line between British India and Afghanistan as he was sceptical of the efficacy of a forward border. His observations were based on his travels across the Pashtun lands and stemmed from a pragmatic realism.[47] Certainly, 'Afghan' occasionally meant 'Pashtun' as well, since the term was preferred over 'Pathan' by the indigenous people. While Campbell differed with the Forward Policy of British India in the 1880s, and the eventual Indo-Afghan borders might have been pushed west by another hundred or so miles, the Afghan rulers until this day have never shunned their claims over the Peshawar Valley and further east and south up to the western banks of the Indus.

Fredrik Barth was more intrigued by the charisma and leadership among the egalitarian Pashtun societies owing to their traditional cultural orientation with a semblance of balance between the clannish and clerical leadership at the local level.[48] However, Pashtunwali within a defined geography permitted a strong ethnolingual commonality in which land, honour, revenge and the protection of anyone seeking shelter were primed over other segmentary mores. These cultural contours were perceived as merging with religious convictions, which underwrote mistrust and even resistance to any external control or conquest.[49] Barth's pioneering studies opened a renewed postcolonial discourse on Pashtun cultures and norms in which historical narratives based on honour, resistance and hospitality underpinned trajectories including solidarity shown during all three Anglo-Afghan wars dating from 1839 to 1920, and the rest. The Great Pashtun Revolt of 1896–7, among other factors, was significantly inspired by Mullah Hadda, which spread far and wide, and resulted in the Tirah Military Campaign in 1897, the largest of its kind ever undertaken by Britain between the Crimean War and the First World War. In the same vein, the revolt led by Faqir of Ippi in Waziristan before and after the Partition, to a great extent, appears to have been a model for Mullah Omar and the Taliban.[50] Haji Turangzai's revolt against the British and then his support for Pakistan fall within the same tradition of jihadist resistance against non-Muslim intervention, espoused by a charismatic religious leader often in cahoots with khans. This tradition, certainly, had indigenous roots, but its ideological and organizational motivation came from the Deoband Movement in India, especially its jihadi elements, that sought a more purist form of Islam, sharing an affinity with the local Pashtun austere traditions.[51] These localist yet powerful traditions were occasionally change resistant as, for instance, seen in the case of King Amanullah Khan, who had to abdicate his throne in 1929 largely because his reforms were perceived as both alien and offensive. The government led by President Daud Khan (1973–78) and the subsequent communist regimes until 1992, despite several incentives, failed to learn from their past and ended up annoying conventional power brokers and local stakeholders of traditional values.

This is not to say that the Taliban are formed in a total rejectionist mould, yet their strength lies in the local power mechanics and cultural interfaces in which charismatic leadership such as Mullah Omar, Baitullah Mehsud and others, by using Islamic values in a uniquely austere, Pashtun way, assumed supreme leadership. In addition, it is quite vital to remember that the Pashtuns – on both sides of the border – are not anti-modern societies. Rather, it would not be ahistorical to suggest that given their location in the proverbial eyeball of global warfare and espionage, they are at a serious crossroads where forces of change and continuity compete as well conflict for ascendance.[52] It is a different matter that, like several other non-Western societies, rural and tribal Pashtuns are receptive to many features and attendant attributes of modernization yet resist the cultural legacies of hegemonic westernization. While post-1979 surveys and comments lionized the Pashtuns for their valorous resistance to the Soviet presence on their soil and for largely causing the dissolution of the Soviet Union, post–September 11 studies and hasty treatises have often ended up denigrating them for their 'traditionalism'. This discourse only attributes all the negativities to these people, including primitivism, sexism, unbridled violence, aversion to democracy and debate, and some inborn enchantment with the death culture.[53]

Orientalism Reborn!

The Saidian model of Orientalism and the entire tradition of postcolonial studies inclusive of an uneven relationship based on power and its multiple ramifications have posed serious challenges in erstwhile differentiated understandings of non-Western communities and societies. Equally reticent in being labelled as a Left or Liberal, contemporary critique of social studies and humanities, especially of literature, history and anthropology, the counterdiscourse resists the objectification of non-Western peoples. This *othering* of indigenous and colonized societies was perhaps the most serious and enduring aspect of imperial legacies in which, other than knowledge, an understanding of class formation has remained hostage to Eurocentric views of the world at large. Accordingly, like precolonial histories, the issues of resistance or self-redefinition, creeds and culture were either totally denigrated or were relegated to some obscure margins of academic discourse. Thus, it was imperative to re-mould non-Western people themselves so as to liberate them from infantility, violence, localism and superstitions, which had permeated for too long. White explorers, conquerors, warriors, missionaries, scholars and even Western women working as travellers or medical missionaries became the redeemers. It is quite interesting to note how some of these traits of discussing and even 'discovering' the tribulations of Muslim women still remain a cherished area of treatises, which again is a major preserve of their Western counterparts. Here gallantry, patronization, critique, moralism and sensationalist pedantry combine to transmit specific imagery.[54] Naturally, postcolonial studies have often challenged the ethos of such early discourses, which permeate at all levels, including among the postcolonial elite of the former colonies, as knowledge capital still remains very region- and class specific. Historical, religious, literary and anthropological studies undertaken during earlier times are confronted with these intellectual challenges, which make it pertinent to offer fresher analyses free of apologia or rhetorical defensiveness.

Such an intense intellectual polarization is quite explicit in the case of the Pashtuns among whom, for a long time, ethnicity, tribal mores, some inborn propensity to violence and a preference for masculine dominance have been the salient features of narratives embodying a strong sense of hierarchical superiority and self-ascriptive authenticity. Since the colonial era, anthropologists, like colonial officials, have often looked at the Pashtuns as a distinct ethnic configuration in which local, clannish and inherently anti-modern mores prevail, while leadership remains a perennial contest among charismatic figures who use tribal honour, resistance and Islam to establish their populist credentials. In a Darwinian way, the ultimate winner in this contest will rule the roost until displaced by external forces and some newer rival. In other words, ironically, the Pashtuns have to be seen as distinctly different and stuck in a time warp of localism and personality-based cliché. Barth's studies, undertaken during the 1950s, could have been produced in the 1920s when Swat's Yusufzai landlords followed an egalitarian model of clan-based relationship, overseen by a benevolent khan or a wali at the top. Basically, it was a top-down model, which despite its enduring impact, ignored peasants, an emerging middle class and steadily changing relationship between the state and societal stakeholders.[55] The romanticization of the Pashtuns and the idealization of a Wali-led Swat as a kind of utopia wedged between the tribal wilderness and a rapidly encroaching urbanization of corruptive magnitude to the east certainly made Barth's study of Swat a prototype of Pashtun society and even quite pioneering given his European but non-colonial background.

Nationalist imperatives of a new state like Pakistan, its fracas with Afghanistan over the Pashtun regions and its prompt induction into the Cold War, turned its Frontier into a new *frontier*, and a strong element of romanticization began to re-emerge in contemporary literary and historical narratives.[56] This was the time when serious historical works also began to appear and, despite their rigorous research, at one level viewed the Pashtuns as synonymous with the entire Afghan society, while concurrently differentiating them from their neighbours all around. Ideas for a Pashtun state in an age of centralizing nation states did not appear that alien, and relations between the Pashtuns and the Raj, and subsequently between the Pashtuns and Kabul and Islamabad, provided the mainstay of newer studies, often beginning with a Caroevian narrative of Pashtun origins, tribes and their history of five millennia.[57] The issues of class, gender, local leadership and migrations were often absent from such Barthian 'high histories' and 'culturelogues', which vacillate between grand narratives of 'tribes' and 'strong men'.[58] The hippie trail of the 1960s certainly exaggerated the mystique of exotica, otherworldliness and rawness of the Pashtuns, which fell in line with the colonial and early nationalist narratives, and equally fitted in well with the Cold War imperatives, in which a benevolent West was needed once again to thwart an external threat, besides breaking the logjam of stalemated traditions. It is not surprising that from such a perspective the Pashtuns emerge both as raw but equally rooted in their traditional cultures, the primitiveness of which could be cherished and further exceptionalized, yet which had to give way to the imperatives of modernity through education, state building and middle-class nomenclature.[59] Such strongly held images were certainly helpful during the anti-Soviet resistance, when Pashtun society was once again overwhelmingly imagined to be masculinized and homogenous. Ironically, here its *archaic* tribal norms were now being idealized as a meritorious asset that had, in the first place, motivated them to pick up arms against the evil empire. Their traditional penchant for independence and daredevil attitude, unlike the previous mantra of 'becoming modern', were appropriated as the mainstay of jihad and worth celebrating. A new emphasis on Pashtunwali thus became an academic and political urgency, for example, seen as a geopolitical attribute, which a few years down the line returns as a haunting spectre. The ensconcement of Al-Qaeda and other jihadis from elsewhere, especially after September 11, hastily returned the Pashtuns to the hinterland of civility and modernity, and once again the Taliban became the poster boys of a violent, sexist and annihilative community, totally deprived of humanity or respect for life and its basic needs. Now they came to personify the notoriety attributed to Muslims during and since the Crusades and become the prototypes of a decadent, disorganized and destructive Orient that the West had in fact tried to transform in yesteryear.

The West's own preoccupation with race and racism, including scientific racism and neo-racism, has been unnerving, only to be replaced with the recourse to ethnicity as a major socio-political reference and determinant behind pluralism. It is not only a more palatable and milder conceptual framework, but also it can surmise the hierarchies without being too crude and irksome as 'race' has been during the early modern era. It is quite interesting to note that the salience of ethnicity as a hydra-faced, catch-all phrase happened in the United States during the 1960s, and then spread to the rest of the world with varying momentum. It certainly helped subjects such as anthropology and sociology, though the Marxist and Liberal groups have often remained wary of it, and instead, sought to define plural communities in reference to larger categories of nationalities. While for the Left, class became a superordinate, for most historians and political scientists, given their disciplinary domains, the role of civilizations and state structures remained the high tidal marks. In the same vein, theories of modernization reiterated the centrality of the middle class in social engineering, including an expected levelling of the society and knowledge capital, and the forming of the very state which would have a transformative impact for all. Unlike the Marxist abhorrence of the middle class as the problematizing bourgeoisie, here it was a redeemer both for the state and society. Ethnicity was never seen as a major roadblock towards this process in which larger and more effective forces of modernization would usher in greater interdependence and material success, transforming all types of ethnicities into stakeholders. In other words, ethnicity, unlike class, if handled with care could graduate from a liability to an asset.[60] Until ethnic movements violently began to threaten states – essentialized under the Westphalian system and anchoring the international systems – ethnic pluralism was viewed only as a form of collective self-definition. But owing to the volatility of post–Cold War strife in places like the Balkans, Africa and South Asia, political scientists began to define it as a nefarious and anachronistic retribalization, running averse to the entire paradigm of a levelling modernization. Ethnic dissidence, curiously, caused a convergence of the erstwhile polarized liberal and conservative positions, with some observers even suggesting a new world order based on 'Empire Lite'.[61]

Is It Class, or Culture?

Given the above-discussed conceptual maze-like context, one may have to be quite careful in using it as the most vital trajectory in studying the Pashtuns or any other such societies, over and above demarcations engendered by class, internal power struggles and external realignments. Nancy Lindisfarne, despite a self-confessed 'anthropological bias', underlines the role of class, gender and imperial hegemony in understanding historical and contemporary Pashtun experiences, and attempts to go beyond the usual strands of ethnographies employed in studying Swat and the Afghan Taliban. She is certainly not comfortable with the Indus being a cultural border between South Asia and West Asia, though she is not dismissive towards this major strain of traditional ethnography.[62] She is sensitive to the role of the state, which poses serious roadblocks for regional anthropologists who, as in cases such as Akbar Ahmed, Ashraf Ghani, Askar Mousavi, Jamil Hanafi and Nazif Sharani might be co-opted by the former itself. In other words, their professional specialization, owing to pressures as well as inducements, might fall prey to the top-down narratives, which seems to hold sway over the local narratives.[63] She refuses to see the state – national and imperial – as a benevolent transformer or a neutral determinant, in the same way as she is hesitant in positing clerics, including the Taliban as demonic forces. Weary of warfare and the Great Game, she finds herself closer to Gilles Dorronsoro, who is wary of equating the Pashtuns with the Taliban.[64] However, Dorronsoro seems to be focused only on the Afghan Taliban, and his analysis predates the emergence and prevalence of the TTP as a congeries of numerous and unremitting militarist campaigns much beyond the ideology of resistance and class fissures.

Lindisfarne could equally be criticized for seeing in the Taliban – at least on this side of the Durand Line – a movement that 'combine(s) Islamist ideals and class politics to emphasize egalitarian feeling and mobilize support'. In her appreciation of their egalitarianism, she is not alone in seeing the anti-imperial nature of the [Afghan] Taliban, yet without qualifying them as distinct from their Pakistani counterparts, it may not be holistically true for all. Fraternal feelings abound with a greater sense of mission and heroism, yet there are powerful manifestations of summary injustices, ruthless retribution and material travesties based on seeking favour or funds through ransom. To her, the Taliban, in an ideological context, must be seen as a retort to foreign [American] imperialist ventures, which ignored gender deprivation in the 1980s when it suited the occasion and picked it up when it needed to demolish the Taliban after September 11. Even the Western claims of creating democratic and mundane institutions and freeing women in Afghanistan not only smack of Islamophobia and imperial expediency but also reflect a nefarious selectivity:

> The invasion of Afghanistan was pro-secular, the invasion of Iraq anti-secular. In impoverished, war-torn Afghanistan, the United States's 'terrorist' enemies are the right-wing Sunni Taliban, while tribalism and gender have been manipulated in favour of Karzai's US-backed secular regime. In oil-rich, the 'terrorist' enemy was Saddam Hussein and his secular, originally leftist, regime. In Iraq, ethnic and sectarians divisions have been leveraged in favour of separatist Kurds in the north, and Shi'ites over Sunnis elsewhere.[65]

In other words, it is the permanence of imperial interests that can conveniently gloss over serious contradictions yet cohere and gel together due to enduring Islamophobia. The emergence of a middle/middling class in Pashtun regions including Afghanistan, the FATA and Swat, squeezing political and economic opportunities both for the khans and peasants, clearly merits elaborate research at the local level. Certainly, locating politics in Pashtun lands beyond certain *given* parameters of cultural forces or inborn traits of some exceptional ethnicity merits serious attention, though, like any other historical developments, explanations may always abound in diversity and their mutual disagreements. No single factor can fully explain a social phenomenon such as the Pashtuns, yet tools like culture, class and creed, and determinants including foreign interventions amidst media portrayals go a long way in understanding the ambivalence bordering on hostility which these Gandhara lands seem to invoke.

Chapter Two

IMPERIAL HUBRIS: THE AFGHAN TALIBAN IN ASCENDANCE

'These are detestable murderers and scumbags, I'll tell you that right up front. They detest our freedoms, they detest our society, they detest our liberties.'

Canadian General Rick Heller, 16 July 2005[1]

'The Taliban made some terrible mistakes, and I do not condone them. But I am also certain that we need a better understanding of how and why they made those mistakes before we condemn them. Many worse things have happened to Afghans than the Taliban government of 1996–2001 [...] In the end the Taliban are only people, and surely deserve to be treated as such. I know they are capable of learning from their mistakes and of changing their minds.'

James Fergusson[2]

Other than the various mainsprings of external interest in Afghanistan and the trans-Indus regions in general, and the Pashtun cultures in particular, geopolitical developments during the 1980s and then specifically after September 11 understandably came to focus on the Taliban. Along with its reductionist portents, such a discourse reveals some shared themes such as political Islam, Taliban militancy and the security imperatives of the regional and global actors, which collectively converge in imparting or reiterating specific images about Muslim and especially the Pashtun communities. The juxtaposing of Islam with violence and Islamist movements as terrorist outfits cannot be seen in isolation, as they have become brand names and identikit for most Muslims. Irreverent of their ideological, denominational, class and national pluralities, such simplified views, more like those of the erstwhile communists and Jews, have unleashed severe ramifications. Appreciation of Muslim mundane dilemmas like those of any other human society is often absent in them, or it may reflect sheer indifference if not bland hostility. Certainly, there are numerous areas in which Muslim groups and states could perform better, yet their political and economic issues, especially those linked with some external factors need to be analysed objectively within their generic contexts. After all, the evolution of various forms of political Islam such as Hamas, Hezbollah, Islamic jihad, the Muslim Brotherhood, the Moro Liberation Army, the Jammu and Kashmir Liberation Front, the Hizbul Mujahideen, the Taliban and such other formulations overwhelmingly sought sustenance in political and economic grievances in which disempowerment, a grave sense of injustice, sustained oppression and dislocations had continued. Surely, the Taliban represent a form of political Islam who used their faith as a legitimizer and a bonding factor that would inspire their followers to the extent of resisting and even attempting to eliminate their adversaries. This form of Islam grew on a sense of divine mission as a holy struggle in which martyrdom became the ultimate objective. In the process they incurred, or did not even shirk death through acts of self-immolation such as suicide bombing, which were solely rationalized through an uncritiqued conviction, which may be seen as a kind of death cult. Nevertheless, the Taliban in Afghanistan are a political movement, which arose due to a particular set of stark realities in that country at a particular juncture, especially amidst a pervasive post-Soviet dismay. Historically, they evolved as a response to warlordism, moral drift and political chaos and, in a formidable way, they have reflected the rural, poor (under) class of their own societies, in which a strong sense of belonging, struggle for a noble cause and even dying for their faith converged with the frustrations of being have-nots. Mostly consisting of war orphans who largely grew up in the sordid atmosphere of refugee camps in Pakistan, the Taliban became the mouthpieces of a disenchanted yet ambitious youth culture that saw their families, like their country, having fallen victim to external invasions and internal nihilism. These 'Oliver Twists' of a tormented land soon reached self-actualization as a power to be reckoned with whose sustenance and enduring prowess for all these long and arduous years have further created a strong sense of purpose and self-esteem.

These Afghan Taliban include the first generation of mujahideen who fought a taxing war against the Soviet war machine that cost more than one million deaths, in addition to dislocating more than five million Afghans into refugee camps in the neighbouring countries. Given the total population of the country, still below 16 million in 1990, the huge proportion of fatalities, added to several million maimed and handicapped, along with the devastation of infrastructure, the cost to an already poor nation was stupendous. But the heroics of Afghanistan were soon overshadowed by two concurrent developments: firstly, the former allies left the people high and dry following the Soviet withdrawal, and secondly, without a proper transitional arrangement across the country and outside Kabul, regional, tribal and ethnic warlords parcelled the entire land among themselves. Here, kidnaps for ransom, the elimination of opponents, gun and drug running and a total absence of development schemes became the order of the day. Despite a Moscow-supported regime in Kabul, led by Doctor Mohammad Najibullah, Afghanistan had fallen victim to internecine civil wars and anarchy, and any tangible plan for the repatriation of refugees failed to mature. Afghanistan became a neglected land mass of dispersed and dismayed human localities in which the local criminal elements assumed overlordship. While one reads an enormous amount of material – often journalistic – on extreme acts committed by the Taliban against women and minorities, it is quite rare to encounter any serious works which might exhaustively contextualize their emergence and prevalence. The Taliban have been seen as inherently barbarian chauvinists who enforced their unilateral writ by sheer force and would not even shirk from imposing severe punishment for minor transgressions, and who equally ensured a very puritanical, humourless and even lifeless kind of existence. Authors such as Ahmed Rashid saw in them a growing threat to Western and regional security imperatives in addition to posing serious challenges to the civil liberties of the masses, while Western journalists such as Christina Lamb viewed them as a negative and pernicious retort to decency, who through their medieval and often irrational attitudes, ensured a pathetic subjugation of women.[3] Needless to say, such narratives provided justification for the post–September 11 military campaigns in

Afghanistan and the calibration of a new system, which was meant to bypass the Taliban while espousing higher moral ground through the empowerment for Afghan women. External observers, including nongovernmental organizations (NGOs) and visitors to Afghanistan during the 1990s, had often echoed the security threats that the Taliban posed to the rest (non-Pashtun Afghans such as the Tajiks, Hazaras and the Uzbeks) besides frowning upon their politicking, which was seen as rooted in ethno-sectarian unilateralism.[4] To some people, Afghanistan had fallen into an unfathomable abyss whose new rulers, unlike the deposed royalty and a small thin layer of the Kabuli middle class and professionals in the Diaspora, had begun to take the country back to some dire existence.[5] From a post-Soviet perspective, while an ebullient optimism marked the beginning of West-led globalization, concurrently views about Islam as the new destabilizing force began to gain currency, and here the ideology of jihad propounded by groups such as the Taliban was translated into a new global threat. Amidst the premises of a clash of cultures and the end of a familiar form of history, such Muslim activists – soon to be known as jihadis – became the 'others' who manifested a new form of totalitarianism with their reach across the familiar territorial and ideological boundaries.

It is only in the recent past that one comes across the view from the *other* side, with Taliban leaders and supporters such as Mullah Zaeef and Samiul Haq providing inside views of the movement and its career. Their long sustainability also led to a greater receptivity to a more dispassionate analysis of 'the Taliban phenomenon'.[6] Inherently Pashtun and comprising past and new fighters from Afghanistan, the Taliban are the culmination of specific circumstances that prevailed in the country in the 1990s, and are simultaneously a transformative movement like several others that have often evolved among Muslims, which embody utopianism by mixing an Islamic ethos with political activism. They might have been the beneficiaries of some external support – tacit or direct – but are essentially a home-grown development, which certainly included a large section of Afghani Pashtuns who had experienced resistance as well as migrations in previous years. Simplifying the creation and prevalence of a movement such as the Taliban merely to the Pakistani ISI or the American CIA is too reductionist an explanation, though mutual contacts and facilitations happened frequently. In the same manner, viewing them as merely an offshoot of Al-Qaeda, overlooking the leadership, goals, purview and strategies is again not the whole truth. There is no doubt that their leaders shared a common world view, especially in the 1980s when Arab Afghans like Osama bin Laden ventured in to fight the Soviets, yet the Taliban have mainly focused on their own country-specific programme. Here, as often articulated by Mullah Omar and others, it has been resistance against the presence and intervention of the foreign (non-Muslim) forces of their (Muslim) lands besides ensuring the promulgation of a sharia-based polity, both purported to establish ultimate peace and distributive justice. Even if some of their leaders might be based in Pakistan's FATA or elsewhere, they have avoided getting embroiled in the internal affairs of Pakistan. This is not an ordinary policy postulation, especially when one looks at Pakistan's variable role of an erstwhile ally to a total adversary, aligned with non-Muslim invading forces in a neighbouring Muslim country. This must have been agonizing to the Taliban leaders, who presumably enjoyed closer proximity with Pakistani civil and military leaders in the near past and who did not even encourage or assist the Pakistani Taliban in carrying out violent attacks within Pakistan. The American pressures on Pakistan to mount more operations against the Taliban leaders and supporters including Jalalud Din Haqqani or the Quetta Shura were resented by its people, and especially drone attacks added to the existing ire, yet the Afghan Taliban continued to abstain from any venture against the Pakistanis as such. By default, the CIA and other such external intelligence agencies might have worked with the Taliban at some levels, but after 1998, following the Al-Qaeda attacks on the US embassies in East Africa and retaliation by the Clinton administration, that interface came to an end.[7] Instead, the CIA and other Western agencies began to strengthen their relations with the Northern Alliance, which became more pronounced after September 11. The United States, Britain and some other European forces reportedly undertook specific military operations on Pakistani soil while targeting the Taliban and their non-Afghan supporters, which, to a great extent, generated resentment against Islamabad among several Pakistani Islamists.

Attributing the evolution and sustenance of a formidable movement such as the Taliban to the Pakistani ISI is a rudimentary view of a formidable situation and ignores other complex and indigenous factors that solidified the Afghani Pashtuns behind Mullah Omar. In addition, such a hypothesis appears to have an exaggerated view of the capabilities of the ISI, which in its own front yard has been unable to stop suicide bombings and attacks on its own installations and other security institutions. The ISI has not been able even to contain ethnic conflict in Karachi, the financial and strategic hub of Pakistan, and crediting it with forming a whole new movement and then sustaining it through its limited means for all these long years, besides running a kind of proxy war without local intent, appear far-fetched premises. They equally belittle the intensity of the local grievances and networks which spawned the Taliban in the first place and carried them through until in 2013, when the White House nonchalantly decided to negotiate with them, much to the ire of the Karzai regime. Certainly, Pakistani intelligence agencies, especially the ISI, were quite close to Afghan mujahideen of various ethnic backgrounds, including some individuals in Hamid Karzai's regime, yet their main preferences were Afghan Pashtuns. Their relationship with Ahmed Shah Masud, General Muhammad Fahim, Abdullah Abdullah, Burhanuddin Rabbani, Karim Khalili, Ismael Khan and others in the Northern Alliance were variable, but one can say the same thing about their relations with Gulbuddin Hekmatyar, the Pashtun leader of Hizb-i-Islami, who, during the late 1990s, turned into a pariah from being a favourite asset. September 11 allowed Indian intelligence agencies such as the Research and Analysis Wing (RAW) to strengthen their relations with the Northern Alliance and some anti-Islamabad dissidents and Pakistani exiles, which made the ISI even more dependent upon the Pashtun elements. Karzai's own overtures to India, often accompanied by rebukes to Pakistan given his nostalgia for his Simla days, also did not help diversify the Pakistani interface with the Afghans. At a powerful level, the evolution of an assertive Pashtun factor within the Pakistani security and civil establishments, freer contacts between the Pashtuns on both sides as compared to the Persian-speaking Tajiks or Hazaras, and Pakistan as the favourite destination for the displaced Afghan Pashtuns understandably solidified these contacts. Numerous Hazara and Tajik refugees used Pakistan both as a new home as well as the staging post for migrations abroad, and despite their affinity with Iran or other regional neighbours, Pakistan provided them a needed and secure channel. Khalili often lived in Islamabad and during the 1980s moved between Islamabad, Tehran and the West, whereas Abdul Rashid Dostum would prefer Turkey, but his fellow Afghan Uzbek refugees used Pakistan in their settlement in Turkey or elsewhere.[8]

Mullah Salam Zaeef, one of the founders of the Taliban movement and a lifelong associate of Mullah Omar, dismissed the view of his party as being totally Pashtun and instead mentioned Talib governors and ministers from amongst the Tajik and Uzbek communities. He was equally dismissive of the allegations that the Taliban, during their rule, carried out massacres in Bamiyan and Mazar-i-Sharif, though he certainly acknowledges that without any proper authorization, some Talib hotheads destroyed the Bamiyan Buddhas in 2001. He has been critical of the United States and other Western powers for attacking his country and occupying it for their own purposes, which conflicted with Afghan interests, boding unnecessary tragedies for his war-torn country. His agonizing internment at Guantanamo Bay owed itself to US unilateralism and was equally facilitated by the Pakistani ISI who, in total of contravention of diplomatic protocols, handed him over to vengeful Americans. Zaeef was certainly not a diehard extremist who would deny education to Afghan girls nor did he believe in isolating Afghanistan from the rest of the world. In an interview in his office in Islamabad, well before September 11, Zaeef rejected various familiar allegations as nefarious misperceptions and spoke as a progressive voice of a movement that sought stability, peace and co-existence in his country – away from warlordism and surrogacy.[9] However, his return to Kabul and confinement in his house did not deter him from acknowledging the venerable title of Amir ul Momineen – leader of the faithful – for Mullah Omar amidst a reinvigorated optimism as well as nostalgia for the Taliban tenure when Afghanistan was comparatively peaceful and free of suicide bombings and where drug production had gone to its lowest point.[10] At some stage, he might re-emerge as an influential intermediary between the external forces and his own leadership both in Afghanistan and across the borders, yet like everybody else he stayed watchful while waiting for the planned withdrawal of the troops by 37 nations from his native soil. Either the Taliban of 2016 may prove different by co-opting the rest or Afghanistan might sadly return to internecine warfare with people seeking revenge as well as patronage. A country ravaged by sustained warfare perpetrated by one superpower after the other, along with their numerous and equally unaccountable collaborators, certainly seeks peace and amity, yet may equally find itself at another ambivalent crossroads. While a post-NATO Afghanistan is highly desirable among most Afghans, as is suggested by several recent studies based on interviews and polls, its future internal politics and implications for its neighbours such as Pakistan, Iran and the CARs may vary from regional co-operation to reinvigorated conflicts. While the Northern Alliance may retain its own pro-India and pro-NATO inclinations, the pro-Taliban Pashtuns may tread carefully in dealing with Islamabad. A sense of mistrust had swept in following Pervez Musharraf's total alignment with the United States in September 2001, and it was certainly not Mullah Abdus Salam Zaeef alone who held a pronounced anti-Pakistan sentiment; rather, it was shared by a whole generation of those who suffered at Bagram, Pull-i-Charkhi, Guantanamo and elsewhere.

Already by early 2013, the war in Afghanistan led by the United States and other NATO countries, with its gigantic human, economic and ecological costs, was being characterized as 'misconceived' by Sherard Cowper-Cole, until recently the British ambassador to Kabul and the special British envoy for Af–Pak.[11] James Fergusson, a British journalist with several works on military history and a keen observer of NATO's longest war in a rather desolate and far less developed country, echoed a similar recurrent sentiment when he advised a negotiated settlement with the Taliban. His volume written during the closing days of Gordon Brown's Labour Government highlighted the age-old predicament of external powers in Afghanistan in which a quick and rather prompt entry into Kabul or Kandahar was always ebulliently viewed as a penultimate triumph. Fergusson repeated a pervasive cynicism toward the war in Afghanistan that had already cost his own country billions of pounds in addition to the lives of about 500 troops, with no end to the stalemate: 'The insurgency is still expanding and Afghans have lost confidence in our ability to stem it, as well as in our ability to establish an alternative government in Kabul that is truly worthy of their support. A negotiated settlement with the Taliban looks increasingly like the West's only way out of the mess'. He further noted, 'Our strategy to date has been dominated by military rather than civilian thinking, and it is failing in large part because we continue to misunderstand the nature of the opposition'. To Fergusson, the Taliban were an ideological force that needed to be understood and engaged in a dialogue, and a continued usage of force was destined to defeat the purpose.[12]

The invasion of Afghanistan undertaken by President George W. Bush had become a multifaceted war against the Afghans in general and the Pashtuns in particular, with the American expenses by 2013 already gone well over $1 trillion in addition to numerous fatalities and causalities. The war that involved well over 130,000 US soldiers – many more than their Soviet counterparts during the 1980s – and other than massive Pashtun deaths, had already destabilized Pakistan along with exacerbating a pervasive sense of Muslim alienation. Amidst this dilemma, a number of studies began to challenge the erstwhile uniformist view about the Taliban, that is, their ferocious primitiveness and vulnerability before the most powerful forces. A sense of triumphalism based on Western invincibility had seriously begun to erode, along with a fresher outlook about the insurgency and its ideological and ethnic portents. Such a major change among politicians, diplomats, journalists and academics displayed a sense of dismay as well as a new realism that had been lacking in earlier rash hypotheses and self-congratulatory analyses. Simultaneously, the detailed memoirs by Mullah Abdus Salam Zaeef, a senior member of the Taliban and a close associate of Mullah Muhammad Omar, offered a persuasive alternative narrative, which equally underpinned the resilience of both the Guantanamo-returned former ambassador as well as of his colleagues in the 'movement' and its ideology. However, before we can surmise Zaeef's autobiography, it is vital to revisit some of the representative scholarly and miscellaneous works on the Taliban, which formed as well as substantiated a specific Western view on this movement.

Ahmed Rashid's *Taliban: Islam, Oil and the New Great Game in Central Asia* was one of the pioneering full-length works which studied the Taliban in reference to the ethnic, regional and global politics of the 1990s. The book appeared soon after the conquest of

Kabul by the Taliban and the establishment of an emirate under the leadership of Mullah Muhammad Omar, at a time when Afghanistan had begun to attract global attention, especially in reference to its form of political Islam, which appeared raw and energetic but was still characterized by several contradictions, especially in reference to women, media and religious minorities. Rashid, a former Cambridge graduate of Pakistani origins and one-time a leftist ally of Baloch activists who were striving for a united (Greater) Balochistan comprising the regions of Pakistan, Iran and Afghanistan, had turned to journalism in the 1980s and reported for Western newspapers before writing for the *Far Eastern Review*. Originally from Lahore, Rashid, in his radical days, had been based in Kabul like some other dissidents and witnessed the overthrow of Daud Khan in April 1978 in a communist coup, followed by the arrival of Soviet troops in December 1979. By then, Rashid – 'one of Lahore's finest exports' – had developed first-hand knowledge on Afghanistan and its new communist rulers, who soon began to face resistance from disparate Afghan tribal groups, often lumped together as mujahideen, or holy warriors.[13] During that time, in his native Pakistan, General Zia-ul-Haq had put paid to the civilian government of Zulfikar Ali Bhutto in July 1977, followed by a full-fledged Islamization of the legal, educational and financial institutions of the country along with the providing of sanctuaries and support to Afghan mujahideen who had begun to attract serious attention from the CIA, MI6 and some anti-Soviet regimes. A few months before the Soviet invasion, Iran – a mainstay of Western influence under the shah – had undergone its Islamic transformation under the spiritual leadership of Imam Ruhollah Khomeini. Political Islam with its three indigenous and certainly distinct manifestations had arrived in Southwest Asia generating diverse responses from around the world. Rashid, a liberal commentator and a world apart from his communist days, was confronted with a populist version of Islam that, to him, was newsworthy due to its uniqueness and regional ramifications. Rashid was writing mainly for Western readers and displayed some specific views about the Pashtuns and Afghanistan, and perceived the Taliban mainly as a regressive movement. However, to be fair to his erudition and intentions, he is not sparing of external interventions, though he carelessly subscribes to orientalist stereotypes of the Afghans, as he notes,

> Anyone who has been touched by an Afghan or visited the country in peace or in war, will understand when I say the country and the people are amongst the most extraordinary on earth. The Afghans have also been affected by one of the greatest tragedies of this century – the longest running civil war in this era that has brought untold misery. Their story and their character involve immense contradictions. Brave, magnificent, honourable, generous, hospitable, gracious, handsome Afghan men and women can also be devious, mean and bloody-minded.[14]

Certainly, every human society has its contrasts and dilemmas, yet Rashid's portrayal seems to echo nineteenth-century Kiplingesque and other contemporary caricatures. His first chapter, in a usual journalistic way, begins by his recounting the killing of a murderer in the Kandahar stadium in a quick, Taliban style in which the victim's relatives are allowed to undertake the execution since they had refused to forgive him in lieu of blood money. About 10,000 spectators – both men and children – saw the gory spectacle, which, to Rashid, typified a callous, premodern practice justified in the name of sharia.

To him, the Taliban were a nihilist reality for the people of Afghanistan in which 'fear, acceptance, total exhaustion and devastation after years of war and more than 1.5 million dead have forced many Afghans to accept the Taliban ways of justice'.[15] The next day, while visiting the Taliban governor of Kandahar, Mullah Mohammed Hasan, he was shocked to see Carlos Bulgheroni, chairman of Bridas Corporation, negotiating for a proposed pipeline. Soon, he was to see the Argentines compete with Unocal in seeking a similar arrangement with the new rulers.

Rashid felt quizzical over the Soviet motivation behind attacking Afghanistan in 1979, which had cost them more than 45 billion US dollars and a retreat that was partly facilitated by the Americans and other allies whose subversive assistance to the mujahideen cost them just 4 to 5 billion US dollars.[16] Rashid found in the Taliban an inherently rural group of southern Pashtuns who had developed camaraderie around the 38-year-old Mullah Omar and operated in quite a secret way. Most of these leaders had suffered war injuries, and their experience of governance and diplomacy was almost nil, though they enjoyed the support of the Pakistani defence establishment, including the ISI, simply because after the Punjabis, the Pashtuns accounted for 20 per cent of the country's armed forces. He recounted the delegation led by General (retired) Naseerullah Babar through Afghanistan in September 1994, which had been facilitated through ISI officials such as Colonel Tarrar (known as Colonel Imam and at one time head of the Pakistani consulate in Herat). Babar, Benazir Bhutto's interior minister, was himself a Pashtun and undertook this delegation not only to personify Pakistani trade ambitions vis-à-vis Central Asia but also to let the Taliban test their prowess by curbing warlords who often waylaid regular traffic between the two countries. It is not surprising that soon after marginalizing the local warlords, the Taliban were able to capture Spin Boldak, the Afghan town on the Pakistan–Afghan border. This prompt action symbolized dramatic results, which other than highlighting Taliban prowess, showed the lack of ability of the Kabul regime, which had been engrossed in a civil war among its various mujahideen constituents such as Hekmatyar, Masud and Dostum. Other than fighting among themselves and turning Kabul and its environs into rubble, their ethnic and sectarian escapades with the Hazara Shias represented another tragic spectacle of anarchy and gruesome violence. Away from the factional fighting in Kabul and the regional potentates in Herat, Bamiyan and Mazar-i-Sharif, here the youthful Taliban shared a cherished brotherhood that grew around a common cause of bringing about an Islamic order in a chaotic country. Many of them had valiantly fought the Soviets and were scarred by those experiences, but had been equally energized by their own sense of mission and purpose.

On 4 April 1996, after capturing Herat, a camera-shy Mullah Omar had hoisted the Prophet's shawl before a cheering crowd of his comrades and students, who by September had been able to capture Kabul and were well on their way to reaching Shomali Plains and Badakhshan – the stronghold of the legendary Masud. The conquest of Kunduz by Mullah Dadullah followed the ouster of Dostum from Mazar. Though both actions claimed thousands of lives, they ensconced Omar's followers as the rulers of 90 per cent of their nation's land mass. The initial attempt to capture Mazar in 1997 had been unsuccessful, resulting in large-scale Taliban deaths at the hands of Uzbeks and Hazaras. The Hazaras were singled out as responsible for the mass graves of 2,000 Taliban found by

Dostum's men near Shebarghan in Jowzjan province. Eventually, the Taliban were able to make inroads into the Dostum-led alliance by winning over some powerful warlords such as Malik Pahlawan, who changed sides, enabling a Taliban victory that had been vitally assisted by the Pashtuns who were settled in and around Kunduz. The Hazaras, led by Karim Khalili and Ali Mazari and stigmatized by predominantly Sunni Afghans, became the focus of revenge for having murdered Taliban troops during their earlier retreat. Masud had roughed up the Hazaras in 1995, and now in 1997, despite large-scale Iranian, Indian and Russian military assistance, their alliance with Dostum and Masud could not stop the Taliban onslaught and it fell before their ascension. Like the founder of Afghanistan, Ahmed Shah Abdali, mainly Pashtun warriors from southern and eastern regions had once again risen to their tribal – Ghilzai and Durrani – traditions and wrested the reins of power from Tajik, Uzbek and Hazara contenders. While many Kabulis were definitely alarmed over the rapidity of these transforming events at the behest of rural-tribal outsiders, given the extent of large-scale destruction of their city, they yearned for some externally imposed stability.

Other than their sudden evolution and a rapid conquest of most of Afghanistan, their policies towards women and minorities – in a unique and certainly exclusive version of Deobandi Islam – began to attract global attention. Rashid, like several other analysts, found a strong gender animus in their policies which went beyond keeping women confined to *chaadar* and *chaardiwari*, as he noted: 'The Taliban's treatment of women drew enormous adverse publicity and international criticism when Emma Bonino, the European Commissioner for Humanitarian Affairs and 19 Western journalists and aid workers were arrested and held for three hours by Taliban religious police in Kabul on 28 September 1997'.[17] They had irritated the Taliban for taking photographs of women, which the Taliban considered sacrilegious as well as an effort to malign their rule by the Western NGOs. However, to their foreign visitors, they often justified their restrictive policies due to the traditional conservative mores of their society, which, unlike the Kabuli urbanites, sought a limiting public role for their women. For the Taliban, this might have been realpolitik given that their constituents mainly came from rural and tribal backgrounds, but for the outside world this was a rolling back of basic human rights of half of the Afghan population:

> Taliban leaders repeatedly told me that if they gave women greater freedom or a chance to go to school, they would lose support of their rank and file, who would be disillusioned by a leadership that had compromised principles under pressure. They also claimed their recruits would be weakened and subverted by the possibility of sexual opportunities and thus not fight with the same zeal. So the oppression of women became a benchmark for the Taliban's Islamic radicalism, their aim to 'cleanse' society and to keep morale of their troops high.[18]

Rashid, like some of the early observers, viewed the Taliban basically as a deviant and extreme form of purist Islam that might have been an aberration in the country. Needlessly, he failed to see the complexity and endurance of the Taliban and offered a rather cursory and understandably negative portrayal of the movement.

While analysing the traits of contemporary versions of political Islam across the board, Rashid found certain commonalities among them, including the role of a charismatic leader who often uses the ideology of jihad and martyrdom to enthuse his followers. Concurrently, as a liberal Muslim, he did not find political Islam, including the Taliban brand, to be properly programmatic, offering alternatives so as to resolve the diverse challenges confronted by Muslim communities and countries. To Rashid, deliverance lay only and strictly in progressive Western models of modernity, which to him, at a generalist level were supposedly secular. In contrast, political Islam – called Islamism by him – was a world apart from the socio-ideational realties of Muslim societies, including Afghanistan, as he observed:

> The Taliban interpretation of Islam, jihad and social transformation was an anomaly in Afghanistan because the movement's rise echoed none of the leading Islamist trends that had emerged through the anti-Soviet war. The Taliban were neither radical Islamists inspired by the Ikhwan, nor mystical Sufis, nor traditionalists. They fitted nowhere in the Islamic spectrum of ideas and movements that had emerged in Afghanistan between 1979 and 1994.[19]

Certainly, many Muslim modernists in recent years have found it convenient to categorize political Islam into revivalist, syncretic and traditional moulds, yet may not comprehend the inherent diversities and overlaps within these three strands. To Rashid, the Taliban *were* an ahistorical phenomenon, which did not comprehend the syncretic traditions within the Afghan cultures, and by superimposing their form of rigid Salafism they were 'bucking the entire trend of Afghan history because they have no understanding of it'.[20] In the rise of the Taliban at the turn of the century, Rashid had found a new great game in Southwest Asia that included regional as well as global actors due to oil politics and strategic gains, yet that could prove fatal for countries in the neighbourhood.

Rashid's view of his own country was that of a weak state on the brink of a precipice where the Taliban model of political Islam as well as the result of Taliban primacy next door entailed serious costs. In a way, he was partially right since like the proverbial blanket, Pakistan could not ignore the developments next door nor could it really please all the contenders, and thus like everyone else, it made its own choices within a limited remit. The return of Osama bin Laden to Afghanistan in 1998, September 11 and then the backlash of this event spilt over the Durand Line, exacerbating Pakistan's own instability, but again the neighbours could not create proverbial China walls:

> The Taliban's new model for a purist Islamic revolution has created immense repercussion, in Pakistan and to a more limited extent in the Central Asian Republics. Pakistan, an already fragile state beset by an identity crisis, an economic meltdown, ethnic and sectarian divisions and rapacious ruling elite that has been unable to provide good governance, now faces the spectre of a new Islamic wave, led not by the older, more mature and accommodating Islamic parties but by neo-Taliban groups.[21]

Most probably, he was pointing towards the wider sympathy for the Taliban model in addition to the growth of parties such as JUI and JI, which despite Musharraf's rhetoric of 'enlightened moderation' formed their own governments in 2002 in the North-West Frontier Province (NWFP) and Balochistan. These parties were soon bypassed by the TTP as a diehard umbrella of vociferously militant groups pursuing their own distinct agendas besides zeroing in on Pakistan's state and civil infrastructures. However, the sustenance and steadfastness of the Afghan Taliban, despite the toughest and sustained campaigns by NATO and ISAF, witnessed a greater populist following of the former, positing them as more than a passing phenomenon. The Taliban stood fast against challenging odds over a longer period of time, which helped them regroup during the waning years of NATO's involvement in Afghanistan, but this victory could also bode well for newer challenges and even a neo-orthodoxy within this predominantly Pashtun movement.

A Neo-fundamentalism, or Rural Islamism?

Amidst the brutal chaos and unremitting violence in Afghanistan, the Taliban's emergence and then their prevalence all over the country during the 1990s through their defeat of former mujahideen like Ahmed Shah Masud, Gulbuddin Hekmatyar, Burhanuddin Rabbani, Abdur Rasul Sayyaf, Sibghatullah Mojjeddedi, Abdul Ali Mazari and Nabi Mohammedi, was not a minor feat. Policymakers, academics, spies and journalists were all baffled by their rise, and a rise which, even to their leaders like Mullah Omar, Mullah Ghaus, Mullah Hasan, Mullah Rabbani, Mullah Dadullah and Mullah Muttawakil must have been no less astounding. Capturing Kabul was not a minor attainment for otherwise rural Pashtun 'outsiders' who might have enjoyed support from across the Durand Line, yet their own resilience, enthusiasm and valour cannot be underrated, especially when the existing regime of Mojjeddedi and Masud had been well ensconced and could afford to continue its enduring brawls with Hekmatyar's Hizb-i-Islami and Mazari's Hazara-based Wahdat-i-Islami. Amidst this taxing imbroglio, while Afghanistan and especially its capital were put on the receiving end of an internecine warfare, Dostum, for a time, carried on with his familiar policy of changing alliances to suit his own interests as well as autonomous power in and around Mazar. Soon after their entry into Kabul, the Taliban had hanged Najibullah, the Moscow-dependent president of Afghanistan, who had survived the Soviet debacle for some time until the mujahideen overthrew him in 1992, and he lived in a UN safe house as a virtual prisoner. His dead body was allowed to hang by a pole in Kabul by the new rulers, yet many Kabulis resigned themselves to an existentialist view of this transformation both out of compulsion as well as out of pragmatism since the Taliban had brought an end to factionalism and unremitting urban destruction. The Hazaras felt bruised, as their travesties incurred a grievous wrath a few weeks later in 1997 when a regrouped Taliban triumphed over a Dostum-led alliance of Uzbeks and Hazaras. Dostum took off for Turkey as he had done off and on, and Iran's efforts to salvage the last bastion of resistance against the Sunni Taliban proved futile. However, their support for Dari-speaking Tajik leader Masud continued, as he was once again confined to Panjshir Valley following his ouster from Kabul. Masud tried to reawaken his contacts with supporters in Moscow, Dushanbe and Tashkent, but to no avail. The latter, like Iran, felt threatened by the Pashtun-led political Islam that could be a model for their own clusters of Islamist opposition. Iran's reasons for unease with the Taliban were ethnic, religious and certainly geopolitical. At one level, the Taliban's ascendancy represented a triumphant Sunni orthodoxy to their northern and eastern borders, while at another level, they were the old enemies, unlike the Persian-speaking Tajiks who had often bickered with Persians. At yet a third level, they were perceived to be a threatening trajectory of a Saudi-Pakistani-American alliance which could further isolate the Shia regime in Tehran. The United States and the European Union were certainly ambivalent towards this new major development in Southwest Asia, and given President Bill Clinton's own personal travails besides challenges in the Balkans, this region, following the Soviet withdrawal in 1988, had once again turned into a distant 'periphery'.

Initially, Afghanistan under the Taliban did not register a major academic interest, yet the press reportage continued with more focus on the Taliban's strict laws on public behaviour, which were seen not merely puritanical but also inherently anachronistic and sexist. The Ministry of Virtues was passing a quick succession of laws meant to control public behaviour, but other than their unilateralism and intolerance in several cases, their implementation through quick judicial proceedings in the name of sharia often became newsworthy, earning the Taliban an image problem. Thus, while their political and military exploits seemed astounding, their sociocultural epithets were seen as compromising the imperatives of a tolerant, peaceful and plural civil society. In lieu of peace and stability, Afghans, especially in cities, were now experiencing strictures of various types, all justified in the name of honour and faith. Amidst such denunciatory news coverage, the earliest work on the Taliban was an edited volume by William Maley, which included several chapters by Afghan scholars and international contributors. *Fundamentalism Reborn* offered multidisciplinary perspectives on the Taliban, though every analysis appeared to be tentative due to the immediate and ongoing nature of their incarnation. At one level, the editor saw in them the continuation of an age-old tradition of madrasa education which produced clerics, while at another they were seen part of a wider phenomenon of seeking recourse to Islam with varying degrees of emphasis on its political and ideological characteristics. Malet referred to Winston Churchill's encounter of 1898 with some of these 'wandering *Talib-ul-ilms*, who correspond with the theological students in Turkey [and] live free at the expense of the people'.[22] Certainly, the comments not only reflected a Churchillian-Victorian imperial view of Muslim activists in post-1857 South Asia but also exhibited resentment towards the Pashtuns in general who had taken up arms all the way from lower Chitral to the western reaches of Balochistan. These revolts all across the trans-Indus regions of a mainly Pashtun population were seen as machinations of 'mad' mullahs who had been inciting their followers against Raj in the name of jihad. Needless to say, Churchill and many other adherents of a 'Forward' policy during the Great Game, witnessed intermittent revolts in these regions all the way until 1947, seeing major anomalies in their formations. The Tirah Campaign of 1896–7 was the largest of its type that had engulfed Swat and adjoining areas of Malakand, along with Kurram, Waziristan, Khyber, Orakzai and adjoining tribal territories, including the Afridi region of Tirah.

Malet, among other factors, found the Taliban detention of the journalists accompanying Emma Bonino on 29 September 1997, in Kabul as a turning point in affirming their tyrannical practices. Still, he saw 'less Afghan blood on their hands than the Soviet army, associates of the Khalqi dictator Hafizullah Amin, or the Hizb-i-Islami of Hekmatyar'.[23] Amin Saikal felt that the personal ambitions of various mujahideen leaders, despite their agreeing to a power-sharing (Peshawar) agreement of 24 April 1992, were largely responsible for fracturing the polity, which was further exploited by external forces such as Pakistan. As an Afghan nationalist, he felt that, despite engineering an amiable agreement, Pakistan, through the Taliban, simply sought 'cross-border ethnic clientelism'.[24] According to Anthony Davis, the whirlwind rise of the Taliban in the mid-1990s was owed to a 'bruised pride of Afghanistan's Pashtun community, whose political dominance of two and a half centuries had been rudely challenged by newly-assertive minorities'. His biographical note on Colonel Sultan Amir – known as Colonel Imam – was the earliest one on an ISI official who, following his training of mujahideen groups in Balochistan during the 1980s, headed the Pakistani consulate in Herat. Imam had, in fact, helped Babar's initiative in 1994 that had not only facilitated the movement of the trade caravan from across Quetta into Kandahar and beyond but also had equally paved the way for the visit of several Islamabad-based Western ambassadors into southern Afghanistan without the knowledge of the Kabul regime led by President Rabbani. Ironically, Davis identifies Imam as a Pashtun military officer, though, in fact, he came from Punjab and was called Imam because he often led the mujahideen and their successors in prayers. They respected him for his devotion, though it is a different thing that the Pakistani Taliban eventually killed him in 2010 while recording his murder on camera.[25]

Ahmed Rashid's piece in Maley's collection noted a vocal 'Pashtun grid' within the Pakistani high command supportive of the Taliban, since during that period both the army and the ISI were headed by two Pashtun generals. In addition, the Pakistani defence establishment viewed with grave suspicion India's growing influence upon the Northern Alliance now ensconced in Kabul, though Richard Mackenzie found American foreign policy towards the Taliban simply ambivalent and 'broken down under the width of its own contradictions'.[26] Anthony Hyman and other contributors looked at Russia, CARs, Iran and Saudi Arabia being watchful of rising Taliban power where their mutual ideological, ethnic and political interests conflicted, reaffirming that the Taliban were not beholden to any specific external force. Olivier Roy's paper differentiated the Taliban as a traditional form of orthodoxy with fundamentalist portents and strictly rural roots, which had been consolidated through madrasa education in the NWFP. He differentiated this kind of Taliban-based trajectory as quite ethnic, narrow in scope and outreach and intellectually less rigorous than Islamism, which to him, was a more modern, urban and better organized trajectory. While the Taliban's exposure to external influences was only confined to their schooling in the Frontier and Balochistan provinces of Pakistan, Islamists such as Rabbani, Mojjeddedi, Sayyaf and a few others from northern Afghanistan had a wider interaction across the Muslim world. Both groups were anti-Western, and in their own respective ways were deeply impacted by movements across the Muslim world, including the First Gulf War of 1990–91. To the French analyst, the Taliban were the most conservative of their type and carried little attraction outside predominantly Pashtun regions, as he noted:

> The Taliban have no foreign policy. Their only strategic alliance is with Pakistan. Theirs is a purely Afghan movement which has been instrumentalised by Pakistan, whose constant goal since the Soviet invasion has been to turn Afghanistan into a vassal country by playing

on the Pashtun ethnic groups and on fundamentalism [...] But there is no danger of a Taliban spillover elsewhere: the movement is strictly Afghan, Pashtun and tribal. They are the expression of a maverick fundamentalism, strangely unfitted for the contemporary world ummah they think they embody.[27]

In hindsight, some of these views did not prove correct as the Taliban, instead of disappearing, put on a resilient and enduring struggle, and in the process found thousands of acolytes far and wide in the neighbourhood.

Like other manifestations of political Islam, sometimes called Islamism as well, such as the JI, the Muslim Brotherhood, Hezbollah and Hamas, the Taliban attracted an enormous interpretive historiography, though areas like geopolitics and gender often dominated such studies.[28] According to Mohammed Ayoob, the Taliban, in a monolithic sense, shared a romanticized view of a mythical golden age that needed to be restored through austere resistance and the imposition of sharia.[29] Roy looked at political Islam as a sociological phenomenon, which aggregated younger and disaffected sections, though he rightly believed that movements like the Taliban were both state- and society oriented. These groups not only wanted to capture power and change the political system but also they were equally committed to transforming their respective societies in a rather purist way.[30] Amidst a host of media outpourings often wondering at the Taliban's *easier* ascension to power in Afghanistan and their travails with Masud, three other areas often attracted major attention from analysts. Their version of political Islam and promulgation of its legal dimensions called *Hudood*, along with their treatment of women and ramifications for other regional states had been the major preoccupation of both the media and academia. Despite the paucity of first-hand information, these studies often saw in the Taliban a whirlwind development destined to run out of steam within the ever-changing vortex of local loyalties and external intervention. Their escapades with the Iranians, Indians and hobnobbing with Al-Qaeda not only added to their critics but also allowed a supposedly closer proximity with the Pakistani ISI. At one stage, Pakistan's Foreign Office, Military Headquarters through the ISI and the Frontier government in Peshawar were seen as pursuing three parallel foreign policies towards Afghanistan, thus making it appear as if Islamabad itself was not so certain about the reach as well as the future impact of this new major force on its western borders, which had already begun to gain sympathy in many opinion circles. Kamal Matinuddin, a retired Pakistani general and a former head of the Institute of Strategic Studies (ISS) in Islamabad, published a book expressing some praise as well as curiosity about this crucial force across the Durand Line. Given his own penchant for strategic analysis within the global and regional contexts, Matinuddin did not shower any exaggerated praise upon the Taliban and instead offered a more realistic and even critical analysis in which the role of madrasas such as Darul Uloom in Akora Khattak and others in Karachi and Balochistan were seen as providing the ideas as well as models. He, however, highlighted the role of free-for-all violence within Afghanistan as the most vital reason behind the Taliban and their receptivity among a wider Pashtun population that was tired of war and warlordism and desired an early return to normalcy.

While offering details on the military capabilities of regional warlords and mujahideen commanders, Matinuddin found the Taliban to be totally untraditional since proper training in military know-how and other more specialized areas of strategy, espionage and planning seemed to be absent: 'The Taliban are not to be compared to an organized army. Their commanders do not carry out a military appreciation. There are no assembly areas, forming-up places, or start of lines before an attack is launched. No fire plans are made. A large number of rockets are fired in the general direction of the objective, accompanied by a hail of bullets from automatic weapons, and hopefully the rival militia surrenders. The war booty so obtained helps them to fight for another day'.[31] To an urbane military thinker, the Taliban's military thrusts were seen as more spontaneous than as properly ordained, yet had worked given the youthful enthusiasm for a deeply ingrained righteousness of their cause and loyalty to the leadership. However, Matinuddin had a mixed message for Pakistan and other neighbours wherein he advised more care and restraint instead of rushing for quick and uncritical support which could only cause a backlash from non-Pashtun and non-Taliban Afghan elements:

> Pakistan's humanitarian and economic assistance to the Taliban was based partly on a desire to promote its national interest – they occupied the areas through which the road to the landlocked Muslim republics led – and partly to put military pressure on Rabbani and Masood, who had bitten the hand that fed them. However, by supporting the Taliban against Rabbani and Masood, Pakistan highlighted its policy of giving preference to the Pashtuns over other ethnic minorities. This was a negation of the declared statements of the Pakistan leadership that they had no favourite in Afghanistan.[32]

He did not question Pakistan's decision to recognize them as the new rulers of Afghanistan following their capture of Kabul, yet did not agree with its timing. It had materialized at the time of the Taliban's ouster from Mazar-i-Sharif after its earlier conquest by them, though subsequently they were able to consolidate themselves in Dostum's stronghold. His scepticism of their politicking persisted, yet he appreciated their handling of a hijacked Indian airliner that had landed at Kandahar airport on Christmas Eve in 1999 with 300 passengers aboard. On its way to New Delhi from Kathmandu, the plane had been hijacked by Kashmiri militants who, among other demands, mainly sought the release of three colleagues from Indian prisons. The aircraft remained on the runway for eight days as negotiations between the two governments continued, and the hijacking came to an end without bloodshed:

> Contrary to what western nations and some people in Pakistan believed, the Taliban behaved in a dignified and mature manner. They did not act like uncivilized people; intolerant, trigger happy and unmindful of internationally accepted norms. The Taliban allowed the aircraft to land in Kandahar on humanitarian grounds just as Pakistan and UAE had done a day earlier. They condemned the hijacking and refused to give political asylum to the hijackers. They warned the hijackers not to harm any of the passengers or else they would storm the aircraft. The Taliban provided fuel to the aircraft to keep the passengers warm.[33]

Matinuddin had urged Pakistanis to dissuade the Taliban from global isolation by pursuing more humanitarian policies without defying world opinion in several crucial areas. In the same vein, Islamabad was encouraged to 'exercise greater influence on the Taliban to ensure that they do not act against Pakistan's national interests. It must persuade the Taliban to encourage the return of Afghan refugees [...] The Durand Line is a very porous border but efforts must be made to check free movement across it'. He concluded his volume by stating, 'Seminaries in Pakistan where Afghans are being imparted religious education must be screened to ensure that they do not become hot beds of terrorists'.[34]

Peter Marsden, an Arabist with some first-hand experience with the British aid agencies in Afghanistan, put an interesting light on the Taliban's version of political Islam and its interface with the outside world, especially the West. His volume, like those by Rashid, Maley and Matinuddin, was an early account of the mainly Pashtun movement that sought stability as well as a virtuous life by transforming both the state and society strictly within their own country. However, he still noticed significant global ramifications in their message and policies, as he noted: 'The Taliban are but one manifestation of the impact of the Afghan conflict but they bring into focus a web of factors spanning interface between Islam and Christianity, developments within Islam as a religion and as the basis for a political ideology, international power politics and international economy. Every effort to clarify the situation raises further questions, and there are no easy labels with which to define the Taliban'.[35] To him, the Taliban did not have a cogent ideology; instead, it manifested a creed, which inculcated as well as expected a passionate commitment. His word of warning at that stage to the West was not to browbeat them for their adherence to their creed given that the former enjoyed a wider global power and self-belief in its dominance: 'This superiority breeds guilt and awkwardness and makes it difficult to criticize non-Western regimes. Were the relationship a more equal one, the process of dialogue would be much easier because the Taliban would also be less defensive about what they perceive to be the threat from the West to Afghanistan's religious tradition'.[36] Further on, he was more emphatic in his evaluation of Muslim-Western relations in which historical memories of past developments such as the Crusades and colonialism transmit painful responses, which might be aggravated by pursuing a polarized and self-congratulatory discourse. While discussing the Taliban creed, he distanced himself from the term 'Islamic fundamentalism', which he thought was quite pejorative and noted,

> The Western vision of Islam is firmly anchored in the crusades, with images of holy warriors, fired with the passion of martyrs, storming the battlements of some crusader castle. Within the Western psyche there appears to be an almost paranoid fear of Islam as something wild, mindless and potentially overwhelming. As attitudes towards women have changed within Western society, particularly during the present century, there has also been a perception of Islam as a religion that is oppressive towards women.[37]

Marsden found in the Taliban a Muslim-wide phenomenon in which radical Islamists were seeking redress from unjust and often unrepresentative systems, which, in most cases, were monopolized by a pro-Western or westernized elite. Looking at the Arab Spring and even Turkey, one may find some justification in this view, in which class and injustice become the major props for putting regimes 'under increasing attack from radical movements within their own borders for being too accommodating with the West. Such movements have found favour with the most impoverished sections of society, acutely conscious of their lack of access to the riches enjoyed by privileged elites within their own countries and of the affluent lifestyles of Westerners'.[38] He found two dominant features in the Taliban movement: the Pashtunwali and the predominance of ulema, making it into a uniquely Pashtun version of Islam in which the seminaries played a vanguard role yet stopped short of offering a new political ideology. They certainly benefited from the traditional salience of clerics in Afghan society, and a pervasive abhorrence against the mujahideen facilitated their predominance. In other words, they were able to further marginalize khans, generally seen as conservative and vulnerable to materialist temptations. Their rural roots from traditionally Pashtun-dominated areas betrayed a sense of distrust of urban cultures, which to them were often centres of some decadence waiting to be cleansed through a tough arm-twisting. No wonder, their harsh policies affected women the most in Kabul and Herat. Other than a strong patriarchal orientation, their exclusive Sunni credentials turned harsh towards the Shias of Bamiyan, though their suspicions of their fellow Sunni Tajiks and Uzbeks had more to do with ethnicity and a quest for power because the former had apprehended a given Pashtun irredentism since the time of Ahmed Shah Abdali.

From across the Durand Line, support for the Taliban came both from Pashtun clerics and a host of other Islamists such as JUI, which had been already divided into two rival factions led by two Pashtun cleric-politicians – Maulana Fazl-ur-Rahman and Maulana Sami-ul-Haq. Both had been the products of seminaries in the KP and had inherited mantle of religious leadership from their respective fathers. Rahman's father, Maulana Mufti Mahmud, was a Deobandi alim from Dera Ismail Khan, whereas Haq's father had, in fact, founded the Deobandi Seminary at Akora Khattak, situated by the Grand Trunk Road just outside Peshawar. Both religio-political leaders rivalled each other, including in gaining greater influence with the Taliban and enjoying a personal relationship with Mullah Omar. In fact, Omar had been a student at Akora Khattak like other Afghan refugees and future Taliban leaders, whereas Rahman's branch of JUI(F) is a formidable political force both in the KP and Balochistan besides often sharing power with various regimes in Islamabad.

Pakistan's other major Islamist party, the JI, founded by Syed Mawdudi in 1941, had sought an Islamic revolution in Pakistan and espoused a Pan-Islamic creed, yet was initially ambivalent and even slightly critical of the Taliban brand of Islamic activism.[39] The JI has been mainly an urban and small-town party of educated lower-middle-class Muslims, sharing commonalities with the Muslim Brotherhood, and had been a vociferous supporter of Afghan jihad during the 1980s. It was often called General Zia-ul-Haq's B team, which through its strong-arm tactics took control of campuses besides facilitating his dubious referendum of 1984.[40] After the death of Syed Mawdudi in 1978, Maulana Tufail Muhammad, who like Zia-ul-Haq, hailed from eastern Punjab and worked in a close alliance with the martial law dictator, led the JI. Under his leadership, the JI transformed itself into a party of agitation, not shying away from using force against anti-Zia civic groups. Their close collaboration with Hekmatyar, Rabbani and Mojjeddedi stemmed both from doctrinal commonalities and a shared ideology of defiance against external and internal opponents. The JI, unlike the JUI(F), lacked a grass-roots vote bank and mainly depended on street power, campus control and now the military regime. Afghanistan and Zia-ul-Haq's repressive Islamization helped the JI in establishing think tanks, in addition to gathering more funds from external sources. Thus, it is understandable that its sympathies were prioritized towards the Mujahideen and that the Taliban were seen as rather new and even naive entrants lacking the literary and pedagogical attributes that the JI had traditionally banked on.[41] However, the rapid conquests by the Taliban, which caused a superimposed stability in the war-torn country, as well as the new JI leadership facilitated a more sympathetic attitude towards the former. Qazi Hussein Ahmad followed Tufail Ahmed as the new emir and, himself a Pashtun from Nowshera, he took a strong stance on Islamization and closer ties with the Taliban. Following September 11 and the Western invasion of Afghanistan, the JI, once again and more like the JUI, benefited from a pervasive anti-Americanism, and both the parties joined a coalition called the MMA, which was able to form governments in the trans-Indus provinces of Balochistan and the KP. Musharraf, like Zia and other military generals, had introduced amendments to the constitution to suit his personal rule besides keeping the mainstream parties away from national politics, which benefited the MMA in 2002 elections. By inducting the MMA into the government, Musharraf added a political defence against his own rule in addition to softening their street agitation. At another level he was able to impress the Americans with his indispensability, given the salience of Islamists such as the MMA in Pakistan. It is a different thing that Pakistan's prerogatives of governance, more like parties such as the PPP and Muslim League were relegated to a periphery, allowing a curious interdependence between Musharraf and the MMA, which continued until his decline in late 2007. The ouster of the Taliban following the Western invasion only added to the support for the JUI and JI, though they were again bewildered by the rise in suicide bombings and attacks on Pakistani civic places, often undertaken by the Pakistani Taliban. Both the parties, out of their own interests, shied away from criticising this self-immolation that had been bleeding both the countries profusely, and in their criticism and rallies they only blamed the United States for the rising spectre of violence in Southwest Asia.

The Taliban might have appeared rustic, raw and even medieval to secular and liberal groups, yet for many Muslims in South Asia and elsewhere, especially the younger unemployed clusters, they symbolized a new form of empowerment that could defy both the internal and external forces. However, given their strong Sunni denominational specificities and exclusionary attitudes towards Mazari's Shias of Kabul and Hazarajat, the Iranian religious leadership also felt uncomfortable with their *new* neighbour to the north. In his Friday sermon, Ayatollah Ali Khamenei, the spiritual Shia leader of Iran, had denounced the Taliban ascendance and refused to accept their version of Islam. He said, 'In the neighbourhood of Iran, something is taking place in the name of Islam and a group whose knowledge of Islam is unknown has embarked on actions having nothing to do with Islam'.[42] The Taliban's rural roots are uncontested facts, and despite their scepticism and even opposition to urban elites, they appear to be changing with the times. As we shall see in the next chapter, Antonio Giustozzi believes that the older Taliban of the founders' generations were superseded by a neo-Taliban in 2002–3, with more receptivity towards newer technologies to spread their messages in addition to running the insurgency. The misplaced priorities of the ISAF, in which defence and military campaigns were prioritized over political dialogue, provided ample ammunition to the neo-Taliban, who were again helped by the structural weaknesses of the Kabul regime. To him, 'the insurgency cannot be described in terms of a rural jacquerie against changes imposed from an urban-based government, there are elements of rural revolt which contributed to make the insurgency possible'.[43] Such views prioritizing negotiated settlements through the co-optation of various forces and groups across Afghanistan were suggested more vocally in recent years, though Western emphasis has often been on a military-led strategy and, with the Karzai regime feeling insecure, any such move added to its own vulnerability. In another report for Chatham House, the same author along with Theo Farrell noted that British militarist policies in Helmand only helped rehabilitate the Taliban among the locals, who otherwise had felt alienated. The co-option of some local toughs, minute checks on the peasantry and efforts to eradicate poppy in the area allowed the Taliban to regain their lost ground. Initially, following the invasion in October 2001, they had decided to lie low and bide their time until the Coalition committed some blunders and pushed the Pashtun peasants towards the Taliban. Based on interviews with more than 100 field commanders and Taliban activists, the report not only recorded the waste of human lives and resources but also equally witnessed the re-energization of the Taliban both in Helmand and across the Durand Line: 'What we find is an insurgency that is driven both by a strong unifying strategic narrative and purpose – jihad against foreign invaders – and by local conflict dynamics: rivalry between kinship groups and competition over land, water and drugs. The manner of the Taliban return to Helmand shows clear intent to retake the province'.[44] It meant that the future of regions like Helmand was to be a drawn-out war of attrition between the Taliban, the Afghan National Army (ANA) and the Afghan National Police (ANP) – something that might be replicated in several other eastern and southern regions: 'In short, the future struggle for Helmand is going to be a straight test between the Afghan organizations that have evolved through the conflict – the ANA, the ANP and the Taliban'.[45] In a way, the lack of substantive interface with the rural Pashtun regions, help from across the Durand Line, the hot-headedness of the urban elite in single-mindedly pursuing their campaigns for control without comprehending the rural sensitivities and the ramifications of the invasion of Iraq definitely re-energized the Taliban.[46] Here, their rural roots, the network of ulema spearheading resistance and support from younger elements such as in Pakistan allowed the Taliban to sustain themselves.[47]

Chapter Three

MASCULINITIES IN CONFLICT: WESTERN PEDAGOGY AND THE RETURN OF THE AFGHAN TALIBAN

'The Americans are about to talk to the Taliban not to get them to lay down their arms and ship them to the Solomon Islands, but as a face-saving exercise. They want to exit Afghanistan sans too much humiliation. In so many words they are telling the Taliban, look we are getting out; make our departure easier. That's it, if only we could read the writing on the wall.'

Ayaz Amir[1]

'For my father's generation of Afghan men, America was not the land of opportunity but a place to die. Exile was the end.'

Fariba Nawa[2]

The Taliban, like several other Islamist groups, have been a frequent subject of predictable journalistic and academic outpourings often reiterating only a vicious and sexist side of their ideology, which inherently banks on staunch Wahhabi, Salafi and Deobandi postulations. Given the pervasive views on Islam and especially following September 11, such a premise became the dominant and perhaps the only narrative of its type in English and other Western languages.[3] Amidst the longest and the immensely taxing war that more than 30 nations have fought in Afghanistan, any alternative academic or media view of Talibanist views of Islam or their ability to withstand and even embarrass the world's most powerful states has certainly been non-existent.[4] It is only recently that the Taliban have begun to use IT, especially websites, though their usage of mobile phones, pamphleteering and messages through human carriers are still the preferred modus operandi. In addition, sympathetic mosque-based networks and tribal contacts facilitate mutual communications, though their younger supporters in Pakistan and elsewhere have been more IT-savvy than the pioneer generation, who were nevertheless still able to surprise everybody with their rapid mobility, prolonged and even effective campaigns and by their survival against the odds. Soon after September 11 and the invasion of Afghanistan, the Taliban were subjected to a 'hammer-and-anvil policy' based on being squeezed from all sides.[5] Pakistan, which participated in this policy, carried out several military operations in the FATA in addition to rounding up thousands of Afghan, Pakistani and other international Islamists from across its lands. The suicide bombings in Madrid, Bali and London – other than hundreds of such kamikaze onslaughts in Pakistani and Afghan towns and markets – intensified general hostility towards this militancy, which was causing stupendous civilian losses. As a consequence, Al-Qaeda, the Afghan Taliban and their Pakistan counterparts in the TTP were all juxtaposed as subscribers to one and the same version of political Islam with the unitary espousal and perpetration of violence and terror. Other than fighting well-equipped NATO and ISAF troops through exposed conventional attacks which cost the Taliban major losses, their recourse to suicide bombings through strapped-on explosive vests was seen as equally insidious and even foolhardy. This form of indiscreet self-immolation was perceived as a nihilist act of blind faith based on adulation for a death cult, and with Iraq, Afghanistan and Pakistan witnessing such occurrences more frequently – and not always against the foreign forces – it only solidified reductionist views about Muslims.

Suicide attacks have often been viewed as an aimless yet costly form of self-immolation, possibly happening out of some penchant for existentialist martyrdom, though Muslim clerics and even other opinion groups within these societies have hesitated in openly questioning this form of new and debilitating intra-Muslim violence.[6] A few high-profile critics such as Muhammad Tahir-ul-Qadri[7] and Javaid al-Ghamdi[8] – both from Pakistan – criticized suicide bombings vocally and through their research tried to prove that any such acts had no juridical basis in Islam and thus cannot be viewed as martyrdom.[9] Retaliatory attacks on critics, including pro-Kabul and pro-Islamabad clerics, and on local politicians, as well as the harassment of journalists and independent writers deterred people from openly challenging the perpetrators of such self-immolation. Violent incidents and the resultant loss of human lives – in general of civilians – were often justified as a collateral cost for some higher and nobler aims. Elements of personal frustrations, family losses, hurt pride or even an uncritical view of martyrdom due to brainwashing have spawned suicide bombings, though there is the possibility of a strong residue of manipulation and misdirection on the part of 'handlers' and peers.[10] Suicide bombings have been a major weapon of the Afghan Taliban in their overall military strategy against foreign occupiers and their Afghan collaborators, justified in the name of jihad. In the case of their Pakistani comrades, fighting in Afghanistan against non-Muslim invaders might have been a major pull factor, yet targeting people and places within their own country could be rooted in a wide variety of reasons. Here, other than personal and class factors, the theological *othering* of collaborators providing succour and support to anti-Muslim forces is certainly a major jihadi instrumentation that becomes a cause célèbre. For sectarian firebrands, in their vitriol against groups such as Shias and Ahmadis, this again is rooted in the theological rationalization of their being viewed as outside the pale of Islam, with their killings being perceived justifiable. The ideology of *takfir* (declaring someone an infidel) has played a crucial role in all the cases of suicide bombing in Muslim regions where clerical decrees and powerful brainwashing underpin a very exclusive definition of being a Muslim. The police and security forces, along with politicians of these respective countries are also often categorized as kafirs for aligning themselves with external, non-Muslim elements at the expense of their fellow compatriots.[11]

Pakistani Islamists, belonging to almost 60 different organizations, may share a broad doctrinal consensus with a loosely structured TTP and could have benefitted from military training with some Pashtun and Punjabi Taliban in the FATA, yet they come from all the various ethno-regional diversities in the country. Unlike the earlier suppositions of their being largely Pashtun tribal teenagers misled by some mischievous mullahs, urban, middle-class and well-placed militants have also been visible in such terrorist campaigns.

Omar Saeed Shaikh, the mastermind behind Daniel Pearl's kidnap and murder in 2002, was a British Pakistani and a graduate from a prestigious London college. Faisal Shahzad, notorious for leaving a truckload of explosives in Manhattan in 2010, was the son of a senior air force official who grew up in Karachi and lived in the United States. In the same way, former military officials such as Ilyas Kashmiri have been in the forefront of jihadi attacks against their former military colleagues and bases. More significantly, the attacks on Debra Lobo, an American university teacher in Karachi, followed by the murder of a civil society activist, Sabeen Mahmud – both happening in April 2015 – were committed by a group of university graduates who, like the perpetrators of September 11, were previously known for libertine lifestyles.[12] The leader of this well-placed gang, Saud Aziz, was a former graduate of a prestigious business school in Karachi and, following a very liberal lifestyle, had become a militant and through the co-optation of like-minded angry younger men carried out numerous target killings in Karachi. Their major operation targeted a busload of Ismaili Shias on the morning of 13 May 2015 when they began their killing spree after boarding the vehicle, which was taking the passengers to their schools and workplaces. After killing 47 people, they took off on motorbikes, but due to the expertise of the police and security agencies were apprehended within a week, followed by their confessions. Pakistanis were shocked to see some of their highly educated, urban and prosperous fellow citizens treading the nihilist paths. Such arrests and discoveries reinforce the fact that, unlike the previous liberal views about militants being the downtrodden rural and tribal youths fallen out of safety nets, some middle class elements had also joined the bandwagon out of their own convictions.[13]

In the outside world, especially across the West, within the prisms of an orientalist view of Islam, the acts of suicide bombing have been seen steeped in a jihadist ideology, though many commentators may occasionally recognize geopolitical drivers behind this phenomenon. Yet the dominant narrative defines it as a *Muslim* cliché, which allows some form of Islamic rationale for sacrifice on the part of perpetrators and innocent bystanders, presumably for a higher cause. The earlier precedents of the Japanese harakiri, self-immolation by the Buddhist monks in Vietnam or the suicide attacks by Tamil fighters in Sri Lanka are not often fully explored, nor are the invasions of Afghanistan, Iraq and Palestinian territories considered as mundane props underpinning desperation and defiant negation, both couched in an act of self-kill to cause more deaths. Such selective views have often converged with the spotlight on madrasas, especially of Salafi and Wahhabi types, which evolved out of Sunni traditions and may manifest political and militant tendencies. Accordingly, madrasas such as the Madrasa-i-Haqqania in Akora Khattak or the Qasmia Madrasa in Binory Town, Karachi, were posited as Taliban factories.[14] While there are Muslim groups all across the world who may find affinity with the Taliban out of an element of resistance or simply to defy their own peers and political elite, still it is very rare to find a sustained account of the Taliban version of recent politics. In that sense, the autobiography of Mullah Salam Zaeef – originally written in Pushto – is a welcome work that offers an alternative view on the Taliban ascendancy besides placing a searing light on the sordid realities of detentions, renditions and dehumanization which have happened under the aegis of a superpower and its regional and global allies. Here Ambassador Zaeef's personal experiences in Pakistan leading to his dramatic arrest at the behest of General Pervez Musharraf's regime, and then a tortuous and prolonged incarceration at Guantanamo offer a powerful counterpoise to analyses embodying geopolitical discourse or unilateral demonization.

Zaeef (1968–) grew up amidst the turmoil and uncertainties of his native country following the turbulent events of 1978 and the subsequent Soviet invasion that led to massive human rights violations, including the displacement of millions of Afghans as well as the callous loss of over a million human lives. A poor country located at the crossroads of history and geography became the centrepiece of a Cold War rivalry in which Afghan blood, as in recent times, flowed mercilessly and stupendously. Zaeef's adolescence in Zangiabad, a small town near Kandahar, was certainly interrupted due to the loss of his parents, combined with dislocations from one place to another until he became a refugee in Pakistani Balochistan, and like many other young Afghans, began to participate in jihad at the tender age of 15. Here his religion and love for his country proved the main props besides surely the examples of his peers who had been fighting a holy war considering it the highest and noblest cause. His contributions in the resistance won him the close confidence of several senior Taliban commanders, including Mullah Muhammad Omar. To Zaeef, the Taliban had emerged during the anti-Soviet resistance and were not a subsequent development, as is seen by Ahmed Rashid, William Maley, Robert Kaplan and several other noted authors on the subject. Zaeef's traditional education as a cleric – mullah – and the bonhomie with some leading Pashtun scholars, immersion in Islamic studies in madrasas on the Frontier (Khyber-Pakhtunkhwa) and exposure to various guerrilla operations equipped him with a greater sense of worldly wisdom in addition to a fervent belief in the Taliban way as the only viable option for a war-torn, factionalist and stigmatized country.

Zaeef's account is not a typical autobiography focusing only on personal achievements; instead, it is the story of the rise, tribulations and rediscovery of an ordinary Pashtun young man who found himself at the interchange of so many hostile and even brutal forces. It is certainly a reportage of a tormented country which has been subjected to some of the worst bombings laced with radioactive material, where generations have spent a lifetime being uprooted and where hastily dug graves kept on proliferating all across the horizon with no end to this agony in sight. No Afghan was involved in global acts of violence and terror such as September 11, July 7 or the Madrid and Bali bombings, but for several decades, the country has been terrorized and violated by all those who have often spoken the loudest on human rights, democracy, gender empowerment, civilizational achievements and the protection of natural environment. Afghanistan is not only an exposé of the world's imperious hypocrisy but also an amazing story in human patience, forbearance and resilience. It is a different matter, however, that one has only heard about security-related issues and, except for occasional references to a weak Kabul regime, the human suffering of the Afghans, especially its Pashtun regions, have not received any major attention. Zaeef's book does not explain several subjects, like the Taliban's escapades with Shia Hazaras, destruction of the Bamiyan Buddhas, suicide bombings, their views on women's education and their interface with the Pakistani Taliban, though his is the best defence of the (Afghani) Taliban so far. Even after all the suffering that he endured – despite his violated diplomatic immunity – Zaeef is quite enamoured of Mullah Omar and all his Talib colleagues; however, he is unforgiving in his scathing criticism of George W. Bush, Pervez Musharraf, Barack Obama and their allies who have not only caused miseries for his native land but, according to his conviction, turned the war on terror into an unabashed multidimensional campaign against Muslims. Certainly, he did not explain the closer interface between Osama bin Laden and the Taliban, yet reiterated his own government's plea for a trial of Bin Laden through a non-partisan court following September 11. His account appears symbolic of the Taliban resilience and their undiminished belief in the validity of their cause and commitment of every sort to fight and even die for it. Amidst all the demonization of the Taliban, contrasted with their unlimited supply of fighters and the ever-increasing tempo of a countercampaign, it is all the more vital to read Zaeef as an archetypal figure. Averse to all early Western triumphalist pronouncements, the Taliban phenomenon sustained itself and might not disappear if Zaeef's account and the objective realties in Afghanistan and the tribal Pakistani regions are viewed as indicators of things to come.

At the very outset of his work Zaeef censors Bush for being more worried about his own life than those of Afghans and others, as soon after September 11, 'in order to save his own life, [Bush] was living in the air. He would land for short periods only, for a press conference or some other important event, and wore a flak jacket in the White House. But how many lives did he play with in Afghanistan? How many people did he murder? How many homes and villages did he destroy? This will never be forgotten'. In the same vein, Obama 'stood with his wife and daughters on the Capitol Hill, [and] he delivered his inauguration speech behind sheets of bullet-proof glass. But now, with the invaders' surge he will take the lives of many Afghans. President Obama! You should know that the lives of our children are just as important to us as your daughters' lives to you!' Addressing Presidents Bush and Obama on the sanctity of human life irrespective of ethnic or national origins, Zaeef is unremittingly critical of the American leaders and speaks his mind like a deeply hurt nationalist: 'Your life is important to you, and that blackguard Bush's life is important to him. This is why I wrote this memoir so that people should understand that the lives of others are also important'.[15] This critique is coming not from a rhetorician but from a person who, despite his diplomatic immunity, was arrested, humiliated and then tortured in Islamabad, Peshawar, Bagram, Kandahar and at Guantanamo concentration camp. His sentiments certainly reflect those of a vast majority of Muslims, and especially Pashtuns, and perhaps that is why NATO and its allies have been unable to contain defiance in a small and immensely poor country which, just in the case of the United States, has cost around a trillion dollars in expenses in addition to the extensive loss of lives on all sides.

Zaeef's account begins with the large-scale destruction that he saw on his repatriation from Guantanamo, and unlike exaggerated reports of transformation of his country, he only witnessed more dismay and desolation in Pashtun areas which, in cases like his own native region, had been a crossroads of history. He then reverts to his own early career, remembering his father, who was a noted cleric but passed away when Zaeef was only seven, and like the deceased peer, began to study Islamic studies under the supervision of some of his father's colleagues until life was no longer safe following the Soviet invasion and he left for Pakistan as a war refugee. Like his return from Guantanamo, his re-entry into Afghanistan as a teenage warrior only alerted him to the sad realities of his homeland where a profusion of fresh graves dotted the landscape. His training and operations against the enemy in the company of other mujahideen – some of his future Taliban colleagues – hardened him into a guerrilla fighter in addition to helping him develop closer amiability with his comrades, which he remembers with celebratory respect: 'May God be praised! What a brotherhood we had among the *Mujahideen*! We weren't concerned with the world or with our lives; our intentions were pure and every one of us was ready to die as a martyr. When I look back on the love and respect that we had for each other, it sometimes seems like a dream'.[16] Other than Mullah Muhammad Omar and Mullah Rabbani Akhund, he became close to Mullah Obaidullah Akhund, Mullah Mazullah Akhund, Mullah Najibullah and Mullah Feda Mohammad – the mujahideen stalwarts and the future founding members of the Taliban.[17] This camaraderie was to strengthen following the pernicious warlordism that evolved in Afghanistan during the 1990s, until some of these clerics met in late 1994 and formed the Taliban movement, and began to punish and sideline local thugs and regional overlords.

Their jihad came to an end in 1989 following the Soviet withdrawal from Afghanistan when these fighters returned to their villages to tend to their lands, families and mosques, and gradually became the bitter witnesses of the acrimonious lawlessness and moral degradation of their country. To Zaeef, moral issues along with disorderly misbehaviour by Afghan warlords led to the formation of the movement, though the desire to the effect had preceded this significant development, which took place in a mosque:

> The founding meeting of what became known as 'the *Taliban*' was held in the late autumn of 1994. Some forty to fifty people had gathered at the white mosque in Sangisar. *Mawlawi Saheb* Abdul Samad, *Mullah* Mohammed Omar Akhund, *Mullah* Abdus Sattar Akhund and *Mullah* Sher Mohammad Malang all spoke, outlining their responsibilities [...] *Mullah* Mohammad Omar took an oath from everyone present. Each man swore on the *Qur'an* to stand by him, and to fight against corruption and the criminals. No written articles of association, no logo and no name for the movement was agreed on or established during the meeting.[18]

Initially, they remained confined to the Punjwei–Sangisar area until a major breakthrough happened which led to their climactic rise across the Pashtun lands. Aware of and inconvenienced by the multiplicity of check posts created by the warlords, ordinary Afghans, especially the business people, yearned for a stable order, whereas a vast majority of people were discomfited with the moral turpitude of some of these warlords. Numerous warlords were involved in serious crimes such as gang rapes of women, who could be simply disembarked from the buses plying between towns. The nearest check post for the Taliban founders was that of Daru Khan at Maiwand, run by Pir Mohammad, Saleh, Bismillah and a group of ruffians who refused to relent and persisted with their coercive and sexist practices. As the negotiations failed, the Taliban issued an ultimatum for the surrender of weapons and the release of hostages that these warlords and their followers possessed. Using guerrilla tactics, they surrounded the post from all three sides, and the warlords, overawed by their determination, fled, leaving the bodies of two abused Herati women and a whole cache of RPGs and Kalashnikovs. Clearing the area from bandits and rapists brought the Taliban an enviable prestige as well as money, and they began to expand their operations to other areas. Their reputation, resolve and public support helped them in consolidating their control as the checkpoints began to be dismantled with the warlords gone and the ordinary public able to move across more freely.

A spectacular attack on a similar check post in Spin Boldak on the Pakistan–Afghan border took only 15 minutes and the vital truck route was restored, with the warlord Akhtar Jan fleeing for his life, whereas his troops joined the Taliban. Soon, Kandahar city was surrendered by Mullah Naqib, allowing the Taliban to claim the historic centre of the Pashtun heartland, and now Herat, Kabul, Jalalabad and Mazar-i-Sharif appeared as possible targets, while a new administration based on the Taliban's understanding of the Islamic penal code began to take shape: 'The old habits of keeping boys, adultery, looting, illegal checkpoints and the government of the gun were over. An ordinary life was given back to the people, and they were satisfied for the first time in years'.[19] Zaeef relished the return to normalcy, and almost two decades later he could see his country still being far from a stable and peaceful dispensation. In September 1995, the Taliban defeated Ismael Khan, a former Mujahid colleague and a Tajik Sunni leader who ruled the southwestern region as a personal fiefdom, and within the context of an emerging strict Sunni Pashtun movement, had begun building up linkages with the Iranians. The latter had been deeply perturbed by the rise of a vocal and increasingly powerful Sunni force to their northeast, and despite Khan and other Tajiks being Sunni, the former began to form bridges with them as well as with Abdul Rashid Dostum, the Uzbek warlord in Mazar-i-Sharif. Khan was a rarity among the numerous post-1992 commanders who had filled the power vacuum in the absence of a central government and 'had actually served people'. Generally known as the 'prince of the west', he built some institutions and collected customs duties on trade with Iran, yet with the arrival of the Taliban, his former associates deserted him and joined hands with Zaeef as the new governor of Herat.[20]

Being the governor of Herat must have been a learning curve for Mullah Zaeef, and while appreciative of the infrastructure created by Khan, he began to win the confidence of the local people, while Khan survived the Taliban wrath and, instead of being executed, was put in a dungeon. After Herat, Kabul fell to the Taliban, and Mullah Omar asked Zaeef, a close confidante, to head the National Defence Ministry, ensuring supplies for troops deputed to fight Ahmed Shah Masud and Dostum. Led by Mullah Dadullah, the Taliban were confronting the combined forces of Tajik, Hazara and Uzbek leaders, who later came to be known as the Northern Alliance. The Shia Hazaras were led by Sayyid Mansour Nadiri, while the Uzbeks were led by Abdul Malik, the latter often prone to changing sides. The conquest of Kabul had allowed the Taliban to ensure advances to the north and, except for Panjshir Valley, they were able to capture Dostum's territory, followed by the conquest of the Hazara region of Bamiyan in 1998. By confining Masud to his valley, the Taliban now controlled vital Central Asian trade routes as well as having access to potential natural resources in the region, though their control was often contested on ethnic grounds, which also caused severe retaliatory policies and practices. The Taliban were quite confident of their control of almost 90 per cent of the country's territory, and Zaeef was deputed by the Kandahar-based Mullah

Omar to supervise all the major mining and industrial projects, mainly concentrated in the north:

> At that time, the chemical factories, a hydropower plant, the gas sector, refinery sector, the cement factory, coal mines and factory, the factory for refining marble and precious stones, salt mines and other heavy industries were all located in the northern provinces and had been divided among various *jihadi* commanders. Due to the war and what often amounted to neglect, all these industries were damaged and run down'.[21]

By that time, tensions with Iran also began to escalate, though foreign companies such as Unocal and Argentine's Bridas began to display some interest in working with the Taliban to explore the possibility of establishing gas pipelines across the country to build energy corridors between Central and Southern Asia:

> 'Iran shared a border with all three parties and worked hard to derail our plans. It made every effort to destabilize Afghanistan and to scare off investors. Their idea was that the pipeline would pass through Iran instead of Afghanistan. Noor Sultan Nazarbayev, the President of Kazakhstan, was against this, however, and promoted the pipeline route through Afghanistan as originally agreed. The leader of Turkmenistan was also interested in Afghanistan'.[22]

Pakistan, by then ruled by Benazir Bhutto's PPP, was providing logistical and financial support to the Taliban and could see in them a new power base that would not be beholden to India. The ISI, the political authorities in Islamabad, the provincial government in the NWFP and General (retired) Naseerullah Babar – a Pashtun supporter of Bhutto and the Taliban – joined hands to offer sustenance to a new Pashtun power emerging in Afghanistan's southeastern areas while expanding itself into a formidable force.

For Afghanistan, history was repeating itself, and once again the Pashtun factor from the Southeast – like under King Ahmed Shah Abdali during the 1740s – was to change its destiny in a decisive mould. On the one hand, it had a new regime in Kabul which lacked a cross-ethnic consensus and often pursued policies which were seen coercive, yet on the other hand, regionally and globally it had begun to attract attention for all kinds of reasons, including the possibility of some increased energy sector dividends. These events gradually pushed Afghanistan into a new great game with external forces seeking to abet their own local allies, and other than Taliban ministers and Al-Qaeda's Arab leaders, ambitious individuals such as Hamid Karzai and Zalmay Khalilzad offered to operate as intermediaries between the Taliban and external prospectors such as Bridas and Unocal. Along with the regional warlords, these suave Afghans with dual nationalities were certainly motivated by a wide variety of personal and other such reasons, and represented a group of Afghan Diaspora who sought stability and the modernization of their country in a close interface with the United States and other Western powers. Within the country itself, the Taliban, in the meantime, had implemented their form of sharia law, which, despite bringing an end to schismatic fighting around Kabul and the Pashtun regions of Afghanistan, disallowed female participation in government departments. Men were ordered to grow beards in addition to tending to religious obligations more seriously, and a ministry, like its counterpart in Saudi Arabia, was installed to ensure public morality and, moreover, it did not shirk from passing strict penal punishments for both men and women. The Taliban soon began to raise global concerns owing to their strict restriction on women's participation in the public sector and female education and to stern laws governing personal morality. Their escapades with the Shias, their blasting of the historic Bamiyan Buddhas and their allowing Osama bin Laden to stay on within the country as a special guest all led to an increased censoring of this increasingly fundamentalist dispensation. Ordinary Pakistanis enthused by their purist version of Islam, and likewise some other Sunni Muslims from across the world developed their own fascination with the Taliban, who were seen as raw, defiant and courageous role models for cleansing Muslim societies of all forms of corruption, inertia and indolence. This romantic view of the Taliban along with their growing critique in the Western media and by human rights groups went hand in hand, but became more intense following the US embassy bombings in East Africa in 1998, which were masterminded by Bin Laden's Al-Qaeda, with its headquarters in eastern Afghanistan. The loss of hundreds of lives in Kenya and Tanzania in the full glare of cameras and the US retaliation under President Bill Clinton's orders, broke off all the back-door diplomatic channels between Kabul and the West, though Pakistan, Saudi Arabia and the United Arab Emirates retained an ambassadorial relationship with the Taliban regime on a reciprocal basis, and Zaeef was soon deputed to Islamabad as an envoy.

Zaeef is unrelenting in his criticism of Pakistan, which may be due to the policies of its various regimes, and also because of his own humiliating handover to the CIA by the ISI, yet he is fully conversant with the strong commonalities and historic bonds between the two neighbours. Here relations went beyond the usual diplomatic protocols and involved enduring channels such as culture, religion, ethnicities and language, which allowed both the countries a whole arena of informal interface and trade. Officials on both sides were cognizant of a powerful US presence and interest in Southwest Asia through various means at the disposal of the only remaining superpower, and were often quite discreet in mutual parleys, which appear to be anathematic to a more blunt, rural and direct Zaeef – totally new to the complex art of diplomacy that he found to be a rather dubious art based on suspicion, eavesdropping and even sheer duplicity. ISI officials and likewise Pakistani diplomats had their own interests and worries vis-à-vis Kabul, though Zaeef found a closer affinity with trans-Indus Pakistanis, who according to his perception, came from Pashtun and Baloch stocks, unlike the Punjabis and Sindhis – the two most populous groups to the east of the Indus.[23] Soon, he became aware of the adulation for the Taliban among clerical groups in the country in addition to a popular groundswell among the ordinary populace.[24] Sympathies for the Taliban, other than a strong Sunni sentiment and shared ethnicity, evolved due to a greater sense of grief for ordinary Afghans, especially after 1998 Tomahawk attacks, and a growing sense of anti-Americanism in the Muslim world. For numerous ordinary Pakistanis – away from the bitter realities of the country itself – the Taliban offered an incorruptible alternative to their perception of a westernized Muslim elite who, to the former, lacked integrity as well as the capabilities to govern in a more sovereign way. An affinity for the underdog and a growing concern over Islamophobia underwrote this sympathy for the austere Taliban, while modernist and reformist Pakistanis feared an encroaching Talibanization of their own country, where women, minorities and civic groups would suffer from misplaced zeal and uncritiqued dogma.

Zaeef has been unforgiving of Musharraf for his 'cruel and hypocritical behaviour towards the *Taliban* and other Muslims', which to the Afghan ambassador stemmed from an unlimited greed and personal ambitions:

> He made a business out of his Muslim brothers in Afghanistan, working to sell people for money to the infidels after 11 September. Most of these ended up in Guantanamo. He has left a black stain on Pakistan's history; one can already hear the voices of the true Pakistani people rising up, denouncing his reign for what it was: a betrayal of Islam. His book has angered so many with its self-proclaimed righteousness; it will stand as a testament to his dishonourable rule.[25]

Certainly, it is a strong retort to Musharraf and his *In the Line of Fire* for being a front-line partner of the United States and other allies and for turning his country into a battleground against its neighbours and co-religionists. Zaeef provides details on parleys that Mullah Omar held with the Pakistan interior minister and the ISI chief soon after September 11 to show Pakistan kowtowing to a vengeful Washington, and he could even foresee mighty American forces heading towards his country.[26] His parleys with the ambassadors and cautioning Mullah Omar on the tumultuous developments soon after September 11 reached a frantic stage until he felt exasperated and sought political asylum through the UN, which, to him, had itself become a bandwagon for American policies:

> Each time the *Taliban* utilized their Air Force, the UN would condemn them for causing civilian casualties. This appears to be quite ironic given the countless civilian losses Afghanistan has sustained in the past years at the hands of ISAF and NATO [...] The UN has changed. It has become a tool that is being used by countries of the world against Muslim nations like Afghanistan and Iraq. What we witness today is unprecedented. America is swallowing the world, brutally bombarding and killing thousands of innocent people in Iraq and Afghanistan, turning hundreds and hundreds of villages into rubble. How can they be allowed to disgrace, kill and detain Muslims around the world in the name of a war against terrorism? How can they hold people for years without telling them their fate or taking them to court?[27]

Here Zaeef not only speaks as a marooned and aggrieved party but he also pronounces his dissent as a vocal ideologue, and certainly his own humiliation and incarceration at Guantanamo, followed by his close observation of post–September 11 Afghanistan have steered him to that point. Zaeef was overwhelmed by the messages of support he began to receive in Islamabad from the world's Muslims in which even poor women were donating their jewellery to help his country through the massive predicament and its aggravated human problems. Afghanistan was under a horrendous threat once again, and in addition to mass demonstrations across the world, volunteers and dissenters began to arrive at the embassy to express their solidarity, as he notes: 'When a fellow Muslim came to me seeking help to make the journey, I would look him over from head to toe and ask about his life, his behaviour, his career. Strong, handsome young people were coming. They wanted my assistance, but what feelings were in their hearts? What emotions had brought them to me?'[28] He contacted Zalmay Khalilzad, the Afghan American academic-turned-diplomat, but the latter had other priorities on his mind, and like most observers and past companions, the Taliban were history – at least for the time being – as the United States prepared for an unprecedented reaction. He tried to explain to him and others that the Taliban were not beholden to Pakistan, though it is not clear whether the former Afghan ambassador might have opined in the same vein about Osama bin Laden.

His handover to the Americans by Pakistani security agents, while the former denuded him along with kicking him, did not leave any residue of affection for either government, as he sadly notes:

> That moment is written in my memory like a stain on my soul. Even if Pakistan was unable to stand up to the godless Americans I would at least have expected them to insist that treatment like this would never take place under their eyes or on their own sovereign territory. I was still naked when a callous American soldier gripped my arm and dragged me onto the helicopter. They tied my hands and feet, sealed my mouth with duct tape and put a black cloth over my head. That was in turn taped to my neck, and then I was shackled to the floor of the helicopter.[29]

For the Americans, he was a major prize, while for the Pakistani handlers it must have been one more act in surrogacy. His humiliation in incarceration continued in his own native land and at Guantanamo, which corroborates similar other accounts of sordid treatment meted out to internees – well over and above the moral and international conventions.[30] His selection of case studies of Arab, Pakistani and Afghan internees in Kandahar is a painful account. For instance, an old Afghan was dragged in the prison and ordered to stand still long hours, which he could not, whereas to snatch an Arab while engaged in his congregational prayers, they threw Zaeef to the ground and pressed his head into the floor while the other soldiers took the praying Arab away. Zaeef had been leading the prayers, and the soldiers could have waited, but they would not miss an opportunity to humiliate these prisoners. Their ages as well as nationalities were quite diverse, but they were grouped together as the deadly enemies of the United States and thus worthy of any kind of punishment.

His account of four years at Guantanamo is certainly revealing and painful, though it was equally instructive for him to know from other internees the fate of many Taliban prisoners who perished while in the custody of the Northern Alliance, especially in Kunduz, Mazar-i-Sharif and Shomali Maidan. Zaeef's ordeal at Guantanamo offers a first-hand account of vengeance, derision and torture that these Muslim inmates – deposited in this legal and moral black hole – had to endure, and how some people became even more resilient, while a few turned into spies for the authorities. 'Many times the holy *Qur'an* was abused; the soldiers deliberately used it as a tool to punish us.

More than once we collected all the *Qur'ans* and handed them back to the authorities because we could not protect them. But instead of taking them back, we were punished'. His summation is that '[p]risoners are the weakest people in the world. A detainee in Guantanamo, however, is not even a person anymore. He is stripped of his humanity as each day passes'.[31] The abuse of inmates at Guantanamo, who in most cases were poor, innocent or just happened to be in the wrong place at the wrong time, has been detailed by Zaeef in a section which reads as an eye-opener and as a charge sheet against the US government. Not only were elderly people being dished out inhumane treatment but also many of these people were ordinary toiling men like butchers, shepherds, barbers and petty shopkeepers; however, they were defined as the most dangerous people by President Bush and Secretary Donald Rumsfeld. 'For four years they had tricked the world into believing that they had detained terrorists without any proof, any law or any formal accusations being made, throwing us into cages'.[32] Zaeef was finally released, interestingly, on 11 September 2005, and landed at Kabul airport the next day to be housed in a special residence in the capital.

And after his release, Zaeef posited a formidable question:

> Why is America continuing to spill blood? Why do they continue to play this game, destroying buildings in the name of fundamentalism and terrorism? What other human rights will disappear into the greedy maw of America? Will this monster finally devour itself? Will it consume the whole world? [...] No one answers the sword with *salaam*. And you cannot wash out blood with water [...] But it seems clear these days that America cannot tolerate anyone but itself, and this may lead to its collapse [...] It is a fact that America has lost its reputation as a peaceful and humanitarian country. Throughout the world America is now regarded as selfish, reckless and cruel [...] Peace seems unlikely. It is what we all pray and wish for. If more violence is to come, then we Afghans will once again be the victims. Our soil and that of our neighbours will bear much of the sorrow.[33]

Zaeef has invited the United States and its allies to look critically at the lessons from Iraq and Afghanistan:

> America should take a look at Afghanistan's history: we have been invaded many times before. How many troops did their predecessors bring? And why did they fail? They should look at Iraq. A million lives were lost while 300,000 US soldiers were there, and the killing continues to this day. Americans should know that they are no longer thought of as a people of freedom and democracy. They have sown the seeds of hatred throughout the world. Under their new banner they have declared a war on terrorism and terrorists, but the very term 'terrorist' is of their own making. The *jihad* against them will never stop as long as America doesn't take steps to correct its mistakes.[34]

Certainly, it is a sad verdict and a blunt message that comes from Kabul, where Zaeef now resides, keeping a low profile and wondering about the state of affairs to come.

Zaeef's views about the role of the United States and other leading NATO nations were certainly hardened as, other than his personal anguish, he witnessed no major improvements or even peace in his country. By identifying Afghanistan and the United

States as 'now bitter enemies', he was not convinced of the liberal use of the term 'terrorists' and invited Gulbuddin Hekmatyar, the Northern Alliance and other elements of resistance to close ranks with the Taliban to defy the foreign forces, which to him were mainly occupying forces that were inherently against Afghan and Muslim interests. His views were certainly hardened. As he observes, 'The diabolical United Kingdom and stubborn America will widen the gap between Muslims and other religions. They will create an atmosphere of distrust and suspicion'.[35] It is certainly a strong verdict in the line of the Huntingtonian clash of religions, and in the light of various opinion surveys on both sides, could be a bitter reality of the post–September 11 era. In his closing chapters, Zaeef keeps coming back to Afghan history, the United States and her policies towards the Muslim regions, and it is no surprise that attitudes on both sides have certainly hardened over the past decade and that in that case Southwest Asian geopolitics has played a crucial role in these divides:

> Afghanistan is the most oppressed country in the world. Afghans take their revenge in silence, even if they have to sacrifice themselves in the process. No Afghan, least of all a Pashtun, believes that America is doing anything other than killing people and sowing hatred. The primary goal of the invasion was to render Afghanistan powerless; even those Afghans who at first marched to the American tune are starting to feel this way.[36]

This is definitely a strong verdict and a powerful summation, and could also explain the continued defiance and unmitigated hostility towards the American troops and their allies. Such a sentiment equally became the bane of support for the Taliban, providing them with sustenance and an unending supply of volunteers to commit suicide bombings, plant remotely controlled improvised explosive devices and engage in guerrilla attacks on all kinds of installations, as well as participating in 'green turning on blue', with pro-Taliban soldiers killing their own American trainers and counterparts. When Zaeef opined on a pervasive hostility towards the United States, he made it resound with what many Muslims, especially the Afghans, tended to believe:

> America has been quite successful in bribing people in Afghanistan. They started handing out sacks of dollars to the Northern Alliance – beginning in Panjshir – to get them to use their ground forces against the Taliban. After the American forces descended during the collapse of the Taliban, they accelerated the bribing process and they continue it to this day. But America used its money for other things as well, hiring puppet spies among the Afghans to strengthen its position, and by putting a bounty on the heads of the leaders of the Taliban and Al Qaeda. They exploited the poverty of Afghans to the utmost.[37]

He cautions them against their prolonged stay and ends his book by returning to his native Kandahar: 'They [the Americans] are on unfamiliar territory and they know little about Afghanistan. Today the situation in my birthplace of Kandahar looks like an unhealthy amalgam of the worst of the Russian times and the civil war that followed'.[38] He ends his work by being sceptical of President Obama, while gloomily leaving the fate of his country only with God. Given the diminution of the NATO presence in Afghanistan and Ashraf Ghani aiming for peace and reconciliation in addition to building a regional consensus with Pakistan, China and Iran, there may be an opportunity for a needed breakthrough in the country. Here, Mullah Zaeef and his associates could help persuade the Quetta Shura, the Haqqanis and other resistance groups join peace negotiations in the largest interests of Afghanistan, where everybody is tired of war, violence and intervention.

Chapter Four

UNDERSTANDING PAKISTAN: GEOPOLITICAL LEGACIES AND PERSPECTIVES ON VIOLENCE

'With each blast, massacre and killing, Pakistan as a state, fails one more time. How many citizens will be slaughtered or blown apart by militants before our delusion gives way to reality? Pakistan stubbornly continues to live in a state of denial, refusing to acknowledge that it is being brutally attacked by a bloodthirsty enemy from within and without. Already driven to the wall, the only mindless response that the state has to offer is yet more barriers, check posts, bunkers, statements and resolutions. To many, it is still not obvious that we are on a suicidal path and unless we can take proactive and radical measures, the violence could only conclude in total collapse of the state.'

Naeem Sadiq[1]

'In the absence of a true national identity, Pakistan defined itself by its opposition to India. It turned its back on all that had been common between Muslims and non-Muslims in the era before partition. Everything came under suspicion, from dress to customs to festivals, marriage rituals and literature. The new country set itself the task of erasing its association with the subcontinent, an association that many came to view as a contamination. In trying to turn its back on its shared past with India, Pakistan turned its back on itself.'

Aatish Taseer[2]

Since the Pakistani state came into being in 1947, it has frequently faced scepticism about its rationale, formation and its future as a nation-state, especially for being located in a testing geopolitical region and frequently stumbling from one crisis into another. The creation of the country – divided into the mainland Indus Valley and the lower Gangetic Delta – accounts for a sizeable number of South Asia's Muslims, themselves making a clear majority of the world's Muslim population, the country has often been seen as a caesarean birth of an otherwise widely assumed united India. Partition was thus viewed as a *negative* process, with the onus of its responsibility falling upon Muhammad Ali Jinnah (1876–1948) and the All-India Muslim League. In the Indian nationalist parlance, other than Jinnah and the Muslim Leaguers and their nostalgic *Turk* followers, the British imperial interests were also held responsible for this *divide-and-quit* dictum, nefariously employed by a weakened, opportunistic and receding imperial power.[3] Thus, the founders of Pakistan, since its inception, were seen as being in cahoots with Western powers intent upon vivisecting an otherwise ordained united *Mother India*, often invoked as *Bharat Varsha*.[4] For such nationalists as well as ultra-right groups, Pakistan's founders and dwellers were the *foreigners*, and that is where Hindu Mahasabha and its recent and more vocal reincarnations such as Shiv Sena, the BJP and Kar Sevaks have cast aspersions on the very loyalty of India's own Muslim population. Urdu, Ayodhya, Mathura, Sir Syed Ahmed

Khan, Kashmir, East Pakistan, Gujarat and Wali Deccani became the *others* and, to such opinions, Pakistan, Islam and non-Indianness came to be juxtaposed together.[5] There is no doubt that even within India, such denunciatory and exclusive views have been countered with powerful ripostes by eminent scholars and civil society activists, yet in the process the concept of Indian identity itself came under an interesting and disputatious purview.[6] This is not to suggest that both India and Pakistan are solely focused on mutual negation since every collective identity is a fluid and multidimensional phenomenon that cannot be explained through a single factor. In the same way Indians have been attempting to define their Indianness within the context of an ascendant and exclusive Hindutva, so too have Pakistanis been engaged in self-reckoning which, given their pluralism, geopolitical location and the attendant external pressures, is even more a cumbersome process. Almost 70 years since the dissolution of the Raj, both India and Pakistan, and likewise other South Asian nations, should have enough credentials and confidence to define the parameters of their collective identities away from solely depending upon some external trajectories, or fear complexes.[7] The newer generations, changed demographics, respective texts, historical narratives and parallel icons and preferences have surely been anchoring their own distinctiveness, though it would be equally unfair to dismiss the concurrent genuine and even mass-based desire to seek a closer and peaceful regionalization. In this chapter, while looking at the broader issues of Muslim identity in South Asia, we try to review a few selected academic and literary works on Pakistan.

The debate on Pakistan, in reference to India, Islam, ethnicity and certainly the geopolitical denominators, has been a persistent reality, and the intense interplay of local, regional and global developments since September 11 has put Pakistan in the proverbial bull's eye. Nuclearization, terrorism, Talibanization, sectarianism and jigsaw-like relations with India, Afghanistan and the West all have become salient features of this discourse, which reverberates in daily media reports, talk shows, surveys by think tanks and certainly through visual presentations and serious academic material.[8] The role of forces such as the Islamists, the army brass, political leaders, ethnic cohorts and the Pakistani Diaspora, especially in the West, has never been under such a multidimensional scrutiny, and this is not merely confined to Western or Indian channels since the country has its own visible share of chattering classes, media and rhetoricians, all pointing towards the presence of a vocal civil society.[9] The ongoing violence in Pakistan, both by Pakistani perpetrators and external forces, is certainly rooted in a plethora of complex factors and, like any other historical development, defies a single-factor explanation. Pakistan's entire population is certainly affected by parallel spectres of violence, and a common moroseness has been too evident to be ignored, especially during the worst monsoon floods in the country when ethnic, sectarian and militant forms of collective violence also remained unabated.[10] Ramadan in 2010 had ended in a surreal way, with policemen guarding places of worship from suspected suicide bombings, which, since 2006, have targeted police and military posts, markets, schools, mosques and such other places of public gatherings.[11] While the CIA-led drones kept raining Hellfires on hamlets in the FATA with an unacknowledged official Pakistani connivance,[12] the target killings in Karachi both by hit squads loyal to the MQM and the ANP – otherwise coalition partners in the PPP-led regime (2008–13), continued unabated.[13] In Balochistan, following the murder of Nawab Akbar Bugti in 2006 on the orders of General Pervez Musharraf, the simmering resentment against Islamabad and non-Baloch citizens, especially the Punjabis, assumed further momentum. Stories about 'missing' Pakistanis following September 11 and especially in Balochistan have abounded on national media with police and intelligence agencies – often called 'deep state' or 'a hidden hand'– getting the flak from the civil society and the Supreme Court. Between 2007 and 2013, amidst instability in Swat and adjoining regions along with frequent suicide and drone attacks, it felt as if the country was experiencing the proverbial million mutinies and the official writ of the state had dwindled to a select few barricaded townships.[14] The spectacular attacks on a Peshawar school on 16 December 2014 and a Shia mosque in Shikarpur in January 2015, followed by a similar suicide bombing in Peshawar and the killing of 47 Ismailis on a bus in Karachi on 13 May 2015, amongst others, happened at a time when the Pakistani official writ seemed to be gaining better ground in its fight against militancy.[15]

Despite the unprecedented floods of 2010, the army's riposte to Hussain Haqqani for allegedly writing a message to Admiral Mike Mullen seeking help for political leadership against the generals and the ISI – which played out before Pakistan's Supreme Court and soon after, US Navy SEALs swooped in on 2 May 2011 – the incipient political system carried on. Holding free and comparatively fair elections under a commonly agreed caretaker government and a revitalized election commission, amidst various forms of threats and violent attacks, was equally re-energizing for civic institutions and public opinion, though the country remained lodged in a precarious security situation. Not only had a political administration for the first time bequeathed power to its elected successor and that too after completing its five-year tenure, but even the presidency itself was going through a similar process. Here, in September 2013 the incumbent Asif Ali Zardari, after completing his full five-year term, bowed to the new electoral verdict, which again was not a mean accomplishment for the country and its political stakeholders. Both Nawaz Sharif and Imran Khan initiated peace parleys with the Pakistani Taliban during 2014 amidst a downturn in violence and the CIA's discontinuing the drone attacks for a short while. A de-escalation in the violence was visible, yet it refused to disappear altogether, and Rawalpindi, Sibbi, Peshawar, Islamabad and Karachi experienced taxing bomb blasts in public places. Drone attacks soon resumed following a short thaw, and by early 2015, North-western Pakistan had already experienced almost 500 CIA-operated drone attacks causing numerous and under-reported civilian deaths. But following the deaths of four Western hostages in North Waziristan as a result of a similar attack in February, President Barack Obama apologized to his nation in April 2015, which to his critics only betrayed an exclusive concern for non-Pakistani casualties.[16]

Violence: Plural Forms, Multiple Manifestations

A salient form of violence underwriting 'Pakistan's reputation as the epicentre of global terrorism and a rogue state',[17] especially following September 11, is owed to geopolitical developments, and here initially FATA and subsequently the entire country became a hotbed of suicide bombings, target killings, attacks on security forces and the state infrastructure, including communal places such as shrines, houses of worship, markets and schools. This violence was further augmented by state policies, including rushed operations against militants in several regions, which then underpinned a greater amount of retaliatory escalation often justified in the name of jihad, resistance or sheer revenge. The second form of violence is sectarian, in which denominational differences have become too volatile, with *takfir* assuming a private and public prerogative for several groups. Here the conflict between the Sunnis and Shias and between the Deobandis and Brelwis is further exacerbated by a wave of so-called majoritarianism, whereby the citizenship of Ahmadis, Shias or even groups such as Zikris becomes disputatious, as if Pakistan might only and solely belong to a so-called majority. The third spectre of violence is ethnic which, earlier on, involved both the former wings of the country. In East Pakistan, it deteriorated into a civil war that arrayed West Pakistani troops and their local Islamist and Bihari supporters – often seen as the linchpins of the Pakistani state – against the Bengalis, whose lingual separatism had grown into a full-fledged Bangladeshi secessionism. Similarly, tensions between the Punjabis and Pashtuns across the Indus regions were germinated with the induction of various changes under the Raj, yet they assumed greater intensity following the scuttling of democracy and the rights of smaller groups under schemes such as the One-Unit in West Pakistan in 1955.

Given the unprecedented mobility in the region in 1947 and ever since, the pluralization of the lower Sindh registered a new form of urban militancy, which has been periodically volatile since the 1980s. Ethnic tensions between the Baloch nationalists and the rest, and the assertion of Muhajir and Sindhi identities since the 1970s have often been volatile and even multiplied due to longer authoritarian rule interspersed by military operations, in addition to the demographic mobility in urban centres such as Karachi, Hyderabad and Quetta. The fifth kind of violence in Pakistan is tribal by nature, which, owing to easy access to weaponry and other modernist linkages along with a unique and destabilizing class formation, has escalated in the tribal regions of the KP, lower Balochistan and rural Sindh. Tribal violence, amongst other factors, is owed to geopolitical developments in Southwest Asia, besides the traditional determinants such as the control of land and other resources. Relations between the khans and mullahs, often in mutual conflict since the 1980s, provided a significant fillip to violence on the Frontier, whereas the Sunni-Shia conflict in the Kurram Agency, or in Quetta and Jhang found impetus due to Saudi-Iranian competition which occasionally played out as a proxy war in countries like Pakistan, Iraq, Lebanon, Bahrain, Yemen, Syria and Afghanistan. Fingers have been frequently pointed towards the United States and other anti-Tehran actors for fomenting agitation against Iran by fuelling sectarian violence in Iraq, Afghanistan and Pakistan.[18]

Whose Violence?

Following the above identification of major forms of violence, it is certainly pertinent to pinpoint particular causes that trigger such violence. Across the globe, trajectories such as class, caste, colour and creed have been, in general, viewed as operative behind most of the collective and even individual incidences of violence. The leftist interpretations often look at economic stratification as spawning conflict, which, in some cases, might be justifiable so as to create a classless, Marxist or socialist utopia. However, the caste and colour factors underpinning racism, apartheid, slavery and even postcolonial unevenness in sociopolitical relationships have also been viewed as the most significant causes for multiple forms of discrimination. In collaboration with other sordid realities, including economic disparities and political disempowerment, dissensions of these types trigger violence. Response to such violence, especially in the post-Columbian era, has been anchored on multiple strategies varying from agitation to armed defiance, non-violence and even accommodation and appeasement, while some polities might have tried to combat it through constitutional and legal frameworks, including positive discrimination and special incentives. For instance, Frederick Douglass in the antebellum United States sought agitation as an effective means of abolishing slavery and Jim Crow laws, while earlier, African American slaves such as Duke Vesey and Nat Turner raised the flag through active rebellion. However, Booker T. Washington, more like Sir Syed Ahmed Khan, advocated the acquisition of education for African Americans as well as the assimilation of Western knowledge and polytechnic instruction. In more recent years, Mahatma Gandhi, Khan Abdul Ghaffar Khan, Nelson Mandela, Desmond Tutu, the Dalai Lama, Abdul Sattar Edhi and Dr. Martin Luther King Jr. have pursued non-violence to neutralize violence itself – something that we find quite at home with the Sufis, Bhagats and several Buddhist monks.[19]

Culture or creed as a major cause for collective violence is linked with the regimented forces of religion, beliefs and culture, in which a strong and exclusive conviction in self-righteousness turns coercive, especially towards minorities and vulnerable groups. Here, almost every religion has built its case on solely appropriating the entire space, while denying similar claims by its counterparts. This moral crusade is not just confined to the three Abrahamic traditions. It is even widely shared and practiced by almost every religion and creed, including Buddhism, as seen in Sri Lanka and Myanmar.[20] In recent times, the European colonization of the world, the enslavement of millions of Africans and the extinction of native and indigenous communities in the Americas and Australasia happened largely due to this unshaken self-belief in taking *culture* to 'uncivilized' people.[21] The elimination of the Mayas, Incas and Aztecs, and likewise other Native communities in the Western Hemisphere might have been the result of an economic and physical control of their lands and resources, but was largely justified through a moral crusade when conquistadors, Pilgrims, Puritans and their successive generations often attained the status of saints, chosen to undertake a civilizational mission among the heathens. In the same vein, the colonization of Afro–Asian lands by the European powers not only gave an impetus to wider missionary enterprises but it equally encouraged evangelization of the world, besides its literary redefinition.[22] This Christian mission was shared by most of the empire builders all the way from Hernando Cortés, Francisco Pizarro, Bartolomé de las Casas, and Vasco da Gama to Walter Raleigh, William Penn, King Leopold, Robert Livingstone, Cecil Rhodes, Lord Cromer and the Lawrences. Christianity benefited the most from this Europeanization of the world, and colonial paradigms went in tandem with the evangelization of these newly conquered continents. Other than Catholic–Protestant or Armenian–Orthodox proclivities, the imperial rivalries often criss-crossed such religious loyalties, but overall there was a transregional, tacit understanding on helping the missionaries in India, Africa, China, Australasia and all the other subjugated continents. Such powerful realities intermingled with the racist and even long-held discretionary views of Muslims, and an entire discourse based on hegemony and civil versus uncivil – called orientalism – emerged in the West.[23] Of course, some countries such as Germany or Sweden initially did not possess colonial empires in the non-White regions, yet missionary fraternity and a widely shared belief in a civilizing mission also allowed scholars in those areas to ride the proverbial bandwagon. The discretionary role of the Church in the antebellum South and Nazi Germany is certainly well documented.

The culture-based unevenness and attitudinal hegemony leading to mass-scale violence also had its intra-European features, and was not solely focused on non-European worlds. For instance, the long tradition of discriminating against Gypsies – Romas as they are called now – and the Jews has been a persistent fact, which, occasionally, assumed sectarian features whenever a so-called official majoritarian religion, in its racialized forms, attempted to marginalize minority groups even from amongst their fellow Christians. However, the worst kind of collective violence occurred all through the twentieth century, in which imperialism, racism and interstate conflicts led to some of the most devastating wars, genocides and other forms of collective violence, as witnessed in the Holocaust and the ethnic cleansing in the Balkans. Here, Europeans engaged in killing fellow Europeans with a view to achieving total elimination, simultaneous with their involvement in the colonies through the powerful trajectories of religion, politics and racism, brewing the most horrible form of collective violence ever perpetrated in human history. No wonder the twentieth century is so far viewed as the most violent century in the known human history, not only because the population groups both on the sides of the perpetrators as well as the victims were extensive but also because following the Second Industrial Revolution, modern states had become even more efficient in causing large-scale human misery. As seen in the two World Wars; the nuking of Japanese cities; and the mass murder in Vietnam, Afghanistan, Yugoslavia, Rwanda, Congo and more recently in Iraq, Syria and Southwest Asia, the industrial and scientific underpinnings of modern violence have transformed it into a mass-scale enterprise and not a sheer powercentric imbalance.[24]

While one may classify trajectories such as caste, class, colonialism, culture and creed as the 'traditional' underlying factors behind collective violence, the more recent debate on modernity itself raises serious issues about the ongoing forms of violence. Here, not just the radical groups such as Al-Qaeda, Hindutva proponents, or the Zionist settlers have pursued violence but also states have persisted with unbridled bloodshed in pushing for their own discretionary agendas and self-interest. The postcolonial states have justified violence against their own population groups in the name of patriotism and national security, whereas the developed states have used all kinds of rationales, including security, self-righteousness and enlightenment to pursue militarist and collective punishment and that too vis-à-vis non-combatant civilian groups, often furtively called 'collateral damage'. Vietnam, Lebanon, Chechnya, Afghanistan, Iraq, Syria, Myanmar and Pakistan are the recent and ongoing case studies in this second form of statist violence, while, in between, Yugoslavia, the Caucuses, Kashmir, Palestine and the sub-Saharan regions have been subjugated to direct or indirect cavalcades originating from some of the most 'enlightened' regions of the world. Ironically, owing to propaganda, self-altruism and greater economic interests, most citizens in both the developed and developing regions often end up supporting their regimes in pursuance of such violence. The lack of independent multilateral forums or their subjectivity, weaker peace movements and pervasive desensitization to violence heaped upon 'others' – especially if they belong to *different* religious traditions, cultures and complexions – help states pursue such discretionary policies. In the same vein, multinational corporations have been operating as state-like conglomerates in squeezing greater interests by committing greater violence on natural resources, causing a significant environmental degradation. The debate about modernity has certainly divided many contemporary thinkers, and its erstwhile adulation has often given way to cynicism towards Euro–American modernity, which, other than transcendent westernization, may also feature some other testing ingredients.[25] While some authors may view the West European Enlightenment as ushering in both modernity and progress and thus being totally sacrosanct, others would see in it a larger, diffused and often turbulent human reality, which may direly necessitate some revisiting.[26]

Islam and Violence

The ongoing focus on Islam as a major instrumentation for global violence, including intra-Muslim feuds, is often perceived as a Western construct rooted in the early modern era when the Europeanization of the world exacerbated class-based and ideological dissensions, and even transmutations among Muslims. However, the Crusades, Mongol invasions and then the Inquisition and expulsions from the Iberian Peninsula often posited Muslims as victims rather than the perpetrators, though the Catholic view following the Ottoman conquest of Constantinople often justified anti-Muslim and anti-Morisco cleansing from across the north Mediterranean regions. The evangelical component of colonization and its resistance by Muslim groups in Afro–Asian territories only exacerbated anger towards Islam and, often in cahoots with racist typologies, Christianity was posited as a more tolerant, cultured and forward-looking alternative not only to Islam but also to other 'Eastern' religions. The Christian colonials, in their self-righteousness, viewed Christianity as synonymous with a superior Western culture since it conveniently benefited both the empire builders and the ecclesiasts.

The missionary-administrator-scholar reconstruction of Islam, especially during the nineteenth century began to reverberate more forcefully following September 11, and amidst a host of writings, visual presentations and websites, a reinvigorated form of neo-orientalism has established itself as a dominant discourse. Writers such as Bernard Lewis, V. S. Naipaul and Daniel Pipes; journalists and activists like Paul Berman, Oriana Fallaci, Bat Ye'or (pen name of Gisele Littman), Melanie Phillips, Pamela Geller, Robert Spencer and Ann Coulter; and a whole array of generals, politicians and evangelical groups, especially from amongst the Christian-Zionists, have lent a significant impetus to this new and more intense form of neo-orientalism.[27] Amidst a growing wave of Islamophobia across Europe, Russia and North America, ultra-right political groups also began zeroing in on Islam by juxtaposing it with immigration, conversions, crime and a stark unevenness in gender relations, as is evident from electoral results in countries and regions like France, the Netherlands, Austria and Scandinavia. Quran-burning bishops and xenophobic racists find close company with neo-Nazis such as the English Defence League, (EDL) with its vicious, coercive agitation focusing on mosques and Muslim neighbourhoods, which may be reflected in the diatribes of hateful politicians such as Geert Wilders and trajectories including Pegida and the National Front (FN). Undeniably, neo-racism through its Islamophobic trajectories seems to have institutionalized itself at various levels and 'hating Muslims is now the public face of racism'.[28]

Anti-Muslim diatribes are quite frequent and may seek justification in the name of freedom of expression, even though they may be explicitly racist and pernicious such as Wilders equating the Quran to Adolf Hitler's *Mein Kampf*, or may even burn the Muslim holy book to vent their own animosity, as well as causing riots so that Muslims can be further blamed for being problematic. Like erstwhile anti-Semitism, the abhorrence for Islam in all its variations has the insidious ingredients listed earlier, and thus violence against Muslims cannot be explained through a single trajectory. It varies from the sheer invasion of Muslim countries and regions, to the detailed profiling of a vast section of the world's population, to internments, renditions, profiling, harassment and sheer discrimination at jobs.[29] Violence becomes quite nefarious when it assumes written, audio and visual forms, and certainly adds to 'the clash of cultures and communities', obfuscating all other bridge-building efforts. Incidentally, even the highest citadels of learning are no exceptions when it comes to exceptionalizing Muslims, and an entire generation of academics keenly follows scholars such as Lewis and Pipes in their negative portrayals of Muslims.[30] A glaring example is a Harvard academic, Professor Martin Peretz, who is also the editor-in-chief of the Washington-based magazine the *New Republic*. While his university planned to honour him by creating an endowed chair in his name, Peretz fulminated in his magazine by observing, 'Muslim life is cheap, most notably to Muslims ... So, yes, I wonder whether I need to honour these people and pretend that they are worthy of the privileges of the First Amendment which I have in my gut in the sense that they will abuse'. Many challenged his views, including Professor Stephen Walt, who wrote to him through the *Boston Globe*: 'If you had said this about Blacks, Jews or Catholics, it would be a scandal'. Given his avowed support for Israel, Peretz used his columns for such a diatribe, though, ironically, compared to the stormy reaction over Helen Thomas's criticism of Israel, his comments did not gather any visible media reaction. Thomas, a respected journalist, had criticized Israel's anti-Palestinian policies and also the continued displacement of these people by a predominantly European Jewry, whom she told to 'go home' to Poland and Germany. She was widely denigrated as a Jew hater, with the *New York Times* and *Washington Post*, among several media outlets, taking the lead in denouncing her.[31]

Irrespective of neo-orientalist and neo-conservative views of Islam – often steeped in derogation and suspicion besides justifying anti-Muslim [often state-led] violence – one has to accept the fact that intra-Muslim violence is also a recurring reality. It is not always rooted in respective views of Islam as reflected in denominational diversities, since it may again be linked with the issues of politico-economic power in addition to complex *local* and extra-regional causes which add fuel to the fury. Despite a greater theological aversion to intolerance as ordained in Islam's classical sources, intra-Muslim violence has been a frequent visitor to Muslim communities all the way from 632 CE to the present.

Its personal, ethnic, sectarian, imperial (for instance, amongst the three Timurid empires, or the erstwhile Ummayyid-Abbasid rivalry) and interstate varieties (the Iran-Iraq war and such other recent precedents) are too obvious to ignore, though there are ideals for a supra-regional, supra-denominational embodiment which has equally enthralled the communities, especially during the current difficult times. This reality of schisms and conflicts has often contrasted with the recurrence of an ideal for a shared ummah, and even amidst a Westphalian reality of scores of Muslim states and the presence of numerous Muslim minority communities across the globe, such a duality is a historical fact. The desire for a united Muslim world gained a major following during the colonial period with proponents like Jamal-ud-Din Al-Afghani, Shibli Nomani, Muhammad Iqbal, Syed Ameer Ali, the Ali Brothers, Muhammad Abduh and many more. Other than these pan-Islamists, religio-political parties such as the Jamiat-i-Ulama-i-Hind, the Muslim Brotherhood, Khaksar Movement, Majlis-i-Ahrar, Jamaat-i-Islami and some of the early leaders of the Iranian Shia clergy always propounded a Muslim globalism. Disenchantment with the postcolonial inertia of the Muslim ruling elite, border conflicts and a continued surrogacy to external powers certainly helped strengthen the idealism for a substantial Muslim fraternity, and this kind of sentiment has been rooted in modern education, mobility and the evolution of a Muslim middle class. However, in our contemporary era, other than the idealization of a Muslim caliphate – *khilafat* – the desire for greater Muslim interdependence has also been articulated forcefully by Muslim intellectuals and activists settled in the Diaspora. These sections have often used pen and brainstorming sessions to offer a more modernist, self-confident but forward-looking *Muslimness*, whereas activists such as Hizbul Tehrir have often opted for a more vocal and politics-based activism. The Muslim student societies on Western campuses have often operated as vanguard groups in propounding the desire and need for worldwide Muslim unity, though following September 11 and July 7 many of them have been under official and media invigilation. This is not to suggest that pan-Islamic views and groups dominate the discourse, as the national, ethnic and denominational diversities do underline many parallel or even opposing affiliations and priorities. In addition, the liberal Muslim groups are more focused on human rights issues, the development of civil societies and a broader acceptance of democracy and modern political systems, and for them regionalization and bridge-building with the West and the rest are greater imperatives than just focusing on a single, united *Muslim* identity. To them, Muslims are as diverse and plural as any other such populous community, and efforts instead need to be directed towards attainable and sustainable goals and those too based on empowerment and shared heritage, and not by assuming exclusive or rejectionist strategies.

Pakistan: Partition and Recent Perspectives

Pakistan, since its inception as an idea and then as a country, has been one of those few postcolonial case studies which, in some familiar realms, has attracted an enormous historiography. An enormity of scholarly and journalistic works – including those by the present writer – abound the libraries and Internet sites. Owing to their repetitive nature which comes from focusing on well-familiar themes such as Islam as the bane of its rationale as well as predicament, the military and mullahs being its nemesis, and obliging and often corrupt politicians operating as the 'enemy within', these works routinely fail to break new ground. Pakistani expatriate scholars have often fallen into the same trap by internalizing an essentialized problematic of Pakistan by virtue of its 'caesarean' separation from *Mother* India, its failure in establishing an enduring democratic system despite all the efforts and public ethos to that effect and its continuous travails with India and the West.[32] No wonder that, despite being overstudied, Pakistan as a society remains underresearched, and that is where the monotony in these narratives has become all too overpowering. The net result is an expected continuum of doom and gloom, including the epithet of being 'a greedy country'.[33]

Farzana Shaikh's early historical study, based on her doctoral research, was a timely attempt at investigating the quest for a cohesive political community anchored on a historical and intellectual ethos of worldwide Islam within a specific South Asian context.[34] She tried to move the discourse on Pakistan's evolution from the prevalent paradigm of high politics of a few powerful men at the top, nudging her reader to seek a long-term explanation of this country's evolution, especially after the post-1857 trauma. Shaikh, in her recent work, might be right in suggesting that there are multiple forms of Islam and that, in the same vein, there are numerous perceptions of Pakistan, which render the plural country into a hotbed of diverse and even contentious interpretations at various levels.[35] Well, that should not be a unique perspective, especially for any scholar, since we are talking about a populous and immensely plural part of the world, and it must not come as a surprise that even countries like the United Kingdom, Belgium, Italy and Spain may have similar challenges, though of course with several substantial differences. Yet, collective identity is always a fluid and evolving paradigm, and in that sense a period of 70 years may still be meagre. Even Israel, often mentioned in Shaikh's volume, has serious ideological problems, not only vis-à-vis its Arab population but also amongst its own Jewish Zionist hard-core citizens, who differ over the nature and direction of their very Jewishness. Yes, India had a better start since it inherited the mainstream institutional framework from the Raj; has been advantageously located away from the restive frontier region; and was lucky to have a long list of founding fathers who, unlike their mostly flamboyant Pakistani counterparts, built up enduring institutions. However, even the very *Indian* identity is comparatively quite young and still evolving, though claims by Jawaharlal Nehru and others of its historicity are no less trivial. But then the real India, in a way, was the Indus Valley as recorded in *Rig Veda*, unless we are talking about Hindustan, though the Indus Valley, curiously, never forsook its adolescence.

Despite her interviews with a vast array of generals, Shaikh seems to follow the usual critique of the military as an exploitative institution, which roped in jihadis, especially in 1971, and then again during the 1980s and 1990s to wage civil and regional wars, as if the latter had no autonomous agency of their own. The military is definitely the strongest pressure group in the country, and as in Turkey, Indonesia, Venezuela, Nigeria, Egypt, Myanmar and such other places, it views itself as the guardian of a state, surrounded by hostile forces. The army's operations in Swat, FATA and elsewhere have cost it large-scale human losses and casualties, and its eye-to-eye stand against a continuous Indian hostility have the support of the Indus Valley people who, by the way, make up almost 80 per cent of this country's population. However, their negligence of or even suspected complicity in presumably sheltering Osama bin Laden in Abbottabad, as documented in the report by the Abbottabad Commission, once again raised serious concerns about the supra-professional priorities of the generals. It would be ideal if the generals stayed aloof and let the politicians establish constitutional politics, but let us not forget that the general-presidents have been either brought in by their external backers or were provided fuller protection as surrogates. Shaikh lists all the contentious and discordant ideological and structural areas, including the ambiguous idea of a Muslim versus an Islamic state, the predominance of the military and mullahs, and a less savoury record on reformism, even often at the risk of repetition, and comes closer to Hamza Alavi's interpretation of a Muslim salariat playing its own chequered game of interests.[36] Alavi's understandably class-based analysis presupposed a pre-existing Muslim upper middle class in British India, which may be an exaggerated view given the economic underdevelopment and disparate nature of Muslim communities, but that is a different subject altogether. To Shaikh, the elite interests constantly ignored the quest for a consensus identity and that became Pakistan's most major malaise. Several Pakistanis may like to go along with her way of thinking, but putting the entire onus of responsibility on Pakistan as an errant runaway from a pristine Mother India or acting as 'America's sullen mistress' warrants a similar view from 'the other side of the mountain'.[37] Shaikh's angry book has to be read in conjunction with Anatol Lieven's volume that, instead of high politics, the army and Islam, focuses on the societal dynamics in the country that sustain it and may eventually endure its various challenges.[38]

Jaswant Singh, a former BJP foreign minister of India, was determined to study Jinnah with a fresher perspective so as to seek out the factors behind the division of the subcontinent. His book caused some uproar among his own colleagues due to their strong reservations against Pakistan and Jinnah, but in Pakistan it was well received, with Singh enjoying superb and cordial hospitality across the Indus lands. Initially, his own ultra-right party expelled him for writing this book on Jinnah – the Quaid-i-Azam (great leader) – but given his high profile and a lifetime commitment to his country and Hinduist ideology, he has been taken back into the BJP's fold.[39] To Singh, himself a devout believer in the uniformist origins of an otherwise ancient and plural but inherently Hindu India, the idea of Muslim separateness was always a 'fallacious notion' because, to him, 'India's foundation is Vedic'. Even the periodization of Indian history such as 'the Muslim era', according to Singh, is wrong, as he believes in the indivisible nature of Indian history and instead blames the Indo-Persian hagiographers for constructing such a false consciousness.[40] That emphasis on distinctness, according to Singh, created an *imagined* separateness of Muslims, which was further regimented by the Europeans. In this context, he defines the stormy events of 1857 as a watershed when Muslim separateness began to evolve through Sir Syed Ahmed Khan until it matured into the demands for separate electorates, and the formation of the All-India Muslim League in 1906. For a while, and quite often, Singh's narrative eulogising a unitary India while critiquing British machinations takes its reader away from Jinnah himself and turns into a familiar nationalist account of the known political history of the decades preceding 1947. To him, the false consciousness anchored on this growing separatism and internalized by an otherwise astute lawyer became a solidified demand for Muslim rights initially seeking parity with the Hindu majority before turning into a full-fledged struggle for sovereignty. 'It has to be understood that there was an inbuilt conflict of interests between a Muslim majority working the 1919 reforms, and a highly literate, professional and political aware urban Hindu majority, suffering the unintended adverse consequences of the 1919 reforms'.[41]

While Jinnah as a proponent of Hindu-Muslim unity tried to cultivate a closer relationship with Gandhi, B. G. Tilak, G. K. Gokhale and the Nehrus, most of the Congress leaders either ignored him out of sheer snobbery and arrogance or merely derided him as a spoiler. As early as 1915, on his return from South Africa, Gandhi did not properly appreciate Jinnah's sincerity for a united nationalist cause and instead, unnecessarily, hinted at his Muslim origins. Motilal Nehru always reciprocated towards Jinnah until he came under the Mahasabha pressure in 1927–28, but his son, Jawaharlal, often looked down upon Jinnah, as is noted by Singh: 'Nehru's private judgments about Jinnah, shaped by intensely personal and emotional factors and aversions, certainly intruded into all his dealings with Jinnah'. Even Gandhi went on vacillating between his claims for an all-India leadership – over and above creeds and castes – and a strict Hindu identity. Patel and several others in the Congress fold refused to accept the genuine concerns and demands of Muslims from various regions and classes, and during the war years Jinnah was able to establish himself as 'the sole saviour' of India's Muslims. After forming ministries in nine provinces in 1937, the Indian National Congress (INC) not only refused to reach out to the League but it also blatantly undertook measures to finish off the latter at places like the UP. Here, Jinnah was finally able to bring the Muslim leaders of Bengal and Punjab together since they all felt apprehensive towards the INC's hegemonic policies and its majoritarianism. To Singh, the INC's irreverence towards the League and other Indian parties, while trying to present itself as the only political voice of the entire land, betrayed an imperious attitude and proved no less than a 'Himalayan blunder'.[42] The INC leadership, especially V. Patel, was heading towards the partition, more so after rejecting the Cabinet Mission Plan of 1946, which had been, in fact, accepted by Jinnah and the League, and guaranteed a federal India. No wonder, in the aura of personal squabbles, rushed expediencies and free fall into vanities, 'India's independence was being reduced to farcical casualness'. Lord Louis Mountbatten's arrogance formally sealed the fate as his vehemently pro-INC adviser, V. P. Menon, began drafting the partition plan, which was promptly seen and approved by Nehru. Jaswant Singh rightly laments, 'It had taken Menon exactly four hours to draw up the Plan changing the face of India, also that of the world'.[43] Singh mourns partition, as is expected of a Hindu nationalist, and patronizingly finds the creation of Pakistan as stemming from misperception, wrong policies and thoughtless ventures, which, to a great extent, underpinned the malaise facing this Indus Valley nation.[44] Again, only reducing the entire discourse to political ambitions of a few individuals while ignoring the societal imperatives, Singh decrees Pakistan as soon descending into a jihadi state, rented out to Western interests and thus becoming a distant reality from what Jinnah might have desired of it in the closing days of his life.

Pakistan: A Counterperspective in Fiction

Away from the sordid realities of South Asian politics characterized by interpersonal squabbles and interparty dissensions, many literary works by South Asian writers, especially those of Pakistani origins, offer a unique and even alternative perspective on the region and its recent tumultuous history, including Partition and post–September 11 violence that has seemed to be unremitting, with Pakistanis killing Pakistanis in the name of revenge, sectarianism or ethnicity. While earlier writers, especially in Urdu, focused on brutality that happened in the wake of 1947 on all sides, the younger generation of Pakistani writers, often writing in English, has focused on the nihilist nature of this violence. Faiz Ahmed Faiz, Saadat Hasan Manto, Intizaar Hussain, Abdullah Hussain, Quratul Ain Haider, Nasim Hijazi and several others have enriched Urdu literature both in poetry and prose.[45] Bapsi Sidhwa, Salman Rushdie and a few other South Asian writers have used fiction to focus on recent history and communal discord, which certainly remains a major preoccupation, but the newer generation has diversified its thematic focus.[46] Here, Kamila Shamsie, Nadeem Aslam, Mohsin Hamid, Daniyal Mueenuddin, Muhammad Hanif, Suhayl Saadi, Aquila Ismail and several others in the same younger group have articulated their anguish and shock through English fiction, while a whole generation of new singers and artists have tried to appropriate a more humanistic dimension of Pakistani cultures.[47] One may focus on an author who owns up to both India and Pakistan, besides her own upbringing in the plural cultures of North America. Away from nationalistic, jingoistic and hyped-up geopolitical narratives, Shauna Singh Baldwin's fiction offers a fresher, warmer and reflective perspective, though no less melancholy either. Her two historical novels reconstruct the story of South Asian history in the pre-1947 era, often reliving through the past the biographies of some known [female] Indians, whereas two collections of her short stories are of a more cosmopolitan nature in which immigrants settled in North America find themselves at several historical and even inquisitional crossroads. *What the Body Remembers* is a novel about two Sikh women married to a landowning Sardariji from Rawalpindi, who has an engineering degree from Balliol and lives a very disciplined life trying to combine both East and West in his person and profession.[48] His privileged life is, however, beset by the lack of any offspring from his first wife, Satya, a dynamic woman in her own right, until he is persuaded to marry Roop, from Pari Darvaza, a small hamlet not too far from the Rohtas end of the Salt Range. Roop's father was a Sikh by conviction, though originally from a Hindu background, yet is devoted to his creed and is an industrious farmer whose wife's early death leaves him with two children. Brought up in a multicultural milieu, Roop sees her husband only after marriage and settles well in Rawalpindi with both Sardarji and Satya. The births of her children bring in joy in the household but also engender tensions, which often converge with the rising communal dissension in a plural Punjab until events turn riotous. Harrowed by personal frustrations, yet still inherently faithful to her religion and husband, Satya is empowered by political developments in India and is no longer comfortable with the status-quo attitudes of an Indian upstartish middle class. Her own end at Punja Sahib in Hasan Abdal, imbued with a reawakened political consciousness, coincides with the sad mayhem across Punjab, where all the four communities take it out on one another. Sardarji's family, including Roop with her baby daughter, is able to make it to Delhi, only after harrowing escapes through a senseless communal melee. In their 'escape', they are helped by faithful friends, including some Muslims, yet all around it becomes a telltale of bloodshed, dislocation, morass and mass migrations.

Nora Baker is known in British history as the first woman to have been awarded the George Cross, but very few people would know that she was a young Muslim woman who had been allegedly killed by the Nazis on the allegation of being a successful British spy. Noor Inayat Khan was the daughter of an Indian Muslim Sufi mentor, a classicist and non-conformist of genteel traditions, and a great-granddaughter of Tipu Sultan, who died fighting the East India Company in 1799. Noor was born to her American mother in Moscow, where Inayat Khan had been holding concerts of Indian classical music in addition to imparting Sufi training to his acolytes. Noor has attracted very few serious historical works, and not enough is known about the circumstances leading to her tragic death at a time when the war was itself coming to a close.[49] Shauna Baldwin's novel *The Tiger Claw* is certainly a dexterously organized story of Noor and her work in Paris with the French resistance as well as her own life as a Sufi Muslim who sought employment with the British intelligence due to various mundane reasons.[50] Benefiting from extensive research in Britain, India, France and Germany, Baldwin was able to interview several knowledgeable people along with the immediate members of the Khan family in their native Baroda. The novel's heroine, Madeleine, is both an asset and a dilemma for her British superiors since she is a *native* woman from the colonies but with a unique and cosmopolitan pedigree, while for the French she is almost local, though a bit exotic. For the Germans, such as her inquisitor, Ernst Vogel, she is a *mischlinge* (mixed breed), but still in the league of fabulous Indian princesses. Her arrest and then torture until her execution – not necessarily by her tormentors – are surely quite tragic, and the novelist is at her best in conveying the sense of pathos as well as resistance exhibited by a petite woman of resolute fortitude. Baker/Madeleine is known as a writer of children's stories and leaves her narrative surreptitiously in her dark cell.

While Baldwin's heroines in her two novels are three South Asian women, along with a host of other ordinary men and women, her short stories cover a wider canvas and induct the Ukrainians, North Americans, South Americans and Europeans, as well as a fair representation of South Asians. Here again, the characters are mostly immigrants who, otherwise well-established law-abiding citizens, often get trapped in the whirlwinds of events such as post–September 11 xenophobia and other forms of racism. Her story 'We Are Not in Pakistan' is about a Pakistani American grandma who is Christian and, along with her American husband, has been settled in the United States. Kathleen is her granddaughter whom she daily accompanies to her school, whereas the grandpa, Terry, is often busy watching football matches on television and is a retired diplomat. Terry and grandma had met long time back at the US embassy's dance parties in Pakistan and got married and moved to the Midwest, where their daughter, Safia, married a local man. Kathleen often argues with her grandma over her insistence on some of the traditional mores, which, according to the younger lady, are not American per se. For instance, Kathleen is often irked by her grandma's insistence on the Pakistani-style of modest dressing, while the granddaughter keeps reminding her that they were in the United

States and not in Pakistan – the latter existing more like an abstract for her. Grandma was herself born of an Iranian Christian mother in India and an Anglo father, but culturally is more akin to Pakistani Muslim women. She still has one of her older address books containing the names and contacts of her close relatives and friends from Pakistan who had been living in the United States, and quite a few of them 'disappeared' following September 11 as US Department of Homeland Security and US Immigration Service personnel chased them away with one excuse or the other. Some of them have already been repatriated to Pakistan; several are languishing in detention centres unknown to many of their relatives; and other harassed individuals are seeking asylum in Canada.

On a normal day, Grandma disappears, and the entire household initially takes it rather lightly, expecting her return any time, but after a day or two Kathleen, Terry and Safia all become immensely concerned. Safia, because of her employment at the airport, remembers that the home security and immigration officials often connive to arraign unsuspecting residents of Pakistani origin. She is convinced that her mum has been whisked away by the same people, as she tells Terry: 'I'm just saying we have to be careful. Remember that woman right here – no, in the suburbs somewhere – what was her name? The Immigration guys barged in while she was in the shower, and next thing she knew she was on her way back to Somalia, leaving her husband and children behind ... Have you any idea how difficult it to stay legal? It's damn near impossible. Lose a job that brought you here or get laid off before you have enough money saved for the trip home and two months later you're illegal. Take nine credits instead of twelve on a student visa and you can be deported. And now they just take away your passport and you're stateless. Can't prove you're from anywhere'.[51] Certainly, this is an untold chapter of a recent unwritten history in which a large number of Muslims, especially Pakistanis, in the United States have 'disappeared' and, unknown to their relatives and authorities, are lost somewhere in no man's land. The rounding up of most of these people owing to sheer xenophobia is initially owed to a suspicion of their being potential terrorists – irrespective of age, profession or gender – and with no tangible evidence available, it begins to bank on some immigration-related technicalities. As a consequence, the suspect ends up in an obscure recess of US and other West European detention centres. The last longish story in this collection, 'The Distance Between Us', is about a Sikh academic who teaches in Santa Barbara and is a frequent victim of racist abuse, largely because he is a non-White and also because many Americans mistake him for a Muslim due to his beard and turban.[52] Our selection of the above authors – a Muslim woman, a Hindu male politician and a Sikh woman – offers us a flavour of some of the recent writings on the Indus Valley people and their histories, structural dynamics and the grievous fallout from the ongoing transregional geopolitics.

Chapter Five

UNDERSTANDING CIVIC SENTIMENTS AND MOVEMENTS IN PAKISTAN: STALEMATED CYCLE, OR A WAY FORWARD?

'Regardless of who takes over, Pakistan continues to teeter on non-governability. Its own version of the Taliban with ties to the Afghan Taliban, are complicated by the strong mysterious influence of the ISI, the country's intelligence service. Any prognosis of the political economy future of the system is hazardous. Karachi, Pakistan's largest city, seems to be virtually in the hands of the local Taliban, and northern Waziristan, at the border with Afghanistan, is but one target under frequent attacks by militants.'

Gustav Ranis[1]

'Pakistan was the great mistake of his parents, the blunder that had deprived him of his home. It was easy for him to see Pakistan itself as a historical blunder too, a country insufficiently imagined, *conceived of the misguided notion that a religion can bind together peoples (Punjabi, Sindhi, Bengali, Baloch, Pathan) whom geography and history had long kept apart, born as a misshapen word, 'two Wings without a body, sundered by the land mass of its greatest foe, joined by nothing but God', whose East Wing had subsequently fallen off. What was the sound of one Wing flopping?'*

Salman Rushdie[2]

In a detailed report – not so uncommon in Western media – a British newspaper, while commenting on the enormity of the security and governance-related problems of Pakistan, highlighted a special report on its front page: 'CORRUPT, BANKRUPT, ELITIST, EMBATTLED, VIOLENT, EXPLOSIVE: Is Pakistan Falling Apart?' Patrick Cockburn had been touring a flood-hit country in 2010 and saw the large-scale devastation first-hand amidst daily reports in the Pakistani media speculating on midterm elections, a military coup and an ongoing polarity between the executive and judiciary. Not too unaware of Pakistan's multiple forms of predicament owing to human and natural factors, he further observed, 'Pakistan is undoubtedly in a bad way, but it is also a country with more than 170 million people, a population greater than that of Russia's and is capable of absorbing a lot of punishment'.[3] Past comments like, *why Pakistan?* have given way to *whereto Pakistan?* and *what kind of Pakistan?*: 'Careers have been made out of predicting the imminent break-up of Pakistan', noted an editorial in the *Guardian* on 15 July 2009 appreciating the general Pakistani resolve to resist militancy and extremism. The British daily, known for its liberal values, further observed,

> But even for the resolute, the events of March and May were hard to take. Militants appeared to strike any target with impunity, be it the visiting Sri Lankan team or the offices of the

Inter-Services Intelligence agency in Lahore. Many, too, doubted whether the army would have the political will – let alone the military resolve – to take on [Pakistani] Taliban in Buner and Swat. But it did, triggering the exodus of nearly 2 million refugees in the process. Now that the first refugees are starting to return after two months of sporadic fighting, it is time to assess the outcome.[4]

Pakistan survived the worst floods in history; multiple forms of violence, especially following the killing of Osama bin Laden in 2011; and a subsequent escalation of violence by the Pakistani Taliban on all kinds of security and soft targets. As seen in the last chapter, the country just in the early half of 2013 experienced 1,300 incidents of violence – often well orchestrated and costing innocent human lives – while more than 1,000 Shias had been killed by the Sunni militants during 2011–13, with more deaths to follow in 2015. Located in a difficult geopolitical zone with often hostile neighbours and internal ethno-sectarian schisms which frequently erupt into targeted killings, the Indus country found itself in the throes of hope and despair. Its chattering classes, deeply disturbed over the state of affairs in the country, pondered over various strategies seeking peace, consensus and development. While politicians and judiciary tried to create an overdue institutional balance, media, activists, artists, Internet forums, writers, bloggers, lawyers, journalists and human rightists intensified their respective campaigns. Irrespective of variant views in the Western media, argumentative Pakistanis and other grass roots have often been cognizant of the fact that their country is confronted by severe domestic and regional threats, and requires a better understanding and assistance from the rest, and, most of all, a more vigilant and responsible commitment to certain collective ideals. Like civil societies elsewhere, these societal voices are aware of their limitations and the herculean nature of their job in which consensus on questions such as 'what type of Pakistan?', 'whose Islam?' and 'what kind of future and its pathways?' may occasionally appear like a charade. Most of all, violence perpetrated by both the societal sections and security agencies against human rights activists and probing journalists has certainly remained undeterred. For instance, from 2009 to 2013, 69 journalists lost their lives while performing their duties. Karachi, KP and Balochistan proved to be the most trying places for investigative work, with human rightists and journalists often caught between various threats.[5]

Worries about Pakistan, its comparatively weaker democratic set-up, bruised institutions and the direct impact of a prolonged military campaign led by 30-plus nations in the neighbourhood amidst daily Predator drone attacks on tribal Pashtuns, besides the recurrent jihadi and ethno-sectarian attacks, certainly did not present a positive picture of the Indus Valley nation. Other than a subdued optimism across the country and scepticism about its viability amidst the proverbial million mutinies, the debate about its rationale and its governance largely moved on to its people and their ethos. Often characterized as a security state or garrison state,[6] or described by Salman Rushdie as the 'unmentionable country across the border',[7] and with opprobrium falling on the civil and military bureaucracy, the intermittent spates of violence have spawned serious questions about the forces of ideology – not just mullahs and madrasas – state and society. Surely, one cannot stay indifferent to the high politics of military and elite pressure groups, but the evolution of militant groups eager to use arms and violence against both the security forces and ordinary citizens took everybody by surprise. Given these groups' religion-based exclusivity, many observers may only view them as reactionary elements that are intent on a senseless annihilation, while others may find faults with their discretionary espousals of Islam. The blame game focuses on madrasas, brainwashing by peers and politicization by some manipulative elements such as the TTP, Lashkar-e-Jhangvi (LeJ), Anjuman-i-Sipah-i-Sahaba, Pakistan (ASSP), TNSM, LeT, Jamaat-e-Daawa (JeD), and other constellations in the FATA, southern Punjab and Karachi. In this perspective it might not be possible to locate or even acknowledge their class dimensions, in which landlessness augmented by a 'land mafia' and economic stratification owing to a traditional monopoly by khans and feudals, along with an entire ideology of resistance both against the Western and surrogate forces underpin this phenomenon. At another level, it may not be just the landless peasants and have-nots practising religious, political and ethnic violence but also they could be a strong constellation of an emerging middle class in which demographics might have gone wrong, or a Jihadi sentiment had been internalized. Thus, while it is crucial to liberate the analysis of Pakistani politics from a single-factor preoccupation with the state and elite monopolization, there is also a need to seek out the class dimensions of these militants-activists. And in between lies a loose, largely unrecognized and often informal sector of civil society that features all the diversities of Pakistan's demography. Undeniably, Pakistani cyclic problems of governance have been seen rooted in a predatory nature of its generals – the most powerful state within the state – all the way from Ayub Khan to Pervez Musharraf – and may also stem from a muddled relationship between religion and politics. The subtleties of an ethnic pluralism often vulnerable to hostility instead of reciprocity have equally aggravated the pangs of 200 million inhabitants of the Indus Valley. This land of unique, active and varying ecology and enriching history has been the recipient of undiminished migrations and invasions from across its western borders all the way since antiquity, and in the process has been both the beneficiary and the victim of unending and equally tumultuous developments. It has certainly been the vanguard of South Asian defences and even redefinition, in which forces of history, demography, cultures, religions and geopolitics have underpinned an unending plethora of vulnerabilities as well as vitalities. In addition, it has been a home to millions of refugees from the east and elsewhere, especially during the dissolution of the Raj, only multiplying newer dynamics and challenges.

This land of immigrants, refugees, Sufis, *bhagats* and adventurers which has often banked on the humaneness of its inhabitants has never been far away from the global spotlight, and especially following the cataclysmic developments such as September 11 and the Western invasion of Afghanistan. The single-factor military trajectory against predominantly Pashtun Afghans often hastily defined or grouped as Taliban, pushed Pakistan, once again, to emerge as a front-line state in an ambivalent and ever-expansive campaign, which succeeded only in alienating a clear majority of the world's Muslim public opinion.[8] It is not merely in the FATA such as Khyber, Waziristan, Bajaur, Kurram, Orakzai and Mohmand, where clerics – often mobilized by their own views of political Islam and ethnicity – took up arms against fellow Pakistanis, even in the otherwise cosmopolitan and immensely hospitable valleys like Swat or cities such as Karachi and

Quetta turned into cauldrons of militancy. Amidst daily bomb blasts, frequent drone attacks, intermittent suicide bombings and eventually a volatile civil war, Pakistanis earnestly debated their old and new history while dilating on an Islamic ethos of peace and war. Gradually, by a clear majority, they filed behind the armed forces and civil society to defy the abrasive encroachment by some of their fellow citizens, who were intent upon transforming the country in their own specific way – often denoted as 'Talibanization' by the chattering classes. It was clear to most Pakistanis that forces like the TTP and their numerous discretionary affiliates basically wanted to capture political power to recast the polity in their own ways and would use undefined terms as sharia and jihad to establish their views and practices over the rest of the public. While some Pakistanis might agree with the TTP or the sectarianism of the LeJ and ASSP, most felt uneasy with their violent means and obscurantist ideas. Like the West's own escapades with the Muslim world, in Pakistan, a whole raft of issues varying from creed, culture, class and geopolitics have assumed salience, whereas individuals such as Zia-ul-Haq, Musharraf, Nawaz Sharif, Benazir Bhutto, Asif Zardari, Imran Khan, Akbar Bugti, Asfandyar Wali Khan, Altaf Hussain, Baitullah Mehsud, Hakimullah Mehsud, Waliur Rehman, Hafiz Saeed, Ilyas Kashmiri, Maulvi Fazlullah and several others are apt to fade away in the long-lost memory of a turbulent and ever-changing history and larger systemic issues, along with serious economic and related challenges which have been the centre of public attention. Pakistan's battleground features conflictive ideas, charged-up individuals and groups and a system that takes longer to deliver, while ordinary people expect prompt solutions to their economic problems within an enduring peace. Ordinary people are stakeholders in their country and its future, yet are bedevilled by numerous problems, including volatile hair-splitting over the nature and shape of that future. This remains the crux of issues both for the state and civil society in the country, and this tug of war in Pakistan may resemble several other postcolonial polities.

As suggested above, one occasionally comes across predictions of the sixth most populous country falling apart due to internal combustive forces and external pressures, interventions and daredevil military operations against its people on its own soil. Following its bifurcation in 1971 due to domestic mismanagement and external intervention, and then a continued legacy of misgovernance, especially under military dictators, factionalist politicians have often underpinned such doomsday scenarios. The dissolution of the Soviet Union and especially of Yugoslavia in 1990–1 provided substantive parallels for such a possibility at a time when the country's three familiar Ks had stalemated in chaos and schisms. The heightened regional tensions with India over Kashmir and, as reflected in an undiminished arms race, inclusive of nuclearization manifestly neutralized the peace initiative of the Lahore Summit. The fracas over Kargil, followed by a coup led by General Musharraf did not allow any harmony between these two neighbours, and following September 11, Pakistan came to be increasingly seen as what Prime Minister Manmohan Singh called 'the epicentre of world terrorism'.[9] It suited both Musharraf and Delhi to pursue a policy that exceptionalized Pakistan as a society direly threatened by the terrorists who had to be reined in through brutal force. The voices for better bilateral relations on both sides, often known as the Track II and Track III channels, proved ineffective as Pakistan by virtue of its Muslim credentials became the focal point for all kinds of geopolitical and even explicitly Islamophobic campaigns. Terrorist attacks on the Indian parliament, the massacres in Gujarat, the waylaying of the Samjhota Train and then the Mumbai attacks not only added distance and depth to the yawning gap in Indo-Pakistani relations but also equally neutralized their respective civil societies from operating in a more persuasive way.[10]

This section touches upon several areas connected with the definition, scope and the working of a diverse and often misunderstood civil society in Pakistan and its complex but crucial interface with the state apparatus and institutions, along with a similar interaction with their societal counterparts. Due to space constraints the effort here avoids going into greater detail, as each of the following questions merits a separate study in itself:

- Is civil society a new or even an alien subject in studying postcolonial societies such as Pakistan?
- Other than historical narratives, most studies on Pakistan so far have often chosen to focus on state formation, its operations and its elite constituents, with sparse references to class formation and to the changing views on ideology, religion, ethnic configuration, gender and vocalization on these issues. Why, in our recent though still infrequent analysis, have we begun to allocate some space to the dynamics, challenges and future dimensions of civil society?
- Is the concept of civil society as anathematic to the religious and other ideological groups, including ethnic rhetoricians as it is to the state itself, such as the army, bureaucracy or the co-opted land-based elite?
- Is there a conflict between Islam and civil society per se? In other words, can they both be harmonized or even synthesized?!
- Can any civil society be class specific? In other words, is it a strictly middle-class phenomenon in which urbanization, education, economic trajectories and an overall profession-based and not a kin-based associational alterative can lead to better governance?
- Do Muslim societies, in general, have an assertive middle class, and can this middle class be redemptive while keeping in mind the political preferences of Neo-conservatives and the ultra-rightists in the West and their Muslim counterparts such as the Salafis and Wahhabis? Not confining it to only mainstream Sunni groups, can one include similar strands from amongst the Shias and Ahmadis, largely excepting the smaller constellations such as the Ismailis or Memons, in which endogamous priorities might underpin its own kind of exclusivity?
- Who forms and constitutes the civil society in Pakistan? Can we define an 'argumentative' Pakistani?
- How far the parameters of civil society groups such as the Black Coats, judges, journalists, human rightists and political parties generate consternation not just within the official hierarchies but also their unrestrained enthusiasm may equally worry concerned citizens. Events in Lahore, with lawyers attacking judges and having fracas with the police in 2011 were seen as both an aberration as well as a trespassing of some accepted frontiers of this proactivity. In other words, civil society is to limit the statist writ in those areas in which human rights and egalitarianism may be jeopardized, but can the former itself turn into a whip?

- How do we fit the role of education, of the eradication of poverty and of gender rights into an empowered civil society, or vice versa, so as to create an alternative discourse for coexistence, peace and a forward-looking outlook to steer the country away from a logjam? (Here the ideal role of state and civil society could be to work in tandem with each other to create a better educational curriculum, an emphasis on sports, a celebration of pluralism in and around the country and greater respect for the weaker elements in the society.)
- How does Pakistan's own location, its rather imbalanced and status-quoist politicking – often monopolized by given pressure groups – impinge on the composition and workings of its civil society? (Here the role of intelligence agencies, surrogacy by the political elite to military and mullahs or even to external [Western or Middle Eastern] dictates can be analysed at greater length.)
- Quite significantly, the civil society is not merely a reactive phenomenon, which may be somehow rooted within the domestic quagmire of ideas and realities, but it is certainly linked with a complex array of regional and global geopolitical and ideological factors. Is it possible to study Pakistani civil society away from the issues and legacies of Partition, or its relationship with India and Afghanistan (and even Iran!) and certainly the North Atlantic geopolitical involvement in South Asia?[11]
- Can the Pakistani demand for a corruption-free system, efficient on delivery and slow on extraction, provide a united platform for bringing about systemic changes as well as bonding diverse forces of society – both from the right and the centre?
- Is there a nationwide consensus on Pakistan as a single political unit or are there various alternative views? How should civil society react to them?
- How can the rights-based movement coalesce men, women, sects, minorities and diverse ethnicities and plural views together under the umbrella of civil society? Who would articulate this vision and who can lead such a campaign to usher in this needed unity in views?
- Is civil society in Pakistan a hostage to the state and religion as such, and can women, private groups and an independent media, aided by the judiciary and minimal foreign pressure on 'do more to kill more', help the former?

Pakistan's civic groups desire a sustained peace and security against violence which is owed to six main trajectories involving the United States, the TTP, ethnic militant militias, Baloch separatists, Sunni majoritarians and the Pakistani security forces. Since 2006, the total human losses have been stupendous and, according to a study by the Campaign for Innocent Violence in Conflict (CIVIC), just in 2009 they outdid every other region on earth: 'In 2009, an estimated 2,300 civilians were killed in terror attacks alone with many more injured. Counting losses from Pakistani military operations and U. S. drone strikes, civilian casualties in Pakistan likely exceed in number those in neighbouring Afghanistan'.[12] Interestingly, the CIVIC acknowledged Pakistan as the only actor in a juxtaposed warfare in West Asia that tried to reach the affected war victims, as it noted: 'Of the warring parties involved in the conflict, the Pakistani government is the only one with efforts to directly help civil war victims. All compensation and assistance mechanisms should be applauded, but significant gaps remain that allow most civilians suffering losses to go without any help'.[13] It is, however, interesting to note that following the arrest of Raymond Davis in Lahore on murder charges in late January 2011, the drone attacks stopped all of a sudden for four weeks, besides there being a sudden downturn in the suicide bombings, which unleashed opinions across the country that some American elements had been involved in campaigns to destabilize their country.[14] And when President Barack Obama made a statement for Davis's release on the basis of diplomatic immunity, Pakistani suspicions were further solidified. Following the personal interest shown by Obama and Secretary of State Hillary Clinton, Senator John Kerry undertook a prompt visit to Pakistan, which led to the view that Davis must have been quite an important figure with access to some sensitive information that could further affect bilateral relations, which had already nosedived.[15] A commentator on a Pakistani website, echoing the pervasive critique of Western policies and their fallout for the country noted:

> A strange alliance is that the US and NATO has [sic.] granted to Pakistan and its people whereas these two are the only entities violating Pakistan's sovereignty for near a decade. Not even Pakistan['s] rival India has done what these friends have done. Drone attacks, clandestine operations, troop incursions, sabotage and then the operatives like Raymond Davis is what Pakistan and Pakistanis have got […] Not many people know that more than 32,000 people have either been killed or sustained injuries because of the America's war on terror since 2001. Other than loss of around 32,000 Pakistani lives, country's economy, as per an IMF report in 2010, had suffered a loss of over $80 billion and more importantly, the confidence of the Pakistani nation is shaken on its state. What for?[16]

As discussed in the previous chapter, the Pakistani death toll from multiple forms of violence had already doubled the mentioned figures, in addition to the total loss to the country's economy running into well above $100 billion. Thirteen hundred incidents of violence, recorded in just the first six months of 2013, underlined the variety of fronts and strategies used by diverse militant outfits targeting civil and military officials, rival ethnic groups, Shias and international mountaineers.[17] While the Pakistani army began a major operation in North Waziristan in June 2014, the militants retaliated by attacking the Army Public School in Peshawar on 16 December, killing 146 children and their teachers. Earlier, Jundullah had carried out a spectacular attack at the Indo-Pakistani border post of Wagah in October, which showed resilience as well as ever-changing strategies by the militants in selecting a wide variety of targets causing maximum human loss, along with receiving stupendous media coverage. The attacks on Shia mosques in Shikarpur and Peshawar in early 2015 and then the targeted killing of 46 Ismailis Shias on a bus in Karachi on 13 May only underlined the surreal nature of intra-Pakistani schisms. On 16 April, a group of well-placed Sunni militants in Karachi tried to kill Debra Lobo, who had been teaching in Lahore and Karachi for decades. She survived, but was repatriated to her native United States. A week later, on 24 April, the same group of militants was able to gun down Sabeen Mahmud, a noted civil society activist with a global profile. It appeared that the Pakistani state and civil society were faced with 'a million mutinies', and long after September 11 the malady had already become a long haul.

Civil Society and Islam

Scholarly and media debates about Pakistan's problems of security and governance have often neglected its societal configurations in which parallel forces of revivalism and reformism, nationalism and regionalism, and pacifist activism and alarmist militarism have spawned diverse currents. By monolithicizing Islam as a unifying or divisive force and by solely focusing on high politics, the crucial forces of gender, sect and class are made rather marginal in most scholarly works on this country, which otherwise has attracted a massive historiography. Works published during the first 50 years of Pakistan's history, in general, viewed politics as a *given* secular pursuit, and its Muslimness [in a monolithic sense] was exceptionalized as a baffling case of raison d'être; thus, national cohesion was presumably anchored on some arcane religious determinant.[18] From this perspective, a *Muslim* state was somehow considered oxymoronic and its governance an impractical proposition. In the early 1990s, very much like Fukuyamian ebullience, both Islam and modernity were seen as multilayered processes heading towards sameness owing to overriding market forces and liberal democracy. This short-lived optimism was soon overtaken by religion assuming a more vocal role and refusing to be a junior partner in places like India, Israel, Russia, the United States, the EU nations and certainly the Muslim world.[19] This ideological shift happened against the backdrop of a weaker Left, tarnished secularism (France, India and Turkey) and a bruised multiculturalism (the United Kingdom, France, the United States and the Netherlands) as religio-political forces sought a quick ascendance on the basis of majoritarianism.[20] September 11 and the George W. Bush presidency proved a high mark of Neo-conservatism, which had started its journey rather aggressively during the Reagan era amidst a major ideological shift in the North Atlantic regions. Several years later, with most of West Asia in tatters, we can witness this hegemonic Right itself turning into a battleground and being confronted by a serious economic crisis which seems to be shaking the ideological moorings of the capitalist ethos.[21] President Obama engendered an immense level of hope in repairing North Atlantic-Muslim relations, besides rolling back military involvement across the Muslim nations; instead, he visibly came to depend on the Pentagon and intelligence agencies, which had no qualms in carrying out 'signature assassinations' and prolonged campaigns targeting Muslim communities. Under the Obama administration – 'high on steroids' – the drone attacks became even more frequent and deadlier; Iraq and Yemen got mired in civil war; Syria, Libya and Egypt felt confused about American policies and the Israelis felt no urgency for rolling back their settlements on occupied lands. The Arab Spring proved chimerical for many Arabs, while Washington was found to be lacking a comprehensive policy on West Asia and appeared more like it was 'in a retreat'.[22] There was disappointment with the Obama administration, which was high on vocal pronouncements and low on delivery, despite the early goodwill, and which dismayed many of its former supporters in the United States itself, and often his remarks about a self-respecting American society over and above racial divides were met with scepticism.[23] Obama's expression of regret on 23 April 2015 over the inadvertent killing of two Western hostages in the FATA, while saying nothing about Muslim victims of drone strikes, only betrayed a partisan expediency.[24]

As a matter of fact, political Islam, seeking allies from amongst civil society and reformers and politicking through the ballot box instead of bullets, is a distinctly constructive and emerging development, and here countries like Turkey, Malaysia, Indonesia, Bangladesh, Tunisia, Senegal and Pakistan deserve fresher perspectives.[25] Political Islam, in all its manifestations, has often been simplistically maligned as a global threat and reduced to catechisms of extremism and terror. While there are forces among Muslims which – as seen in Egypt during 2013–15, or in ISIS – seek recourse to bullets for a variety of reasons, there are even more sectors across the board which see no conflict between Islam and democracy or universal empowerment, including the rights of women and minorities. This latter view was previously known as Islamic Modernism during the colonial era, and it can still re-energize postcolonial Muslim states towards *Muslim democracy* – akin to the Christian democracy of Western Europe. Parties such as the All-India Muslim League, Egypt's Wafd, Nahdlatul Ulama in Indonesia, Turkey's Adalet ve Kalkınma Partisi (Justice and Development Party), the Tunisian Al-Nahada and even religio-political parties like Jamiat-i-Ulama-i-Hind, the JI, the Muslim Brotherhood, Hezbollah and Hamas all have practised electoral politics and can certainly play a crucial role in neutralizing their extremist counterparts by developing interdependence between modernity and tradition, as well as between religion and politics. Such an interface, hopefully, could strengthen various workable forms of Islamic democracy.

During the dissolution of the Soviet system, Ernest Gellner, no less impressed by the momentous changes yet nevertheless unlike Francis Fukuyama, acknowledged the existence of civil societies among Muslims, which could help them better adjust with the changing realities.[26] Gellner did not live to see the post–September 11 dramatic events inclusive of the invasion of West Asian regions and a rising and often unstoppable tide of Islamophobia, but ever since, an entire generation of experts on Islam and Muslim societies has evolved across the Mediterranean. Led by time-tested experts such as Bernard Lewis, Neo-conservative think tanks and writers as varied as Oriana Fallaci, Daniel Pipes, Gisele Littman (Bat Ye'Or), Raphael Israeli, Robert Spencer, Pamela Geller, Anne Coulter and V. S. Naipaul, these numerous experts have found Islam simply oppressive and Muslims only accustomed to authoritarianism and misogyny. Other than this sustained academic and media-based perspective on Islam, the Muslim Diaspora is also posited as a fifth column working in cahoots with European liberals to change the religious and political cartography of the West.[27] As predicted, this discourse sees sociopolitical problems confronted by Muslims essentially as an *Islamic* priori, and unless Islam underwent some holistic transformation like the sixteenth century Reformation, Muslims would continue hopelessly bleeding themselves and others, besides coercing their women and deputing their youths to commit mass murders.[28] The decimation of Palestinian resistance by stigmatizing Hamas and by the frequent Israeli invasions of Gaza and southern Lebanon amidst a constant denigration of the Iranian position on regional security, often in league with conservative Sunni monarchs, proved to be a crucial ingredient of this tradition. Consequently, at one level, it may appear like 'a clash of fundamentalisms', as opined by Tariq Ali, while concurrently it is the disempowerment of Muslim voices given the security-centred regimes in the Muslim world and the private and public nature of animus elsewhere.[29] Mahmood Mamdani's work is an interesting comment on this situation, in which this rather complex development has been shown exclusively as an *Islamic* trajectory, though Khaled Abou El Fadl and several other noted scholars do not absolve Muslims of their problematic both with Islam and Modernity.[30] While several Muslim scholars may highlight the humanness of Islamic heritage even during times of duress,[31] some others may find sociological and theological issues rather too complex but no less exciting.[32] Scholars such as Tariq Ramadan[33] find no inherent conflict between being a Muslim and a Westerner, while Shabbir Akhtar may even detect a competent level of self-sufficiency, enabling Islam not only to go through its contemporary predicament more smoothly but also emerging even stronger from all kinds of assaults and challenges.[34]

Amidst this polarized debate on Islam's ability, or incapacity, to coexist with the societal demands of universal empowerment, substantive democratization, the prioritization of mundane progress and civic imperatives, the discussion on civil society in cases such as Pakistan has assumed greater significance. The view of Islam being inherently an (Arab) imperial religion à la the Naipaul strand stands refuted by three or four significant developments in the Muslim regions. Firstly, the overthrow of the long-time military dictators in Indonesia, Tunisia, Libya, Pakistan and Egypt, despite their authoritarian apparatchik and external crucial support in the name of security, has shown that Muslims per se are not endlessly resigned to dictatorships of ideologies and personalities and can muster their forces for change by overcoming all kinds of differences. The way the multidisciplinary constellations have harnessed communication highways and have persisted with zestful resistance is certainly the strongest retort to the view that Islam not only lacks civil societies but also, in effect, suppresses them. In a powerful way, the revolutionary movements across the Middle East are emancipating Arabs from a debilitating self-deprecation brought on since 1967 when external forces began to dictate more vehemently often in collaboration with the region's obliging regimes.[35] While acknowledging the impact of these changes on the Arab world, Prince El Hassan bin Talal noted in a comment, 'A new generation has come of age. Creativity, new communication technologies and the use of rational peaceful protest have restored Arab self-esteem'.[36] Even since Egypt's countercoup on 3 July 2013, hopes for a democratic redemption have not been dampened, though the polarization of the society has been quite volatile. Secondly, one can foresee similar civil society–led movements in other Muslim countries, though the road to democracy and empowerment is paved with nails and this is not an easily attainable goal. Thirdly, this is not the first or the last time that Muslim societies have been confronted with harrowing roadblocks. Serious challenges in the past, including the Crusades, Mongol invasions, the Inquisition and expulsions from Spain, colonization and the post–World War I dismay pervasive across the Middle East did not consign Islam to the dust bin of history.[37] Instead, Muslims have been able to turn to a new chapter in their career through some element of survivability and adaptability, which might have allowed some observers to see an inborn recourse to 'modernism'.[38]

Political Islam and civil society are evolving paradigms in any given Muslim community and share a complex interface, but the momentous developments in the Middle East,

Southeast Asia and North Africa, besides the civil society movement in Pakistan from 2007 to 2012, show the evolution of their positive interdependence. If allowed to gradually attain an agreeable ideological consensus in these case studies, it might become difficult for serious analysts to posit Islam as inherently and perpetually hostile to civil society. Respect for human rights, participation in democratic processes, defining corruption as a moral (as well as political) issue and demands for independent judiciary and critical media are some of the attributes of this form of political Islam, which does not require to be pigeonholed as 'moderate'. It is reformist, generally peaceful, certainly populist and inherently anti-hegemonic. In some cases, it has assumed the form of Muslim feminism, and has even begun a serious dialogue with secularism. The examples of Muslim opinion groups in India and a serious receptivity to Turkish, Senegalese, Moroccan and Indonesian models allow many Muslims to become stakeholders and even effective defenders of secular institutions without embodying the extremes of apologia or aggression.[39] However, it is true that not enough comparative research has been undertaken on Muslim polities and civil societies since the academic focus both in historical and political studies has been state-centric, or just confined to anthropological studies of smaller units.[40] This scholarly duality of preoccupation with high politics, as contrasted with segmentary and micro-entities has ignored the vast sociocultural terrain in between, and could explain the paucity of material acknowledging the existence of civil societies in these echelons. This does not mean that the civil society is strictly a middle-class artefact, as it is not fair to see it only as a modernist – pseudo-Western – constellation. For instance, the lawyers' movement in Pakistan in 2007–8, anti-Taliban demonstrations in Pakistan following the attacks on Daata Durbar in Lahore in 2010, protests outside Islamabad's Red Mosque in 2014–15, the congregations of civic forces in Tahrir Square in Cairo in 2011–12 and earlier anti-Ben Ali campaign by Tunisians involved diverse classes and demographics of these respective places.

Conceptualizing Civil Society in Pakistan: Variables and Contours

The existence of a vocal and argumentative Pakistani civil society, despite numerous fissures and roadblocks, cannot be denied. The movement for the country itself despite several political and religious disincentives, the persistent demands for democratization, resistance against martial law and now against militancy, coercion and corruption surely substantiate its presence. In more recent times, the two-year-long movement for the independence of the judiciary amidst a cross-regional consensus and fuller participation in electoral politics have been its shining hours. In addition, undiminished debates on political corruption, increasing disgust with militancy – often shared by the chattering classes –, the quest for peace with India, non-interference in Afghanistan and a tangible relationship with the West are other substantive sectors of this civic tradition. It often seeks recourse to visual and literary expressions, anchoring idealism for a tolerant and transparent order. More pronounced in English publications but also vocally shared in specific Urdu literature, debates, music, plays and seminars, these civic sentiments have found their expression, which cannot be denied simply because it may not have high-profile role models, or has lacked a 'deliverer on a white horse', though younger people and women in 2013–14 had often visualized Imran Khan in that role. Pakistan is quite a unique polity amidst postcolonial Muslim states where a rich and well-established tradition of multiple political parties and opinion groups has persisted despite various totalitarian onslaughts and selective violence. Demands for a transparent system, equal rights for all citizens, without of course offloading religious dictums and meaningful decentralization have been significant areas of this quest, which itself features moments of hope and phases of despair. The contours and components of Pakistani civil society need to be studied in reference to class, demography, ideology, ethnicity, media, gender, relations with India and the West, some of which we may take up individually.

1. Class Dimension of Pakistani Civil Society

With regards to a traditional analysis of Pakistan, other than a binary view of Islam as a homogenizing asset or a divisive liability for the country, and the state-versus-society paradigm, class-based studies routinely touch on feudatory sections arrayed at the expense of landless peasants. Here, in a classical Marxist paradigm, Pakistan is presupposed to retain a petty bourgeoisie, though it is criss-crossed by sectarian and ethnic divisions, and manifests both progressive and retrogressive strands. Even the anti-colonial clerics could qualify as a radical proletariat – not by intent but by content – who might be intellectually 'archaic', yet are politically progressive and could still be harnessed for a larger transformation. Improvement on the classical Marxian view of the Pakistani bourgeoisie called the *salariat* again fell short of defining or even taking into account the emerging vast array of civil society in which growing sections of humanists; professionals such as lawyers, artists, authors and media critics; and women's associations had begun to sound vocal alarms on local and national problematiques of human rights.[41] In most cases, these clusters have been the beneficiaries and even the instruments of Westernized modernization, which is supposed to precede the spectre of a classless revolution. While traditional groups such as Sufis and other charitable institutions operate all across the country and reveal a persistent aspect of civic initiatives, Pakistani civil society is still an evolving middle class, mostly an urban dispensation. Other than mosque- and shrine-based charity networks or individual waqf activities as seen during national disasters, the vocal cadres of civil society consist of successful NGOs like the Edhi Foundation. Other clusters sponsoring educational, judicial, gender and political activism such as the Women's Action Forum (WAF), Aurat Foundation, Pakistan Institute of Peace Studies (PIPS), Pakistan Institute of Local and Political Development (PILDAT), Sustainable Development Policy Institute (SDPI) and several others are mainly urban. Some of them often earn opprobrium from religious and other critical elements, but the role of the Citizens Foundation, the Agha Khan Support Programme, the Sahara Foundation, Shaukat Khanam Cancer Hospital and such other *modernist* ventures, including the HRCP, bar associations, press clubs and numerous Internet groups are effective in their own ways.[42]

2. Ideological Mishmash

Other than the existence or even possible fluctuations of this middle class for all the above reasons, suppositions about its ideological orientation and the antennae of tolerance are equally worth debating.⁴³ It would be ahistorical to pigeonhole and straightjacket this civil society as either totally secular or holistically orthodox since in many areas it is conservative per se, and then in several domains it appears quite progressive. Pakistani civil society has its own traditional and modernist components and they come from various walks of life, and it would be erroneous to reduce the country's complex socio-ideological populace into only two groups of fundamentalists/orthodox and modernists/secularists. There are several grey areas in between besides the overlaps, where one notices a voluntary and not always forced appropriation of Islam, Pakistaniat, democracy, rights-based empowerment and economic progress. Surely, there are disputations on issues such as 'what, or, which' type of Islam, Pakistan and modernity to form, rather a tangible and viable consensus, though this form of debate and interface have often been acrimonious for more than a century. According to Yonginder Sikand, a typical Pakistani was not a bigot, as he noted in his an earlier work: 'the average Pakistani Muslim certainly is not a bearded, Kalashnikov-wielding, vehemently anti-Hindu or anti-Indian monster [...] For the average Pakistani Muslim, Islam is an integral part of his or her cultural identity, but it is not something that dominates every act or thought'. To him, 'discourse [is] dominated by economic, personal, caste, *biradari* (brotherhood) and regional issues'.⁴⁴ To Sikand's other compatriots such as Subhas Kapila, unlike India's liberal political institutions, Pakistan has regressed into a military-plus-mullah gridlock. Thus, Pakistan may not even have a civil society, and consequently remains decades and miles behind India.⁴⁵ It is certainly true that even ethnic militants, Taliban networks and organizations such as LeT have their own charity programmes geared for a greater public outreach. Other than these groups, the main political parties, especially the religio-political parties, seek dividends through charity work, often during natural calamities.

3. South Asian Legacy: Ambivalence or Rejection?

Following 1857, South Asian Islam's own dynamism and plurality were confronted with serious concerns about a possible 'Andalusia syndrome', and that is where parallel views and movements began to evolve. Questions about Islam being a confident part of Indian civilization or India being a significant part of Muslim civilization received varying responses in a changing political atmosphere. Here, the imperial, demographic, local and interest-based factors played a major role in diversifying opinion among South Asian Muslims. Partition, as seen earlier, happened for all the historical reasons and forces, and one may continue discussing its imprints for India and Muslims forever, yet one has to accept the fact that the founding generation on both sides of the new borders was not willing or even prepared to make it into a holistic 'cut-off' for South Asia. In the same vein, one cannot reduce the formation of the fifth-largest state in the world to a single-factor explanation such as the fear complex, the egocentricity of a few individuals or the high politics of three major political forces in the subcontinent. However, the post-1947 sundering of relationships, warfare, the partition of Pakistan, the arms race and the respective historical narratives often based on selectivity and othering have made partition into an on-going and even totalistic process. As a result, civil societies in all the three countries have been compelled or even impelled to serenade to respective nationalist narratives, and more often have not been able to establish cross-border contacts. Here the role of all the three states has been similar in being abrasively discretionary. A select few individuals moving across the borders idealize people-to-people contacts, but they too have their narratives of frustration owing to official nonchalance. The lack of regionalization has left the Pakistani, Indian, Afghani and Bangladeshi civil societies on their own and the situation in India is slightly different given the larger areas and more diverse population groups involved, though it also remains territory bound and cannot defy the official writ beyond a certain point.

The bitter relations with India and the separation of East Pakistan with the decisive help from Delhi, certainly caused the salience of a visible West Asian orientation in Pakistan. The denial of Indianness became a more accepted norm, at least in textbooks, and India was reduced to a non-Muslim *other* that was eager to put Pakistan into an ever-squeezing nutcracker. The nuclear tests of 1974 and 1998, India's march on Siachen Glacier, the construction of dams in the Valley amidst an undiminished defiance in Indian-held Kashmir, the Kargil escalations and the attacks in Mumbai often marginalized people-to-people contacts on both sides. In such a dangerous void, only the mistrust and hostilities flourished, besides spawning an ambivalent if not outright hostile attitude towards India or Pakistan's Indian past. In the same vein, India equally distanced itself from its north-western historic roots even to the extent of Hinduizing the Indian history and ethos all the way back to the Aryan period without giving any space to the Dravidian or West Asian antecedents that had only further pluralized India following their indigenization. Thus, the deconstruction of a regional cold war becomes a major prerequisite for all the respective civil societies, and especially on both sides of the Wagah-Attari borders where a single-factor preoccupation based on sheer rejection should give way to a more tolerant reciprocity.

Opinion polls across two countries, often conducted by civic groups, including the media, reveal several positive signs, and they owe it to the untiring work by pacifists on both sides. Opinion surveys conducted among 42 Pakistani villages and six major cities in India revealed interesting strands. For instance, it was

> found that terror has receded greatly in the minds of Indians as the first thing they associate Pakistan with, dropping from top-of-mind for 75% of those polled in December 2009, to 42% in December 2010. Last year, 82% in Mumbai and 74% in Delhi associated Pakistan with terrorism, but these figures are down to 49 and 46% respectively. The association of India with Kashmir has reduced in Pakistan, but it is still top of mind at 53%. 14% instantly associate "India" with a hope for better relations while 14% fear attack from India. Awareness of the Kashmir issue has quadrupled to 42% in India, with 17% showing awareness only after launch of Aman Ki Asha as against an awareness of only 4% before it was launched' [...] As many as 73 per cent of the respondents in Pakistan and 68 per cent in India affirmed that 'Pakistan–India relations feature in my thought'.[46]

With the ascension of Sharif's regime, peace and trade with India seemed to head new priorities, but following the Indian elections of 2014, any radical breakthrough in the stalemate did not happen. India did not seem to undertake any substantive measures to break the logjam, and there was a worry that this enthusiasm from Islamabad might once again fizzle out due to lack of any substantial reciprocity.[47] In addition, it was felt that the Congress government did not like looking less tough vis-à-vis Pakistan, given the BJP's juggernaut, now headed by Narendra Modi, who was not known for any soft corner for Muslims in general and Pakistan in particular. By the time civil governments led by the PPP and ML took over responsibility, militancy in the country had already mushroomed into several parallel trajectories. Both the state and civil society, for the next decade, became the main targets of the militants, with the general populace lodged in a morass. In December 2015, following Modi's flying stop-over in Lahore and reiteration of both Delhi and Islamabad to continue with parleys re-energized hopes for a breakthrough in Indo-Pakistani logjam.

4. Indus Valley Legacies in the Borderland

True to its challenging location as the bridgehead among the central, southern and western regions of Asia, and also because of its alive and vigorous and even conflictive pluralism – unlike other regions of the subcontinent – Pakistan's history and politics have tended to be tumultuous. The country may resemble a fidgety youth whose adolescence somehow remains undiminished and instead exudes an unstoppable vibrancy mingled with truancy. Like India, Pakistan thrives on a rich folk culture with an eager middle class waiting in the wings, while simultaneously it is imbued with an unending energy and exuberance traditionally characterizing Central Asian communities. It may be fighting 'a million mutinies' largely spawned by a vast array of activists often propped up by religious radicalism, sectarian chauvinism, ethnic nihilism or political activism, yet it still has a unique blend of its own persona that any keen observer may not fail to notice.

Pakistan's misplaced emphasis on the external and regional dimensions of its security, irreverence towards governance by the power elite, especially the generals and their Western backers, and the annihilative invasion of Afghanistan in 2001 followed by the FATA turning into an explosive battleground have collectively ignited the powder keg that waited in the form of an overwhelmingly youthful demography. Accounting for 65 per cent of Pakistan's population, many from these youthful clusters refused being pushed over by the Bush-Musharraf-Karzai combine that singularly and very insidiously pursued coercive policies. The Western military invasion of Iraq and the intensity of the campaign in Afghanistan featuring massive bombardments, large-scale and ironically unaccounted for Afghan deaths not even recorded as statistics and then the expansion of this militarist intervention into the Pakistani Pashtun regions pushed the country to a precipice. There is no doubt that other than Baituallh Mehsud from South Waziristan or Mullah Salam Zaeef from Kandahar, there are thousands of Pashtun affectees of detentions, renditions and aerial killings – all subsumed under the pernicious paradigm of the 'war on terror'. By killing indiscriminately and focusing only on a military-based strategy on both sides of the Durand Line, the United States and its allies have transformed millions of Pashtuns and their sympathizers into sworn enemies. Amidst a pervasive anti-Americanism rooted in partisan American foreign policy in the Muslim regions, taking revenge against the West and its allies became the core ideology of these Southwest Asian groups, leading to the unrestrained bloodshed in Kabul, Peshawar, Mumbai, Karachi,

Quetta, Islamabad and Lahore. Irreverent to the consequences of such heinous violence directed against civilians and by consciously targeting the police and security forces, these radical elements sought their revenge in the tribal tradition of *badla*. Following an attack on the police academy in Lahore and similar other such attacks on ISI headquarters in Lahore, Rawalpindi, Peshawar and Kohat, Baitullah Mehsud before his death in a drone attack in August 2009 had voiced his determination to continue with this retaliation against aerial attacks which multiplied under the Obama administration. Mehsud's successor, Hakimullah Mehsud, extended such retaliatory ventures to other places such as Diamer, Sukkur and Multan. To the forces intent upon resisting and defying Washington and its allies, the political downturn of leaders such as Jose Aznar, Michael Howard, Tony Blair, Musharraf, George W. Bush. Zein al-Abedin bin Ali and Hosni Mubarak is crucially linked with their participation in the war on terror, widely perceived as a new crusade against Muslims. Musharraf, like Zia-ul-Haq, underrated the level of public resentment over his unqualified loyalty to Washington, and in the same vein the general berated the forces of civil society, which genuinely demanded a systemic overhaul to stem the growing threat of Talibanization.

5. Gender and Minority Rights in Pakistan

For Pakistani civil society, like many other places, the empowerment of women and ethno-religious minorities is a major challenge as well as a significant area of public discourse and the resultant historiography. Featuring in serious studies and public efforts, gender rights and equal citizenship are a noted area of contestation between the reformists and conservatives within the state and society. Here, discretionary views on sharia as reflected in policies implemented by Zia-ul-Haq, such as the Hudood legislation, separate electorates for minorities and additions to blasphemy laws, have unleashed two parallel strands dividing both the proponents and antagonists. While, research and statistical information on crimes against citizens such as honour killing or karo-kari, attacks on non-Muslim groups and high-profile events such as the murder of Governor Salman Taseer in 2011 in Islamabad and the attack on a Christian church in Peshawar in 2013 may portray Pakistan as a society of a coercive obscurantism, they equally underline the existence and increased importance of vital think tanks such as the HRCP. Where generals and parliamentarians might have shirked from assuming a more vocal public stance against segregative and discretionary policies, sections of vocal social critics have attempted to flag their dissent. The arrival of argumentative Pakistanis might be a recent development and not risk-free, but the emergence of vocal women has been a reality of the past three decades. The regimes led by Bhutto, Sharif, Musharraf and Zardari might have routinely backtracked on the issues of universal human rights and equal citizenship amidst basic freedoms, the generation of Mukhtaran Mai, Malala Yousafzai and Asma Jahangir offers parallel spectrums of the same sentiment. Partly inspired by such women activists and partly due to finding themselves locked between a stalemated judicial system and a male-centred jirga tradition (assembly of tribal elders), some housewives even decided to pioneer an all-women jirga to deal with serious issues of domestic violence and honour killings in which victims are predominantly women. This 25-member-strong jirga came into being in the summer of 2013 in Mingora, Swat, and despite various reservations about the archaic nature of the system, it speaks volumes about the increased awareness among women in moffusil areas. It may have its own problems in areas like implementing verdicts, yet its moral and symbolic significance cannot be underestimated. Tabbussum Adnan, the founder of this Pashtun women jirga in Swat, was aware of various threats and hurdles, but still felt that women's predicament could not be left to the police and legal processes. Nor could they be left to the sole discretion of a male-dominated jirga, in which decisions were made without women ever being heard in their defence.[48] Of course, dynastic and conservative politics with an opportunistic interface between pir and feudal, khan and mullah, military and mullah persist, yet greater economic demands, widening education, growing media access and the search for some synthesis between religion and politics, nationhood and ethnic identity and trust between the rulers and the ruled would further strengthen this arm of civil society.[49]

6. Political Parties and Civil Society

Pakistan is surely a unique and even endowed polity for having retained a zestful tradition of national, regional, ethnic and ideological parties, which reach various segments of this diverse and plural society. The struggle for Pakistan was led from a political platform, and despite intermittent authoritarian policies and totalitarian regimentation, even the survival of political parties itself is not a minor achievement. One may hold several reservations against the dynastic and even despotic wherewithal of the leadership of most of the political parties, yet the infusion of fresher blood, greater recourse to local issues, an alert media and an awakened judiciary allow more space for politicking, though patronage and patriarchy will remain the major features of this party politics. Pressures on the political parties are immense and so are the expectations, which are gradually turning into a greater accountability and respect for constitutional politics, reforms in the electoral system and a judiciary attempting to put itself into a more centre stage position. Criticism of politicians, their tardy, dynastic and even personalist politics will remain supreme, and it will slowly turn towards the other three powerful pressure groups: the military, mullahs and ethnic ideologues. This is an area that helps civil society immensely, and here input by the latter is more effective through lobbying, petitioning and even direct strikes.

7. Khaki Forces and Civil Groups

Traditionally, the generals have been abhorrent of civic voices, including those of politicians, and have often worked in cahoots with the civil bureaucracy, preferring centrist policies. Like elsewhere, the contempt for these voices based on denigration and fear has been symptomatic of thinking at the senior level, all the way from Ayub Khan to Musharraf. Their speeches, books and policies portray politicians as nefarious, irresponsible and corrupt, who have to be 'cleansed' and held accountable. But such rhetoric does not make much impact after long periods of military rule in the country, which in all cases ended either in the total humiliation of the perpetrators or the decapitation of their manufactured systems. Generals ride the proverbial tiger rather too quickly and easily, but find it hard to ride down, and in the process become dependent upon crafted, partisan and temporary pseudo-political systems, which fizzle out with their own decline. Thus, political systems based on constitutional primacy and supported as well as protected by an independent judiciary and a critical media remain the ideals in places like Pakistan, and that is where politicians have a golden opportunity to dig in their heels to help strengthen their institutions. The role of a 'secret hand' or 'deep state' alluding to intelligence agencies in their political manoeuvrings has not earned any positive dividends nor has their frequent failure in stemming militancy and violence, which allows politicians to retain initiatives in their hands. It appears that there is more space for a critique of the defence establishment, no romanticism for another war and instead a greater expectation from it in fighting militancy and disorder. This is not to suggest that the ISI, Military Intelligence (MI) or other such agencies have become totally apolitical and transparent, yet certain echelons have begun to claim their space by reaffirming their basic rights, and through a better usage of social media, ordinary Pakistanis adore their soldiers, especially when they have been dying in such large numbers while fighting militants of all types. However, civil society, like politicians, remains weary of generals, and it will take many more years and institutionalized efforts in strengthening civic institutions. This aspect of civic efforts aiming for good governance, respect for individual freedoms and trials only through a regular judicial system is being helped by courts which reprimand agencies on issues such as 'the disappeared Pakistanis', who in most cases are believed to have been the victims of this 'hidden hand'.

8. Arts, Literature, Media and Print Capital

It is interesting to note that post–September 11 decade, with all its traumatizing impact on the country, has also been a period of immense literary and artistic creativity in addition to the flowering of a vibrant and even daredevil media. Writers in English, Urdu and other languages have focused on socio-ideological issues in a Faizian way, in which love and romance are themselves interconnected with the collective agony and pain. Kamila Shamsie, Muhammad Hanif, Daniyal Latifi, Mohsin Hamid, Nadeem Aslam, Daniyal Mueenuddin and many more have produced some of the finest literature on a multiplicity of themes, whereas younger music groups such the Strings, Vital Signs, Laal and Junoon, along with individual singers Aatif Aslam, Rahat Fateh Ali Khan, Ali Zafar, Shahzad Rai, Ali Azmat, Raheem Shah, Zeek Afridi, Hadeeqa Kiyani, Abrarul Haq, Arieb Azhar, Jawad Ahmad, Salman Ahmad and others have variably tried to articulate themselves through their lyrics.[50] Here the appropriation of Pakistani locales, folk cultures, Sufi paradigms, historical themes and regional vocabularies has heralded an artistic renaissance, which to a great extent owes itself to volatile challenges that this youthful society is confronted with. In the same vein, a vocal media has played a vanguard role in the rolling back of Musharraf's Emergency and other unilateral curbs, helped the lawyers' movement transform itself into a nationwide struggle and, in the process, has discovered its own vitality. In some cases, it has begun to take on extremism and violence perpetrated in the name of religion and ethnicity, and is equally censorious of corruption, official strictures against the media or other organs of civil society. This visual media may have its own commercial and ideological incentives, but, in general, it is bold, raw and noisy, and provides needed a platform for all kinds of issues. Certainly, the websites and like-minded chat groups have made deeper inroads into the body politic of Pakistani society, along with offering multiple platforms for discussion and dialogue. Some of these groups involve diaspora Pakistanis and Indians from across the border, and certainly include a large number of women from various walks of life. However, its coverage of human travesties such as corruption, kidnaps, honour killings, hostage taking, gunrunning, kowtowing to external pressures and debates involving younger people, ulema, civil society activists, housewives and role models have been taking place with competitive intensity. More than 40 television channels may still devote more time to religious telecasts, but this kind of conservatism does not go unchallenged among the argumentative Pakistanis.[51] However, Pakistan being so diverse and its various ethnic, class and ideological groups jockeying for listening ears and gaining a greater profile disallow a straightjacket view of a society fixated in some eternal time warp.

The above résumé does not mean Pakistan in 2016, three years after holding an unprecedented and uninterrupted transfer of power through elections, was out of woods as violence in the FATA, Afghanistan and across the Indus Valley continued to pose a persistent security concern, and the blowback from Western policies in collaboration with Islamabad was hurting every Pakistani, especially with daily reports of civilian deaths. Pakistan's predicament was going to take some time and a raft of domestic, regional and global ameliorative efforts was awaited to steer it out of morass. Stories about a possible 'Arab Spring' fizzled out due to political gradualism operating fairly, in addition to women and younger Pakistanis having opted for mainstream politicking through platforms such as Imran Khan's PTI. Any revolutionary form of upheaval or change was not expected for several other reasons: firstly, Pakistan is too diverse and, after seeing the military in power for so long, and religious elements dishing out only disharmony, there is no stomach for a countrywide transformative movement. However, it stays 'perpetually on a knife edge – extremists plot and explode bombs, senior politicians are assassinated, society seethes with discontent. A slim upper crust floats in a bubble of wealth and privilege – the local version of Hello! offers coverage of upper-class parties – while the poor grind along under soaring food inflation and 12-hour power cuts'.[52] Secondly, an unnerving geopolitics and violence, along with acute economic issues and a serious energy crisis have also reshaped public opinion against any extra-constitutional politics. Thirdly, regional states and an increasing proportion of Pakistani stakeholders are not enamoured of a major state falling into pieces, which may itself reject Stephen Cohen's prediction of the country dissolving in the next four to five years.[53]

Younger people in Pakistan, including a vocal section of its civil society, idealize Imran Khan as a 'third force', yet like India, the plural nature of their country and the ambiguous and often problematic politics of its three proverbial A's (Army, Allah and America) may necessitate sustained and institutional frameworks to lead it out of its malaise which, after all, might be difficult yet not impossible.[54] In the same vein, the overdue consensus between religion and politics, empowerment and equal citizenship, and nationalism and regionalism has yet to emerge to gel diverse trajectories together. However, successful elections and a peaceful transfer of power, the salience of political parties and, most of all, the resonance of civil society led by daring black coats and voiced by a critical media still offer some iota of optimism. The army is not eager to strike back, as there are serious question of legitimacy and professionalism, especially following the assassination of Osama bin Laden, and also it is a different Pakistan where people are tired of authoritarianism and militarism. Extreme forms of religious activism have already created a more humane riposte, whereas critique of the United States continues due to Washington's single-factor obsession of killing more and more people on both sides of the Durand Line, along with a complete profiling of Pakistani phones and e-mails. In this context, India is not seen as a threat, and there is a keen desire for regional cooperation, though civil society and activists frequently feel dismayed with Delhi's continued irreverence towards bilateral negotiations, especially when they could strengthen democratic and moderate forces on both sides. Surely, domestic dissensions and external travails would keep Pakistan in a precarious condition until substantive reforms, an enduring peace within and without, and universal education might steer it out of this dilemma. The Indus inhabitants have stakes in these preconditions, though they will have to come forward vocally to invalidate violence from all its various sources in addition to sharing a greater responsibility to remove the malaise of corruption, tax evasion, economic disparities and political inequities. It is certainly very encouraging to see 12,000 NGOs active on several fronts and its expatriates contributing more than $13 billion annually, yet only a million Pakistanis paying tax out of a population of 200 million does not offer a positive example. Pakistan remains quite open and supportive to foreign investments, and its citizens do not lack in entrepreneurship, yet its huge agricultural sector, which absorbs a major work force but does not contribute enough towards revenues and development needs to be overhauled through land reforms, agricultural tax, introduction of cash crops and a more equitable usage of water and energy resources.[55]

Chapter Six

THE UNITED STATES AND PAKISTAN: FRIENDS OR FOES!

'You are so cheap [...] we can buy you with a visa, with a visit to the US, even with a dinner [...] we can buy anyone.'

A US spy to Shuja Pasha, the former ISI chief, in the report by Pakistan's Abbottabad Commission[1]

'But the C.I.A. continues to run America's secret air war in Pakistan, where Mr. Kerry's comments underscored the administration's haphazard approach to discussing these issues publicly. During a television interview in Pakistan on Thursday [1 August, 2013], Mr. Kerry said the United States had a "timeline" to end drone strikes in that country's western mountains, adding, "We hope it's going to be very, very soon."

'But the Obama administration is expected to carry out drone strikes in Pakistan well into the future. Hours after Mr. Kerry's interview, the State Department issued a statement saying there was no definite timetable to end the targeted killing program in Pakistan, and a department spokeswoman, Marie Harf, said, "In no way would we ever deprive ourselves of a tool to fight a threat if it arises."'

Mark Mazzetti and Mark Landler[2]

By 2014, the Afghan war being fought by the United States in collaboration with Canada, Australia, Japan and several other European nations had already become the longest military involvement in American history, and during its second phase rather assumed the uncharitable title of 'Obama's war'. For many critics, it may be the third Vietnam in recent history following the earlier United States-Vietnam conflagration and the Soviet entanglement in Afghanistan in the 1980s – often called Moscow's Vietnam by many observers, including Zbigniew Brzezinski. In fact, by 2013 a continuously restive Afghanistan had already become the biggest security challenge to the United States with its serious and ever-expansive implications for Southwest Asian nations such as Pakistan and beyond. The former National Security Advisor, in his inaugural lecture at a conference in Dallas in 2009, had vocally highlighted the dangers of Washington's ongoing policies in a country where people were fiercely independent and religiously motivated, and given their terrain and past history determined to fight foreign forces on their soil. According to Brzezinski and other analysts, Muslims in general and Afghans in particular viewed these forces as inherently Christian who, in league with the acrimonious traditions of the past, had joined together to attack a Muslim nation and thus had to be resisted.[3] In another interview for a widely watched BBC television programme, Brzezinski felt that the war in Afghanistan, with its unexplained reasons and rather misplaced targets, had already inflamed a major section of world population and, if it continued, could result in a serious threat to US primacy in global affairs within two decades.[4]

Such widespread concerns about a prolonged war in Southwest Asia with its serious impact on the world's Muslim communities became even more pronounced when the

United States began to pressure Yemen, declaring it a new home for Al-Qaeda and overlooking its own limitations along showing with a diminished view of objective realities on the ground. As highlighted by a noted Israeli analyst, the growing quarrel with Iran, the instability in Iraq and the continued volatility in Southwest Asia certainly did not justify the expansion of already costly and highly dubious escalations in another fragile Muslim country.[5] Barack Obama's overtures towards the Muslim world following the damage incurred during the George W. Bush era seemed to be faltering as the president could not make any headway on the chronic Israeli-Palestinian issue nor could he initiate a clear policy for West Asia except for the withdrawal of troops from the two war-torn countries. Continuation of the policies largely banking upon military offensives in West Asia, including frequent drone attacks, troops deployment and the absence of a conducive approach towards the 'Arab Spring', amidst reluctance to curtail Israeli settlements in the Occupied Territories did not offer much optimism about the new administration in Washington. In the same vein, US-Pakistani bilateralism, which had entered its sixth decade, was witnessing the most decisive and equally problematic phase in its security-centred career. Most Pakistanis viewed the US policies in Afghanistan causing a multiple rise in militancy in their own country, with Pervez Musharraf and then Asif Ali Zardari having acquiesced to unmitigated US demands and pressure for using military in the Frontier regions. Pakistanis, who by tradition have usually shown nonchalance towards religio-political parties in elections, had never witnessed Taliban-style assaults before and were now fighting an enemy within. Attacks and constant flights of the CIA-operated predator drone aircraft had not only caused thousands of civilian deaths, including women and children but also they had unleashed a new cycle of violence in which bereaved Pashtuns and their supporters began to wreak revenge on fellow citizens.[6]

Our effort in these pages aims at highlighting multiple legacies and issues underpinning the US-Pakistani relationship without ignoring its interface with the regional (South Asian) and global (Muslim and European) cross-currents.[7] Following some preambling statements and a conceptual understanding we may focus on strands and strains engendered since September 11. This may help us understand the aura of mistrust between the Pakistanis and Americans despite the often-repeated official mantra of greater mutual understanding. It is from among the Pashtun tribes – especially in the KP and across the Durand Line in Afghanistan – that most of the defiance to external presence and the resultant militancy accrues, though equating trans-Indus Pashtun regions with an abrasive fundamentalism and 'a crucible of world terrorism' only betrays rancour.[8] At a pervasive level, discretionary policies towards Muslim travellers and citizens settled in the West or the profiling of nations like Pakistan are also linked with post– September 11 developments, and thus the events in Pashtun regions are not confined to the Hindu-Kush and Indus territories, but in fact they reverberate everywhere. At a personal level, at the Dallas International Airport, the author, despite his 35 years of academic and personal associations with the United States, was especially quizzed for more than an hour, which reminded him of the treatment that Muslims often receive while travelling away from their homes even though they may possess Western passports and proper professional identification. 'Were you born in, or near Peshawar?' was the first question from the US Customs official, ensconced behind the glass cabin, and it summarized the entire mindset that seems to have prevailed at various levels.

His other questions, of course, varied from the colour of the author's eyes to the location of the Roman city of Bath, which is otherwise designated as a World Heritage town.[9] It is rather amusingly anomalous that the author's own birth in an area stigmatized for tribalism has an interesting parallel with his permanent residence in an English university town, otherwise famous for its own unique form of tribalism.[10]

It is important to induct above personal details as most Muslim professionals, including those settled in the West are, overwhelmingly, cosmopolitan individuals and are sensitively aware of the challenges and expectations resting on their shoulders given their crucial role as cross-cultural intermediaries. However, suspecting, profiling and quarantining these individuals is not only highly regrettable but also equally disadvantageous to the national and global interests of the United States. One cannot undervalue the need for security checks, yet there is selective interrogating and screening of Muslim individuals through specific quarantining, who otherwise possess all the required documentation, prior visa and other personal details which are already available in the official data banks. As confirmed by WikiLeaks and Edward Snowden's leak of classified documents, the intelligence agencies and the Department of Home Security certainly have the complete profile data of most Muslims, especially Pakistanis, and this selectivity only smacks of discretion and impropriety, in addition to alienating a vast section of alert Muslim opinion. Perhaps these policies of singling out individuals for prolonged questioning are purposefully motivated to discourage Muslims from travelling altogether, especially to the United States, hitherto itself celebratory of immigration, pluralism and mobility. As several individual experiences of Muslims notables and the grass roots reveal, the United States seems to have certainly closed its doors on the world's Muslims.[11] The military engagements in Afghanistan and the related instability in West Asia are worrisome issues within Europe as well, and such fears are not confined to only South Asians or Muslims.[12] The Europeans and others, in general, believe that the Bush administration caused irreparable damage to trans-Atlantic relations through a rabid unilateralism, irreverence towards global institutions like the UN and by undertaking a sudden retreat from the Kyoto commitment. The decision to attack Afghanistan amidst feelings of anger and revenge was supported by the European Union (EU) nations so as not to fail their senior North Atlantic partner, and they willingly participated in the military invasion. However, the crucial and even daredevil attack on Iraq and Libya, and the continuation of a taxing and purposeless war in Afghanistan seriously eroded the moral high ground, if there had been any. The Afghan invasion with its attendant human costs and lack of any tangible achievements in addition to Pakistan becoming a casualty of the CIA drones and their lethal legacies deflated erstwhile support for US military-based policies.[13]

While September 11 was a travesty, the invasions of Afghanistan, Iraq and Pakistan have also allowed the simultaneous elimination of countless Muslims in Chechnya, Kashmir, Gujarat, Gaza, Southern Lebanon, Sinjiang, Myanmar and in several other places where long-term political grievances were promptly redefined as terrorist movements by the respective authorities. In addition, multipronged discretionary campaigns have featured renditions, undocumented detentions, numerous disappearances and the fulsome profiling of millions of Muslims. It appears as if September 11 proved a field day for all kinds of forces seeking their pound of Muslim flesh since the entire legacy of violence has now been ascribed only to transnational elements, with the states rather becoming altruistic forces with no checks on their unilateral policies. Such policies were unleashed at the behest of powerful lobbies, and here the Bush administration led the crusade, with the retort coming from jihadi and such other groups. As a consequence, the vast majority of the world's Muslims have been caught in this crossfire, and the Fukuyamian end of history has quickly turned into a fantasy, leaving an open field for those who only desired polarization and the use of unbridled force. Dick Cheney, Donald Rumsfeld, John Ashcroft, Paul Wolfowitz, Richard Perle, John Bolton, Zalmay Khalilzad, Paul Bremer and other important officials came to characterize an aggressive, dangerous and evangelical America which imperilled everybody's interests, as a supercilious neo-conservatism in league with the military-industrial complex overtook the national ethos.[14] This cabal of ideologues heading most of the important US departments and numerous think tanks only affirmed the primacy of neo-fundamentalists as proverbial 'Strangeloves'.[15] The situation did not change under Obama, and instead seemed to be 'business as usual' in which institutional imbalances within the US government remained unrepaired.[16] While Richard Holbrooke, and Hillary Clinton on a few occasions might have desired fuller political engagement and not a total dependence on military campaigns, the Pentagon and CIA seemed to carry decisive precedence in the White House. Mixed signals of negotiating with the local forces such as the Taliban often betrayed a great sense of confusion and drift within the Obama presidency. Concurrently, policies in the Middle East did not reveal any significant breakthrough or a fresher input.

US–Pakistani Bilateralism: Legacies of Mistrust

The US–South Asian relationship has often been seen as an interface between a core and a periphery, underwritten by the Cold War dictates on the part of the United States and propped up by the regional imperatives of the countries like Pakistan, Afghanistan and India, which pursued their own regional cold wars.[17] The US–Pakistani bilateralism during the 1980s was also seen in reference to Alvin Z. Rubinstein's model of the influence relationship, which dilated on the mutual camaraderie of the ruling elite on both sides.[18] Several analysts, especially from the Pakistani side, saw this bipartisan relationship in consonance with a balance-of-power premise, which suited both the parties in their own respective interests. Since the 1950s, the security dimension of this bilateralism was prioritized over every other consideration, though cultural diplomacy during the Soviet control of Kabul also became pronounced.[19] Following the revolution in Iran and the Soviet invasion of Afghanistan during 1979, Pakistan – an erstwhile forgotten and even stigmatized ally – was quickly rediscovered to become the front-line state. Here, Pakistan's democratic imperatives and progressive values were seriously compromised to fully protect and project General Zia-ul-Haq (1977–88), who ran the most oppressive and conservative regime in an immensely plural and politicized country. While Zia was being supported to the hilt, Pakistani civil society withered as a result of his discretionary and dictatorial policies often at the behest of secret agencies, and this is where Karachi, Kabul and Kashmir (the three Ks of the Pakistani predicament) evolved to haunt the generations of the Indus land.[20] An additional and equally crucial dimension of this relationship was the direct interface between Pakistan Army's General Headquarters (GHQ) and the Pentagon, and between the CIA and the ISI, with the result that all other channels were peripheralized and the Pakistani state was reduced to a security state.[21] Western global prerogatives during the closing phase of the Cold War overrode the democratic and developmental prerequisites of Pakistan, which only consolidated the primacy of the generals, intelligence agencies and politicians willing to kowtow to the khaki echelons and their external backers. The co-optation of religious groups such as the JI into the Afghan jihad both by General Zia-ul-Haq and the United States consolidated this triangular relationship, which provided a steady backup to the mujahideen, who were being sustained by similar support from Muslim jihadis elsewhere. Many of these fighters might have come on their own, but major prodding by the CIA and facilitation by the ISI and similar other intelligence outfits created a nexus of conflictive forces who were united only to further their respective interests. Pakistan's familiar triumvirate of three A's (the Army, America and Allah) also evolved during the 1980s, and eventually the Soviet exit from Afghanistan was made possible through Pakistani-US collaboration. The CIA prided itself on this momentous achievement.[22] However, Pakistan, like Afghanistan, was left high and dry during the 1990s by Washington and instead was slammed with sanctions due to its nuclear programme that it had always claimed to be its deterrent against a potential threat from India. While Benazir Bhutto and Mian Nawaz Sharif tried to create more space for political forces – otherwise seriously dented by the above triumvirate since Zia – their own naiveté and incessant bickering on non-issues did not help them. In the meantime, Karachi and Kashmir remained restive, often beyond the control of political leaders, who showed similar drift on Afghanistan.

Musharraf definitely lacked justification for overthrowing the country's democratic set-up on October 12, 1999, but lukewarm criticism from the Clinton administration – as was later the case with General Abdel Fattah el-Sisi's coup in Egypt in July 2013 – only encouraged the impetuous general in further mutilating the political institutions of his country. Governance became a dire issue in an immensely plural country where only a decentralized and consensual democratic structure could have gelled divergent forces. Musharraf was initially seen as a pariah in the West, until September 11, once again, put Pakistan into a front-line role for the US-led invasion of Afghanistan. Musharraf soon began to be projected as a responsible ally and a global statesman by his Western friends, exactly the way a ruthless General Zia-ul-Haq had been earlier heralded in the North Atlantic regions.[23] Once again, Pakistan's democratic and related internal security imperatives were imperilled for an ambivalent and insidious war on terror, and Musharraf's hasty participation in an ever-prolonging campaign turned Islamists and other anti-Western forces against his own regime and then his country at large. After 2005, Pakistan itself became a battleground with a proverbial million mutinies raging and Musharraf positing himself as the last bastion against an impending Talibanization of this nuclear state. Pakistani civil society struggled against Musharraf's one-man rule and radical constitutional amendments to suit his personal interests, and activated itself further following the general's dismissal of the Chief Justice on 9 March 2007.[24] Here on, quite opposed to Pakistan's civic dictates, Washington and London, until the summer of 2008 attempted to sandbag Musharraf, even at the expense of Pakistan's democratic processes and in contravention of prevailing public opinion.

Musharraf's ad hoc measures failed to contain the militancy in the country, and instead his expediencies only added to its intensity with the FATA and Swat becoming even more restive. In addition, relations with India did not improve despite his various dramatic gestures such as a visit to India and a retreat on Kashmir. While Pakistan's nuclear weapons often registered negative reportage and critical comments in Western Europe and North America – despite the country's vanguard role and attendant costs in a controversial and explosive war on terror – India was increasingly seen as a trustworthy global actor. The Bush administration put added energy into US–Indian bilateralism by committing the United States to providing dozens of nuclear reactors to Delhi at a time when its closest ally suffered on many fronts, including long power blackouts. Reports on American plans to capture Pakistani nuclear assets in any future emergency, often authored by well-known analysts such as Seymour Hersh, were angrily commented upon at various levels especially when Pakistanis, given their location and following a multiplicity of media channels, were well informed on several issues impinging on their own safety.[25] In 2015, in a longer piece on the killing of Osama bin Laden, Hersh raised several vital issues about the possibility of Pakistani–Saudi collusion on keeping the Al-Qaeda leader in a safe house and then his elimination in a joint ISI–CIA move which featured its own phases of mistrust and ambiguities.[26] Thus, we can see how the US–Pakistani relationship, despite almost half a century of cooperation, failed to develop into an enduring mutuality and instead experienced numerous aberrations on both sides. Pakistanis often saw themselves as the aggrieved party by having been used and then forsaken. In addition, their own affinity with Muslim issues, in contrast with an ongoing multifaceted campaign focusing on Muslims and emanating from a number of quarters, did not allow any sustained cordiality. It is no wonder that the grass roots in the Indus Valley occasionally blamed the United States, India and Israel directly and indirectly for instability in their country.[27]

Pakistan–United States Bilateralism: A Perennial Roundabout, or an Ambivalent Crossroads!

Volatility around Pakistan's borders, precariously intersecting its inner ethnic and doctrinal pluralities, assumed violent proportions after September 11, nefariously feeding into an angry cynicism amongst a vast majority of its citizens. They have been deeply disturbed over the enemy within, perceived to be working in cahoots with the enemy from without, as they vehemently desire to steer out of these surreal and taxing goings-on. Islam and Pakistan, both horizons away from a commonly agreed consensus, have remained the familiar reference points, yet the violence around them and often in their name only exacerbates a pervasive bewilderment.[28] While the outsiders may sweepingly call it 'a failing state', 'the epicentre of world terrorism' or 'a possible Afghanistan or Somalia only a hundred times more lethal', the historical resilience of its people and even of some of its institutions is certainly not a minor feat. While it increasingly became almost impossible for Pakistanis to travel abroad given the serious suspicions held by most of the regimes and societies both in a less-sympathetic neighbourhood and the world at large, amidst such ever-increasing discretionary restrictions and incrimination, one did not fail to notice the mellowness amongst its populace at large. Given external scepticism about Pakistan since its inception, its frequent recourse to military dictatorship and the severance of its eastern wing, followed by the post–September 11 negative critique at various levels somehow made its dumbing down a familiar phenomenon.[29]

Pakistan is in the throes of a serious predicament, which is hydra-faced and has been seriously affecting public morale, national security, institutional infrastructure and country's economy besides seriously compromising its global profile making it almost impossible for Pakistanis to attain spatial mobility.[30] Pakistanis are overwhelmingly bewildered at the frequency, variety and intensity of violence being perpetrated against them. At one level people, in general, believe that this is all owing to post–September 11 invasions, and especially the military campaigns in Afghanistan and Pakistan, as feared all along, caused this maelstrom. According to some opinion groups, Pakistan was the unintended victim of this perfidious war on terror while to many others it was the *real* target due to its nuclear programme and a sustained multidimensional hostility from numerous external forces. Here in public parlance, India, the Zionist lobbies and even many sections within the United States administration were held responsible for destabilizing the country and making it ungovernable. While there is a growing realization that the perpetrators and victims are overwhelmingly Pakistanis, still the money, training facilities and vital logistical support are believed to be facilitated by the mentioned sources that have their own discretionary agendas converging with several regional and local enmities. Thus, at one level, there was violence as a response and reaction to the US-led operations in Afghanistan and intermittent drone strikes in the FATA, which was to be resisted in the name of jihad and here Pakistani security forces and government became the enemy by aligning with the *Western, Christian* and *anti-Muslim* forces. Allegedly, Black Water, the CIA, RAW and the Mossad were perceived as working against *Muslim* interests, and even some tribal chieftains who otherwise supported Islamabad were suspected of helping anti-Muslim forces and thus were targeted quite often. The Pakistani government, under Musharraf, the PPP and the ML was viewed as fully colluding with the former forces, and thus its khaki and civilian personnel and institutions had to be destroyed. Even while the ML and Imran Khan pursued negotiations with the Pakistani Taliban, violence attributed to sectarian, ethnic and splinter groups continued in urban and tribal regions including Islamabad, Karachi and Peshawar.

Here the Afghan Taliban led by groups such as Sirajud Din Haqqani, the elusive Quetta Shura or similar anti-Western forces led by the Pashtun warlord Gulbuddin Hekmatyar, were considered holy warriors despite the fact that these groups mostly declared their nonchalance and impartiality towards Pakistan's internal conflicts. They reiterated their impartiality off and on, yet grew on support from non-Afghan fighters including those from the KP, Punjab and elsewhere. Afghanistan, even after 14 years of military operations and CIA missions including the drone attacks and monetary inducements to tribal chieftains, did not obtain total peace. Even while NATO troops were withdrawing from Afghanistan in 2014, the graph of multiple forms of violence did not register any significant downturn, though the large-scale participation in the elections in April also reaffirmed a pervasive desire for peace. Pakistani–US bilateralism suffered greater strains over issues such as Washington's increased pressure on Islamabad to mount more military operations in tribal areas; seek out greater cooperation with Kabul even if the Karzai regime had kept accusing Pakistan for most of its domestic vulnerabilities; and an increased public uproar over drone attacks. In addition, bilateral relations suffered the most in the wake of the operation by the US Navy SEALs in Abbottabad on 2 May 2011, resulting in the death of Osama bin Laden, followed by the American attack on Salala Post on the Pakistan–Afghan border on 26 November 2011 which killed 24 Pakistani soldiers. Earlier, on 27 January, Raymond Davis, a CIA contractor, had killed two Pakistani motorcyclists in Lahore, raising a storm of protests for him to be put on trial. His escapade happened just a few weeks after the conviction of Afia Siddiqui, a Pakistani neuroscientist with a doctorate from Brandeis University who had been tried in the United States for her alleged connection with Al-Qaeda, and in September 2010, a court in Manhattan, while upholding the charges, sentenced her to prison for 86 years. Simultaneously, senior US civil and military officials routinely kept accusing Pakistan of providing sanctuary to the Taliban and Al-Qaeda, as it appeared like a convenient alibi to paper over frustrations arising over such a sustained and costly engagement in Afghanistan.[31] While the most powerful alliance in world history could not explain its own failure in blocking the movement of militants across the Durand Line, its pressure on Pakistan, along with leaks to the Western media of frequent stories of alleged Pakistani culpability, only betrayed the fragile nature of this security relationship. It is not surprising that with this kind of backdrop, US public opinion has often been either hostile or simply unfriendly to an ally nation which had been in the forefront in providing logistical and active support to American involvement in a neighbourly Muslim country. The American rebuke of Pakistan often chose to overlook the diverse and equally perverse forms of violence with which Pakistan itself had been confronted, in which a more dispassionate analysis could have been in order instead of sheer condemnation.

Secretary of State Hillary Clinton tried to offer a personal touch to her diplomatic efforts by using public diplomacy to reach broader sections of Pakistani society. Her empathy with Benazir Bhutto's children and the advantage of closer ties with Nawaz Sharif, to some extent, were helpful through the stormy phases, yet events like attacks on a Pakistani military post in Salala and an increase in drone attacks, along with the Abbottabad operation greatly added to the tensions and mutual suspicions. Washington's almost desperate and total dependence on the Karzai regime and lack of any initiative to work towards a broad-based negotiated settlement in Afghanistan led to a stalemate, especially in 2011 when the United States–Pakistan strategic dialogue was disrupted. Kabul under Hamid Karzai often used Pakistan as a routine alibi for its own security failings, and Islamabad suspected a closer Kabul–Delhi axis working in league against its interests, with Washington often seen as a benign party that could have otherwise broken the Indo–Pakistani and Pakistani–Afghan logjams. Following Admiral Michael Mullen's strong rebuke of the ISI in 2011, Pakistanis felt that the United States was being insensitive to their dire security imperatives. A kind of grudge and sense of victimhood on all sides became more explicit as the security situation in Southwest Asia kept deteriorating, along with the interstate relationship taking a nosedive. With the ascensi

Nawaz Sharif as prime minister in 2013 and his eagerness to repair relations with Kabul, Washington and Delhi seemed to be offering some thaw. John Kerry, Hillary Clinton's successor at the State Department and a frequent visitor to Pakistan, in his meetings with the Pakistani civil and khaki leadership presented a quid pro quo in which Washington would show greater accommodation to Pakistani security limitations, while the latter would accept reduced drone strikes though reluctantly, and simultaneously would try to persuade the Taliban to negotiate with Kabul. The resumption of US–Pakistani strategic dialogue and efforts to repair a damaged bilateralism were being welcomed cautiously on all sides, though drones and the future course of possible negotiations with a Taliban reluctant to offer an olive branch to a rather unpopular Karzai regime posed formidable challenges.[32] The killing of Hakimullah Mehsud by a CIA-operated drone-led missile on 1 November 2013 seriously dented any hope for negotiations with the TTP, as had been promised by Nawaz Sharif and Imran Khan during their respective election campaigns. The decisive operation had happened immediately after Nawaz Sharif's visit to Washington and was followed up by a similar strike on 21 November on a seminary in Tal near Hangu – the settled district of KP – immediately spawning roadblocks by Imran Khan's PTI. This strike well inside Pakistani 'settled' territory triggered road closures by the PTI for lorries carrying NATO supplies across the Khyber Pass. Other than the US objections to the Iran-Pakistan-India pipeline project, the lack of any resolute effort for forging better Indo–Pakistani relations surely gave a temporary dimension to this bilateralism, which, otherwise, could have been quite beneficial at several levels.[33] The US–Pakistani relationship has often fluctuated and at times appears lacking in long-term objectives and trust-based sustainability, as was noted in a report: 'U.S.–Pakistan relations are fluid at present, but running a clearly negative course: still based on several national interests shared by both countries, yet marked by levels of mutual distrust and resentment that are likely to catalyse a new set of assumptions for future ties'.[34] The Western military drawdown has eased pressure on Pakistan and could eventually allow China to play a more co-optative role by indirectly nudging all the parties towards a workable consensus, though Kabul–Taliban bilateralism remains the most vital determinant.

American Predictions of a Failing State

While official American censoring of Pakistan became more vocal under Obama, the intelligence surveys and some academic analyses equally turned sceptical of Pakistan's survival as an independent state. Widely reported in the Pakistani media and shared by social networks, predictions about Pakistan as a failing state and an epicentre of world terror only alienated a major section of public opinion. Following are a few examples of some interesting studies, which often portrayed a doomsday scenario for the country and have been amply highlighted in the Pakistani and Indian media with their own respective searchlights on their contents. In December 2000, while depicting global trends by 2015, a CIA report saw Pakistan as a fractious and isolated state that 'will not recover easily from decades of political and economic mismanagement, divisive politics, lawlessness, corruption and ethnic friction'.[35] A 2005 study by the US National Intelligence Council and the CIA, reported in the *Times of India*, characterized Pakistan as a failed state by 2015 where bloodshed and civil wars would turn the territory into a 'Yugoslavia-like fate' amidst a struggle for control over its nuclear weapons and a fierce Talibanization.[36] In an editorial comment in the *New York Times* in 2007, two leading defence analysts, Frederick Kagan and Michael O'Hanlon, alerted US authorities to prepare contingency plans to retrieve Pakistan's nuclear arsenal in view of a feared dissolution of the country. They noted, 'The most likely possible danger are these: a complete collapse of Pakistani government rule that allows an extreme Islamist movement to fill in the vacuum; a total loss of federal control over outlying provinces which splinter along ethnic and tribal lines; or a struggle within the Pakistani military in which the minority sympathetic to Taliban and Al Qaeda try to establish Pakistan as a state sponsor of terrorism'.[37] In a similar piece just before the elections of February 2008, Selig Harrison also reiterated Pakistan's dissolution on ethnic lines, with the Pashtuns and Baloch going their own respective ways and leaving Punjab with the 'rump state' of Pakistan.[38] A 2008 report by the US Intelligence Council and the CIA, *Global Trends 2025*, found Pakistan to be a high-risk country with the possibility of melting down. Identified as a 'wildcard', Pakistan was predicted to dissolve, with its Pashtun regions separating from the country.[39] In January 2009 a Pentagon report suggested that Pakistan, over the next 25 years, could experience a 'rapid and sudden' collapse due to sectarian and civil warfare, necessitating the involvement of the US forces in the country.[40] Such prescriptive comments flagging preparedness for a possible involvement by the US forces to take control of Pakistani nuclear facilities appeared amidst reports of operations by American paratroopers on Pakistani soil. A media report on 3 September 2008 claimed a commando raid by US Special Forces, assisted by military helicopters, had killed 15–20 Pakistanis including women and children.[41] The *Guardian*, in fact, confirmed such periodic raids, which had been happening frequently since 2003, with Washington intent upon even more strikes.[42]

Surely, the above-mentioned predictions and reports further dampened Pakistani hopes for a positive future and, in several cases, underwrote a widening critique of the long-term American objectives in the region. Most of these reports suggested that the United States was only concerned about Pakistan for being a nuclear Muslim state and desired to control its enrichment and militarization facilities by destabilizing that country. Such anti-American views found currency among various quarters of public opinion, though several voices kept alerting people to the threat from within and around. Other than internal uncertainty, Pakistan's geopolitical security issues appeared to have become even more complex, as was noted by a politician–columnist: 'Strange the workings of history – our military geniuses under Gen Zia sought strategic depth in Afghanistan. It is the Taliban and Al-Qaeda which have acquired strategic depth in Pakistan'. The United States sought a negotiated way out from Afghanistan after a 13-year-long war with unprecedented human and material costs on all sides, but the aborted parleys with the Taliban in Qatar and their de facto vetoing by Karzai turned them into a farce. Other than Karzai, Pakistan had itself been left in a quizzical situation whose earlier offloading of the Taliban and campaigning against them and their comrades-in-arms in the FATA caused real concerns related to their encroachment on the Pakistani state itself:

> The Americans are about to talk to the Taliban not to get them to lay down their arms and ship them to the Solomon Islands, but as a face-saving exercise. They want to exit Afghanistan

sans too much humiliation. In so many words they are telling the Taliban, look we are getting out; make our departure easier. That's it, if only we could read the writing on the wall [...] At least Karzai knows what is what. We get used like a box of tissues again – the first time under Zia, the second time now – and still think we are 'stakeholders' in the Afghan game. There's no end to our talent for make-believe, even as the tide of history is being reversed.[43]

Imperatives and Options

Pakistan's cost in lives, resources, property and morale has been endlessly higher owing to this decade-long militancy spawned by smaller sections on the margins of society. One may seek out multiple reasons for this increased violence: the global clash and post–September 11 geopolitics have certainly provided the impetus, with Muslim countries and communities being targeted holistically for the crime of a few miscreants. The pressures on obliging Muslim regimes and their ill-thought-out policies against their own people have made it into a self-immolating phase in which Somalia, Iraq, Afghanistan, Egypt, Pakistan, Saudi Arabia, Yemen, Libya and Syria witness soldiers and militants fighting it out among themselves, resulting in intra-Muslim violence.[44] The issues of political and economic empowerment certainly merit serious consideration as most of the activists and militants are otherwise have-nots who are using political Islam not only as a dehegemonizing force against the rich and equally arrogant Western powers but are also arrayed against their own regimes, which they see as corrupt surrogates. In other words, coercion and corruption underline the malaise, which is rooted in an authoritarian elitism. Other than its political and economic casus belli, ideologically, several interpretations of political Islam abound, and some of them within the Salafi/Wahhabi paradigm have taken upon themselves to pursue *takfir* (declaring people un-Islamic). Another larger factor is rooted in the dichotic and inefficient nature of religious and modern instruction – both lacking substantive reforms and mutual interface – though it would be unfair to incriminate the entire madrasa (seminary) system.

The view of militant Islam as an anti-Western trajectory is beyond doubt given all the historical, colonial economic and ideological root causes, yet defining it as anti-modern and anti-empowerment would be fallacious.[45] Militants have no qualms in using modern weaponry and information technology, though they vehemently oppose Western political and cultural norms. Thus, it is important for policymakers both in the United States and elsewhere not to solely bank on military strategies featuring assaults, detentions and aerial attacks, and rather initiate sociopolitical alternatives in which dialogues, democratization and economic development supersede discretionary policies. There is a greater need for building up cross-cultural and cross-sectional bridges instead of stigmatizing Muslims. The Obama administration had been losing favourable ground within and outside the United States and could have instead focused on resolving conflicts that germinated a pervasive anti-Americanism that skyrocketed during the Bush years. In addition, there was a greater urgency to strengthen multilateral institutions like the UN besides involving neutral Muslim states in the proper reconstruction processes in war-torn countries such as Iraq, Libya, Syria and Afghanistan.

Violence in Pakistan has unleashed its own cycle and retains similar portents for the region to the east given the historical traditions, geographical proximity and also because of the anomalous and conflictive nature of the Indo–Pakistani relationship, which does not allow sufficient leeway for healthy alternatives. Instability of this type does not respect any borders, and India, like Pakistan, may witness its own familiar and not-so-familiar cycles of violence if its policymakers keep on pursuing a self-congratulatory view of their own exceptionalism and immunity from violence next door. In addition, a desire to demand or seek a greater pound of Pakistani flesh is not judicious at all given that Pakistan is, realistically speaking, the first and most formidable line of defence for India against any form of instability, whereas India's huge size, complex and often contentious pluralism and its overstretched security paraphernalia can also render it vulnerable to some unfamiliar and painful future.[46] It is vital both for South Asia and the United States to undertake substantial steps towards regionalization between India and Pakistan aiming for cordial relations, which will help them contain militancy besides obviating the possibility of any major conflagration owing to some future terrorist attack.[47] Here Washington with its immense clout in both countries needs to be proactive and supportive.[48] Surely, the Pakistanis, and likewise the Afghans, themselves have to take vital decisions on the issues of their national security, governance, peace and harmony, while tackling challenges such as violence, poverty, the misuse of religion and the spillover from extra-regional geopolitics. The Indus Valley has to rise, once again, to seek out its own inner dynamics while banking on its rich history and a vast reservoir of human resourcefulness, and certainly it cherishes and deserves a better existence. These people in turmoil are understandably mellow and slightly unsure given the multiplicity and intensity of the challenges they face and a vast array of inimical forces, yet their own destiny is, once again, poised to determine the future of the entire South Asia.

Chapter Seven

THE EUROPEAN UNION AND SOUTHWEST ASIA: PERCEPTIONS, POLICIES AND PERMUTATIONS

'The Western media propagates an image of a romantic Afghanistan, one that cannot be conquered or tamed. Its people are warriors whose only purpose is to resist and fight; they are unruly natives unwelcoming to modern society. Afghanistan is a mystery that no outsider can unravel or know [...] American and British policies and military strategies have been based on these perceived notions, as if Afghans were not capable of change or progress, as they were frozen in time and with tribal mentalities.'

Fariba Nawa[1]

The EU, through its numerous individual members and multilateral agencies, and Southwest Asia inclusive of Pakistan and Afghanistan, both have maintained a multi-dimensional relationship, which since September 11 was definitely overshadowed by security-related priorities. Development, governance, poverty reduction, education, gender rights, and assistance in reforming infrastructure found their way within official pronouncements, but frankly speaking it was the pre-eminence of security-related concerns which brought these regions closer together, though in no less ambivalent a way. Despite the salience of security and geopolitical imperatives, the historical, Diasporic, academic, commercial and cultural interfaces have, in recent years, tended to be either overlooked or get de-emphasised on both sides, whereas winning the war, fighting terrorism and neutralizing extremism resounded as a familiar mantra and fait accompli. In one sense, this relationship is almost as old as the EU itself. In 1952, its earliest incarnation initiated its presence in the Indus lands, though most of the West European nations had already established ambassadorial posts in Karachi and Kabul.[2] The earliest phase in this newer relationship was characterized by mutual curiosity in addition to a modicum of assistance in some infrastructure-building areas. Both sides were still in the early processes of their respective redefinition, which again, in a rather curious way, stemmed from post–World War II geopolitical considerations, interests and imperatives. The ideological division of Europe preceded the partition of the subcontinent just by a few years, though a generation down the decades it has successfully overcome that sundering.[3] In contrast to Europe, the boundary contestations over Kashmir and the tribal regions had already engulfed India, Pakistan and Afghanistan in an acrimonious relationship, which, despite enthusiasm for people-to-people trajectories, has been less than cordial. Issues of divided communities and natural resources, the transfer of people often caught in haphazard and even painful migrations –some of the world's largest ever – along with active warfare over unresolved issues such as Kashmir unleashed a South Asian cold war that refuses to abate.

Like post-1945 Europe grievously and insidiously divided by a taxing Cold War, the post-1947 South Asia has been a hotbed of interstate, ethnic and ideological rivalries featuring regional polarities. Like many of the current 27 EU nations, South Asian nations found themselves gnawed at by regional fault lines, which only catapulted them into seeking assistance and even patronage from the flag carriers of a contemporary global polarity. Thus, in the way Europe became a battleground for East-West rivalry, South Asia also turned into an arena of regional conflicts that pushed it into the global cold war either through a willing co-optation dictated by respective geopolitical interests or because of the pull factors from extra-regional powers. Certainly, Afghanistan and India, in their own unique ways, either tried to stay away from global alignments or aimed at seeking benefits from both the warring sides.[4] After the Sino-Indian war of 1962, India sought closer collaboration with both the blocs, whereas following the Indo-Pakistani war of 1965, Pakistan, exhibiting its disappointment with the Western powers, sought proximity with the People's Republic of China.[5] In 1971, India, with active Soviet assistance, helped midwife Bangladesh, while during the 1980s, Pakistan became a conduit for the United States and other Western powers assisting the mujahideen in their resistance against Soviet troops. Since September 11, both India and Pakistan have pursued a new era of the regional game in war-torn Afghanistan by cultivating closer commonalities with their favourite ethno-regional allies, whereas China, Russia, Central Asian republics and Iran have keenly watched the new buzkashi unfurl in their immediate neighbourhood.

The EU, Undefined Parameters, Unlimited Ambitions

The rationale behind the evolution of the EU was meant as an antidote to the millennia of intra-Europe wars of global dimensions since this association is a multilateral alliance of shared political ideals, regional interests and common concerns. Despite its reticence on geopolitical imperatives and ambitions, this growing alliance is rooted in these vital concerns and embodies a consensus on keeping Europe safe and secure from intra-Europe wars and invasions, especially from the east, though this realm has been allocated to NATO, history's largest and most enduring military alliance.[6] The EU and NATO evolved out of similar imperatives, shared apprehensions and inclusive ambitions, though intra-European feuds and long-drawn battles have turned subterranean. By strictly focusing on military and security affairs, NATO appears to retain more cogent and coherent remit featuring well-defined and extensive components. It is a different issue that in its longest active war, its limitations as well as its munificent powers became even more apparent.[7] In contrast, the EU is still evolving, often contested and somehow constrained by the respective interests and trajectories of its various states, and unlike NATO, it deals with a plethora of old and new areas. The EU, despite a visible establishment which deals with international affairs and is led by commissioners, does not have unitary EU-wide policy postulations. It may never have a single policy, yet in areas like aid, human rights and the environment it certainly exhibits a cogent viewpoint. However, active foreign and defence policies are left to the United States, NATO and the respective member states. These institutional 'ambiguities' of the world's largest Caucasian club not only underpin an unending process of mediation, negotiation and arbitration but they also make its policies and processes cumbersome, expensive and contentious.[8] In a military crisis such as in the former Yugoslavia, or the ongoing warfare in West Asia and the Ukrainian-Russian dispute, the North Atlantic countries, including the West European nations, have found it easier to bank on US leadership within NATO, but in the cases of political policy and diplomacy, the EU, much like the UN and the Organization of the Islamic Cooperation (OIC), has been generally found lacking in convergences, united will and consensual action. These restraints still do not diminish the profundity and outreach of its public diplomacy and the similar respective trajectories of its individual governments.

The EU is definitely the most successful multiregional alliance in political, cultural and economic areas, but unlike the Association of South East Asian Nations (ASEAN), it is still unclear or even hamstrung on intra-state diversities and proclivities, and that is where it reverts to American leadership and the NATO umbrella. However, eight South Asian nations, despite being part of the South Asian Association for Regional Cooperation (SAARC), have been unable to move multilaterally on any substantive front. Even the basic right of mobility for their one and a half billion South Asians remains a distant dream, not to mention political and security issues. Suspicions and restrictions disallow any such grass-roots and people-to-people interface. When it comes to resolving regional conflicts over territory, water resources, goods and drugs smuggling, illegal migrations and ecology, the SAARC is as ineffective as the OIC, though interestingly some other such alliances such as the Organisation of African Unity (OAU) seem to be more proactive.[9] On the same Asian continent, ASEAN itself is a brilliant example of substantive multilateralism in which, irrespective of the distinct and divergent cultural and political features of each member nation and in spite of their mutual squabbling more like in South Asia, they have binned warfare into a forgotten past. The ASEAN, other than investments in education and infrastructure, has been behind the "tiger" Asian economies as they have been reaping the benefits of such an enduring and uninterrupted peace in an area where wars, natural disasters, ethnic cleansing and displacements had been consistent until a few decades back.[10] In contrast, despite their pious pronouncements and periodic summits, both the OIC and SAARC have never outgrown their stalemated status as 'talk shops' or 'social clubs' of the power elite, which are strong on pronouncements but acutely deficient on regional policies. The Arab League and the Gulf Cooperation Council seem to be following a similar route of mutual squabbles, and have been found lacking in rigour and leadership, as observed during the tumultuous 'Arab Spring' and crises in Iraq, Syria, Libya and Yemen.

Other than the problematic of being an alliance of diverse cultures and economies with varying degrees of external engagements, the EU's strength and challenges emanate from both the United States and NATO. The latter often determines the agenda and strategies when it comes to external geopolitical issues, though both vacillate between admiration and muted criticism of their political and bureaucratic elite counterparts headquartered in Brussels but spread across the 27 nations through an ever-increasing flotilla of international [European] bureaucracies of overwhelmingly white men and women. While statewide plurality is reflective within the EU's constituents and a plethora of its organs, and it may contest or even leave aside grey areas, the EU also denotes Europe's own historic, cultural, racial and imperial specifics, encouraging some of its leaders and ideologues to speak of it as a distinct and strictly *Christian* club. Post–September 11 tensions and anxieties amidst a growing accent on exclusive nationalism(s) in almost all the EU nations have considerably pushed the EU towards this narrowly defined and *racialized* cultural paradigm.[11] It has also nefariously exacerbated internal fissures which often, other than strong Islamophobic and anti-immigrant manifestations, boil up in the form of inter-ethnic travails such as the Greek-German fracas witnessed in the background of the economic turndown in 2013–15.

In addition to the above-mentioned ambiguities, the EU's greatest challenge is to synchronize respective state/nation-based identities and interests with those expected or idealized from a regionalized and consensual Europe-wide embodiment. Here hyped-up issues of sovereignty, distinct constitutional identities and separate histories coalesce with grudges and reservations over economic contributions or a lack of them as well as threats to jobs, housing and facilities for the 'natives'. In other words, the age-old issues of ethnicity, class, systemic choices and diverse economies all seek shelter under an ambiguous yet highly insidious panoply of sovereignty and patriotism. These powerful pulls for 'national sovereignty and interests' over and above 'dictatorship' from Brussels, amidst dwindling job markets and increasing competition from Asia, intensify intolerance especially against 'outsiders'. Like the erstwhile Jewish presence in Europe, Muslims, Africans and the travelling communities frequently come under the spotlight, though an increased Islamophobia subsumes a major share of this ire. Islamophobia may not be expressed too often in a crude way, yet takes many shapes and subtleties varying from bans on minarets to male circumcision and halal meat, along with a large-scale but routinized profiling of Muslim Europeans.[12]

Southwest Asia: War Zone of Undefined Parameters

Like the EU nations and member states, South Asia appears a rather coherent and well-defined region – at least from the outside – if one looks at the forces of geography, ecology and political economy, and it becomes tempting to see it like a well-defined cultural and economic monolith. Bordered by the highest mountains to the north and the Indian Ocean to the south, and by rather fluid dividing lines to the west, while being distinct from the Burmese border in Southeast Asia, this most populous region named after the Indus [i.e. India, Hindustan, Hindi, Hindvi and Hinduism], despite persuasive commonalities is as diverse as sub-Saharan Africa. Plurality features through religions, sects, languages, ethnicities, class structures, castes, demographic variations and elite formation, along with the various parallel traditions and discourses of political history. Both democracy and dictatorship continue to feature in the short political history of contemporary South Asia, as do the challenges of political instability, religious extremism, majoritarian hegemonies and certainly the issues of sharp inter-class differences. The forces of modernity and tradition, unlike in East Asia or Latin America, have rendered this region into a hotbed of local and statewide dichotomies, which may often boil over in the forms of Taliban, Hindutva, Maharashtra nativism, Sunni statehood, Khalistan, Greater Balochistan, Pashtunistan, peasant revolts in Jharkhand, Muslim Bengali primacy, and Buddhist and Sinhalese unilateralism. These ethnic, class, caste and ideological chasms reflect fault lines going beyond the territorial borders – like the divisive water resources – of the eight nation states luring their respective governments into a form of essentialized regional competition which may not shy from turning into full-fledged inter-state conflict.[13]

Whereas the EU, Western Europe and the now vast regions of Southern and Eastern Europe are regionalized, banishing political and religious wars and border conflicts into a distant memory, South Asian nations have not even begun their journey towards regionalization. Other than a mutual trust deficit, the bilateral and regional commerce and shares in investments across the borders have been dismal, and instead transactions still happen through some third-party facilitation such as Dubai. Emphasis on a masculine form of nationalism with military muscle and blue navies, along with nuclear arms (at least in the cases of the two larger regional states), the common strategies on similar challenges or sharing civil experiences and institutions are visibly absent. Internalizing rival historical narratives, mostly justified by conflictive ideologies and competitive ethnicities and religions, newer generations in South Asia are mutually as far apart as Mongolia and Patagonia. Here both the EU and ASEAN are often posited as positive alternatives to regional incongruities, yet the ruling groups, powerful institutions and stakeholders do not permit any breakthrough. Disputes like Pashtunistan, Kashmir and divisions over the distribution of water resources, along with allegations of interference in each other's affairs and the sheer use of force are offered as the causes for this malaise. The periodic summits, media exchanges, meetings at global forums and cricket matches usually lead to increased expectations, which soon vanish under 'business as before'. Trade first, or the resolution of conflicts first, has already become a monotonous narrative, with governments unable or unwilling to offer a major breakthrough, unleashing a gaping void, which is mostly filled in by the security agencies, hate-seeking rhetoric and marauding xenophobes.[14] The people-to-people relationship for post-independence South Asians, unlike the unprecedented mobility across the various boundaries within the EU, remains an elusive dream.[15] Thousands of miles of barbed wire, well-lit watch towers and concrete bunkers vigilantly monitor inter-state borders, as people-to-people contacts stay non-existent.[16] Thus, whereas the EU may still be an undefined and half-realized [or even too ambitious!] project, its precedence for regions including South or Southwest Asia is no less trivial.

Despite this entire raft of convergences and divergences between the two distant but increasingly proximate regions, it is vital to locate the mutual perceptions on *both* sides to see how they underwrite their attitudes and even official policies in which religions, cultures, conflicts and concerns often seem to predominate. Following those historic and regenerated perceptions and even stereotypes we shall have an overview of mutual covenants and commitments which have caused the EU's growing, though often ambivalent involvement in Southwest Asia and vice versa. Our next section of this study certainly focuses on the areas in which future policies could be operational in the larger interests of both the subcontinents.

Politics of Perceptions and Misperceptions

While national interests and, to some extent, ideals may play a pivotal role in the formulation and implementation of foreign and defence policies of any state, the subtle role of images and misperceptions, however, is equally crucial in underpinning such trajectories.[17] As seen in the 1930s and during the Cold War, views about various communities – religious, ethnic or ideological – helped spawn several decisions, including policies towards the Soviets, Nazis, Jews, colonized peoples and capitalist societies. Religion, literature, travelogues, the media (in more recent times), the impact and reporting of global events such as West European empires, or September 11 itself are more glaring examples in which the former operated as formidable facilitators for discourses such as orientalism, Islamophobia, neo-racism and anti-Westernism. That is why most countries in Europe and North America have been investing major sums in pursuing public diplomacy through educational exchanges, programmes run by the USAID, Fulbright fellowships, Woodrow Wilson grants and similar elite-centred activities through the British Council, Department for International Development, the Goethe Institute, La Maison Française and such other mediums.[18] In a world of competition and conflicts, the realpolitik drives such policies in which, in the name of aid, development and public welfare, training and exchange projects are undertaken mainly geared towards favourable image building. While the colonial powers, often unabashedly, undertook the enterprise of class and elite formation – the brown sahibs, as they are known – their successor states and related multilateral organizations such as the EU have become quite sophisticated, subtle and indirect in pursuing similar goals. Here, moralized goals such as the eradication of poverty, illiteracy, gender imbalances and epidemics are put forth within the realm of public diplomacy either through the host country's official bodies or facilitated by NGOs.

Historical Burden in Image Making

Historically speaking, Europe has for centuries embodied and pursued the Europeanization of the world, which during the modern era often manifested itself in the White Man's Burden, and in the postcolonial period has operated as a junior partner in the United States-led hegemonic Westernism. Non-Europeans calibrated Europe as a monolithicized, distinct and essentially *different* community during the Middle Ages, especially in the wake of the Crusades. This homogenized view of Europe was based on the premise of a 'Christian West' – an ultimate *maghreb* – which, interestingly has refused to disappear and remains one of those unique and permeating formulations in human history which have defied time and change. Europe's pre-Christian interaction with non-Europe was through the Greeks and Romans, and here cultural differentiation existed, yet without a religious/Christian accompaniment. This old *West* competed with the rival *East*, which moved between ancient Egypt and ancient Persia. South Asia did often come in, but only in reference to an ancient polyglot of cultures or as a harbinger of trade opportunities, as was the case during the Roman era. The Persians, since the arrival of the Aryans on both sides of the Suleiman Mountains, shared a rivalry as well as temptation over the Indus lands, whereas the ancient Greeks took Punjab as 'the land's end'.[19] Annexation of the Indus Valley by the Persians and then its conquests by the Greeks/Macedonians under Alexander proved a turning point since their mutual rivalries opened the way for the evolution of the classical Hindu empire with a brief though no less glorious Buddhist interregnum under Emperor Ashoka. Along with the Persian cultural influences, Central

Asia deeply impacted the Indus Valley and North Indian plains. Other than the Persians, Greeks and Central Asians, ancient Hindustan – a perennial borderland – was deeply impacted by a new West Asian thrust under Islam. Islam itself had been the beneficiary of the continuum of Persian-Roman warfare that had weakened both the empires – a process that happened in India as well.

The evolution of Islam and the salience of Muslim caliphates defined Europe as a land of setting sun that had become predominantly Christian due to the Byzantine Empire's adoption of this Middle Eastern religion. While Muslims could control the Mediterranean regions such as Anatolia, Iberia and North Africa, the interiors of Europe largely remained unpenetrated by Islam except for scholarly and clerical contacts that persisted all along via Sicily and Spain. The Crusades certainly caused the first major and prolonged encounter between the *Maghreb* and *Mashreq*, and here other than politics and military warfare, Christianity and Islam became emblematic of this first-ever, sustained and equally taxing clash of cultures.[20] In addition to these two communities, Jews found themselves at the crossroads as well and often sought to move out of harm's way. Scholarly and commercial exchanges between Muslims and Europe proved enduring, though most studies and populist images only focus on warfare, violence, conquests and hero-versus-villain narratives. Muslims of Sicily and Spain saw religion and politics combined in this Christianized Europe, and contemporary maps, books and literary pieces ushered in the centrality of religion in this West.[21] The Crusades were crucial, volatile and far reaching, but the balance of power between the two sides remained undecided until the Mongols destroyed the remnants of the caliphate and Muslim regional powers, along with grievously bruising a greater sense of their self-confidence. The Mongol invasions from the east and the north coincided with the third and the subsequent series of the Crusades, and though Islamic civilization escaped total annihilation, its political power was deeply jolted until the Mongols turned to Islam and new Turkic empires came into being. Though, politically, Muslims created a new era of land-based empires, the confidence deficit proved enduring, and the imperial and clerical prioritization of conformity over creativity took a strong hold.[22]

While the Mongols in the east accepted Buddhism and established empires in China and Tibet, in the western regions they and their Turkic compatriots founded the Mughal, Ottoman and the Safawid empires, which injected fresher blood into Muslim cultural and political trajectories besides halting their feared decline. This major transformation after all the wanton destruction amidst the Crusades and the Mongol invasions helped Muslims for a time, until modernity heralded a new, ambitious and vigorously Christian Europe. From the Andes to the Caucuses and Siberia, and from Cairo to Cape Town the world encountered a confident, conquering and civilizing project unleashed by some of the smaller nations of Western Europe. Led by Iberian regimes and followed by other monarchies all the way to Moscow, this expansion not only happened amidst the denigration of the non-Western and non-Christian peoples but also it equally refurbished a Crusades-like self-righteousness. The era of modern (European) empires had arrived not merely in a familiar form of conquest and plunder as often rightly attributed to the Conquistadores, but in a more holistic way, heralding the curious but no less significant combination of control and culture, in which other than economic and political primacy, Christianity found a new lease on life in the vast swathes of the 'new' and 'old' continents. Historian John Darwin may trace in Tamerlaine's empire the beginning of a modern era of empires, but that may not be applicable to every land-based empire. However, Chris Bayly's focus on a modern imperial era dating from the 1770s sounds more persuasive.[23]

It appears that the relationship between Europe and the rest of the world became uneven, complex, hegemonic and discretionary in more recent times and that the erstwhile aspects of conflicts and commonalities were taken over by more institutionalized and intricate forms of control and conquest. The transmutation of colonialism into a more complex imperialism in the nineteenth century, accompanied by neo-racism and the infantilization of non-Western peoples and cultures, along with the creation of a new class of brown sahibs certainly created enduring images of the colonized. In our times, Frantz Fanon, Mahatma Gandhi, Rabindranath Tagore, Nelson Mandela, Mao Zedong, Malcolm X, Aimé Césaire, Muhammad Iqbal, Desmond Tutu, Martin Luther King Jr., Leopold Senghor and other intellectuals and activists have attempted to create a greater sense of equality and empowerment across religious, ethnic and class-based boundaries. Still, despite the independence of the former colonies, a raft of civil rights laws and political correctness in addition to the evolution of the civil societies in the former colonies that unevenness and misimages in its wake still persist. Colonialism might have receded some time back, but military interventions, including sheer invasions and a firm control over global financial, technological and informational institutions disallows the emergence of a postcolonial world based on mutual respect, interdependence and equality. Sadly, in many cases, racist typologies such as Islamophobia; the profiling of non-White communities, especially Muslims; and the cooperation of a postcolonial elite have re-energized this unevenness that grows on historical factors and the geopolitical interests of powerful states. That is why when the term 'globalization', on the heels of Fukuyamian triumphalism, became a new mantra in the 1990s, numerous observers simply viewed it as another name for abrasive Westernism. In any case, the inadequacy of solely modernity-based democracy, discreet control over multilateral institutions and policies, the salience of geopolitical interests over and above the spirit and prerogatives of a global interdependence and invincibility of market-based economy have further exposed the serious problems with this adage.[24]

On the non-Western side, the images and misperceptions about the North or North Atlantic region persist and need serious revisiting to obtain a more dispassionate balance and greater receptivity for sharing the responsibility of the malady at home. For Muslims in particular and the world at large, *West* evokes envy, awe and ambiguity. Its multiple control over global institutions, elites, policies and resources, contrasted with the harrowing issues of poverty, exploitation and violence, becomes even starker. Here, remotely controlled technologies as seen during the two Gulf wars and more recently in Libya and in drone attacks on six Muslim nations underwrite these three major views of the West. While there is an eagerness to acquire Western standards of living (often without westernization!), there also exists a shared sense of inequality and religious divide. The critique comes from both the religious and liberal elite who seek a redress, but in their own respective ways, though both may also idealize resistance of one kind or the other.

With the overall weakness of the liberal traditions, augmented by the issues of coercion and corruption of the local westernized elite, the recourse to Islamism is certainly an ideological as well as an economic fallout of these stark imbalances. Political Islam and Hindutva with their many manifestations reflect the mentioned views and images of the West, and pose as panaceas for manifold issues. It is a different thing that these ideologies may be quite successful in challenging and even *displacing* the systems and status ante, yet are often found wanting in *replacing* systemic wherewithal. The Islamists of various hues and persuasions cite culture, religion and certainly the history of East-West relations to substantiate their case against the *Crusaders, colonials* and *Zionist-Christians*, bound together to humiliate the world of Islam. It is no surprise that their counterparts such as the neocons apply similar typologies from the past while promising utopias in the future.

The above resume is not meant to show that the East-West or the North-South relationship is only one dimensional and perpetually hostage to the forces of negativity and rejection, though ignoring them would be equally at our own peril. Concurrently, it would not be conducive to overlook the inherent unevenness in inter-state and societal schisms, which allow misperceptions a greater role in adding to divisiveness, besides refurbishing extremist forces on all sides to bulldoze 'silent majorities'. Of course, we live in a power-centric world where the strongest military and economic prowess can override multilateral prerogatives, and that is why some people may even yearn for a multipolar world with varied power centres.

National Interests versus Multiple Prerogatives and the EU

Without any irreverence towards the EU and its rootedness in a greater desire for peace and mutual interdependence, the pull factors such as 'distinct' histories, cultures, economies, foreign policy, institutional frameworks and, certainly, the primacy of national interests push it towards positions such as unilateralism, bilateralism (France and Germany earlier on, or the United Kingdom and the United States all along), or even towards sheer introversion in which foreign policy and involvement are vital but not as binding as domestic interests and priorities. The latter model is often seen in Scandinavia, where foreign policy issues are judged under a rather different light unlike France and Britain, though during the first Gulf war and again after September 11 these domestic and global strands converged. In addition, in the case of Afghanistan we have been witnessing the EU-wide alliance that has inducted both Germany and Japan into the longest warfare of their recent histories. However, in all its various agreements and proclamations towards other regions, including Southwest Asia, the EU has highlighted areas of regional peace and development as its two main objectives with trade and aid spawning many of the former. While each EU nation pursues its own policies regarding relations with Afghanistan and Pakistan, and since September 11 areas like terror have gained salience, the common strands across national boundaries can be found geared towards 'state building' and 'capacity building'. Here sectors including peace, education, gender empowerment, equal citizenship rights, control on drugs, migration and even regional cooperation are hoisted as vital domains. In other words, irrespective of the volume of trade and investment by each member state vis-à-vis Afghanistan and Pakistan and the intensity of 'engagement', the EU-wide consensus in certain major areas exists without unleashing any intra-EU conflict or competition. The informal and formal parleys both at the EU level and in Kabul and Islamabad have featured a shared sense of purpose and policy, which can be explained due to warfare with the Taliban. Despite private and popular reservations, the governmental unity in fighting the Taliban and making Afghanistan more amenable to some modicum of modern governance remains a shared objective. In the same vein, Pakistan's territorial integrity, greater peace and neutralization of militant groups keep a broad NATO-EU consensus unshaken and undiminished. With 2014 as the threshold for a 'drawdown', the EU governments were able to pacify their domestic critical and dissenting voices, though everyone felt uncertain about a post-withdrawal scenario. However, the Russo-Ukrainian conflict and the rise of ISIL/ISIS in 2014–15 proved a timely alibi for the Western alliance as public opinion, instead of critiquing expensive and even unneeded engagements in West Asia, was diverted towards newer issues in international politics. Another era of *buzkashi* within Afghanistan, regional contenders vying for influence, Taliban ascendance, or even a regionalized Afghanistan were the possible and no less worrisome scenarios being conjectured at various fora across the EU during 2015. Linked to that were concerns about the capacities of the ANA and its post-2014 role given the 'return' of the Taliban and the Pashtun clusters becoming more salient on both sides of the Durand Line. Concurrently, there was uncertainty about Pakistan's FATA and its future relationship with the rest of the country within the context of an energized Taliban in Afghanistan. But the dismay and exhaustion over an open-ended and inconclusive campaign had certainly engendered a strong element of despair and fatigue in the EU, though one did not witness a sustained debate for alternative approaches towards Muslim regions such as Southwest Asia. A postscript of all the gigantic financial and human expenses incurred in a very long, taxing and often ambivalent and controversial engagement in a challenging region had earlier underpinned a spectre of anxiety, but unlike in the case of the Vietnam War, Europeans, like the Americans and Australians, shirked from any mass-based action.

The EU and Pakistan: Past and Present

The European Economic Community (EEC) and Pakistan entered into a formal treaty agreement in 1962, and consequently this relationship has moved bilaterally as well as multilaterally, involving all the member states. The early phase was quite limited and less visible, yet increased in the 1980s coinciding with two significant developments: firstly, the integration and enlargement of the EEC itself, and secondly, Pakistan's role as the front-line state following the Soviet invasion of Afghanistan in 1979. Other than the presence of about four million Afghan refugees on this side of the Khyber Pass and the more pronounced involvement of certain North Atlantic nations, the ouster of a pro-West shah in Iran in February 1979 made Pakistan a more needed partner in West Asia, though concerns about its nuclear programme also began to figure prominently in the media and other bilateral parleys. Partly, both the United States and the EU nations used this nuclear factor to underwrite their sermonizing on disarmament and also because this kind of pressure and clubbing could make Pakistan more amenable to the Cold

War-related demands of the Western bloc. In addition, such a periodic critique and censoring of Pakistan was meant to allay Indian criticism of Western aid to Pakistan, and thus Pakistanis, criticized for 'not doing enough' against extremists/terrorists, were often baffled by this undiminished spotlighting. They often assumed that the North Atlantic nations were insensitive to Pakistan's security prerogatives vis-à-vis its relationship with a nuclear-capable India and were instead singling them out for their being a predominantly *Muslim* nation pursuing the acquisition of an 'Islamic Bomb'. The French nullification of their treaty with Islamabad for a reprocessing plant in 1976 under US pressure, despite all the security measures and modalities agreed upon and Zulfikar Ali Bhutto's statements regarding Washington's rebuke, created a trust deficit. However, this deficit was often ignored or papered over owing to various convergences over Afghanistan and also because of the ruthless policies of General Zia-ul-Haq's regime that, to a great extent, controlled foreign supplies and assistance to the mujahideen.

It was only in 1985 that the European Commission (EC) established its first office in Islamabad, which was upgraded to a Delegation in 1988, and in 1992, the EC's humanitarian arm opened its office in the country's capital. Subsequent upon the signing of the Lisbon Treaty of December 2009 stipulating significant integration, the Delegation was upgraded, and dealt with development cooperation, trade, humanitarian assistance, energy, the environment and climate change. Run by around 100 staff of various nationalities, the Delegation's head was accredited as an ambassador, who other than dealing with the host government, society at large and NGOs, coordinates the operations of embassies of the 27-member states in Pakistan. The EU and Pakistan are signatories to a number of treaties and memoranda of understanding (MOUs), a tradition that originated in 1976 with the first-ever treaty being signed before its upgrading in 1986, whereas the current nature and realms of relationship are governed under the Cooperation Agreement of 2004. The serious ramifications of September 11, the Western invasion of Afghanistan featuring the cooperation of Pakistan and the economic and related consequences of these events anchored this treaty until the Lisbon Treaty provided imperatives for redefining this relationship. As a result, the EU–Pakistan Five-Year Engagement Plan was signed, which stipulated more assistance and help for the embattled country in addition to developing a common framework to govern subjects such as regional security, counterterrorism, drug trafficking and cooperation in trade and commerce. This treaty also carried the EU's commitment to helping develop Pakistan's civic and democratic institutions along with opening up European markets to more Pakistani goods so that instead of aid, Pakistan can duly benefit from trade.[25] Implementation of these objectives and their assessment were delegated to a joint commission that meets on an annual basis as a monitoring body, steering dialogue on issues like nuclear proliferation, counterterrorism and migration.

It is worth noticing that the EU accounted for 22–25 per cent of Pakistani external trade, totalling 3.4 billion, including textiles, leather, surgical and sports goods, whereas EU exports to Pakistan during 2011–12 totalled around 3.8 billion and consisted of manufactured goods and pharmaceutical and medical products. Following the EU's award of the Generalized System of Preferences (GSP) to Pakistan on 12 December 2013, the country's trade volume was expected to increase considerably. The aggregate

EU assistance to Pakistan since 1976 has been $500 million disbursed through various projects and programmes. Due to parallel contributions from individual countries, with the United Kingdom heading the list both in terms of trade and aid, EU assistance to Pakistan was not extensive until long after the events of 2001. For instance, only 75 million euros had been initially earmarked for 2002–2006, but another $50 million were added due to the country's partnership following the invasion of Afghanistan. The EU also channelled some of its assistance through NGOs along with supporting microfinance small and medium-size enterprises. Following the devastation caused by the earthquake on 8 October 2005 in Azad Kashmir and the Northern Areas, the EU Commission proposed a package of $93.6 million geared towards humanitarian assistance for reconstruction along with helping Afghan refugees. Over the past ten years, EU assistance to Pakistan in areas like rehabilitation and reconstruction has been around $32 million, with most being specified for the KP, where Swat's military operation in 2009 caused the dislocation of two million people from the valley.

On the eve of the first-ever EU-Pakistan Summit held in Brussels on 17 June 2009, Baroness Catherine Ashton, the EU Representative for Foreign Affairs and Security Policy and the Vice-President of the European Commission, visited Islamabad on 4–6 June. In her meetings with President Asif Ali Zardari and other senior officials, closer cooperation in sectors like security, peace and the eradication of poverty through some shared developmental policies was reiterated. Consolidation of a multiparty democratic setup in the country, despite the militancy in Swat and more frequent suicide bombings, reflected new eagerness on both sides. It appeared that unlike during the Pervez Musharraf years, Zardari and Hamid Karzai, at least for a time, were displaying better understanding on regional issues since the EU, given the prolonged instability and volatility in Afghanistan, desired closer cooperation between Kabul and Islamabad instead of trading accusatory charges. The EU-Pakistan Summit included President Zardari and some cabinet members, whereas along with Baroness Ashton, Jose Manuel Barroso and Javier Solana represented Brussels. Understandably, subjects like fighting terrorism, extremism and militancy headed the agenda, with mutual assurances on both sides in the realms of helping civil society, implementing educational reforms and providing better training of the police. In addition, negotiations covered nuclear proliferation, with the EU urging Islamabad's closer interface with the International Atomic Energy Agency. The joint statement reaffirmed support for a secure and stable Pakistan fighting the root causes of violent extremism and radicalization that had caused suffering to the people of Pakistan. Pakistan was promised further humanitarian assistance geared towards rehabilitation processes in the KP as well as an offer of help for good governance, which would include electoral reforms, in accordance with the EU Election Observation Mission. Reportedly, greater encouragement for gender empowerment and human rights also featured under this joint purview. The EU assured its contributions of 485 million by 2013 towards the 17 April Tokyo Declaration of the 'Friends of Democratic Pakistan' that had pledged $5 billion in development assistance. Pakistan's dire energy needs featured in these negotiations, and the EU team committed support in renewable energy area, whereas at Pakistan's insistence they showed more receptivity for a preferential tariff regime (GSP+) on Islamabad's commitment to the ratification of the remaining

UN conventions. For President Zardari, this was certainly quite reassuring and morale boosting at a time when he headed a rather fragile PPP regime, with the KP witnessing daily terror incidents and a vast area of the Malakand Division virtually fallen to the Pakistani Taliban led by Maulvi Fazlullah.[26]

The success of a Swat military operation, which was undertaken by the Pakistani army with political leadership fully backing it from Islamabad and Peshawar, certainly raised Pakistan's profile, and during the worst floods of 2010 the country received significant EU assistance. According to Ashton in August 2010, Pakistan had moved to the top of the EU agenda, though her statement was also meant to repair EU-Pakistan relations, which had recently been impacted by a controversial statement by David Cameron. The British prime minister, in a lecture in India, had lambasted Islamabad for exporting terrorism, which was vocally resented in Pakistan. In a letter to EU foreign ministers in August, while acknowledging the dismay Cameron's statement had caused, an EU official observed to the *Guardian*: 'It damaged the other 26 [EU states] what he said, but it's brought into focus the core issues and the need for a wider and better strategy. Hague himself thought [Cameron's words] were a little naïve and has really backed us in this discussion'. Ashton was reported to have listed the issues Pakistan was confronted with, including floods, terror, development, thorny relations with India and felt that it was 'in the EU's interest that we have a stable and prosperous Pakistan, but also the international community as a whole'. Highlighting some of the issues discussed at the Pakistan-EU summit, she recommended the extension of the reduced tariffs to Pakistan allowing it the GSP, and certainly Pakistan's predicament with floods, internally displaced persons (IDPs) and frequent encounters with violence had softened EU leaders towards a more accommodative attitude towards the Southwest Asian nation.[27]

Contrasted with the US critique of Pakistan amidst more frequent drone attacks, this approach by the EU showed a better understanding of how to engage the country in a more conducive way. While the EU recognized the insidious impact on regional security and cooperation emanating due to Indo-Pakistani schisms, it still encouraged its member states to increase cooperation with Islamabad and Delhi in a mutually exclusive way. Despite his vocal criticism of Pakistan while visiting India, Cameron had also supported more assistance for Islamabad, especially when his country committed itself to a multiyear socio-economic development programme for the latter totalling $800 million. However, the floods of 2010, the British prime minister's criticism and the complex situation in Afghanistan beefed up Pakistan's priority on the EU agenda. The EU's Foreign Policy Division tried to repair the relationship, in addition to rectifying the trust deficit. Here assistance both for rural development and rehabilitation was reiterated along with deliberations in Brussels to help Pakistan in improving its counterterrorism capacities. Supporting the US official line of 'do more' was the obvious objective, though the means and channels were not so abrasive and instead tended to use both individual and EU-wide persuasion without putting Islamabad on the defensive. NATO and Washington preferred to be more direct and accusatory, whereas the EU adopted a low profile and indirect parleys without putting Islamabad, the army's GHQ and the ISI under a negative searchlight.

Other than the EU being Pakistan's largest trade partner accounting for 25 per cent of its exports and 11 per cent of imports, the bilateral trade in 2011 totalled $10.56 billion, with exports accounting for $6.18 billion and imports totalling $4.38 billion. The EU investments for 2010–11 were recorded to the tune of $230 million, and thus both the sides view this relationship as quite crucial and beneficial. EU aid for 2012–13 was around 225 million, mainly centred on rural development, health and governance. Here the evolution of the Pakistani Diaspora has played a crucial role in its various capacities, though the news reports have singularly focused on the issues of radicalization and terror, which are not a choice of the majority. Yet Pakistanis feel impacted by this denigration.

The EU-Pakistan Five-Year Engagement Plan of March 2012, following its endorsement on both sides, delineated the following areas for dialogue geared towards shared objectives:

- political cooperation
- governance and human rights
- trade
- energy
- social cooperation

As delineated in the Pakistan-EU Strategic Dialogue of 4–6 June 2012, published on the eve of a visit by Baroness Ashton, the above objectives, frequent dialogues and the development of a monitoring mechanism became the focal points. The formation of subgroups, assessment of the implementation of the plan, periodic parleys, assurance on the GSP and deliberations on the restoration of suspended NATO supplies as well as concerns over the human rights situation were the main components of this recent round of negotiations.[28] Baroness Ashton's own interview with *Dawn* recognized the upgrading of the relationship, shifting from its erstwhile emphasis on trade and aid to a more political incarnation. She acknowledged Pakistan's regional challenges and dynamics in which issues of security and tackling terrorism were further highlighted. She also saw better prospects for Pakistan in a stable Afghanistan and felt that a broadening of the EU-Pakistan interface in the fiftieth year of bilateralism may augur well for the entire region. She took note of Indo-Pakistani relations, though she seemed to support bilateral negotiations between these neighbours.[29] A year later, applauding Pakistan's elections and a smooth transfer of power from the PPP regime to the ML, the EU's Council on Foreign Relations reiterated its support for Pakistan's efforts towards good governance and the fight against terrorism. More than 100 EU election monitors who, in general, acknowledged their transparency, observed countrywide elections on 11 May 2013.[30] Given this landmark achievement by democratic forces in Pakistan and in view of the EU's better appreciation of Pakistan's domestic and regional imperatives, there was optimism for a more substantive phase in bilateralism.[31] In December 2013, the EU Parliament approved the GSP Plus for Pakistan, permitting many Pakistani commodities an easy entry into the Union. Accordingly, 20 per cent of Pakistani exports were allowed a duty-free entry, whereas 70 per cent would have a reduced tax levy, affording the country a handsome amount in needed foreign exchange by raising the annual trade volume with the EU to $2 billion. The Sharif government presented this as its landmark achievement towards economic reconstruction and development.[32]

Afghanistan and the EU: Warring Allies

The EU's involvement in Afghanistan is more recent, complex, gigantic and no less confusing. Earlier on, amidst sensitivities emanating from East-West rivalry, West European nations had often supported a strong but friendly and conservative regime in Kabul. Over the years, they had worked with the monarchy in Kabul, though its overthrow by Sardar Daud Khan in 1973 raised several concerns. However, with a pro-West shah ensconced in Iran as a regional policeman, and both Pakistan and Turkey closely aligned with the West, such worries did not transmute into major strategic concerns. Staying away from Pakistan-Afghanistan border tussles and dealing with both countries through a low-key diplomacy while keeping them aligned with the West's Cold War postulations underpinned these policies. Individual nation states helped Afghanistan in development sectors by leaving security-related issues largely to the discretion of the United States and Britain. The Saur Revolution and the Soviet invasion in 1978–79 brought in an unprecedented involvement of the North Atlantic nations on the side of the mujahideen and political Islam, and Afghanistan became an active battleground of a heightened cold war until the Soviets withdrew in humiliation and the EU began to focus more on its own immediate neighbourhood. Until 2001, Al-Qaeda and the Taliban were seen as a major irritant yet not a significant security threat, but September 11 and the accentuated US pressure amidst revengeful fury changed the entire geopolitical scenario. During the 1990s and especially during the Taliban era, EU maintained its liaison offices in Peshawar and moved into Afghanistan in 2002 with a major policy initiative for 2003–2007 following the conferences in Bonn, London and Brussels.[33] With the obvious NATO involvement as a warring alliance in Afghanistan, even the newer EU members deputed their troops and military equipment to wage a rather undefined and largely one-sided war that stemmed from revenge and not from any long-term planning and strategizing. Like Britain, other EU nations wanted to be seen as actively participating in this war to establish their own credentials as credible and formidable forces very much in league with the United States. With Russia still not recovered from its own dramatic reincarnation and stalemated in tensions with Georgia, the EU nations wanted to be acknowledged as a confident global actor. However, waging war and funnelling in money and consultants happened concurrently, though over the years, issues of corruption, warlordism and mutual mistrust did not help show any substantial results on the ground. At one level, the EU nations allocated major sums under various heads for the country, but concurrently, their impact was insubstantial, if no less disputatious. White-collar corruption, huge costs for consultancy and a worsening security situation even in the capital rendered the entire programme rather ineffective, and despite looking impressive on paper, the ground realities betrayed a greater sense of despondency.[34]

Amidst an increased anti-Westernism, the EU has certainly faced a dilemma: through its NATO counterpart it was waging war in Afghanistan while concurrently seeking peace, democracy and development in the same country.[35] Ground realities in Kabul and the areas under the control of the Northern Alliance were certainly different, but in the Pashtun regions and distant areas, the suspicion towards non-Muslim forces stayed unabated. Other than these serious contradictions and their anticipated results, the EU has been the second-biggest donor for the Kabul regime and its non-Pashtun alliance. As seen in a British parliamentary report on Afghanistan, the lack of any substantive progress in state building and the eradication of insecurity, especially after the withdrawal in 2014 had already added to fatigue and confusion, which might further increase, given the financial crisis and unpopularity of involvement in Afghanistan and the FATA. The cases against drone attacks and incidents of green on blue, and questions about the continuation of a post-Karzai regime amidst the vulnerabilities of the ANA had further exacerbated uncertainties on all sides. However, the presidential and provincial elections held across Afghanistan on 5 April 2014, with a more than 65 per cent turnout by voters – despite the inclement weather and security threats – re-energized some hopes for a time. Still, for future historians, the multiple involvement by the Western powers – one of the biggest in the post–World War II era – would always prove quizzical, though unlike Vietnam, Algeria or Kenya it might not come back to haunt Western metropolises. Lack of statistics on war-related fatalities especially of civilians, and a continued tradition of resistance and hostility raise several questions about the entire campaign.

While EU publications, especially Strategic Papers and similar reports by the United Nations Development Programme, the Human Rights Commission of Pakistan and the Karachi University's Centre for European Studies offer us copious statistical and related information, there is a still a great need to look at various issues and areas which underlined this complex and ever-growing interaction. Here both the experiences as well as statistics from each member state along with some EU-wide comparison are needed to draw a broad picture. It is true that the perceptions on both (all) sides have been problematic, and here historical burden, augmented by recent geopolitical developments including warfare and interventions further regimented these images. There are groups (Ultra Right, clerical and media based) on all sides which use the issues of immigration, religion and economy to create a sense of mistrust and even fear on all sides. The *Islamization* of Europe and the *Westernization* of the Muslim world could sound far-fetched, but their pernicious and multilayered influences cannot be brushed aside, whether we look at September 11, July 7, the Madrid bombings, large-scale profiling, invasions of various Muslim countries or an undiminished and equally partisan media preoccupation with Islam and Muslims. The world definitely needs better and responsible information on all sides, more channels of mutual understanding and a less trigger-happy aptitude, which may prioritize dialogue and tolerance over and above patronization or sheer denigration. Both the Muslim world and its regions like Southwest Asia, and Europe have to boldly face up to the difficulties of the past and challenges of today, while heading towards more non-interventionist and multilateral approaches. In addition, it may not be just countries like India and Pakistan where people-to-people relationships should be a premier exigency. The developed and prosperous regions including Europe and North America equally require substantial bridge building with the developing world. Remote controlling through some surrogate elite, surveillance or through fighting wars featuring awe and shock, or bombing the skies in the name of global peace, gender empowerment and even cultural uplift will not convince the contrarian and bitter realties on the ground. The EU and its peoples are disturbed by the hardships and inequalities in the Muslim world, but then these have not been totally indigenous developments given the long-time external interventions in those regions. Seeing enemies abroad has sadly led many Western establishments into the rigmarole of hunting for the 'enemy within', which is not a happy spectre whether we seek global peace or domestic integration. Wars and campaigns waged abroad have very powerful domestic components and even accompaniments which need to be readdressed if not in a spirit of some sublime ideals, then at least in the name of sheer national interests.

CONCLUSION: PASHTUN TROUBLED LANDS, UNCERTAIN SOUTHWEST ASIA OR A NEW BEGINNING!

*'This is not our war, it is a foreigners' war; it is based on their goals [...]
America didn't want peace. America should be honest with Afghanistan. What they say and what they do should be the same.'*

Hamid Karzai[1]

'I am a United States Army General, and I lost the Global War on Terrorism.'

Lt. General Daniel Bolger[2]

'Who could have imagined at the end of 2001 that 13 years later the US would be exchanging prisoners with the Taliban? For the US, getting back their only prisoner detaches them further from Afghanistan, the handover of the five leaders is a sign of their legitimacy and strength.'

The Independent[3]

'On initial inspection, Afghanistan has little to commend it as a country worth fighting and dying for. Located in one of the most inhospitable and remote corners of the earth it is the world's fifth poorest state and has become synonymous with instability, terrorism and war.'

Colonel Stuart Tootal of the British Army[4]

'Once, getting very excited, President Karzai told me that, if Musharraf did not accede to some particular demand (I forget what), he, Karzai, would personally head Pashtun march on the Attock bridge across the Indus (the jumping-off point for many invasions in the other direction) and lead an attack into the Punjab itself.'

Ambassador Sherard Cowper-Coles[5]

By 2015, most NATO troops had departed from Afghanistan, and like Iraqis and Libyans, Southwest Asians found themselves bequeathed to the violent forces of disarray. September 11 and its postscript spun an entire vortex of armed trajectories which, despite an avowed hostility towards the 'insidious' West, has metamorphosed into an unending fratricide with ethnic and sectarian violence as its two taxing manifestations. The Afghan Taliban, by virtue of being predominantly Pashtuns, saw themselves bearing the brunt of the West's longest ever military engagement and thus in a plural society like Afghanistan, one could foresee a greater recourse to ethnic particularism. Hamid Karzai, popular in Western metropolises for some time, failed to win over the Pashtuns in addition to causing a major trust deficit in Islamabad. His lack of clarity and courage on reconciling with the Taliban and instead blaming Pakistan for all his domestic woes eventually was followed by a greater mistrust of his Western backers. Though power remained hostage to NATO, ISAF and the Northern Alliance, Ashraf Ghani's greatest challenge remains the re-induction of an ethnic balance and peace within the country. NATO's exit is deemed as a retreat by the Taliban, while some of them may only see in it a well-deserved opportunity to seek out revenge. To others, it might be a reckoning and even a new beginning. In the following pages, while contextualizing these vital global and regional developments, we also take into account how this long-term and immensely costly involvement began to raise some issues within Western circles for review.

Pakistan, an unwilling and equally confused ally in the war on terror, soon turned into a battleground. The jihadists turned back upon the Indus nation, seeking their own pound of flesh, while Washington and Brussels never relented in their pressure on Islamabad, with Delhi watching the gory drama unfold in the Indus lands. The weakening of an official writ became apparent in the FATA and soon in Swat, while Karachi fell back to its own parallel pattern of ethnic and sectarian chaos. While the TTP graduated into an umbrella organization, its constituents such as the LeT, LeJ and Jundullah now operated in even more daredevil ways. Meticulously organized attacks on the army's GHQ, Kamra Air Base, Mehran Naval Base, Karachi Airport, Tarbela Camp and ISI and Federal Investigation Agency (FIA) buildings seemed to become trendsetters for ISIS in its lightning attacks in West Asia. Whereas Generals Ashfaq Kayani and Shuja Pasha had dithered in undertaking a cohesive military campaign in the FATA and Karachi, their successors – Raheel Sharif and Moin Akhtar – spearheaded unremitting and sustained military operations. Simultaneously, the insurgency in Balochistan was brought down to a 'manageable' level by exploiting the volatile differences between the Baloch Liberation Army and United Baloch Army, which surfaced following the death of the charismatic Nawab Khair Bakhsh Marri in June 2014.[6] In their own desperation, the TTP and its affiliates – much like the Afghan Taliban – changed their strategies and intensified targeted attacks on 'soft' institutions such as schools, buses and worship places. Kabul and Islamabad, amidst high-level exchange visits, reiterated joint political and military strategies through intelligence sharing and also sought political and economic support from China. The respective forces of Southwest Asian nation states and political Islam have been engaged in a decisive duel aimed at causing greater harm to the other side, with the polarization already turned into the proverbial Afghan buzkashi. For instance, 2013 turned out to be the most violent year in Pakistan since 2001, when other than ordinary citizens and journalists, politicians from the PPP and ANP were killed in greater numbers. The year 2014 proved costly for Shias and Christians, and ended with the attack on Peshawar's Army Public School in which 146 pupils and teachers were killed by the TTP. In 2015, three major attacks on Shias occurred in Shikarpur, Peshawar and Karachi, followed by the killing of 22 Pashtuns by Baloch militants on 30 May.

Ghani's efforts for parleys with the Taliban could possibly augur a new federal consensus for his country, whereas his attempts to reach out to Islamabad and Beijing may help repair relations with his neighbours. With Beijing and Islamabad willing to help, there is always a possibility of a breakthrough for Af-Pak. Concurrently, other than the military putsch, Pakistan needs a persuasive narrative to counter the steady graph of its own Taliban and several dozen ethnic and sectarian outfits which grow on violence and criminalization. Peace, public safety and economic development will happen only through good governance in both the countries, though greater empowerment of the SAARC may also divert needed resources and energies towards nation building in entire South Asia. In the same vein, policy makers and military strategists in the West need to face up to the long-term consequences of their interventionist policies over and above orientalist dictates since North Atlantic unilateralism simply ends up strengthening a civilizational clash.

The longest-ever war of international and complex dimensions, as pieced together by investigative journalists such as Anand Gopal, has bequeathed its own heroes and villains, though unlike other wars it has not had victors, but rather only losers and a train of legacies.[7] The loss of human life on all sides, the enormity of wounded and war-affected people especially in Southwest Asia, stupendous costs and the destruction of natural resources accompanied by serious cultural and psychological fissures that various faith groups and plural communities continue to experience. Amid a widening chaos in several West Asian regions and with Afghanistan already transformed into an ambiguous and taxing war zone, numerous Western observers, military officials and diplomats have gradually started to urge a *political* solution to the imbroglio, or a plain exit. War weariness has prevailed over the North Atlantic regions, and the lack of any clear policy on Afghanistan after troop withdrawals was seen as sheer drift and indecisiveness. As an ABC-*Washington Post* survey revealed in 2013, only 28 per cent of Americans seemed to be supportive of a campaign in Afghanistan, while former officials and several analysts warned the Obama administration of an Iraq-like implosive situation in the Southwest Asian country.[8] The ascendancy of the Taliban and their presence even in some sections of the nation's capital, and more bloodshed in Pakistan with an aggressive TTP masterminding attacks on military and civil installations and its affiliates, not even sparing mosques, schools and funerals had begun to present a rather disheartening situation all round. Violence on both sides of the Durand Line even during the month of fasting in 2013 appeared to have reached a new nadir. July had already claimed more than 700 lives in sectarian mayhem in Iraq, while in eastern and southern Afghanistan the Taliban mounted more frequent attacks on Afghan forces and ISAF, though the elections held on 5 April 2014 were comparatively peaceful and with a significant turnout.[9] After six months of contestations between Ashraf Ghani and Abdullah Abdullah, the presidential rivals, a power-sharing formula was finally agreed in September through arbitration by US Secretary of State John Kerry, and finally on 30 September they took their oath as the new, post-Karzai executive in Kabul. The cabinet, however, was not complete until the next spring. Under the agreement, Ghani Ahmedzai assumed the powerful position of the president, while Abdullah became the prime minister heading the cabinet yet accountable to the former. The next day, the new government affirmed a security agreement with the United States, which allowed the retention of 10,000 US troops until 2016, with the rest leaving the country over the next few months. Karzai had developed differences with Washington over the last three years of his presidency and persistently refused to sign this agreement, whereas Ghani, a former World Bank official and a finance minister in the post-Taliban government, promised to empower women in his country besides eradicating corruption.[10] Amidst several renewed attacks by the Taliban, the developments in Kabul beckoned both hope and fear, while in the neighbouring Pakistan, the Nawaz Sharif government survived a protracted agitation led by Imran Khan and Maulana Tahir ul Qadri, who had accused the former of corruption and electoral rigging. India under a reinvigorated and newly elected BJP prime minister, Narendra Modi sent mixed messages to a war-weary Pakistan while he sought a higher status for his country given its enhanced political and economic profile.[11]

Slight hopes of a breakthrough for negotiations between the Taliban and the United States in Qatar also did not materialize in 2013 given the long-standing mutual distrust and reservations by the Karzai regime, which seemed to mistrust Pakistan, Washington, London and certainly the Taliban. The Taliban themselves did not want to negotiate with the Karzai regime, which as affirmed by Mullah Omar's Eid message, was not a true representative of the Afghan people and suffered from a serious legitimacy crisis. The negotiations happened amidst hope and fear in 2015, though situation still appeared untenable. Pakistan certainly desired a friendly and peaceful Afghanistan so as to ease its own security situation, which since 2001 had become a two-pronged spectre. It constantly desired a visible Pashtun presence in any newer set-up and, given its long-standing suspicions of India and some of the leaders of the Northern Alliance, would not forego any semblance of interface with the Afghan Taliban. Suspicions and expectations seemed to underlie on all sides, and like in the past, 2015 again ended on a stalemate. Even the hopes for an Indo-Pakistani breakthrough did not happen, largely because of renewed tensions on the LOC and Delhi's own prevarications. The Indo-Pakistani discord was vetoing any progress on Kashmir and Afghanistan, though Ban Ki-moon, the UN Secretary-General, had offered to arbitrate in the event that both the countries agreed to it.[12] Southwest Asia in 2015 remained hostage to the forces of violence emanating from international, ethnic and sectarian dissensions with the Taliban and their affiliates on both sides of the Durand Line operating as pseudoregimes in areas under their tutelage.

Other than the shooting exchanges across the LOC in Kashmir between Indian and Pakistani troops in August, several high-profile incidents of violence and escapades kept occurring frequently, with large sections of the population in Pakistan, Afghanistan and the Indian-controlled Valley ensconced in a pervasive despair.[13] In a spectacular and well-coordinated attacked on the central jail in Dera Ismail Khan in the KP on 29 July 2013, the Taliban insurgents were able to get 250 prisoners released, and despite prior credible intelligence, the security forces including the paramilitaries failed to pre-empt or even defend the break-in by more than a hundred Pakistani Taliban. This event followed a similar major jailbreak in Bannu in April 2012, allowing 400 internees to flee to the hills in the nearby FATA. Some of these inmates had been implicated in serious crimes and were supposedly being kept in maximum security.[14] A few days later, a well-planned suicide attack on a police funeral in Quetta – orchestrated by the TTP or possibly by Baloch separatists – resulted in 40 deaths of quite senior police officials.[15] The well-planned attack occurred on Friday, not only a Sabbath day in the Muslim world but also a time when many Pakistanis were celebrating Eid at the end of Ramadan. Quetta had been just a witness to another orchestrated attack against the Hazara Shias, whereas Peshawar and Karachi continued to face periodic ethnic and sectarian attacks with impunity.[16] The newly installed Sharif administration seemed to be locked in a dilemma on multiple fronts at a time when border forces on both sides of the LOC in Kashmir became engaged in sporadic firing incidents, dampening down hopes for a better relationship between Delhi and Islamabad. Before the elections of May 2013, Nawaz Sharif and Imran Khan were keen on negotiating with the TTP and had demanded an end to CIA-operated drone strikes.[17] Certainly, American missiles might have been killing some selected militants, but they were also radicalizing even more people in Pakistan, Afghanistan and elsewhere, especially from among those who had lost close ones in such predatory attacks.[18] Following the TTP's attack on Army Public School on 16 December 2014, any hope for peaceful negotiations with the Pakistani Taliban died.

As mentioned earlier, amidst a worsening security situation and greater human suffering across the Indus regions, demands for a review of Western policies in Afghanistan had begun to surface in 2012–13. Sandy Gall, a long-time British reporter on Afghanistan and the Near East, offered copious details on 'what went wrong' in Afghanistan especially at Tora Bora and then in Helmand, in addition to the factors behind the general failure of military strategies. He blamed the Bush administration for not mounting a sustained and comprehensive campaign soon after September 11. Moreover, with a thin presence on the ground and that too delegated to the local private Afghan militias, Washington by default helped Osama bin Laden escape into the FATA and then Abbottabad. To the British journalist, the West's banking solely on the Northern Alliance and Karzai did not offer tangible success, as it disallowed any substantial Pashtun co-optation in mainstream politics. Washington, in its pursuit to punish Saddam Hussein, had diverted vital resources to Iraq, which facilitated the Taliban resurgence, duly helped by the Pakistani ISI that viewed the Northern Alliance as only serving its own, and India's interests.[19] Basing his narrative on the failings of the policies pursued by Dick Cheney, Donald Rumsfeld and Tommy Franks, he revisited authors like Peter Bergen and CIA agents, including Gary Berntsen, who blamed the lack of precise and sustained operations for failing to clear the country of Al-Qaeda and the Taliban.[20] It is interesting to note that in his strong rebuke of the Taliban, and despite his sensitivity to the Pashtun population, Gall did not challenge its alienation; instead, like George W. Bush and Tony Blair, he unreservedly acknowledged the Western campaigns as a war against the Taliban. Perhaps, isolating the Taliban from Al-Qaeda through substantive negotiations and inducements, and not solely opting for a militarized policy could have achieved the objectives – something that one hears belatedly from Western commanders and diplomats. By examining the personal accounts of senior British military officials, including Admiral Michael Boyce, Generals Michael Jackson, Richard Dannatt and David Richard and their field commanders in Kabul and Helmand, Gall had sought out failures at various levels such as the shortage of personnel and resources needed for a decisive military campaign in a challenging terrain.

Despite his appreciation for John Reid, Gall is critical of a policy of trivialization of the Afghan campaign, whereas according to the former British defence secretary, the troops were 'to leave [Helmand] without firing a shot'.[21] Gall's sources are 'insiders' –British senior officials with first-hand experience in Helmand – including Henry Worsley, Andrew Mackay, Stuart Tootal, Ed Butler, Frank Kitson and Leo Docherty, who, in some cases, have written about the problematique of the campaign in Afghanistan, or gave statements to the long-awaited Chilcot Inquiry. According to Gall, whose main focus is on the British war strategies and assistance policies, the absence of inter-institutional coordination among the DFID, USAID and their several military counterparts, otherwise geared toward reconstruction and restoration, turned out to be a major handicap in winning over Afghan hearts and minds. Other than these logistical failures often attributed to civil leaders such as Gordon Brown and Rumsfeld, Gall is unsparing of misgovernance and corruption at various levels within the Afghan government. Here, he does not take into consideration the white-collar corruption – the preserve of the armies of consultants and expensive project managers – who, like their Afghan counterparts, did not shirk from pocketing huge sums. To Gall, Pakistan and especially its ISI remain the core problem in Afghanistan since without their covert support for Mullah Omar, Quetta Shura and the Haqqanis, the Taliban could have been decimated a long time back, and here he finds the Indo-Pakistani rivalry as the main cause for Islamabad's alleged support for the Taliban. He does not touch upon the India factor in Afghanistan but, quoting from Matt Waldman's report based on a dozen interviews with the Taliban in Kabul and Kandahar between February and May 2010, he zeroes in on Pakistan both as one of the root causes as well as a solution to the Afghan imbroglio. Highlighting the loss of East Pakistan, Waldman had focused on Pakistani worries of secessionism in the Pashtun regions and hence newer policy postulations: 'Pakistan took steps to counter perceived threat from India and growing Pashtun nationalism. Part of the response was an increasing Islamization of society, reflected in the proliferation of *madrasas,* and greater support for militant Islamist groups that were to be used as proxies in Kashmir and Afghanistan'.[22] Regarding complex developments characterizing Southwest Asia since the 1990s, such a single-factor explanation may always be inadequate as it overlooks Pashtun integration within the countrywide economy, along with professionalization of a major section of this Southwest Asian community. Radicalism of the TTP variety and the defiance of the Afghan Taliban –two distinct and parallel trajectories – cannot be understood only in reference to ISI-led covert support, though some former ISI officials such as Hamid Gul, Imam Tarrar and a few others often expressed their appreciation of the Afghan Taliban.

In recent years, the most serious critique of Western policies in Afghanistan regarding the waging of an unmitigated war against the Taliban even after the apparent neutralization of Al-Qaeda has come from former Western envoys such as Karl Eikenberry,[23] Sherard Cowper-Coles and Nicholas Barrington. A career foreign service officer, Cowper-Coles was sent to Kabul from Saudi Arabia in 2007 as the British ambassador when British troops were already engaged in Helmand amidst frequent reports of British causalities and consequent debate about the very rationale, direction and future course of military campaigns in the country. Subsequently, he left that position to become the UK representative for the Af-Pak region – again another of those ambivalent positions – following the earlier appointment of Richard Holbrooke in that capacity by Washington. The Conservative government in Britain led by David Cameron, apparently, did not feel that enthusiastic for Cowper-Coles, and he left that post after holding it only for nine months. Retirement from the British Foreign Service allowed Cowper-Coles to speak and write about Afghanistan more openly, often reiterating the salience of a political solution to the quagmire by negotiating with all Afghan groups including the Taliban. His views might have looked too radical a few years earlier when Bush and Blair often sounded

CONCLUSION 139

buoyant and even triumphant on Afghanistan, but following the Iraq fiasco and another retreat from yet another Muslim country after long-drawn-out, costly and unpopular warfare, such views did not elicit any major outcry. In addition, it is also worth noting that such critiques of interventionist, military-centred strategies were written by people only during their retirement from endowed civil or military assignments. Pertinent though these views may be, their belatedness only betrayed a kind of whitewash. The fact remains that very few Western officials resigned out of ideological or moral differences with their regimes over polices in Iraq, Libya and Southwest Asia. Instead, several people varying from armed forces to the diplomatic corps, including the huge contingents of consultants, journalists, strategists, think tanks and NGOs flagging democracy, women's rights, universal education and the entire gambit of reconstruction, made careers from these conflicts. It is altogether a painful fact that even after these armies of professionals and specialists had expended billions, both war-torn countries and their respective neighbours such as Syria and Pakistan deteriorated into hotbeds of a million mutinies.

In his post-retirement memoirs, Cowper-Coles finds the Afghan venture purely 'misconceived', which deserved a political approach 'drawing in all the internal and regional parties to a conflict with roots far deeper than the Western intervention of 2001'.[24] Despite a significant hullabaloo and political propaganda regarding turning Afghanistan into a viable state, the results on the ground were found by the former envoy to be to the contrary, as he notes: 'There was virtually nothing to show for five and a half years of Western engagement, apart from the narco-tecture of the drug lords' palaces on stolen land, and an encroaching tide of checkpoints, sandbags and earth-filled barriers of hessian and war mesh'.[25] While finding his bearings in 'Helmandshire', the British ambassador is reminded of the futility of the Western campaigns in Afghanistan by his Russian counterpart, Zamir Kabulov, who confides in him in his own way: 'I have a very warm feeling toverds you, Sheered. You are making ze same mistake as ve did'. A similar view was shared with him and David Miliband by Holbrooke when the latter noted that 'in the Western campaign against the Taliban, we may be fighting the wrong enemy in the wrong country'.[26] But as a conformist and very much part of the establishment, our author was not going to go against the grain, and felt that following 'the humiliation of 9/11, America needed to kick some butt', though one wonders why Britain, Canada, Australia, Japan and the rest of the EU would join the bandwagon without having formulated any major long-term policy alternatives. Cowper-Coles feels that the American troops in mountainous Pashtun areas were sustained either 'by happy pills or the muscular brand of evangelical Christianity promoted by the US Army chaplains, or both'. While positing Pakistanis and Afghans as socially quite similar to each other, he still finds reasons to orientalize the Pashtuns, to whom 'killing foreigners was a kind of national sport – a bit like village cricket in Sussex'. One wonders when was the last time that the Pashtuns ever took to Europe, the Middle East or North America as invaders, though, historically, it has been the other way around. But he is equally aware of the fact that only 3 per cent of the Afghan National Army were Pashtuns from the south, which made reconciliation even more difficult.[27]

He is certainly sensitive to the issues of misgovernance and especially when it comes to the presidential elections of 2009, which proved controversial and strained relations between Karzai and Holbrooke. He, routinely, found the Afghan president confined to a small coterie of advisers and often suffering from a sort of paranoia, especially when it came to Pakistan. Karzai held a 'binary' view of the neighbouring country and expected his allies to choose between Afghanistan and Pakistan, and while 'being viscerally anti-Pakistan, he was profoundly pro-Indian'. This is certainly a very strong observation about the head of his host state that went from a 'hero' to a 'zero' in the eyes of his numerous allies.[28] Karzai certainly had dilemmic relations with his Western backers, to whom he owed his position and safety, but he also resented their authority and unassailable power and, instead, desired to be an effective head of the state in his own right. His love-hate relationship is revealed by the former British ambassador in the middle section of the book especially when things started going wrong for everyone in Afghanistan, and more so when several innocent Afghans were getting killed in allied air strafing. Karzai must have felt that the British and the Americans were trying to dictate to him like the colonial proponents of the 'Forward Policy', and in the process, the Western media and particularly the embedded journalists were only regurgitating official, patriotic and even hyperbolic tunes. The Taliban resurgence, the Helmand fiasco, Karzai's outbursts and intermittent stories of corruption at various levels involving regime officials and Western intermediaries began to find an outlet in leaked reports about the Afghan president, who was accused of suffering from paranoia and exhibiting a bunker mentality. 'Ethnically, he is a lonely Pashtun in a government made up largely of Tajik veterans of the Northern alliance', noted the *Times* on 16 January 2008.[29] Such critical media comments and biting reports on misgovernance and corruption appeared more frequently at a time when Karzai accused the British of assisting the Taliban surreptitiously and had just declared Michael Semple and Mervyn Patterson personae non gratae. Semple, married to a Pakistani and fluent in Pashto and Dari, with extensive links across the region, was the EU Deputy Special Representative, whereas Patterson was the chief political analyst of United Nations Assistance Mission in Afghanistan.

Cowper-Coles's account of his short tenure as Britain's Af-Pak representative is a chronology of his visits and meetings with scores of politicians, diplomats, journalists and academics around the globe. He also discusses his brief interaction with Holbrooke, who appeared to have been sidelined by both the administrations in Washington and Kabul, though he still retained his supporters like Hillary Clinton in the State Department. Towards the end, some of his observations, such as comparison between Western wars in Vietnam and Afghanistan are quite persuasive, though he only focuses on the American aspect, curiously avoiding discussion on the British conundrum. Cowper-Coles does not mince words in acknowledging the fact that a huge proportion of aid either did not get to its intended destinations through a medley of rules or was subsumed by the intermediaries. Yet the facts here are only United States related and again exclude the other donor countries: 'Thus, some 40 per cent of American aid monies allocated to Afghanistan are said to find their way back to the United States, in the forms of consultancy and security contracts, equipment orders, and so on. That is hardly a good way to win Afghan friends and influence Pashtun people. Here, as so often, President Karzai was not wrong in his criticisms'.[30] It would be quite relevant to know whether the EU nations, including Britain with its 'tree-huggers' too noticed such serious discrepancies. Nicholas Barrington retired in 1997 as the British High Commissioner in Islamabad, after completing 37 years at the Foreign and Commonwealth Office with an extensive knowledge of Persian in addition to serving in Iran, Afghanistan and Pakistan since the 1970s. His letters in the British media and two biographical volumes vocally took stock of British and Western policies in Southwest Asia. A critic of the invasion of Iraq and of Blair's unilateralism, Barrington vociferously pleaded the case for negotiations with the Afghan Taliban – long before the publication of Cowper-Coles's memoirs.[31] As mentioned previously, a wide variety of Western analysts belatedly became quite vocal in their reiteration of a political solution to the Afghan crisis through sustained and meaningful negotiations with the Taliban. As witnessed earlier in cases of the African National Congress, the IRA and Basque separatists, direct or third-party negotiations could have been constructive in breaking the logjam. In the same vein, several liberal Pakistanis were not enamoured of parleys with the TTP in view of their serious and genuine concerns about the Taliban model of governance and citizenship, yet neutralizing hostilities and inducting these elements into mainstream politics might retain its dividends. After all, as the following survey shows, the war in Southwest Asia has been a testing and consuming dead end where any kind of sustained and all-encompassing breakthrough for peace could translate into multiple benefits for all.

War without End!

The salience of a policy based on a military surge, drones, midnight raids and an almost complete lack of media coverage from the ground – excluding the embedded type – amidst a growing dismay over the disarray and open-ended nature of this unending warfare allowed the Taliban to be more ebullient. To them, 2014 meant the departure if not the defeat of the biggest and longest military operation ever mounted by NATO and its allies. For Afghans in general, 2015–16 may mean either a totally new era of instability – depending upon which ethnic and ideological cluster group they may come from – while to others it may simply mean uncertainty continuing, albeit under a different name and with newer and older denizens at the helm. Earlier on, NATO forces and US official attention remained zeroed in on the Haqqani group, with Osama bin Laden dead and Mullah Omar almost absent from familiar official statements. Without any rapprochement with the Taliban, Karzai in 2013–14 looked tenuous and even transitional, whereas the Northern Alliance appeared to be holding on in Kabul without weakening its Panjshir fountainhead. In a post-Karzai scenario, in the case of another volatile power contest in Kabul, there could still be a possibility of Karim Khalili's Hazaras and Abdul Rashid Dostum's Uzbeks reverting to the segmentary politics of the 1990s, with Iran and Turkey eager to play even more pronounced roles. A concerned Pakistan might also try to restart its damaged interface with the Taliban whose followers – the TTP – on its side of the border would feel reinvigorated with the triumphal ascendancy of brothers-in-arms. However, in his first-ever visit to Pakistan as president, Ghani remained upbeat following reassurances from Nawaz Sharif and his generals.

Certainly, this is not to deny the episodic or sporadic developments in seeking some semblance of peace in Afghanistan over the years though, in postscript, they virtually failed to transmit any substantive results, leaving Southwest Asia even more volatile and factionalist. As seen earlier, mutual suspicions and dependence on military strategies on all sides, with constant volleys of blame and counterblame, did not concede any centre stage to a negotiated settlement which, other than providing face-saving to the main contenders, could have equally helped some intra-Afghan bridge building. The lack of trans-ethnic consensus and the absence of any enduring NATO-Taliban interface predictably did not augur well for a stable Pakistan or a peaceful Southwestern Asia as a viable postscript to withdrawals or troop reductions. The internal bidding forces long known for mistrust, and often in league with their respective external supporters, appeared to be gearing towards new, taxing great games in the country where peace and security have often refused to stamp their presence. At this crucial juncture, one could periodize variable phases in this 'war on terror' in which polarized parties and fractious enmities have curiously remained the same, though over the years Pakistan itself became another and equally volatile war theatre or arena of various parallel operations. In the latter case, policies pursued by Islamabad towards the FATA-based TTP routinely vacillated between cold and hot phases of operations and negotiations – a pattern one can foresee recurring in the near future. A detailed American report in 2010 had shown that the death toll and casualties on the Pakistani side just from military operations had already exceeded those across the Durand Line: 'Counting losses from Pakistani military operations and US drone strikes, civilian casualties in Pakistan [are] likely [to] exceed in number those in neighbouring Afghanistan'.[32] Despite all the hullabaloo about sovereignty, Pakistan appeared to have allowed the FATA to transform itself from a 'no-man's-land' to a full-fledged 'war land', and ironically relegated it to the proverbial 'badlands' of the colonial years. In the process, excluding Swat, the FATA, to some extent, was ceded to the predatory drone operations at American discretion, while the TTP, for a long time, was able to conjure its own systemic networks and nationwide tentacles. The tribal Pashtuns, like other victims of suicide bombings, target killings and hostage taking, remained locked in between a proverbial devil-and-the-deep-blue-sea situation, without any apparent political or alternative way out of the imbroglio. Even with the NATO withdrawal, the TTP was not expected to surrender its pre-eminence in the FATA and its pronounced role across Pakistan through an effective network of proxies and affiliates which kept the state stalemated on numerous ethnic, sectarian and sheer criminal fronts, along with playing an insidious role in Indo-Pakistani bilateralism. Despite mounting a holistic military operation in North Waziristan in the summer of 2014, the Sharif regime and the Pakistani Army along with the civil society were not so certain of a total neutralization of the TTP and its more than 60 affiliates. More than being the product of regional imbalances, militancy appeared to be both a global and an intra-Muslim development, which needed a long-term dialogue, inclusive developmental programmes and alternative discourse, to wean away younger people from guns and self-immolation.

Periodizing the US-Southwest Asian Quagmire

The various phases of the US-led engagements and entanglements in Afghanistan have been largely anchored on a prioritization of military strategies in which the use of force and some cooperation of 'junior' allies were a preferred modus operandi, ironically pitting the most powerful nations of the world against one of their poorest counterparts. Initially, during the first post–September 11 phase, the US-led campaign, supported by many, justified by an obliging UN and assisted by an enthusiastic EU, betrayed a strong element of vengeance as well as self-righteousness in which an immense usage of firepower and CIA-led bribery for anti-Taliban clusters underscored desired objectives. The goals were mainly to punish both Al-Qaeda and the Taliban concurrently regardless of putting any other alternative strategy in place. This policy worked as the Musharraf regime and the Northern Alliance provided the vanguard as well as the foot soldiers in rounding up the Taliban and Al-Qaeda stragglers, who often ended up at Guantanamo, Bagram, Pull-i-Charkhi and other 'safe houses' across Southwest Asia. During this time, Pakistan was routinely rebuked for auguring peace treaties with its own tribal groups, when it tried to strengthen ties with pro-Islamabad maliks and clerics.

The second phase began inclusive of some political and economic components without the co-opting of affected Pashtun groups, though the military aspect remained preeminent and persistently undiminished. The crowning of Karzai amidst the high-sounding ideals of democracy and women's empowerment had reflected a sense of déjà vu and triumphalism, which now ushered scores of NGOs, 'tree-huggers' and other 'do-gooders' into Kabul, but the basic issues of security and financial resources being adrift began to find sporadic entry in the media.[33] The Bush administration, along with Blair, felt that Afghanistan could still be managed, and in a rush to eliminate Saddam Hussein they now focused on Iraq. In the process both war fronts proved even more problematic. Military might and related engagements, which suffered from legitimacy issues at the moral and popular levels, not only proved exorbitant but were also found acutely lacking in political, social and economic alternatives – the real challenges in both the war zones. Instead, grass-roots radicalization seemed to multiply amidst a grave sense of anger directed at the Western powers and their Muslims allies. This phase helped restore and rehabilitate the Northern Alliance, but several people and groups of a dubious past obtained de facto positions in the set-up in Kabul, leading to a kind of unstated regionalization of the country, with Pashtuns entertaining a serious sense of grief and alienation. Consequently, the traditional Pashtun-non-Pashtun rivalries were acutely rekindled, and Afghanistan soon began to witness guerrilla attacks, increased suicide bombings and target killings of pro-Kabul regional allies. According to the dominant retrospective discourse, the lack of peace and stability – all going against the grain of erstwhile optimism – were attributed to two factors: the war in Iraq and the inability of the Kabul regime to offer a tangible and consensual alternative across the region. In addition, the Taliban were accused of using narco resources to fund their military ventures.

During the third crucial phase, Pakistan was pushed into undertaking military campaigns in the FATA, which, to Musharraf, disallowed the possibility of a direct American interventionism in the country amidst speculative reports on the vulnerability of Pakistani nuclear arms falling to the militants. A bit of arm-twisting of this type along with monetary incentives to the khaki leadership against the backdrop of Musharraf's own vulnerabilities were sufficient enough for Pakistani troops to march into the FATA for the first time since 1947, which proved to be the beginning of a different kind of end, never expected by planners in Rawalpindi. The fourth phase began with Musharraf abysmally isolated and Karzai being routinely rebuked for systemic inefficiencies and endemic corruption. During this phase, the British and American operations in Helmand, contrary to early and equally misplaced optimism, had started to prove costly as more and more Western troops suffered fatalities, along with the TTP now challenging Pakistani resolve and resources across the Durand Line. Not only Musharraf but also even Benazir Bhutto and such other Pakistani leaders and stakeholders had been co-opted to keep an unremitting pressure on the Taliban. Musharraf's ill-planned venture at the Red Mosque in July 2007 to please both the Chinese and the Western critics equally proved inimical since it hastened the emergence of the TTP. Baitullah Mehsud had already brought various regional clerics and militants together and, benefiting from a pervasive anti-Americanism and the Pakistani military's dilemmic situation between its American detractors, critics and Pakistani doubters, he almost rose to the status of Mullah Omar. No wonder, the camera-shy Pashtun from South Waziristan became a self-styled emir, fighting the 'Crusaders' and their paid agents.

The fifth phase of warfare and militancy in Southwest Asia featured the co-opting of the regional warlords needed to shore up grass-roots resistance to the Taliban, who seemed to decisively defy NATO as well as Karzai's writ outside Kabul. While disillusionment with Karzai began to surface quite prominently despite his closer collaboration with the American generals and Zalmay Khalilzad, the peace on the ground became even more untenable. Here Pakistan and its ISI soon began to be seen as part of the problem in the Pashtun regions, and Karzai would not stop short of critiquing Musharraf, who himself felt embattled and even betrayed for not having achieved any breakthrough with India, while several from his own people had been decrying the war on terror as 'not our war'. The banned religio-political outfits succeeded in idealizing the Taliban which was fighting a holy war against the foreign infidels, and the collateral damage costing thousands of Pakistani lives was routinely brushed aside so as to underwrite their sense of martyrdom. The soldiers and generals along with the civil administrators now became the selected targets of the Pakistani Taliban and their allies from across southern Punjab, Swat and elsewhere. The war, instead of winding down, had become more widespread, volatile and immensely destabilizing for two countries. In Pakistan, this was the horrid scenario of a million mutinies with Sunni-Shia, Wahhabi-Sufi, Muslim-Ahmadi, Pashtun-Muhajir and Baloch-Punjabi chasms all turning into parallel volatilities.[34]

The sixth phase in the US-led war in Southwestern Asia began with the advent of the Obama administration as well as the ensconcing of the PPP regime in Islamabad. With a forlorn Musharraf gone, President Asif Ali Zardari surprised his critics by following a conciliatory policy with all his diverse political counterparts, along with softening Kabul's ire, though he followed the GHQ-led dictums on war-related strategies. The severe escalation in suicide bombings, selective attacks on military installations across Pakistan and a rising graph of fatalities amidst basic economic and structural hardships challenged the efficacy of the PPP regime and its ANP partners in the KP. However, the death of Mehsud in a drone attack in August 2009 and greater public support for military operations to wrest control of Swat from Fazlullah and his followers helped affirm Zardari's steadfastness, whose own wife had been presumably killed by the Taliban groups for sharing a closer mutuality with the Western powers in her ideological orientation. Karzai, for a while, stopped criticizing Islamabad for not eradicating the (Afghani) Taliban sanctuaries in the FATA, but now Washington under Barack Obama began to pronounce that critique, and this became the next phase in this drawn-out war on terror in Southwest Asia. However, the resurgence of the Taliban, their persistence in Helmand and well-organized guerrilla attacks against the backdrop of disenchantment in Western public opinion towards this 'unclear' and equally costly war nudged some non-military policymakers in Washington towards seeking some political solutions to the Afghan quagmire. Here, other than the surge, midnight raids by special forces and greater recourse to drone warfare featured 'Obama's war' until speculation about some third-party negotiations began to register a modicum of interest.

This phase, characterized by the seeking of parleys with the 'good' Taliban through some Arab (Saudi and Qatari) interlocutors, made its inception during 2010–11, yet failed to reach any tangible culmination. The Abbottabad operation and an emphasis on training Afghan police and troops were soon prioritized over negotiations with the Taliban, whose fighters had mastered five new effective strategies. Firstly, they seemed to enjoy more support among the rural networks; secondly, the FATA had refused to be pacified, allowing the Taliban unchallenged breathing space; thirdly, the effectiveness of improvised explosive devices had begun to cause serious damage; fourthly, the Haqqanis had proved effective in staging high-profile operations in Kabul and Kandahar; and lastly, but crucially, the Taliban had infiltrated the Afghan police and security forces with green-on-blue attacks becoming more frequent, thus causing increased fatalities as well as demoralization. The Quetta Shura retained links with the Taliban in and around Afghanistan, yet unlike the Haqqanis, it kept a low profile. During this intense phase, interspersed with more violence and the Pakistanis and other vocal groups raising a hue and cry over the drone attacks, Taliban allies began to mount even more deadly ambushes on NATO supply convoys, which eventually were, for a time, scuppered by Pakistan, especially when the TTP started using Afghan soil for its attacks on Pakistan. The proverbial tipping point had come with the killing of 26 soldiers in November 2011 by US troops at the Salala border post in Mohmand Agency, along with the CIA operative Raymond Davis killing two Pakistanis in the busy city of Lahore. The Abbottabad operation by the US Navy SEALs, and other contentious developments during this phase intensified US–Pakistani bickering, and senior American officials including Mike Mullen and Leon Panetta did not shirk from accusing the Pakistani ISI of running a proxy war against their country.[35] Official rhetoric aside on sovereignty and the undesirability of predatory strikes – almost a routine mantra by now – this short interregnum during 2011–12 still helped the PPP regime in reclaiming some lost ground. However, Pakistani civilian and military leaders remained reluctant for an all-out attack on North Waziristan largely because of overstretch in other agencies and also owing to an absence of any forthright change in Washington's policy under an incumbent president battling for re-election. The recent phase features military operations in the FATA, closer collaboration between Kabul and Islamabad and a possible induction of China to help regain some consensus within Afghanistan.

Despite a vivid understanding of Indo–Pakistani schisms and their enduring imprints on the region especially in Afghanistan and Kashmir, as highlighted by advisers like Bruce Riedel, the Obama administration kept avoiding a substantive policy undertaking that could have helped old adversaries break the tense logjam. In this aura of uncertainties, hostilities and vulnerabilities, everyone awaited the rapidly approaching post-drawdown scenarios with a rather grave sense of trepidation. Washington's Afghan policy carried the hallmark of Petraeus–Panetta salience in which the Pentagon and CIA assumed the flagship roles of leading two concurrent wars in Southwestern Asia, with the president routinely signing the 'death warrants' of suspected militants by commissioning missile attacks. The replacement of David Petraeus by John Brennan as the head of the CIA and Panetta's headship of the Pentagon meant even more enthusiastic advocacy for drone warfare and a military-led strategy.[36] The British were equally involved in operating drone strikes, which, according to reports, had accounted to some 300 such operations in Afghanistan, though there has not been any detailed study so far of such British operations in the FATA.[37] The withdrawal of the British garrison from Helmand, leaving behind their extensive landing and residing facilities at Camp Bastion, was finally complete on 24 October 2014, though a civil war situation in Iraq and Syria by then signalled increased American and British involvement in West Asia.

Despite Ghani's appeal for reconciliation made in his first visit to China, the Taliban continued with their attacks, though the global attention now seemed to be more focused on the IS's rapid expansion in the Levant. Ghani's visit to China certainly underlined the recognition of a growing influence of his eastern neighbour, itself imbued with greater economic, energy and geopolitical trajectories, along with his resolve to assuage Beijing's worries about some militants from Sinjiang now aligned with the Afghan and Pakistani Taliban. Beijing had raised similar concerns about militants from the East Turkestan Islamic Movement with Sharif during his visit to China in early November 2014 – a few weeks after Ghani's sojourn. Both the Southwestern countries appeared to repose significant confidence in the Chinese leadership and investments by Beijing in developing infrastructure in areas like mining, energy and trade and possibly the needed political support in facing domestic and regional challenges.[38] In April 2015, Nawaz Sharif and Xi Jinping, the Chinese president, signed several agreements in Islamabad geared towards creating infrastructures such as the road links, railway lines, business centres and energy production schemes in addition to linking China with the Pakistani port of Gwadar. Known as the China–Pakistan Economic Corridor, with a total outlay of $45 billion, there were hopes for a better future in Southwest Asia.[39]

In West Asia, ISIS seemed to follow the Taliban model of undertaking lightning military assaults on territories held by the regimes in Baghdad, Damascus and Irbil, the last being the headquarters of a largely autonomous Sunni Kurdish region in northern Iraq. The former Iraqi Baathists, disgruntled Sunni Iraqis and their supporters from elsewhere had captured vast swaths of land in Iraq and Syria and announced the formation of an Islamic caliphate, promising the restoration of a lost Muslim glory. It appeared as if the borders created by Britain and France – the former colonial states – now faced serious defiance from a new generation of pan-Islamists intent upon restoring the erstwhile Ottoman administrative units in these Kurdish and Arab areas. The Obama administration, confronted by several fronts in South Asia, Middle East and North Africa and often found wanting in terms of any tangible policy options, now appeared to be seeking allies amongst the older enemies such as the Iranian regime, which itself was deeply embroiled in Iraq, Syria, Lebanon and Yemen, trying to shore up its fellow Shia allies who were battling a predominantly Sunni ISIS and similar other radical groups. US–Iranian relations had been sour since 1979, but further nosedived when, following September 11, President Bush included Iran in his 'axis of evil', soon to be followed by attacks on Iranian security forces by Jandullah, an anti-Tehran Sunni militant organization. Abdul Malik Rigi, an Iranian Baloch, who had been often in cahoots with the American intelligence community until he was arrested by Pakistani authorities and handed over to Tehran, led this group.[40] In a major switchover, President Obama in October 2014 sought closer Iranian cooperation by sending a confidential letter to Ayatollah Ali Khamenei urging the latter to help reach an agreement on Iran's nuclear enrichment programme which, until recently, had incurred a severe reprimand from Israel and the United States.[41] After protracted negotiations in Geneva, the Western governments led by Washington were able to hammer out details of a memorandum capping Iranian nuclear research, with the promise of lifting sanctions against Tehran. Largely applauded by many observers, this breakthrough was not liked by Republican politicians in the United States nor by Israel and the Sunni Arab states. It was feared that eventually a Republican-dominated Congress might not ratify the memorandum, leaving Obama's effort at reaching out to Iran in the doldrums. In the meantime, the Saudi–Iranian rivalry appeared to be accentuated due to their dispute over Yemen, Iraq and Syria. Interstate and intrastate conflicts supported by their respective allies in the region appeared to have become a civil war of wider proportions between Shias and Sunnis, with polities and plural communities facing the brunt of an intra-Muslim schism. By 2015, Southwest Asia, however greatly impacted by these developments, seemed to have become a low priority region in global politics.

Southwest Asia: The Way Forward

Post-Karzai, Kabul will have to reach out to the Pashtuns and especially the Taliban so as to build a broad-based consensus, which may even include new political and constitutional reforms in addition to a non-interventionist role by the regional and Western forces. Given the drawn-out warfare with the Taliban, many Western regimes have been reluctant in offering open support to Ghani, yet his main opposition came from the Northern Alliance and such other anti-Taliban clusters. The Taliban staged more than 240 incidents on election day in April 2014, though fatalities were fewer, and even after the installation of the new regime, they kept reminding everyone of their presence by undertaking attacks on security forces in and around Kabul and Jalalabad. It is possible that the Taliban were both suffering from fatigue like the Western governments and pursing a wait-and-watch policy without renouncing their hostility towards Ghani and Abdullah. Simultaneously, the upbeat Taliban detected better opportunities in dealing with the new Kabul regime, especially when its Western backers had opted for a less interventionist role in security matters. Without Western dictates, both the regime and the Taliban had a better chance of negotiating and leading the country towards a sought-after peace, though here the role of the ANA remained quite crucial. Instead of using the ANA against the Taliban, as some external and internal forces preferred, the ideal option all along has been the prioritization of political strategies based on co-optation devoid of confrontationist strategy. In addition, the induction of the Pashtuns into the armed forces is meant to further re-energize Afghanistan's federal system. In other words, a gradualist politics based on negotiations and not on revenge ideally suits Afghanistan and could eventually help co-opt the Taliban as stakeholders in a set-up which may seek its shared roots within a commonly agreed, multi-ethnic framework.

Pakistan, despite its radical turnaround under Musharraf and its eventually finding itself in a nutcracker, has maintained various channels of communications with the Afghan Taliban and avoided any large-scale assault on the Haqqanis, Quetta Shura and other groups on its side of the Durand Line. The Northern Alliance, elements within the Kabul regime and its other backers have long suspected a close Pakistani–Taliban nexus due to Pashtun and India factors – for their own reasons – and that is where substantive efforts are expected from the Kabul regime and also from India and Pakistan to ensure a cohesive and all-encompassing regionalization.[42] While Pakistan must abstain from helping the Taliban-led unilateralism in Afghanistan, India is equally required to avoid arming and assisting a discretionary ANA while spawning an anti-Taliban and anti-Islamabad trajectory.[43] In the same vein, the Kabul regime could ideally pursue watchful neutrality by avoiding involvement in Indo–Pakistani regional rivalries and instead could develop a relationship based on positive engagement. Like Afghanistan, Pakistan's urgency is peace within and around. Here a more thoughtful strategy on dealing with violence is required in which other than the police, army and judiciary, political and economic reforms are needed whereby the FATA, in particular, is fully integrated into the country; the FCR is abolished; economic development is secured and a grass-roots judicial system is fully reinvigorated. While peace parleys with the TTP following the attainment of military objectives could be helpful in neutralizing some of their borderline elements, more robust measures are required to safeguard vulnerable groups across the country from extremist forces. Deweaponization, educational reforms, efficient police and monitoring systems and a greater role for civil society as well as tangible bridge building with all three neighbours – India, Iran and Afghanistan – can certainly allow greater peace and interdependence across the various opinion groups. In the same vein, unrest and disorder in Balochistan and Karachi cannot be left only to the military and ISI-led operations; instead, more holistic systemic reforms harnessing short- and long-term strategies in the spirit of decentralization are urgent. While the country's highest judiciary was vocally helped by the civil society, its lack of reformism at the local and grass-roots levels only disheartened many erstwhile supporters of the superior judges. Legal and judicial reforms have to happen at various levels, and this is a challenge as well as an ideal opportunity for Pakistani politicians to herald a new breakthrough.[44] Both these countries need to undertake vital efforts for peace within, besides resolving their perennial issues of governance so that ordinary people can become stakeholders in peace and development.[45] Here, other than civil society and external forces, domestic consensus through reform, accountability and decentralization has to head the agenda; otherwise, domestic

CONCLUSION

grievances may seek convergence with the regional proclivities and external interventionism, which are already proving too unnerving.

Certainly, the marginalization of the Pashtuns, especially of the secular and moderate elements both in Pakistan and Afghanistan in the preceding decades allowed the resurgence of extremism. The economic and political empowerment of the Pashtuns, especially from war-torn tribal regions can help their reintegration within the national ethos and infrastructure as well as isolating radical groups.[46] Here, instead of mounting punitive campaigns by focusing only on security-related issues, a systemic change in the policies and trajectories is required, which goes beyond the official mantras of 'accommodation' and 'pacification', and in which both Kabul and Islamabad work together over and above partisan expediencies. Kabul's relations with Pakistan require major repair since the latter was deeply concerned about India's growing interest across the Durand Line, where some anti-Islamabad elements such as Pakistani Baloch separatists had been receiving covert financial and political support. In the same manner, Karzai's paranoia about Pakistan and the latter's eagerness for 'strategic depth' have to be shunned by both sides so that reconciliation, reconstruction and the formation of multiple forms of relationship may augur a new beginning for all, and especially for millions of Pashtun victims of this sustained and taxing warfare and militancy. In other words, 2015 signalled older worries and newer hopes for Southwest Asia, though a desire for peace and cooperation resounded even more vocally.

NOTES

Introduction

1. Winston Churchill, *The Story of the Malakand Field Force* (London, Longman Green and Company 1898), quoted in James Fergusson, *Taliban: The True Story of the World's Most Feared Guerrilla Fighters*, (London: Bantam, 2010), 164.
2. John C. Griffiths, *Afghanistan: Land of Conflict and Beauty* (London: Andre Deutsch, 2009), 5.
3. The comment was made following the attack by the Taliban-led Uzbek militants on Karachi Airport on 8 June 2014. See 'Matin', under 'Pakistan's Position on Drones Is Clear: FO', *Dawn*, 12 June 2014.
4. According to a study by Brown University's Watson Institute of International Studies, the war in Afghanistan and Pakistan since September 11 had claimed 149,000 lives as well as wounding 162,000 people. The vast majority of this conservative estimate happens to be civilians. *Dawn*, 2 June 2015.
5. Based on a research study completed at Harvard University in early 2013, the wars in Afghanistan and Iraq had cost the United States $6 trillion, with most of the money going to the care of the war veterans. Prepared by the Nobel Laureate Joseph E. Stiglitz, and Professor Linda J. Blimes, the study shows these two wars being the most expensive ventures, several times over and above the earlier cost estimates. A British daily, in commenting on this report, noted, 'There will be no peace dividend', is the stark conclusion from the 22-page report from the Kennedy School of Government, 'and the legacy of Iraq and Afghanistan wars will be costs that persist for decades'. *Telegraph*, 29 March 2013.
6. Traditionally, during the Cold War decades South Asia was often seen as a peripheral region, though in its final phase, Southwest Asia did become a focal point of a drawn-out warfare. Robert J. McMahon, *The Cold War on the Periphery: The United States, India and Pakistan* (New York: Columbia University Press, 1996). The lower estimate of the British costs for the Afghan campaign as mentioned in the British Parliament, has been £30 billion in development assistance, and £243 billion in security assistance, since 2001. House of Commons International Development Committee, 'Afghanistan: Progress and Prospects after 2014', Sixth Report of Session 2012–13, HC 403 (London: TSO, 25 Oct. 2012), 5. Post-traumatic stress disorder is certainly a major concern for allied troops, and here campaigns in Iraq and Afghanistan have led to numerous suicides and prolonged mental illnesses. Certainly, one cannot obtain such figures for the Afghan, Iraqi and Pakistani population groups, yet under the laws in the North Atlantic regions, one can have access to some statistical information. Figures obtained by the BBC for its investigative programme *Panorama*, reveal that 50 British soldiers committed suicide just in 2012. This was in reference to deployment in Afghanistan and, in fact, exceeded the number of British soldiers killed by the Taliban that year. Out of this total, 21 had committed suicide in Afghanistan while on active duty, and 29 others had taken their lives on return. 'UK Soldier and Veteran Suicides "Outstrip" Afghan Deaths', BBC, 14 July 2013, http://www.bbc.co.uk/news/uk-23259865.
7. Of course, Samuel Huntington's premise reduces history only to a record of conflicts and warfare, while Tariq Ali, given his penchant for a dialectical view of history, may interpret it

as a clash between the Bible-thumping Neo-conservatives and the Salafists such as Al-Qaeda. Tariq Ali, *The Clash of Fundamentalisms: Crusades, Jihad and Modernity* (London: Verso, 2003).
8. According to Bob Woodward, military operations in both Afghanistan and Pakistan (often called Af-Pak in official jargon) became 'Obama's war', in league with 'Bush at War'. See Bob Woodward, *Obama's Wars* (New York: Simon & Schuster, 2011). Some senior advisers such Bruce Riedel, a former CIA official in South Asia, have for quite some time advocated focusing on Pakistan to gain some results in Afghanistan, seeing both countries as congenital twins. Bruce Riedel, *The Search for Al Qaeda: Its Leadership, Ideology, and Future* (Washington, DC: Brookings Institution Press, 2010).
9. This dual view of Muslims seen in a rather reductionist way has been addressed by Mahmood Mamdani and several other Muslim scholars who have often used the Saidian paradigm in their inquiries. See Mahmood Mamdani, *Good Muslim, Bad Muslim: America, the Cold War, and the Roots of Terror* (New York: Pantheon, 2004).
10. Long-time and influential scholars such as Bernard Lewis would refuse to see any positive attribute in the Muslim past and present, viewing Islam as an eternal 'crisis' and a perpetual 'outrage'. These views have received further xenophobic support from writers and propagandists such as Daniel Pipes, Pamela Geller and Robert Spencer, whose outbursts only underline Islamophobic right-wing fascist groups within the West. This is not to say that Muslim commentaries and discourses, despite several original works by intellectuals such as Tariq Ramadan and Khaled Abou El Fadl, are in sync with some of the above-mentioned censoring voices. Ayaan Ali Hirsi, Salman Rushdie, Irshad Manji, Ibn Warraq or other disparate groups of 'ex-Muslims' often echo such derisory views of Islam and Muslim peoples. For an interesting overview using Frantz Fanon as a searchlight, a Muslim academic sees such people, especially from amongst the Iranian Diaspora, often heralding a rather apologetic discourse. Hamid Dabashi, *Brown Skins, White Masks* (London: Pluto, 2011) and *Post-Orientalism: Knowledge and Power in Time of Terror* (New Brunswick: Transaction Publishers, 2009).
11. Paul Berman, *Terror and Liberalism* (New York: W. W. Norton, 2003). Initially, terms like 'Islamism' and 'Islamofascism' would cause a counterargument, but now they are used more routinely since 'political Islam' is seen as a rather more neutral and even mild term, especially when large-scale security campaigns are to be justified.
12. The Frontier Crimes Regulation developed in the 1880s following detailed discussions and research to control the Frontier region, which was still part of Punjab, which itself had been taken over from the Sikhs in the 1840s. To establish a modern form of law and order while borrowing some from customary traditions, these imperial rules have continued to provide a system of indirect government in the FATA even long after independence. Robert Nichols, ed., *The Frontier Crimes Regulation: A History in Documents* (Karachi: Oxford University Press, 2013).
13. Zia ur Rehman and others, 'Governing FATA: The Big Debate', *Dawn*, 6 July 2014, http://www.dawn.com/news/1117447.
14. These tentative figures are based on demographic patterns gathered by the Central Statistic Organization of the Islamic Republic of Afghanistan, http://cso.gov.af/Content/files/Settled%20Population%20by%20Civil%20Division.pdf.But they are contrasted with some others, which claim the population to be around 31 million people, though the last nationwide census in Afghanistan was undertaken in 1979, and since then a province-by-province approach has been followed: http://www.indexmundi.com/afghanistan/population.html.

    According to the Census Organisation of Pakistan, an official body, the country's population, on 4 July 2013 totalled 183,591121: http://www.census.gov.pk/.

    Quoting the UN estimates of 2012, the BBC notes the Afghan population to be around 33 million: http://www.bbc.co.uk/news/world-south-asia-12011353.

    For the Pakistani population, the BBC citation of the UN figures of 2012 finds it to be nearly 180 million: http://www.bbc.co.uk/news/world-south-asia-12965781.
15. Other than historical studies, several recent works on human rights and Indo-Pakistani security issues have spawned interesting comments on Kashmir since the 1990s. See Alastair

Lamb, *Kashmir: A Disputed Legacy, 1846–1990* (Hertingfordbury: Roxford, 1991) and, Victoria Schofield, *Kashmir in Conflict: India, Pakistan and the Unending War* (London: I. B. Tauris, 2010). Nuclearization is vividly linked to the Indo–Pakistani history of discord, quite clearly in the case of Pakistan, though all kinds of exaggerated and even partisan accounts on the subject often call it an Islamic bomb. For instance, Gordon Corera, *Shopping for Bombs: Nuclear Proliferation, Global Insecurity, and the Rise and Fall of the A. Q. Khan Network* (London: Oxford University Press, 2006). The author, a BBC journalist, has certainly depended upon media and Western intelligence reports, shying away from locating South Asian roots behind this competition.

16. For interesting studies devoted to the role of intelligence agencies, see Mohammed Yousaf and Mark Adkin, *Afghanistan: The Bear Trap: The Defeat of a Superpower* (Barnsley: L. Cooper, 2001); George Crile, *My Enemy's Enemy: The Story of the Largest Covert Operation in History. The Arming of the Mujahideen by the CIA* (London: Atlantic Books, 2003); Bob Woodward, *Veil: The Secret Wars of the CIA, 1981–88* (London: Headline, 1988); and Bruce Riedel, *What We Won: America's Secret War in Afghanistan, 1979–89* (Washington, DC: Brookings Institution Press, 2014).

17. This Islamist resurgence was seen not merely as a revivalist paradigm. It was equally interpreted as a rearticulation of an age-old denominational divide between Sunnis and Shias. See Vali Reza Nasr, *The Shia Revival: How Conflicts within Islam Will Shape the Future* (New York: W. W. Norton, 2007).

18. I have discussed these ideological issues in their South Asian and global contexts in my two earlier works: *Jihad, Hindutva and the Taliban: South Asia at the Crossroads* (Karachi: Oxford University Press, 2005) and *Crescent between Cross and Star: Muslims and the West after 9/11* (Karachi: Oxford University Press, 2006).

19. Subrata Mitra, ed., *Ethno-National Movements in South Asia* (Boulder, CO: Westview, 1998).

20. For further details, see Robert G. Wirsing, *India, Pakistan, and the Kashmir Dispute: On Regional Conflict and Its Resolution* (Basingstoke: Macmillan, 1998); *Pakistan's Security under Zia 1977–1988* (Basingstoke: Macmillan, 1991); and Ishtiaq Ahmad, 'Siachen: A By-Product of the Kashmir Dispute and a Catalyst for Its Resolution', *Pakistan Journal of History & Culture*, 27, no. 2 (2006): http://www.nihcr.edu.pk/latest_english_journal/siachen_a_bi-product_of_kashmir_dr_ishtiaq.pdf.

21. Musharraf, of course, has offered his own partisan view of the circumstances leading to the Kargil conflict and apportions blame to Sharif for not showing sufficient courage, while the latter has often blamed the former for his daredevil venture, which seriously isolated the country in the world. See Pervez Musharraf, *In the Line of Fire: A Memoir* (New York: Simon & Schuster, 2006). The BJP, of course, made the Kargil conflict into a major election issue and won a landslide, with both Delhi and Islamabad once again at daggers drawn until, after September 11, Washington modestly tried to restore some normalcy in bilateral relations. Musharraf's own visit to Delhi and Agra, a rather substantive step, failed to achieve any major breakthrough other than a few confidence-building measures until the violent attacks in Mumbai in November 2008 caused a dramatic reversal that is taking its time to thaw. For more on the Pakistani military, foreign policy and militancy, see Husain Haqqani, *Pakistan: Between Mosque and Military* (Lahore: Vanguard Books, 2005); Hassan Abbas, *Pakistan's Drift into Extremism: Allah, the Army and America's War on Terror* (London: Routledge, 2004); Zahid Hussain, *Frontline Pakistan: The Struggle with Militant Islam* (London: I. B. Tauris, 2006); and, Riaz Mohammad Khan, *Afghanistan and Pakistan: Conflict, Extremism, and Resistance to Modernity* (Baltimore: Johns Hopkins University Press, 2011).

22. Under a move that many may call realpolitik or pragmatism, numerous warlords opted to surrender before the Taliban and that is how a kind of superimposed peace returned to rural Afghanistan. In October 2001, amidst military campaigns, Western policy makers followed a similar policy of co-optation of the former regional warlords, and they were showered with money, weapons and positions in the new Karzai-led set-up in Kabul. The emergence of these warlords has only added to the growing weakness of the Kabul regime, and serious

questions about this policy soon came to haunt its backers. Rod Nordland, 'Top Afghans Tied to '90s Carnage, Researchers Say', *New York Times*, 22 July 2012: http://www.nytimes.com/2012/07/23/world/asia/key-afghans-tied-to-mass-killings-in-90s-civil-war.html?_r=0

23. Jason Burke, *On the Road to Kandahar: Travels through Conflict in the Islamic World* (London: Penguin, 2007) and Christina Lamb, *The Sewing Circles of Herat: My Afghan Years* (London: Flamingo, 2003). In her earlier reports and in this work, the British journalist was quite ebullient about the Karzai regime and the post–September 11 developments in Afghanistan, though gradually her reports like those of other Western journalists began to reveal a sense of exhaustion and even despondency.

24. For a recent defence of the Afghan Taliban, see Maulana Samiul Haq, *Afghan Taliban: War of Ideology, Struggle for Peace* (Islamabad: Emel Books, 2015).

25. Often critical in his reports, a Pakistani journalist even felt that Pakistan might be closer to a meltdown. See Ahmed Rashid, *Pakistan on the Brink: The Future of America, Pakistan, and Afghanistan* (London: Allen Lane, 2012); also 'Pakistan: Worse Than We Knew' (a review of *The Wrong Enemy: America in Afghanistan, 2001–2014* by Carlotta Gall) in *New York Review of Books*, 5 July 2014; Pamela Constable, *Playing with Fire: Pakistan at War with Itself* (New York: Random House, 2012).

26. While the United States has been reportedly spending $100 billion a year on its military presence and campaigns in Afghanistan, the expenses for its dozens of other allies from across NATO have been equally significant. For instance, for Britain, other than losing almost 500 soldiers along with several thousand casualties, the total expenditure has been around 37 billion pounds. For a detailed analysis by a former naval intelligence officer with some first-hand experience, see Frank Ledwidge, *Investment in Blood: The True Cost of Britain's Afghan War* (New Haven: Yale University Press, 2014); also, Richard Norton Taylor, 'Afghanistan War Has Cost Britain More Than £37bn, New Book Claims', *Guardian*, 30 May 2013.

27. For further details on Musharraf's coup, the holding of a referendum to become president while still wearing a uniform, and the elections in 2002, see Iftikhar H. Malik, *Pakistan: Democracy, Terror and Building of a Nation* (London: New Holland Publishers, 2010).

28. For further details in a journalistic genre, see Ahmed Rashid, *Taliban: Islam, Oil and the New Great Game in Central Asia* (London: I. B. Tauris, 2002) and Mustafa Hamid and Leah Farrall, *The Arabs at War in Afghanistan* (London: Hurst, 2015).

29. Mark Mazzetti, 'A Secret Deal on Drones, Sealed in Blood', *New York Times*, 6 April 2013.

30. As will be seen later, Pakistan's charismatic political leader, Imran Khan, led marches against drone attacks in 2012, and it became a major issue during the elections in 2013. On his assumption to office, Prime Minister Nawaz Sharif, in his inaugural speech to the new parliament on 5 June 2013, asked for the cessation of drone attacks. *Dawn*, 6 June 2013.

On 20 November 2013, a Predator fired missiles on a seminary in Tall inside Pakistani-settled territory at a time when Sharif was just on his way back from an official visit to the United States.

31. Vali Reza Nasr, *The Indispensable Nation: American Foreign Policy in Retreat* (New York: Anchor Books, 2014).

32. Chuck Todd, *The Stranger: Barack Obama in the White House* (Boston: Little Brown and Company, 2014).

33. For instance, a former senior British general and NATO commander in Afghanistan, David Richard, highlights some of those issues that he had then recorded in his diary. See David Richards, *Taking Command* (London: Headline, 2014).

34. 'The air war in Afghanistan has declined significantly since Petraeus's departure and the end of the troop surge he implemented. But Afghanistan still remains the central battleground for US drone strikes. As of 6 December 2012, the US launched 447 drone strikes in Afghanistan that year, up 5% from 2011'. These aerial attacks have been justified and intensified by President Obama and the CIA Director, John Brennan, on the plea that they were precise and avoided large-scale deaths, though this view has been challenged in a new study by Larry Lewis, a researcher for Center for Naval Research, which has close ties with the US military. It has

been based on figures from mid-2010 to mid-2011, and reports ten times more deaths and casualities than commonly presented. Spencer Akerman, 'US Drone Strikes More Deadly to Afghan Civilians Than Manned Aircraft – Adviser', *Guardian*, 2 July 2013.
35. C. Christine Fair et al., 'The Drone War: Pakistani Public Opposition to American Drone Strikes in Pakistan', Social Science Research Network, December 2012, see: http://papers.ssrn.com/sol3/papers.cfm?abstract_id=2193354. Here the authors make a rather interesting claim that most Pakistanis oppose drone attacks simply because they are misinformed by a specific section of media and opinion makers. Given the wider accessibility to media along with high-profile protest marches across a highly politicized society such as Pakistan, besides the campaigns by relatives and international campaigners such as Reprieve and UN officials, such a premise does not hold any ground. Another recent report also finds drone strikes to be rather beneficial and to curtail violence: Patrick B. Johnston and Anoop Sarbahi, *The Impact of US Drone Strikes on Terrorism in Pakistan and Afghanistan*, April 2015: http://patrickjohnston.info/materials/drones.pdf. Needless to say, both these authors, from the Rand Corporation and the University of California, Los Angeles, respectively, lack the required fieldwork and follow the patterns adopted by the other report mentioned above. It is instructive to see how local authors and artists are using their brush and pen to voice a pervasive sentiment against air strikes. A BBC Urdu report on 4 July 2013 showed this form of creative retort: http://www.bbc.co.uk/urdu/multimedia/2013/07/130704_drone_attack_art_zz.shtml.

    Several reputable organizations, including the Long War Journal, the New America Foundation, and certainly the Bureau of Investigative Journalism and Columbia Law School have frequently exposed the fallacious views about the efficiency of 'taking out' militants through predatory aircraft, and instead have recorded the civilian fatalities along with greater support for militants by proving that these attacks are counterproductive. With more deaths through 'collateral damage', sympathy and support for the insurgents do increase. However, apologists refuse to ascertain the insidious impact of these strikes, and they only echo the CIA's viewpoint on such policies. See C. Christine Fair, 'Ethical and Methodological Issues in Assessing Drones' Civilian Impacts in Pakistan', *Washington Post*, 6 October 2014.
36. In more recent times, Seymour Hersh, in a long article has raised several issues, including possible collaboration between the Inter-Services Intelligence (ISI) and the CIA with Pakistanis fully aware of bin Laden's location, which was allegedly financed by the Saudis. Seymour M. Hersh, 'The Killing of Osama bin Laden', *London Review of Books*, 37, no. 10 (21 May 2015). The White House refuted some of his statements such as concerning the dispersal of bin Laden's body parts over the Hindu-Kush and the absence of any fight at his dwelling or the role of a courier in locating the Arab fugitive. A few days later, a list of bin Laden's reading material was also published, apparently to reinforce the official story, which definitely allocates the entire credit to the CIA and the US Navy SEALs.
37. William Dalrymple, 'Deadly Triangle: India, Pakistan and Afghanistan', Washington, DC, Brookings Institution, June 2013, http://www.brookings.edu/research/essays/2013/deadly-triangle-afghanistan-pakistan-india.
38. For background on ethnic politics in the lower Indus Valley, see Feroz Ahmed, *Ethnicity and Politics in Pakistan* (Karachi: Oxford University Press, 1998); Iftikhar H. Malik, *State and Civil Society in Pakistan: Politics of Authority Ideology and Ethnicity* (Oxford: St. Antony's-Macmillan Series, 1997; and Nichola Khan, *Mohajir Militancy in Pakistan: Violence and Transformation in the Karachi Conflict* (London: Routledge, 2012).
39. Growing economic ties between India and China, along with the high-profile visit by the new Chinese leadership in May 2013, have certainly kept the dispute in a frozen state, yet the claims and counterclaims, in addition to the presence of the Dalai Lama and almost half a million of his Tibetan followers, create a roadblock to a fluent and problem-free bilateralism.
40. For Sino-Pakistani projects signed in April 2015, see Iftikhar H. Malik, 'Hope and Caution: A New Phase in Pak-China Relations', *Turkey Agenda*, 23 April 2015, http://www.turkeyagenda.com/hope-and-caution-a-new-phase-in-pak-china-relations-2333.html,

41. Akbar S. Ahmed, *Millennium and Charisma among Pathans: A Critical Essay in Social Anthropology* (London: Routledge & Kegan Paul, 1976); Nancy Lindisfarne, 'Exceptional Pashtuns? Class Politics, Imperialism and Historiography' a paper presented at a conference in London, 2010; Robert Nichols, *Settling the Frontier: Land, Law and Society in the Peshawar Valley, 1500–1900* (Karachi: Oxford University Press, 2001); and, Mukulika Banerjee, *The Pathan Unarmed: Opposition and Memory in the North-West Frontier* (Oxford: James Currey, 2000).
42. Fredrik Barth, *Political Leadership among the Swat Pathans* (London: Athlone Press, 1959); *Features of Person and Society in Swat* (London: Routledge & Kegan Paul, 1981). For more recent research, see Sultan-i-Rome, *Swat State (1915–1969): From Genesis to Merger* (Karachi: Oxford University Press, 2009).
43. John Keay, *Explorers of the Western Himalayas, 1820–95* (London: John Murray, 1996); Peter Hopkirk, *The Great Game: On Secret Service in High Asia* (Oxford: Oxford University Press, 2001); Victoria Schofield, *Every Rock, Every Hill* (London: Century, 1984); James Spain, *The Way of the Pathans* (Karachi: Oxford University Press, 1972); Alice Albinia, *Empires of the Indus: The Story of a River* (London: John Murray, 2009); and William Dalrymple, *Return of a King: The Battle for Afghanistan* (London: Bloomsbury, 2013).
44. For a wide range of readings, see Mullah Abdul Salam Zaeef, *My Life with the Taliban* (London: Hurst, 2011; Syed Saleem Shahzad, *Inside Al-Qaeda and the Taliban: Beyond Bin Laden and 9/11* (London: Pluto, 2011); and Steve Coll, *Ghost Wars: The Secret History of the CIA, Afghanistan and Bin Laden* (London: Penguin Books, 2005).
45. Samiul Haq, *Afghan Taliban*.
46. For a persuasive commentary on some recent works by Barnett Rubin, Peter Bergen, Vahid Brown and others, see Anatol Lieven, 'Afghanistan: The Way to Peace', *New York Review of Books*, 4 April 2013. Some other works mentioned above are reviewed in our subsequent chapter. Also, Anatol Lieven, 'Pakistan: The Mess We Can't Ignore', *New York Review of Books*, 20 March 2014, http://www.nybooks.com/articles/archives/2014/mar/20/pakistan-mess-we-cant-ignore/.

    Muhammad Iqbal (1875–1938), through his lectures and philosophical poetry, is a pre-eminent intellectual influence who continues to attract a global interest. Professor Fazlur Rahman (1919–1988) immersed himself in traditional Islamic instruction at Deoband and then researched Ibn Sina at Oxford, followed by teaching assignments at Durham and McGill universities. After working in Pakistan during the 1960s, Professor Rahman moved to the University of Chicago and pioneered research on modernity within the Islamic experience. The author of several known works, Rahman remains a pioneer intellectual in the study of Islam and the Middle East. Professor Muhammad Khalid Masud (b. 1939) is a known scholar who has worked in the areas of classical Islamic studies, and other than holding academic positions at McGill and Leiden has been based in Islamabad. For his views on Iqbal, *ijtihaad* and sharia, see *Sharia Today: Essays on Contemporary Issues and Debates in Muslim Societies* (Islamabad: Emel Books, 2013).

    Javed Ahmad Ghamdi (b. 1952) is the author of several works in Urdu and English, and is known for challenging exclusivist orthodoxy. He founded the Al-Mawrid Institute of Islamic Social Sciences in Lahore, and subsequently, due to threats on his life, had to move to Malaysia. His columns and television interviews reach cross-sections of Pakistani reformist groups.
47. A new study by a Pashtun journalist working for Radio Free Europe highlights the lack of political and administrative integration of Pashtuns within the larger state structures on both sides of the Durand Line, where among other factors such as orientalism, a grave sense of disillusionment and alienation has taken root. To him, the marginalization of moderate and secular Pashtuns only allowed the salience of Taliban-like extreme forces. See Abubakar Siddique, *The Pashtun Question: Key to the Future of Pakistan and Afghanistan* (London: Hurst, 2013).
48. It is worthwhile to acknowledge the evolution of an ever-increasing historiography on gender-related issues within the Muslim regions such as Pakistan. Such a discourse, like the civil society

itself, seeks commonalities as well as contrasts with the outside world. For instance, Asma Aftab, *Gender Politics: Falsifying Reality. Feminism: Another Perspective* (Islamabad: Emel Books, 2011).

1 Gandhara Lands: Wrestling with Pashtun Identity and History

1. Rodney Atwood, *The March to Kandahar: Roberts in Afghanistan* (Barnsley, UK: Pen & Sword Military, 2008), 56.
2. The colonial official was involved in the First Anglo–Afghan War (1838–42) and wrote about 'Pathans'. Quoted in Rob Johnson, 'Afghanistan: Unfriendly Fire', *History Today*, July 2012.
3. Charles Allen, *Soldier Sahibs: The Men Who Made the North-West Frontier* (London: John Murray, 2000), 12.
4. In November 2012, long after the military operation and apparent expulsion of the Taliban from Swat, the latter tried to kill Malala, and in the process grievously wounded her for having written the blog. She was rushed to a hospital in Peshawar where her life was saved, yet she had to undergo specialized treatment in a British hospital in Birmingham. She and her family received global media attention as they continued their struggle for the right of universal education for girls. The author has been personally aware of some aspects of the campaign, including Malala's nomination for the Nobel Peace Prize, and her father has been a frequent and lauded speaker at special meetings in London and Oxford during 2012–13. Also, Malala Yousafzai, *I Am Malala* (London: Weidenfeld & Nicolson, 2013). On 10 October 2014, Malala Yousafzai was awarded the Nobel Peace Prize for 2014, and at 17 she is the youngest Nobel laureate.
5. Based on personal interviews in Pakistan and elsewhere; also gleaned from Internet reports and comments.
6. Khadim Hussain, *The Militant Discourse* (Islamabad: Amazon, 2013). Kindle edition.
7. It is quite pertinent to note that inhabitants of the upper Swat Valley are not strictly Pashtun and, in the same way, many *Punjabi* Taliban from Southern Punjab come from altogether non-Pashtun ethnic configurations. So, at one level, the TTP may be a largely Pashtun-led umbrella group based and operative in Pashtun areas, yet it has drawn a cadre of non-Pashtun supporters as well who, with their own idea of jihad, imbued with anti-Shia and anti-India sentiments, joined the former.
8. For an extensive discussion, see Peter Bergen, ed., *Talibanistan: Negotiating the Borders between Terror, Politics, and Religion* (New York: Oxford University Press, 2013).
9. For the Arab dimension of Al-Qaeda and its wider coalitions amidst the Western operations in Afghanistan and Iraq, see Camille Tawil, *Brothers in Arms: Al-Qaida and the Arab Jihadists* (London: Saqi, 2010).
10. Ghani, like the other Western regimes was worried about a vacuum in his country that could only help forces intent upon destabilizing it. On their side, the Chinese did not want Afghanistan to become a hotbed of militants, including their own rebels from Sinkiang. See Zalmay Khalilzad, 'Why Afghanistan Courts China?' *New York Times*, 3 November 2014.
11. More than 100 Pakistani civilians and several members of paramilitary forces – the Pakistani Rangers – were grievously injured in this well-organized attack, which made banner headlines across the world media. The selection of the sensitive site, and the capability to mount the terrorist plan through a young volunteer, causing maximum human losses, allowed the TTP the desired publicity when global attention was more focused on northern Syria and ISIS. It also showed the vulnerability of the Pakistanis security apparatus, which despite some early warnings to the effect, had been once again found wanting in professional vigilance. *Guardian*, 3 November 2014.
12. The Deobandi mosque had enjoyed closer relations with the Afghan mujahideen during the 1980s and had also established a seminary for women, called Jamia Hafsa. During the military

operation in June 2007, several students, who in most cases came from the KP, were killed in crossfire between the military and the militants. The events hastened the emergence of the TTP, and as late as 2013, its impact could be felt in various acts of militancy in the country. For instance, on 22 June 2013, a group of militants posing as Gilgit Scouts attacked a hotel at the mountaineering base camp often used by climbers for Nanga Parbat. In a meticulously organized operation in an otherwise difficult terrain, the militants were able to kill ten foreign mountaineers and one from Pakistan, for which the TTP claimed responsibility. Its Jund-i-Hafsa, named after the seminary, had mounted the attack, and included both the Pashtun and Punjabi Taliban. *Dawn*, 24 June 2013.

13. The TTP factions such as Jundullah/Jundallah (JuA) and Jamaat-ul-Ahrar (JA) seriously differed over their respective loyalty to Mullah Omar and ISIS, and following the suicide bomb attack on 2 November 2014 at the Wagah border post, both factions concurrently claimed the credit for carrying it out. *Dawn*, 3 November 2014. Earlier, in a major suicide bomb attack on 22 September 2013 at a church in Peshawar, masterminded by Jundullah, 124 Pakistani Christian worshippers had lost their lives. Jundullah has been carrying out attacks on Shias in Quetta and Gilgit-Baltistan and, according to some opinion groups, had replaced LeJ as a major militant sectarian outfit. The JA comprises the former TTP leaders such as Ihasanullah Ihsan and Omar Khurasani, who separated from the TTP and Jundullah in August 2014 to support the caliphate proclaimed by the IS. This group was reportedly based in the Bajaur, Mohmand and Khyber regions within the FATA.

14. In a rather damning and judgemental piece, Christopher Hitchens, echoing Salman Rushdie's view of Pakistan, challenged the rationale of US–Pakistani relations, while not finding anything positive in the Muslim country itself, whose accompanying map was shown as being under the threatening shadow of a bearded cleric. He observed:

> 'Here is a society where rape is not a crime. It is a *punishment*. Women can be *sentenced* to be raped, by tribal and religious kangaroo courts, if even a rumor of their immodesty brings shame on their menfolk. In such an obscenely distorted context, the counterpart term to shame – which is the noble word "honor" – becomes most commonly associated with the word "killing." Moral courage consists of the willingness to butcher your own daughter.
>
> 'If the most elemental of human instincts becomes warped in this bizarre manner, other morbid symptoms will disclose themselves as well. Thus, President Asif Ali Zardari cringes daily in front of the forces who [sic] openly murdered his wife, Benazir Bhutto, and who then contemptuously ordered the crime scene cleansed with fire hoses, as if to spit even on the pretense of an investigation. A man so lacking in pride – indeed lacking in manliness – will seek desperately to compensate in other ways. Swelling his puny chest even more, he promises to resist the mighty United States, and to defend Pakistan's holy "sovereignty." This puffery and posing might perhaps possess a rag of credibility if he and his fellow middlemen were not avidly ingesting $3 billion worth of American subsidies every year'. Christopher Hitchens, 'From Abbottabad to Worse, *Vanity Fair*, July 2011.

For a rejoinder, see Christine Fair, 'The Road from Abbottabad Leads to Lame Analysis', *Huffington Post*, 21 June 2011, http://www.huffingtonpost.com/c-christine-fair/.

15. Several issues have been raised about the official American narrative on this mission and also because the Pakistani Army and the Inter-Services Intelligence (ISI) have publicly avoided releasing all the details related to this operation. Four years later, Seymour Hersh's article reawakened some of those questions. See Seymour M. Hersh, 'The Killing of Osama bin Laden', *London Review of Books*, 21 May 2015.

16. Like the Karzai regime, several Western journalists, ironically echoed by some in the Afghan media, routinely blamed Pakistan for the instability in Afghanistan. Carlotta Gall, *The Wrong Enemy: America in Afghanistan, 2001–2014* (New York: Houghton Mifflin Harcourt, 2014); also, 'What Pakistan Knew about Bin Laden', *New York Times Magazine*, 19 March 2014.

17. General (retd.) Shuja Pasha, the head of the ISI, blamed politicians for not being sensitive to nation's exigencies and lacking dynamism and leadership qualities, though the fact remains that Bin Laden had been living in the KP for almost a decade with his large family and even moving between towns of Peshawar, Haripur and Abbottabad. The report went beyond being a mere 'white wash'. *The Guardian*, 9 July 2013. For the complete text of the Abbottabad Commission Report, see http://www.aljazeera.com/indepth/spotlight/binladenfiles/http://www.aljazeera.com/indepth/spotlight/binladenfiles/.
18. Raymond Davies was allegedly being followed by two Pakistanis on motorbikes, and at a busy intersection, he shot them down, though as per protocol, diplomats are not supposed to carry weapons with them. Another US embassy car, while trying to reach the scene, killed a passerby, and despite the arrests and extensive media coverage, neither Davis nor any of his colleagues faced a proper trial in either country. Davis was released in March 2011 and allowed to return to the United States. 'CIA contractor Ray Davis Freed over Pakistan Killing'. BBC Online News, 16 March, 2011, http://www.bbc.co.uk/news/world-south-asia-12757244.
19. Navi Pillay, the UN High Commissioner for Human Rights, at the end of a four-day visit to Pakistan in early June 2012, called for a UN-led investigation of these missile attacks, which have on average targeted tribal areas once every four days under President Barack Obama. 'US Drone Attacks in Pakistan: UN Backs Probe into Civilian Casualties', *Express Pakistan Tribune*, 7 June 2012, www.tribune.com.pk.
20. Following his visit to Delhi, the US secretary of defense arrived in Kabul on 7 June on an unannounced visit and exhorted Pakistan to undertake punitive action against the Haqqani group, deemed to be based in North Waziristan. A day after the suicide attack in Kandahar, which had claimed 24 Afghan lives, he observed, 'We are reaching the limits of our patience here'. http://www.bbc.co.uk/news/world-asia-18350766.

    The former CIA director and secretary of defense has further elaborated on these developments in his recent biography. See Leon Panetta, *Worthy Fights: A Memoir of Leadership in War and Peace* (Harmondsworth: Penguin, 2014).
21. *The News International*, 3 July 2013.
22. The ANP and independent candidates were the main targets of this TTP-led violence, as has been documented in a report by the Pakistan Institute of Peace Studies (PIPS), Islamabad:' "298 people lost their lives and 885 others were injured across Pakistan between January 1 and May 15 in 148 reported terrorist attacks on political leaders, workers and voters, besides 97 incidents of political violence", said the report titled "Elections and Violence Monitoring Report"'. *The Express Tribune*, 25 May 2013. According to the above source, most of the killings happened in Karachi, though, unlike the KP, all such assassinations in Pakistan's biggest city cannot be attributed only to the TTP. For more on PIPS and its reports, see http://www.san-pips.com.
23. This temporary accommodation towards Imran Khan's party (TIP) soon dissolved into thin air as, following elections, two of his legislators were gunned down in Hangu and Mardan. The latter incident involved a suicide bombing during funeral prayers on 18 June 2013, causing 30 deaths and numerous casualties.
24. In general, 60 per cent Pakistanis came out to cast their votes, giving a strong rebuke to such threats, and in Swat itself, a record number of girls began attending school, while art activities and tourism equally caught up on an unprecedented scale. For details, see BBC World Service-Asia (online), 13 May 2013.
25. BBC Urdu Service, monitored in Oxford, 15 June 2013, http://www.bbc.co.uk/urdu/pakistan/2013/06/130615_ziarat_residency_rk.shtml; and Al-Jazeera (English), 15 June 2013 (www.aljazeera.com).
26. A comment the next day in a leading English daily suggested that both a peaceful dialogue and a concerted cleansing operation needed to zero in on the FATA and the TTP. Despite the non-monolithic character of the TTP and other affiliates, their ideological and foregoing policy postulations seem to show a kind of consensus which the new government will have

to harness: 'The TTP's demands are the most critical aspect of the issue. Reportedly, among other things the militants want the non-interference of Pakistan in the Afghan conflict as well as constitutional and foreign policy changes in accordance with their interpretation of Quran and Sunnah. The militants also call for a war of "revenge" against India'. Muhammad Amir Rana, 'The Dilemma of Talks', *Dawn*, 16 June 2013.
27. For further details, see Tahir Kamran, 'Contextualizing Sectarian Militancy in Pakistan: A Case Study of Jhang', *Journal of Islamic Studies* 20, no. 1 (2009): 55–85; Mariam Abou Zahab, 'The Regional Dimension of Sectarian Conflicts in Pakistan', in *Pakistan: Nationalism without a Nation*, ed. Christophe Jaffrelot (London: Zed Books, 2002); and Andreas T. Rieck, *The Shias of Pakistan: An Assertive and Beleaguered Minority* (London: C. Hurst, 2013).
28. 'Quetta: Shia Hazaras Refuse to Bury Pakistan Bomb Dead', BBC (online), 18 February 2013, http://www.bbc.co.uk/news/world-asia-21495975.

    The Hazaras have been well integrated into the Pakistani educational and economic sectors, and other than sectarian and ethnic xenophobia, their achievements have caused serious jealousies at the local level. It is worth noting that Pakistan's first woman pilot in the air force is a Hazara and that the country's second commander-in-chief, Muhammad Musa, was a Hazara. A Pakistani-Canadian academic found the Shia situation quite exasperating in the country: Murtaza Haider, 'Time for Shias to leave Pakistan', *Dawn*, 18 February 2013.
29. On 21 June, a suicide bomber hit a Shia mosque in Peshawar and killed 10 people in addition to injuring dozens of other worshippers. The human loss could have been even greater if the suicide bomber had been able to reach the prayer area since on his entry, he was seen brandishing a pistol and was challenged by a worshipper. To avoid being captured, he blew himself up, but not without causing such a large-scale atrocity on the Muslim Sabbath. On 30 June, there were bomb blasts in Hazara Town in Quetta, which killed around 30 people along with grievously injuring many more. More than 1,000 Hazaras had been killed by December 2012, while their death toll in just the first half of 2013 was above 300, causing many of them to move out of Quetta and seek shelter elsewhere, including Australia. *Dawn*, 1 July 2013. In March 2014, a rather unknown group, Ahrarul Hind, claimed t responsibility for bomb blasts in Islamabad's courts and at security posts in Peshawar as a part of their revenge campaign. The killings in Shikarpur, Peshawar and Karachi in 2015 showed the resilience of anti-Shia outfits, which identified themselves as Jundullah and showed an affinity with ISIS.
30. A nationalist Indian journalist has even opted for such a term to title his recent work. See M. J. Akbar, *Tinderbox: Past and Future of Pakistan* (Delhi: Harper Perennial, 2012).
31. For a historical survey of Afghanistan, see Edgar O'Balance, *Afghan Wars: Battles in a Hostile Land: 1839 to the Present* (Oxford: Brassey's, 2003); Louis Dupree, *Afghanistan* (Princeton: Princeton University Press, 1980); Barnett Rubin, *The Search for Peace in Afghanistan: From Buffer State to Failed State* (London: Yale University Press, 1995); and Olivier Roy, *Islam and the Resistance in Afghanistan* (Cambridge: Cambridge University Press, 1990).

    For a quick outline of the various Afghan parties and their leadership, see http://www.afghan-web.com/politics/parties.html
32. Before his mysterious death, either by some pro-Taliban militants or by Pakistani intelligence agencies in 2011, Syed Saleem Shahzad, a well-informed journalist, offered a first-hand and 'globalized' perspective on the Taliban in which both Al-Qaeda and the Taliban become two sides of the same coin. His information on trans-Indus groups and individuals is certainly comprehensive. See, Syed Saleem Shahzad, *Inside Al-Qaeda and the Taliban: Beyond Bin Laden and 9/11,* London: Pluto, 2011. Militants and security forces had killed about 50 Pakistani journalists during the post–September 11 years.
33. Other than the 'green over blue attacks' undertaken by Afghan troops against their NATO counterparts, September 11, July 7, the Bali bombings, the Madrid blasts, the Mumbai attacks, the Boston Marathon bombings and the organized massacres of Pakistani and Afghani troops over the past several years are owed to a 'middle-class Taliban cluster'. Faisal Shahzad

(2010), Ilyas Kashmiri of Mehran notoriety (2011) and the killers of Advocate Zulfiqar Ali Chaudhary (3 May 2013) have been well-educated scions of some upper-middle-class families of professionals who became radicalized due to a strong religio-political motivation. Faisal Shahzad's father was a retired air marshal in the Pakistani air force, and the Pashtun scientist lived in New Jersey with his wife and family. He was arrested while boarding a plane after parking an explosive-laden truck in Times Square in 2010. As Shahzad confessed during his trial in Manhattan, he was seeking revenge for fellow Muslims who had died in drone attacks in Southwest Asia. Ilyas Kashmiri opposed Musharraf's decision to turn the tables on the Taliban and was further inflamed by Indian attacks on Azad Kashmiri villages and the resultant gang rapes of women who were kidnapped by Indian soldiers. He came closer to Osama bin Laden and, following his murder in Abbottabad, Kashmiri led an organized attack on the Pakistani navy's Mehran Base, destroying two Orion aircraft and killing several troops. Zulfiqar Ali Chaudhry had been pursuing Benazir Bhutto's murder case and was killed by a pro-TTP team led by Omar Abdullah, a graduate militant. Abdullah is the son of a retired colonel who, in fact, planned to kill Musharraf in 2003 and had been court martialled. Omar Abdullah was found in a hospital after suffering injuries during his attack on Barrister Chaudhry on 3 May 2013. 'Suspect Held over Murder of Pakistan Prosecutor Chaudhry Zulfiqar Ali', BBC World Service, 'Asia News', 14 June 2013, http://www.bbc.co.uk/news/world-asia-22905387

34. For this later view, see Alex Strick Van Linschoten and Felix Kuehn, *An Enemy We Created: The Myth of the Taliban-Al-Qaeda Merger in Afghanistan, 1970–2010* (London: Hurst, 2011).
35. Drones have found many cheerleaders from amongst American academia as well who feel that they are the best and most efficient means of deterring and eliminating acts of terror. See Patrick B. Johnston and Anoop Sarbhi, 'The Impact of U.S. Drone Strikes on Terrorism in Pakistan', 25 February 2012, http://patrickjohnston.info/materials/drones.pdf; and, Christine Fair, 'The "Drone Papers" Do Not Reflect All Drone Programs, Especially in Pakistan', *The Huffington Post*, 28 October 2015, http://www.huffingtonpost.com/c-christine-fair/drone-papers-do-not-reflect-pakistan_b_8392652.html.
36. Jo Becker and Scott Shane, 'Secret "Kill List" Proves a Test of Obama's Principles and Will', *New York Times*, 29 May 2012.
37. 'But it's one thing to see murders planned on television and quite another to read that this planning session is occurring in the White House Situation Room in January, 2010, and that President Obama has assumed the grim responsibility of casting the final vote on every death sentence that this jury (so obviously outside traditional legal channels) is handing down.' Francine Prose, 'Getting them Dead', *New York Review of Books* (a blog), 6 June 2012; also Muhammad Idrees Ahmad, 'How Pakistan Can Stop Drone Strikes?' *The Atlantic*, 3 July 2013.
38. 'In years to come, historians will ask how America – after its defeat in Iraq and its humiliating withdrawal from Afghanistan scheduled for 2014 – could have so blithely aligned itself with one side in a titanic Islamic struggle stretching back to the seventh century death of the Prophet Mohamed'. Robert Fisk, 'US urges UK and France to Join in Supplying Arms to Syrian Rebels as MPs Fear That UK Will Be Drawn into Growing Conflict'. *The Independent*, 17 June 2013.
39. Rodric Braithwaite, *Afgansty: The Russians in Afghanistan, 1979–89* (London: Profile, 2011).
40. Other than recent migrations, Pashtun families settled in several cities of India, and for a while, along with some Peshawari families, provided a long line of Bollywood heroes. There have been princely states in British India seeking ancestry from trans-Indus regions. In addition, in Punjab's districts of Attock, Multan and Mianwali, a sizeable number of local residents seek Pashtun ancestry. The Chachis of Attock, Niazis of Mianwali and Durranis of Multan make visible family-based networks of local influentials. Cricket-turned politician and a charismatic leader for younger Pakistanis and women, Imran Khan has often prided himself on his Niazi Pashtun roots going all the way back to |Waziristan. See, Imran Khan, *Warrior Race: A Journey*

through the Land of the Tribal Pathans (London: Chatto & Windus, 1993), and *Pakistan: A Personal Journey* (London: Bantam, 2012).

41. Olaf Caroe, *The Pathans, 550 B.C.–A.D. 1957* (reprint, Oxford: Oxford University Press, 1983).
42. The famous best-selling novel *The Kite Runner*, by Khaled Hosseini, in its initial section, hints towards these ethnic chasms, especially the biases against Shia Hazaras. Khaled Hosseini, *The Kite Runner* (London: Bloomsbury, 2004). Sayed Asghar Mousavi, *The Hazaras of Afghanistan: An Historical, Cultural, Economic and Political Study* (Richmond, Surrey: Curzon, 1998).
43. For a more recent account of the First Anglo-Afghan War, see William Dalrymple, *Return of a King: The Battle for Afghanistan* (London: Bloomsbury, 2013). For some other works focusing on the British Empire in a rather celebratory way, see H. L. Nevill, *North-West Frontier: British and Indian Army Campaigns on the North-West Frontier of India, 1849–1908* (London: John Murray, 1912); Winston Churchill, *The Story of Malakand Field Force* (London: Longmans, 1898); A. P. Newton, *A Hundred Years of the British Empire* (London: Duckworth 1940). For some other works from the colonial era representing the views of spies, military officials, diplomats and others, see Alexander Burnes, *Travels into Bokhara*, 3 vols. (London: Murray, 1834); *Cabool. Being a Personal Narrative of a Journey to, and Residence in that City in the Years 1836, 7 and 8* (London: Murray, 1842); Arthur Conolly, *Journey to the North of India, Overland from England, Through Russia, Persia and Affghaunistaun*, 2 vols. (London: R. Bentley, 1834); Patrick Macrory, *Signal Catastrophe: The Retreat from Kabul, 1842*, (London: Hodder & Stoughton, 1966); William Moorcroft and G. Trebeck, *Travels in the Himalayan Provinces of Hindoostan and the Punjab*, 2 vols. (London: John Murray, 1841); G. Pottinger, *The Afghan Connection. The Extraordinary Adventures of Major Eldred Pottinger*, (Edinburgh: Scottish Academic Press, 1983); and, Florentia Wynch Sale, *Journal of Disasters in Affghanistan, 1841–2* (London: John Murray, 1843).
44. For an overview see, Michael Barthorp, *Afghan Wars: And the North-West Frontier 1839–1947* (London: Cassell, 2002); Jules Stewart, *The Savage Border: The History of the North-West Frontier* (Stroud: Sutton, 2007). Also, Peter Hopkirk, *The Great Game: On Secret Service in High Asia* (London: John Murray, 2006); Elphinstone Mountstuart, *An Account of the Kingdom of Caubul and Its Dependencies in Persia, Tartary and India* (London: Richard Bentley, 1839); E. Cadogan, *The India We Saw* (London: John Murray, 1933); C. C. Davies, *The Problem of the North-West Frontier, 1890–1908 with a Survey of Policy since 1849* (London: Curzon Press, 1974); W. R. Lawrence, *The India We Served* (London: Cassell and Co, 1928).
45. Rudyard Kipling contributed extensively on the Frontier-related themes in his fiction and poetry, whereas the missionaries and generals left their own narratives, which, like recent travelogues, offer an entire spectrum of interesting historiography. See Rudyard Kipling, *Kim* (reprint, London: Dent, 1994); G. S. Robertson, *The Kafirs of the Hindu-Kush* (London: Lawrence & Bullen, 1900); Aurel Stein, *On Alexander's Track to the Indus: Personal Narrative of Exploration on the North-west Frontier of India* (London: Macmillan, 1929); George Campbell, *The Afghan Frontier* (London: E. Stanford, 1879); Lowell Thomas, *Seeing India with Lowell Thomas* (New York: The Saalfield Publishing Company, 1936); (Lord) Frederick S. R. Roberts, *Forty-One Years in India*, 2 vols. (London: Richard Bentley, 1898); Alice M. Pennell, *Pennell of the Afghan Frontier: The Life of Theodore Leighton Pennell* (London: Seeley, Service, 1914); Eric Newby, *A Short Walk in the Hindu Kush* (London: HarperPress, 2010); Geoffrey Moorhouse, *To the Frontier* (Falmouth: Coronet Books, 1986); Victoria Schofield, *Afghan Frontier: Feuding and Fighting in Central Asia* (London: Tauris, 2003); Kathleen Jamie, *Among Muslims: Meeting at the Frontiers of Pakistan* (London: Tauris Parke Paperbacks, 2003); and Rory Stewart, *The Places in Between* (London: Picador, 2014).
46. According to Sir Campbell, by going beyond the Indus, the British had 'overstepped natural ethnographical boundaries of India'. George Campbell, *The Afghan Frontier* (London: E. Stanford, 1879), pp. 39–42.
47. J. L. Morrison, 'From Alexander Burnes to Frederick Roberts: A Survey of Imperial Frontier Policy, *Proceedings of the British Academy*, 22 (1936): 173–83.
48. For a recent biography, see Thomas Hylland Eriksen, *Fredrik Barth: An Intellectual Biography* (London: Pluto, 2015).

49. Fredrik Barth, *Political Leadership among Swat Pathans* (reprint, London: Athlone Press, 1990), and *The Last Wali of Swat: An Autobiography* (New York: Columbia University Press, 1985).
50. Akbar S. Ahmed, *Resistance and Control in Pakistan* (London: Routledge, 1991), 84. For a more recent analysis of resistance among Pashtuns based on faith and culture, see Sana Haroon, *Frontier of Faith: Islam in the Indo-Afghan Borderland* (New York: Columbia University Press, 2007).
51. This kind of view gained academic currency during the 1980s as Afghans, especially the Pashtuns, resisted the Soviet occupation. See Olivier Roy, *Islam and Resistance in Afghanistan* (Cambridge: Cambridge University Press, 1990).
52. Here, one tends to agree with John Gray, who sees modernity in a wider perspective rather than confining it to only Euro-American spheres. See John Gray, *Al Qaeda and What It Means to be Modern* (London: Faber, 2007).
53. The Taliban are seen as 'our' – Western – creation, who lost their innocence and utility a long time ago. See Van Linschoten and Kuehn, *An Enemy We Created*. Also, Thomas H. Johnson and M. Chris Mason, 'No Sight until the Burst of Fire: Understanding the Pakistan-Afghanistan Frontier', *International Security* 32, no. 4 (2008): 41–77.
54. 'I also wore the burka to discover for myself what it is like to be an Afghan woman; what it feels like to squash into the chock-a-block black rows reserved for women, when the rest of the bus is half empty, what it feels like to squeeze into the boot of a taxi because a man is occupying the back seat, what it feels like to be stared at as a tall and attractive burka and receive your first-compliment from a man in the street. How in time I started to hate it. How it pinches the head and causes headaches, how difficult it is to see anything through the grill'. Asne Seierstad, *The Bookseller of Kabul* (London: Little, Brown, 2003), 6.
55. Some of this criticism came from Talal Asad, which Barth accepted, albeit reluctantly, in his subsequent work. See Talal Asad, 'Market Model, Class Structure and Consent: A Reconstruction of Swat Political Organization', *Man* 7, no, 1 (1972): 74–94.
56. For instance, James A. Michener, *Caravans* (reprint, London: Mandarin, 1993); James Spain, *The Way of the Pathans* (London: R. Hale, 1962); *The Pathan Borderland* (The Hague: Mouton, 1963).
57. Other than individual case studies, one can find works on the Pashtunistan issue as well. See Stephen Rittenberg, *Ethnicity, Nationalism, and the Pakhtuns: The Independence Movement in India's North-West Frontier Province* (Durham, NC: Carolina Academic Press, 1988), and Sayyid W. A. Shah, *Ethnicity, Islam and Nationalism: Muslim Politics in the North-West Frontier Province, 1937–47* (Karachi: Oxford University Press, 1999).
58. Akbar S. Ahmed, *Millennium and Charisma among Pathans: A Critical Essay in Social Anthropology* (reprint, London: Routledge and Kegan Paul, 1980); and, Mukulika Banerjee, *The Pathan Unarmed: Opposition and Memory in the North-West Frontier* (Oxford: James Currey, 2000).
59. The Soviets felt the same way about their neighbours who needed help as well as redemption against the local exploiters and their external backers. Tribes and clans were too irrelevant for them since nationality and proletariat were the essentialized trajectories.
60. Works by Nathan Glazer and Daniel P. Moynihan have been quite persistent and influential in this context. The latter, during the post–Cold War years found greater space for his prioritization of ethnic factors in global politics during the 1990s when, other than the former Eastern Bloc and Yugoslavia, ethnic conflicts all across Africa and Asia posed formidable challenges to the entire project of the nation state. See Daniel P. Moynihan, *Pandaemonium: Ethnicity in International Politics* (Oxford: Oxford University Press, 1993). It is interesting to note that both Germany and France underplay the usage of 'race' in the official lexicon.
61. Moynihan felt vindicated, while others assumed that the entire system was threatened by 'failing states' due to internal fissures. See Michael Ignatieff, *Empire Lite: Nation-building in Bosnia, Kosovo and Afghanistan* (London: Vintage, 2003).
62. Nancy Lindisfarne, 'Exceptional Pashtuns? Class Politics, Imperialism and Historiography', a paper presented at a conference in London, 3 May 2010, with due acknowledgement for some of the points made earlier in this chapter.

63. These are some of the known specialists on Southwest Asian communities such as the Pashtuns, Hazaras and Tajiks, but have often worked for the regimes in Islamabad and Kabul holding important positions, or decided to work abroad for multinationals with some occasional vacillations as expatriate experts.
64. Gilles Dorronsoro, *Revolution Unending: Afghanistan, 1979 to the Present* (New York: Columbia University Press, 2005).
65. Lindisfarne, 'Exceptional Pashtuns?'.

2 Imperial Hubris: The Afghan Taliban in Ascendance

1. 'Gen. Hillier Explains the Afghan Mission', *Globe and Mail*, 16 July 2005. http://www.theglobeandmail.com/globe-debate/gen-hillier-explains-the-afghan-mission/article1331108/.
2. James Fergusson, *Taliban: The True Story of the World's Most Feared Guerrilla Fighters* (London: Bantam, 2010), 5.
3. For instance, Ahmed Rashid, *Taliban: Islam, Oil and the New Great Game in Central Asia* (London: I. B. Tauris, 2000); Christina Lamb, *The Sewing Circles of Herat: My Afghan Years* (London: Flamingo, 2003). Recently, there has been an interest in locating the larger context of Taliban ideology, especially in reference to their literature and not just the creed: Alex Strick van Linschoten and Felix Kuehn, eds., *Poetry of the Taliban*, trans. Mirwais Rahmany and Abdul Hamid Stanikzai (London: Hurst, 2012).
4. Amidst the hosts of writings, one can only refer to a few volumes, though papers, special reports and documentaries proliferate in almost all the major languages of the world. See William Maley, ed., *Fundamentalism Reborn? Afghanistan and the Taliban* (London: Hurst, 1998).
5. Barnett Rubin, *The Fragmentation of Afghanistan: State Formation and Collapse in the International System* (New Haven, CT: Yale University Press, 2002).
6. I have borrowed the term from a friend and an author: Kamal Matinuddin, *The Taliban Phenomenon: Afghanistan 1994–1997* (Karachi: Oxford University Press, 1998).
7. Bruce Riedel, *Avoiding Armageddon: America, India, and Pakistan to the Brink and Back* (Washington DC: Brookings Institution Press, 2013), 127–8.
8. This first-hand information is based on personal evidence that I gathered during the 1980s and 1990s in Islamabad, London, Oxford, Berlin, Washington and Istanbul.
9. The Afghan ambassador was quite forthcoming in a conversation with the present author and mentioned his parleys with the Western diplomats based in Islamabad. Interview with Mullah Zaeef, 30 August 2000.
10. In his interview with James Fergusson, he dwelt on these themes in addition to his own efforts for peace in the country. Fergusson, *Taliban: The True Story*, 170–9.
11. Sherard Cowper-Coles, *Cables from Kabul. The Inside Story of the West's Afghanistan Campaign* (London: HarperPress, 2012), xxii.
12. 'The Taliban are the representatives of an ideology as much as they are an army. It follows that we need to win arguments with them, not just battles – and we can't do that without talking to them. How much, in the end, do we really know about the Taliban and their motives? Not nearly enough, I would suggest'. Fergusson, *Taliban: The True Story*, 2.
13. Cowper-Coles, *Cables from Kabul*, 228.
14. Rashid, *Taliban: Islam, Oil and the New Great Game in Central Asia*, vii.
15. Ibid., 4.
16. Ibid., 18.
17. Ibid., 65.
18. 'The gender issue became the main platform of the Taliban's resistance to UN and Western governments' attempt to make them compromise and moderate their policies'. Ibid., 111.
19. Ibid., 87.
20. Ibid., 87 and 212.
21. Ibid., 93.

22. Winston Churchill, *The Story of Malakand Field Force* (repr.; London: Mandarin, 1990), cited in William Maley, *Fundamentalism Reborn?* 14. Even before Churchill, several colonial officials had noted the centrality of Islam in Pashtun opposition to the British. During the First Anglo-Afghan War (1838–42), Henry Rawlinson, the political officer in Kandahar, confided to a friend that the Afghans were annoyed with the British on religious grounds: 'It is indeed the rock upon which we split'. Quoted in Rob Johnson, 'Afghanistan: Unfriendly Fire', *History Today*, July 2012. http://www.historytoday.com/rob-johnson/afghanistan-unfriendly-fire.
23. Maley, *Fundamentalism Reborn*, 23.
24. 'Pakistan's objectives were twofold. The first was to secure a receptive leadership in Kabul that would ensure the transformation of Afghanistan into a Pakistan-dominated Pashtun-ruled enclave and assist Pakistan's goal of wider regional influence, and broader regional political, economic and strategic gains. The other was to enable Pakistan to merge the identity of Pakistan's and Afghanistan's Pashtuns into one and settle once and for all the longstanding Afghanistan-Pakistan border dispute in line with Pakistan's interests'. Ibid., 37 and 38.
25. Ibid., 43–4.
26. Ibid., 86 and 100.
27. Ibid., 210–11.
28. Several writers find these terms similar, while for others there is a thin but crucial difference in their implications. For example, Graham Fuller, *A World Without Islam* (Boston: Littlee, Brown and Company, 2010). Following the Egyptian military coup in 2013, some authors, rather too hastily, felt that Islamism, first introduced by the Muslim Brotherhood in 1928, had been finally discredited. See, Hazem Kandil, 'The End of Islamism?' *London Review of Books*, 3 July 2013, http://www.lrb.co.uk/blog/2013/07/04/hazem-kandil/the-end-of-islamism/.
29. Mohammed Ayoob, *The Many Faces of Political Islam: Religion and Politics in the Muslim World* (Ann Arbor: University of Michigan Press, 2008).
30. Olivier Roy, *Globalized Islam: The Search for a New Ummah* (New York: Columbia University Press, 2006).
31. Matinuddin, *The Taliban Phenomenon*, 59.
32. Ibid., 133.
33. 'The student militia guarded the aircraft night after night clad only in cotton *shalwar* and shorts, with the temperatures falling to 10 degrees below zero. An Indian delegation was permitted to come to Afghanistan despite the fact that New Delhi had not recognized the Taliban regime and was, in fact, supporting their opponents'. They allowed the UN negotiators to work with the Indian interlocutors and were able to get the passengers released in lieu of three Kashmiri militants. Ibid., 227–8.
34. Ibid., 229.
35. Peter Marsden, *The Taliban: War, Religion and the New Order in Afghanistan* (London: Zed Books, 1998), 1.
36. Ibid., 4.
37. Ibid., 57. To him, the Taliban's ideology combined idealism for a sharia rule with mores from Pashtunwali, 66.
38. 'Radical Islam has thus been a response to relative disadvantage as well as to the chaos of civil conflict'. He warned against causing an unnecessary polarization besides a feared tendency 'to brand all Muslims as extremists'. Ibid., 67. In the Taliban he found similarities both with the Iranian Revolution and the Wahhabi Puritanism of Saudi disposition. Ibid., 74 and 77.
39. For the leadership and creed of the JI, see Seyyed Vali Reza Nasr, *Syed Mawdudi and the Making of Islamic Revolution* (New York: Oxford University Press, 1996), and Frederic Grare, *Pakistan: The Myth of an Islamist Peril* (Washington, DC: Carnegie Endowment for International Peace, 2006).
40. In another study, I have looked at the ideological interface between the military rulers and the JI until the latter entered a new phase of oppositional politics in the 1990s. Iftikhar H. Malik, *State and Civil Society in Pakistan: Politics of Authority, Ideology and Ethnicity* (Oxford: St. Antony's-Macmillan Series, 1997).

41. One of the JI spokesmen criticized the Taliban's increasing restrictions on female education and participation in the job market by suggesting that such policies only fed into negative portrayals of Islam. Marsden, *The Taliban: War, Religion and the New Order*, 99.
42. Quoted in ibid., 130. However, Marsden saw various socio-religious strands informing Taliban ideology and activism: 'To summarise, one sees a range of influence in the creed of the Taliban, drawn from Islamic movements in the Middle East, Iran, the Indian subcontinent and Afghanistan. However the dominant influence appears to be that of the Afghan Ulema, who could be perceived as seeking a return to the status quo that existed before the intellectual movements of the 1950s and 1960s set in motion a chain of events from which Afghanistan is still reeling'. Ibid., 87.
43. Antonio Giustozzi, *Koran, Kalashnikov and Laptop: The Neo-Taliban Insurgency in Afghanistan* (London: Hurst, 2007), 230.

    Such views prioritizing negotiated settlements through the co-optation of various forces and groups across Afghanistan, especially the Taliban, were suggested more vocally in recent years, though Western emphasis has often been on a military-led strategy. With the Karzai regime feeling insecure, any such move added to its own sense of vulnerability: 'A stable and peaceful Afghanistan is unlikely to be achieved without the involvement and cooperation of the more moderate elements of the Taliban', concluded a long-time observer: John C. Griffiths, *Afghanistan: Land of Conflict and Beauty* (London: Andre Deutsch, 2009), 280.
44. Theo Farrell and Antonio Giustozzi noted, 'By arriving with insufficient force, aligning themselves with local corrupt power-holders, relying on firepower to keep insurgents at bay and targeting the poppy crop, the British made matters worse. 'Far from securing Helmand, British forces alienated the population, mobilised local armed resistance and drew in foreign fighters seeking jihad'. They describe British troops as 'blindly ignorant of the local politics underpinning [the insurgency]'.

    'Indiscriminate use of fire by British forces alienated locals who were driven from their homes or lost family members,' they write. 'The pressure on what remained an undermanned force meant that the British lacked the presence and tactical patience to develop ties in most communities, and still had to rely on artillery and air power to get out of trouble.' Richard Norton-Taylor, 'UK Forces in Helmand 'Made Matters Worse', Says Report', *Guardian*, 10 July 2013. This came two weeks after General Nick Carter's interview with the same British newspaper in which he criticized Western powers for not having negotiated with the Taliban during the earlier phase. The British general was the deputy head of NATO forces in Afghanistan and, like Sir Sherard Cowper-Cole and James Fergusson, had based his hindsight/lateral view on his personal experiences in the country.
45. Theo Farrell and Antonio Giustozzi, 'The Taliban at War: Inside the Helmand Insurgency, 2004–2012', *International Affairs*, 89, no. 4 (2013): 871. See: http://www.chathamhouse.org/sites/default/files/public/International%20Affairs/2013/89_4/89_4_03_FarrellGiustozzi.pdf.
46. Hassan Abbas, *The Taliban Revival: Violence and Extremism on the Pakistan-Afghanistan Frontier* (New Haven, CT: Yale University Press, 2015).
47. In her latest work with the usual rebuke of Pakistan, a well-known British journalist has attributed the Taliban salience to the support they received from the ISI, as if the entire NATO and ISAF were humbled by the intelligence agency of a struggling country. See Christina Lamb, *Farewell Kabul: From Afghanistan to a More Dangerous World* (London: HarperCollins, 2015).

3 Masculinities in Conflict: Western Pedagogy and the Return of the Afghan Taliban

1. Ayaz Amir, 'So, Finally a Farewell to Arms', *News*, 21 June 2013.
2. Fariba Nawa, *Opium Nation: Child Brides, Drug Lords, and One Woman's Journey Through Afghanistan* (New York: Harper Perennial, 2011), 73.

3. Certainly, there are several other counternarratives as well, but they pale before this powerful and hegemonic discourse which posits Muslims and all kinds of Islamist groups as one monolith which thinks and works alike, with some inherent fascination for violence. Some recent works have tried to look at the Taliban as ordinary human beings, belonging to a wider social mosaic of Afghanistan. For instance, see *Poetry of the Taliban*, edited by Alex Strick van Linschoten and Felix Kuehn, and translated by Mirwais Rahmany and Abdul Hamid Stanikzai (Karachi: Oxford University Press, 2012).
4. In recent times, some analysts have tried to interview some field commanders, ordinary Taliban and other camp followers on both sides of the border. See Antonio Giustozzi, ed., *Decoding the New Taliban: Insight from the Afghan Field* (London: Hurst, 2009); Rob Johnson, *The Afghan Way of War. Culture and Pragmatism: A Critical History* (London: Hurst, 2014); Peter Bergen, ed., *Talibanistan* (New York: Oxford University Press, 2013); and Carter Malkasian, *War Comes to Garmser: Thirty Years of Conflict on the Afghan Frontier* (New York: Oxford University Press, 2013).
5. A recent biography by a former associate of Osama bin Laden shows that there were serious rifts between the Taliban and Al-Qaeda even before September 11 and that the entire Western discourse which viewed them as operating and working in tandem did not reflect the facts on the ground. See Mustafa Hamid and Leah Farrall, *The Arabs at War in Afghanistan* (London: Hurst, 2015).
6. For a critical analysis, see Talal Asad, *On Suicide Bombing* (New York: Columbia University Press, 2007).
7. Muhammad Tahir-ul-Qadiri, *Fatwa on Terrorism and Suicide Bombings* (London: Minhaj Ul Quran, 2011).
8. Known for his rational and more egalitarian views, Al-Ghamdi was quite popular among literate, urban Pakistanis, but earned the ire of orthodox clerics, and there have been threats on his life. He ran his own institute aimed at teaching and pursing research on Islam, and based in a posh locality of Lahore, his television series were meant to answer theological and juridical questions. A former member of Jamaat-i-Islami, but years apart in his ideas and orientation now, Al-Ghamdi had to seek asylum in Malaysia, and his programmes became infrequent.
9. Dr. Tahir-ul-Qadri, a Pakistani cleric based in Canada, is the founder of the Minhaj ul-Quran schools, which take aboard Sufi teachings and practices. There are a dozen such schools in the United Kingdom, though the movement began from Lahore and uses publications as well as television programmes to reach Pakistanis at home and abroad. His whirlwind visit of Pakistan in early 2013, in which he intended to lead a protest march on Islamabad demanding some changes in the electoral system, was skilfully handled by the PPP regime and Pakistan's Supreme Court. In another similar protest and 'siege' movement in 2014, Qadri tried to dislodge the Sharif government, but failed to do so and returned to Canada. However, his 512-page commentary of *fatwa* (edict) was released from London in early 2010, and is a detailed retort to all kinds of arguments in favour of suicide bombing. In an interview he noted, 'They [terrorists] can't claim that their suicide bombings are martyrdom operations and that they become the heroes of the Muslim Umma [global brotherhood]. No, they become heroes of hellfire, and they are leading towards hellfire [...] There is no place for any martyrdom and their act is never, ever to be considered jihad'. Dominic Casciani, 'Islamic Scholar Tahir ul-Qadiri Issues Terrorism Fatwa', BBC Online, 2 March 2010, http://news.bbc.co.uk/1/hi/uk/8544531.stm.
10. Some sporadic interviews with potential or injured suicide bombers in Pakistan often showed younger boys from tribal and rural backgrounds who had been led to believe that their targets were infidels and non-Muslims, though such a view disallows personal intentions as a powerful agency. However, it is crucial to note that the TTP and its supporters in Pakistan, or similar other groups from amongst Shias and Sunnis, are certainly aware of their targets as an element of *takfir* (declaring someone an infidel or non-believer) feeds into their mindset.
11. One could certainly make a list of sects, denominational groups and such other communities from among Muslims, who have often been on the receiving end of *takfir*. Other than Sunni

and Shia militants pursuing this exclusion, intra-Sunni and intra-Shia dissension has also led to such paths. For instance, Wahhabi Sunnis with a strong Salafi orientation may not only view Shias, Ahmadis and Zikris as non-Muslim but also accuse Sufi Muslims of following innovation (*shirk*), and discourage them from visiting shrines and pirs. Suicide attacks, often attributed to extremist purists, have happened at several Sufi tombs in Southwest Asia and Iraq causing numerous deaths. In the same vein, the Twelver Shias have their own reservations against the Ismailis and Zaidis, while both Sunnis and Shias overwhelmingly disagree with the Ahmadis, Zikris, Yazidis and Druze Muslims. The pull towards uniformity, while being apprehensive of growing pluralism has, all through Muslim history, resulted in such *takfir* and accompanied violence, though these acts cannot be attributed to a vast majority.

12. Debra Lobo had been teaching in Lahore for decades before moving to Karachi and becoming the vice-principal of the Jinnah Medical and Dental College. Her attackers had been following her movements until they attacked her on 16 April. Lobo was grievously injured and flown out of Pakistan to her native United States. This author had met her only two weeks before the shooting at a conference at the University of Karachi. See Tim Craig, 'American Wounded in Pakistan in an Apparent Terrorist Shooting, Police Say', *Washington Post*, 16 April 2015. https://www.washingtonpost.com/world/american-wounded-in-pakistan-in-apparent-terrorist-shooting-police-say/2015/04/16/28a4c9c4-e434-11e4-81ea-0649268f729e_story.html. Sabeen Mahmud was a civil society activist who had been protesting against sectarian and ethnic violence, demanding the arrests of firebrand clerics as well as the investigation of missing Baloch activists. Her coffee cum gathering place, The Second Floor (T2F), was located in a busy market area and would often host people of all persuasions to discuss religious and political issues. She had just finished a meeting on Balochistan on 24 April and was driving home when the attackers waylaid her. For more on her, see Lois Parshley, 'The Life and Death of Sabeen Mahmud', *New Yorker*, 28 April 2015: http://www.newyorker.com/news/newsdesk/the-life-and-death-of-sabeen-mahmud
13. For a recent review, see Nadeen Farooq Paracha, 'In Pakistan, Well-To-Do and Willing to Terrorize', *Deutsche Welle*, 28 May 2015, http://www.dw.de/in-pakistan-well-to-do-and-willing-to-terrorize/a-18481412.
14. For more on this, see Christine Fair, *The Madrassah Challenge: Militancy and Religious Education in Pakistan* (Washington, DC: US Institute of Peace, 2008).
15. Abdul Salam Zaeef, *My Life with the Taliban* (London: Hurst, 2010), xlvi–xlvii.
16. Ibid., 43.
17. He is certainly unforgiving of the ISI, especially in the post-Soviet era, and this is understandable given his own arrest by his Pakistani hosts and a humiliating handover to the Americans, which was over and above international protocols on the sanctity of his ambassadorial rights.
18. They determined to implement sharia by curbing vice and crime, and began their work in the area around Sangisar until they started to take on warlords and other opponents. Zaeef, *My Life*, 65
19. Ibid., 75.
20. 'It surprised me that people so quickly turned their backs on him. Still, soon after my arrival people started to visit me each day in an attempt to persuade me to imprison his brother [...] It seemed there was loyalty after all, and I wondered if I could trust the people I was supposed to work with. Ibid., 82–3.
21. Ibid., 94.
22. Ibid., 96.
23. Very much like some anthropologists and even latter-day Pashtun and Baloch nationalists, Zaeef's definition of the Indus as the cultural borderline between two subcultures of Pakistan or as a demarcation point between Southern and Southwestern Asia is certainly curious.
24. He notes, 'At the time, I believe as many as 80 per cent of the people of Pakistan supported the Islamic Emirate of Afghanistan. The dictatorial regime of Pakistan – led by its Chief Executive Pervez Musharraf – disapproved of our close cooperation and our strong relations inside Pakistan. Pakistani officials were very concerned to see this public support for Afghanistan.

Ibid., 117. For Musharraf's viewpoint, see Pervez Musharraf, *In the Line of Fire: A Memoir* (London: Simon & Schuster, 2006).
25. Zaeef, *My Life*, 121.
26. 'My mind raced as I looked at the screen and considered the probable repercussions of the attack. At that very moment, I knew that Afghanistan and its poverty stricken people would ultimately suffer for what had taken place in America. The United States would seek revenge, and they would turn to our troubled country. Ibid., 141.
27. Ibid., 133. It is quite interesting to note that William Maley, the American ambassador in Islamabad, had often been in touch with Mullah Zaeef, and in an impromptu meeting long before September 11 told the Afghan envoy of reports of a possible attack on US soil, which begs pertinent questions about lack of any pre-emption. Ibid., 138.
28. 'Everyone gave what they could, freely and out of solidarity. Many Muslim sisters were giving us their jewellery and other possessions. We collected gold by the kilo. Soon we also started to accumulate blankets, shoes and other much needed goods in the embassy. I still remember the passion of our Muslim brothers, and how much they wanted to help'. Some people came to see him crying as they all feared a dark future for Afghanistan given the intended invasion. Once in Islamabad, on the way to the Embassy, a waving couple who had been trying to see him over the past several days stopped him. He allowed them in: 'The moment they arrived, the woman started crying. Then her husband started crying, too. There was so much sorrow that I also began to cry. My heart was so heavy that all I needed was an excuse. We cried a lot.' Ibid., 158–9.
29. Ibid., 173.
30. For a first-hand account, see Moazzam Begg, *Enemy Combatant: A British Muslim's Journey to Guantanamo and Back* (London: Free Press, 2006). Also, David Rose, *America's War on Human Rights* (London: Faber, 2004); Clive Stafford Smith, *Bad Men: Guantanamo Bay and the Secret Prisoners* (London: Weidenfeld & Nicolson, 2007); Andy Worthington, *The Guantanamo Files: The Stories of the 774 Detainees in America's Illegal Prison* (London: Pluto, 2007); and Mahvish Khan, *My Guantanamo Diary: The Detainees and the Stories They Told Me* (New York: PublicAffairs, 2009).
31. Zaeef, *My Life*, 200.
32. Ibid., 209.
33. Ibid., 224–5.
34. Ibid., 233.
35. Ibid., 226.
36. Ibid., 231.
37. Ibid., 240.
38. Ibid., 233–44.

4 Understanding Pakistan: Geopolitical Legacies and Perspectives on Violence

1. Naeem Sadiq, 'Why We Can't Rid Society of Weapons', *Express Tribune*, 19 July 2013. http://tribune.com.pk/story/578273/why-we-cant-rid-society-of-weapons/.
2. Aatish Taseer, 'Why My Father Hated India', *Wall Street Journal*, 16 July 2011. http://www.wsj.com/articles/SB10001424052702304911104576445862242908294
3. Maulana Abul Kalam Azad and other Nationalist leaders feared that Pakistan, instead of resolving their predicament, would only divide and further marginalize South Asian Muslims. See Abul Kalam Azad, *India Wins Freedom: the Complete Version* (New Delhi: Orient Longman, 1988); also Mushirul Hasan, *Legacy of a Divided Nation: India's Muslims since Independence* (New Delhi: Oxford University Press, 2001) and *Inventing Boundaries: Gender, Politics and the Partition of India* (New Delhi: Oxford University Press, 2002).

   Partition remains a major academic subject among historians of South Asia, and literary figures, especially from Hindi, Urdu and Punjabi strands. In more recent times, biographical works have tried to focus on it as a gigantic human tragedy, in which leaders of all kinds – Indians and the British – are held responsible for their culpability. Stanley Wolpert, *The Shameful Flight: The Last Years of the British Empire in India* (New York: Oxford University Press, 2006); Urvashi Butalia, *The Other Side of Silence: Voices from the Partition of India* (New Delhi: Penguin Books, 1998); Ian Talbot and Gurharpal Singh, eds., *Region and Partition: Bengal, Punjab and the Partition of the Subcontinent* (Karachi: Oxford University Press, 1999); Rajmohan Gandhi, *Punjab: A History from Aurangzeb to Mountbatten* (Delhi: Aleph Book Company, 2013); and Ishtiaq Ahmed, *Punjab: Bloodied, Partitioned and Cleansed. Unravelling the 1947 Tragedy through Secret British Reports and First-Person Accounts* (Karachi: Oxford University Press, 2012).

4. A kind of overarching Hinduization, as preached by numerous Hindu outfits since the 1920s, did engender a sense of unease among Muslims even in majority provinces such as Punjab. In Bengal, following the Famine, the economic interests of a predominantly landless Muslim peasantry began to converge with the League. However, the founders of Pakistan in general were Muslim modernists and not clerical groups such as the Jamiat-i-Ulama-i-Hind. See S. M. Ikram, *History of Muslim Civilization in India and Pakistan: A Political and Cultural History* (Lahore: Research Society of Pakistan, 1989); K. K. Aziz, *The Making of Pakistan: A Study in Nationalism* (London: Chatto & Windus, 1967); and Taj-ul-Islam Hashmi, *Pakistan as a Peasant Utopia: the Communalization of Class Politics in East Bengal, 1920–1947* (Boulder, CO: Westview, 1992).

5. I have raised these issues in reference to the entire region and not just within the perspective of India-Pakistan contestations. For these various themes, see Iftikhar H. Malik, *Jihad, Hindutva and the Taliban: South Asia at the Crossroads* (Karachi: Oxford University Press, 2005).

6. For various perspectives, see Khushwant Singh, *The End of India* (Delhi: Penguin Books, 2003); Sunil Khilnani, *The Idea of India* (Delhi: Penguin Books, 1997); and Barbara and Thomas Metcalf, *A Concise History of India* (Cambridge: Cambridge University Press 2006).

7. There are small sections of Pakistanis, who like their Indian counterparts, find fault with the idea of Pakistan itself and instead idealize a merger, much beyond the religious and political divisions. Asif Siddiqi, *The Reunion of India & Pakistan: Together Forever* (New Delhi: Promilla and Co. Publishers, 2013).

8. While Pakistanis may be dismayed by a monstrous cycle of misgovernance and instability, its intellectuals and thinking sections have been uniquely engaged in dilating on these issues in numerous literary genres. It is not a minor achievement for this country to have a lion's share in the youthful generation of quality writers, many of them even having been shortlisted for prestigious prizes. This is certainly not the place to enumerate all those Pakistani authors from across the disciplines, but a fair representation of 'new' literary personalities can be found in the recent issue of a leading literary magazine. See *Granta* (London), No. 112, Autumn 2010. The 288-page issue is devoted to Pakistan and has contributions from a predominantly Pakistani authorship, along with a small number of their counterparts from elsewhere with interest on the same.

Another major literary and academic collection of diverse, critical and fresher writings has been provided in a newly established British journal. See *Critical Muslim* (London), 4 (October–December 2012).

In the same vein, one could refer to several visual productions such as *Khuda Kay Liyaya, Bol* and others in that self-critical genre which have invited greater introspection on these major issues unleashing violence of a diverse nature. Interestingly, most of this debate is happening on the Internet among younger and diaspora groups, who discursively operate through social media, offering a strong and well-knit arm of the country's civil society.

9. Some of the recent serious comments, other than those referred to further below, have come from a wide variety of authors. For instance, Owen Bennett-Jones, *Pakistan: Eye of the Storm* (London: Yale University Press, 2009); Stephen Cohen, *The Idea of Pakistan* (Washington, DC: Brookings Institution Press 2006); Shuja Nawaz, *Crossed Swords: Pakistan, Its Army, and the Wars Within* (Karachi: Oxford University Press, 2008); Zahid Hussain, *The Frontline Pakistan: Struggle with Militant Islam* (New York: Columbia University Press, 2015); Ayesha Siddiqa, *Military Inc.:*

Inside Pakistan's Military Economy (Karachi: Oxford University Press, 2007); Pervez Musharraf, *In the Line of Fire: A Memoir* (London: Simon & Schuster, 2006); and, Benazir Bhutto, *Reconciliation: Islam, Democracy and the West* (London: Simon & Schuster, 2008). For an overview of some of the recent works on Pakistan, see S. Akbar Zaidi, 'Contesting Notions of Pakistan', *Economic and Political Weekly*, 10 November 2012, 32–9.

10. In the wake of floods, suicide bombings and an undiminished violence in the FATA, Pakistanis often wondered about the limitless scale of violence both by the natural and human forces – ostensibly in competition – and displayed a sense of resignation and surrealism. A greater sense of religiosity along with a shared helplessness were noticed all over the country, where thousands of mercy missions aimed at helping the flood victims were taking place on a daily basis, though the parallel spectre of suicide attacks equally refused to diminish. The spirit of charity and mutual help witnessed during the devastating earthquake of 8 October 2005 was again observed across the Indus lands in the summer of 2010.

11. Other than attacks on mosques, schools and funeral processions, the two most horrid attacks have been on the respective shrines of Daata Gunj Bakhsh on 1 July and of Shah Ghazi in Karachi on 30 September 2010, sent shock waves among Pakistanis of a reign of fear unleashed by a specific element of purist extremists. Since Osama bin Laden's death in Abbottabad on 2 May 2011, there has been an escalation in such attacks in Karachi, Peshawar and the FATA. In addition, attacks on the Hazara Shias in Quetta and drawn battles with the Shia Turis in Kurram have continued unabated with hundreds of deaths. In between there have been attacks on Ahmadis in Punjab, along with targeted killings of pro-government tribal leaders, members of the assemblies and critical journalists. The attack on Christian worshippers in a Peshawar church on 22 September 2013 sent shock waves across the country largely because it caused major human losses and, as admitted by the TTP, the militant outfit conducted it. Unlike other individual incidents rooted in controversial blasphemy laws, it was an outright attack on a place of worship of people defined as people of the book. Mostly Christians and likewise Ahmadis fall victim to 'local' xenophobia in which some cleric or land-grabbing mafia accuse the former of having blasphemed the Prophet or the Quran. As seen in the attacks on Lahore's Ahmadis on 22 May 2010, and the burning of a Christian couple in Kasur on 4 November 2014, miscreants against these vulnerable Pakistanis had misled local mobs.

Karachi has remained quite restive over the past several years in which ethnic violence between the Pashtuns and Urdu speakers *(Muhajireen)* and gang wars between various Baloch groups in Lyari along with target killings of Shias have been persistent. According to the Human Rights Commission of Pakistan (HRCP), 1,726 people lost their lives between January and June 2013, while in 2012 for the same six months, 1,215 murders were reported in the city. For some recent statistics on such communal, ethnic, sectarian and target killings, published by the HRCP, see *State of Human Rights in Pakistan* (Lahore, 2013), 335, http://hrcp-web.org/hrcpweb/wp-content/pdf/AR2012.pdf. (The site carries all the previous detailed annual reports and related comments.)

The scale of violence can be assessed by the fact that just in the first six months of 2013, there were 1,300 incidents of planned attacks in the country. *BBC Urdu Report*, 10 July 2013, http://www.bbc.co.uk/urdu/pakistan/2013/07/130710_terrorism_shumaila_ra.shtml.

12. Richard Holbrooke, the US envoy for Afghanistan and Pakistan, in a press meeting, underlined this civil and military collaboration with the American authorities. Ironically, the day he was holding this meeting, North Waziristan was hit by two missile strikes, killing 14 people. 'Govt, GHQ on Board over Drone Attacks: Holbrooke', *News* (Islamabad-Rawalpindi), 16 September 2010. Under the Obama administration, the drone attacks on Pakistan have registered a major increase, often happening several times a day. Other than Pakistani media and human rights groups, *Long View Journal*, in its report 'Charting the Data for US Airstrikes in Pakistan, 2004–2010', created by Bill Roggio and Alexander Mayer, has kept a complete record of the number of the drone attacks and the resultant reported casualties. See http://www.

longwarjournal.org/pakistan-strikes.php; for BBC archives on predator attacks, see http://www.bbc.co.uk/urdu/pakistan/2010/07/100721_us_drone_attacks_special.shtml.

Such views have been corroborated by Lt. General (retired) Shuja Pasha, the former head of the ISI, who, in his testimony before the Abbottabad Commission investigating the US Navy SEALs operation and the killing of Osama bin Laden, acknowledged that. The commission was headed by a former senior judge, and it submitted its report in February 2013, but it was not released to the public until *Al-Jazeera* obtained a copy. See http://www.aljazeera.com/indepth/spotlight/binladenfiles/http://www.aljazeera.com/indepth/spotlight/binladenfiles/.

Various authorities have looked at drone attacks and their impact on Pakistani society and their multiple ramifications. While some researchers and websites emphasize the moral and human dimensions of drone strikes, others locate the low cost of this weapon against militants, whereas the Pakistanis view it as an attack on their sovereignty. For figures on drone attacks and the fatalities, see http://drones.pitchinteractive.com/.

According to the studies undertaken by the Bureau of Investigative Journalism, the following table highlights the figures:

Time Scale: 2004–11 May 2015
Total US strikes since 2004: 417
Total Obama strikes: 366
Total reported killed: 2,456–3,962
Civilians reported killed: 423–962
Children reported killed: 172–207
Total reported injured: 1,148–1,727

Source: https://www.thebureauinvestigates.com/category/projects/drones/drones-graphs/ (The operations by US special forces and drone missions by the British are not accounted for.)

13. The ANP, a secular Pashtun nationalist party, often raised its voice over target killings in Karachi, whereas Altaf Hussain, the London-based MQM leader, went to the extent of inviting some generals to bring about holistic changes in the country's political economy. Such statements made headlines during the Ramadan. Soon after the 11 May 2013 elections, Hussain, in one of his periodic harangues, threatened the separation of Karachi along with a strong rebuke to journalists and his other critics. Soon, London's Metropolitan Police was stormed with petitions by thousands of Pakistanis to try Mr. Hussain, a British citizen living in suburban London. In the meantime, the British police pursued its investigation of the murder of Imran Farooq, an MQM founder and another exile, who was killed near his home in 2010. In early July 2013, the BBC's flagship current affairs programme, *Newsnight*, carried a well-documented report about Hussain and his alleged role in the murders in Karachi, besides the stories of extortion and money laundering. For the documented report by Owen Bennett Jones, see 'MQM: The London-Based Party Holding Karachi in Its Grip', 12 July 2013, http://www.bbc.co.uk/news/uk-23270342.
14. According to detailed Pakistani reports based on extensive documented statistics, obtained by the Bureau of Investigative Journalism, scores of civilians had been killed in drone attacks during 2004–9, which may partially explain the emergence of the TTP. For details as well as the original Pakistani document, see Chris Woods, 'Exclusive: Leaked Pakistani Report Confirms High Civilian Death Toll in CIA Drone Strikes', Bureau of Investigative Journalism, 22 July 2013, http://www.thebureauinvestigates.com/2013/07/22/exclusive-leaked-pakistani-report-confirms-high-civilian-death-toll-in-cia-drone-strikes/.
15. The attack on 2 November 2014 at Wagah-Attari border post, a scene of popular flag ceremonies, was seen as a direct retort against the military operations in the FATA and Balochistan. The attack on the American teacher, Debra Lobo, on 16 April, and the murder of civil society activist Sabeen Mahmud, on 24 April 2015, were reminders of multiple and equally organized forms of violence in the country.
16. Rafia Zakaria, 'Drones: One White Death Can Change Everything', *Dawn*, 28 April 2015.
17. Ishtiaq Ahmed, *Pakistan: The Garrison State* (Karachi: Oxford University Press, 2013), 470.

18. For detailed figures on more recent Shia killings, see https://lubpak.com/archives/132675.
    Some observers may dismiss it as a conspiracy factor, though it is true that Israel and its supporters elsewhere may very much like to destabilize the Iranian regime due to its strong affinity with Hezbollah, Hamas and other such groups. Journalists such as Seymour Hersh have even mentioned Israeli involvement in destabilizing Iran in the patterns of Iraq, and here Kurdish and other neighbouring regions have often been suspected of such subtle intrusions. See also, Iftikhar H. Malik, 'Sunni-Shia Schism in Pakistan: Going Beyond Old Enmities', TurkeyAgenda, 20 May 2015, http://www.turkeyagenda.com/sunni-shia-schism-in-pakistan-going-beyond-old-enmities-2445.html.
19. The debate about racism underwriting slavery or vice versa has engaged several sociologists, and is often seen in reference to North Atlantic escapades with the slave trade, slavery and a continuing legacy of racism, which were further compounded by religious righteousness and cultural baggage, often known as 'the White Man's Burden'. For a useful background, see Winthrop Jordan, *The White Man's Burden: Historical Origins of Racism in the United States* (New York: Oxford University Press, 1974).
20. In the name of majoritarianism and to have a greater say in political affairs, some monks and their followers have tried to exclude the Tamils and Rohingyas from their perceptions of Sri Lankan and Burmese nationalism, respectively, and have even justified violence against them. Some scholars find this militant tradition rooted in the recent past, where the model of Japanese devotion to country and the Samurai creed came to inspire Nazis like Heinrich Himmler, Karlfied Graf Duerckheim, Walther Wust and Wilhelm Gundert in the twentieth century. Based on personal notes of the lecture by Professor Brian D. Victoria, 'Japanese Buddhism and the Third Reich', Bath Spa University, Bath, 15 May 2013; also, Brian D. Victoria, *Zen at War* (New York: Rowman & Littlefield, 2006).
21. A greater awareness of the rights and predicament of 'indigenous' and 'native' communities certainly owes to global civic groups and scholars, though the documentation of various types is beginning to happen only in recent years. Based on notes from a lecture by Professor Lisa Jackson Pulver, 'Australian Aboriginal People: The State of the Nation', Oxford Talks, Wolfson College, Oxford, 2 April 2013. Also: http://talks.ox.ac.uk/talk/index/11464. Professor Pulver is herself an Australian Aborigine and the first PhD and university academic from her people, and is documenting the facts and figures about the 'native communities' across the world. According to her, there are more than 300 million people in the world who fall under this category.
22. Edward Said, W. E. B. Du Bois, Frantz Fanon, Leopold Senghor, James Baldwin and many other intellectuals from the former colonies have provided an excellent counternarrative to this dictum.
23. Of course, in our times, Edward Said's study *Orientalism* (1978) is the pioneering work in this area, which has led to an ever-increasing discourse on orientalism, cultural theory, postcolonial studies and the colonization of mind. Also, Ziauddin Sardar, *Orientalism* (London: Open University Press, 1999).
24. For more on this, see Samantha Power, *A Problem from Hell: America and the Age of Genocide* (London: Flamingo, 2010).
25. Hannah Arendt, *The Human Condition* (Chicago: University of Chicago Press, 1952).
26. Here the Eurocentric views of Francis Wheen are in conflict with those of John Gray. See Francis Wheen, *How Mumbo-Jumbo Conquered the World? A Short History of Modern Delusions* (London: Harper Perennial, 2004); and, John Gray, *Al-Qaeda and What It Means to Be Modern* (London: Faber & Faber, 2007).
27. I have commented on the outpourings of some of these individuals and think tanks in a few of my recent studies. For instance, *Crescent between Cross and Star: Muslims and the West after 9/11* (Karachi: Oxford University Press, 2006). For an interesting review, see Malise Ruthven, 'Righteous & Wrong', *New York Review of Books*, 19 August 2010, http://www.nybooks.com/articles/archives/2010/aug/19/righteous-wrong/.
28. Zoe Williams, 'Politics Has Changed But Our Urge to Protest Is Undiminished', *Guardian*, 6 October 2010.

29. Even the special reports by watchdogs ensuring equality show that Muslim men and women are often disadvantaged when it comes to seeking employment. One aspect of these Muslim specific policies has been profiling of Muslims by the police and security agencies, often challenged by human rights groups. *Guardian*, 11 October 2010. http://www.theguardian.com/uk/2010/sep/30/police-surveillance-muslims-no-regard-law.
30. For instance, see Bernard Lewis, *The Crisis of Islam: Holy War and Unholy Terror* (London: Weidenfeld & Nicolson, 2003).
31. Chris McGreal, 'Harvard under Fire over Plan to Honour Islamophobic Editor', *Guardian*, 22 September 2010. In the case of Peretz's diatribe, both the leading papers, like a few others, either ignored his comments or hid them in columns further inside their papers.
32. For more on this, see Iftikhar H. Malik, *Islam, Nationalism and the West: Issues of Identity in Pakistan* (Oxford: St. Antony's-Macmillan Series, 1999).
33. An American academic, in her own personal way, has been applying this denigration for a society of 200 million, over and above its complexities and even several dynamics. Other than presuming a popular Pakistani support for drone strikes, ironically her analysis does not go beyond 'the nexus' of scheming generals, capricious militants and inefficient politicians, all united to grab American largesse, especially when Washington DC stays vulnerably naive about their intentions. C. Christine Fair, *Fighting to the End: The Pakistan Army's Way of War* (Delhi: Oxford University Press, 2014).
34. Farzana Shaikh, *Community and Consensus in Islam: Muslim Representation in Colonial India, 1860–1947* (Cambridge: Cambridge University Press, 1989).
35. Farzana Shaikh, *Making Sense of Pakistan*, (London: Hurst, 2009). Faisal Devji views Pakistan as a type of Muslim Zion and thus more than a mere geographical expression. See his *Muslim Zion: Pakistan as a Political Idea* (London: Hurst, 2013).
36. Hamza Alavi, 'Class and State', in *Pakistan: The Roots of Dictatorship*, ed. Hassan Gardezi and Jamil Rashid (London: Zed Books, 1983).
37. Shaikh, *Making Sense of Pakistan*, 208.
38. Anatol Lieven, *Pakistan: A Hard Country* (London: Penguin, 2011).
39. Jaswant Singh, *Jinnah: India-Partition-Independence* (New Delhi: Rupa & Co., 2009).
40. Ibid., 13 and 14.
41. Ibid., 127.
42. Ibid., 233, 237 and 239.
43. Ibid., 417, 420 and 421.
44. An interesting work by an Indian analyst focuses on the history of Punjab since the demise of Emperor Aurangzeb (1707), the Sikh rule, Raj, and then the partition of Punjab and its ramifications for the subcontinent. Rajmohan Gandhi, *Punjab: A History from Aurangzeb to Mountbatten* (Delhi: Aleph Book Company, 2013).
45. Faiz Ahmed Faiz (1911–1984), Saadat Hasan Manto (1912–1954), Quratul Ain Haider (1928–2007), Nasim Hijazi (1914–1996) and Intizaar Hussain (1923–2016) are just a select few familiar names from amongst many.
46. From amongst his many collections of stories, critical essays and novels, one may mention *The Midnight's Children* (London: Vintage, 2008); *Shame* (London: Vintage, 1995); and, certainly *The Satanic Verses* (London: Viking, 1988). Other writers of Pakistani origin who have settled in Britain include Ziauddin Sardar, Aamir Hussain, Rukhsana Ahmed and Hanif Kureishi, along with dozens of Urdu poets and prose writers whose contributions and literary efforts deserve a whole separate volume.
47. The shorter contributions of some of these and other writers appear in *Granta*'s special issue on Pakistan: *Granta*, No. 112, Autumn 2010. Suhayl Saadi, a physician, is a Glasgow-based novelist and playwright who has authored three novels, and his *Psychoraag* (2004) won several prestigious awards in the United Kingdom and Pakistan. Aquila Ismail's novel is partly autobiographical and focuses on tensions between Bengali and non-Bengali East Pakistanis during 1970–1. See Aquila Ismail, *Of Martyrs and Marigolds* (North Charleston, SC: CreateSpace, 2012).

48. Shauna Singh Baldwin, *What the Body Remembers* (Toronto: Knopf, 1999).
49. Shrabani Basu, *Spy Princess: The Life of Noor Inayat Khan* (London: The History Press, 2008).
50. Shauna Singh Baldwin, *The Tiger's Claw* (Toronto: Knopf, 2004).
51. Shauna Singh Baldwin, *We Are Not in Pakistan* (Fredericton, New Brunswick: Goose Lane Editions, 2007), 163.
52. Ibid., 218.

5 Understanding Civic Sentiments and Movements in Pakistan: Stalemated Cycle, or a Way Forward?

1. Gustav Ranis, 'Is Pakistan a Failing State?' *Yale Global*, 25 April 2013, http://yaleglobal.yale.edu/content/pakistan-failing-state.
2. Salman Rushdie, *Joseph Anton: A Memoir* (London: Vintage, 2013), 60.
3. 'Is Pakistan disintegrating? Are the state and society coming apart under the impact of successive political and natural disasters? The country swirls with rumours about the fall of the civilian government or even a military coup. The great Indus flood has disappeared from the headlines at home and aboard, though millions of farmers are squatting in the ruins of their villages. The US is launching its heaviest-ever drone attacks on targets in the west of the country'. Patrick Cockburn, 'Is Pakistan Falling Apart?', *Independent*, 7 October 2010. http://www.independent.co.uk/news/world/asia/is-pakistan-falling-apart-2100865.html.
   While reviewing Carlotta Gall's book censoring the Pakistani ISI and its links with the Afghan Taliban, Cockburn was quite critical of official policies and their ramifications for the country itself. See Patrick Cockburn, 'Double Game. *The Wrong Enemy* by Carlotta Gall', *New York Times*, 25 April 2014.
4. 'Swat is no longer a Taliban fortress and if the resettlement is done with patience and care, and if civil militias weed the militants out, it will not be again. What now has to happen here, as in Afghanistan, is that the provincial government has to emerge from its bunkers and fill the space liberated by combat'. 'Pakistan: Disaster Averted', editorial, *Guardian*, 15 July 2009. http://www.theguardian.com/commentisfree/2009/jul/15/editorial-pakistan-refugees-swat-aid
5. For further details on threats faced by journalists, see Pakistan Institute of Peace Studies, *Media Safety in Pakistan: A Study of Threats to Journalists in Pakistan* (Islamabad: PIPS, 2014).
6. Ishtiaq Ahmed, *Pakistan: The Garrison State* (Karachi: Oxford University Press, 2013).
7. Salman Rushdie, *Imaginary Homelands: Essays and Criticism, 1981–1991* (Harmondsworth: Penguin, 1991), 9.
8. The early Western moralist pronouncements on Afghan women's emancipation from extremists along all the moralist promises of women's empowerment, the curbing of the fundamentalists and ushering Afghanistan – and Pakistan – into some kind of enlightened utopia failed to materialize. A well-known Afghan writer and woman parliamentarian, Malalai Joya, mourned the devastation of her country and the agony of Pakistan, as she observed in an article published soon after the exposé by WikiLeaks. She wrote, 'Wikileaks has exposed some of the truth about the civilian toll of this war against the Afghan and Iraqi people. Afghans hold the US and Nato, and their puppet Karzai, responsible for these war crimes. They claim to fight terrorism, but in fact they are the biggest terrorists in the eyes of our people […] His [Obama's] surge of troops has brought only a surge of violence, and his expansion of the war into Pakistan has claimed many innocent lives. Obama promised "hope" and "change", but Afghans have seen only change for the worse. Here he is now seen as a "second Bush"'. Malalai Joya, 'Any Hope I Had in the Ballot Box Bringing Change Is Gone', *Guardian*, 2 November 2010. http://www.theguardian.com/commentisfree/cifamerica/2010/nov/02/hope-ballot-box-afghanistan-gone
9. Manmohan Singh came out with this statement soon after the Mumbai attacks of 2008, though Benazir Bhutto and several other people had also appropriated this term.

10. The attacks on the Indian Parliament and then on Mumbai assumed a new dimension when, in July 2013, during the court proceedings a former senior security official in India submitted an affidavit alleging that the Indian agencies had masterminded these attacks to facilitate the passing of some specific legislation. 'Pakistan Seeks Clarification on Indian Official's 26/11 remarks', *Times of India*, 20 July 2013. http://timesofindia.indiatimes.com/india/Govt-behind-Parliament-attack-26/11-Ishrat-probe-officer/articleshow/21062116.cms
11. A respectable website, often subscribed to by middle-class Pakistanis both at home and abroad, in a poll found 57% of respondents (1,720) blaming the United States, followed by suspicions of Israel held by 22% (676) for being opposed to Pakistan's nuclear programme. Interestingly, India was seen as only a minor irritant, with 12% of the respondents (308) viewing it as a threat to Islamabad's nuclear arsenals. A total of 3,028 respondents had participated in the poll. See, 'polls', in www.pkpolitics.com.poll, accessed in Oxford on 19 February 2011.
12. Christopher Roger for CIVIC, *Civilians in Armed Conflict: Civilian Harm and Conflict in Northwest Pakistan* (Washington, DC: CIVIC, 2010), www.civiliansinconflict.org/uploads/files/publications/civilian_harm_in_nw_pakistan_oct_2010.pdf.
13. Ibid., p. 5.
14. *Dawn*, 18 February 2011. http://www.dawn.com/news/607061/ji-leader-calls-for-davis-trial-in-at-court
15. Not only the families of the victims in the FATA but also international observers and commentators have often raised legal, moral and political questions about drone attacks. Philip Alston, UN rapporteur, in his report in June 2010, criticized the ramifications of this 'PlayStation mentality'. 'UN Official Criticises US over Drone Attacks', BBC, 2 June 2010, http://www.bbc.co.uk/news/10219962. Also, Philip Alston and Hina Shamsi, 'A Killer above the Law? Britain's use of drones in the war in Afghanistan must be in accordance with international law'', *Guardian*, 8 February 2010. http://www.theguardian.com/commentisfree/2010/feb/08/afghanistan-drones-defence-killing.
16. 'Pakistan's Sovereignty Is a Joke for the U.S', 17 February 2011, http://www.facebook.com/note.php?note_id=195108583849954.
17. BBC World Service (Urdu), 10 July 2013. Also, *Guardian*, 24 July 2013.
18. The resurgence of religion in its millenarian form, according to a leading Western thinker, has been a sustained reality of our era, though it has not been fully accepted as a pervasive phenomenon among all kinds of ideologies and isms. See John Gray, *Black Mass: Apocalyptic Religion and the Death of Utopia* (London: Penguin, 2008).
19. Some of these issues are discussed within the South Asian context in my *Jihad, Hindutva and the Taliban: South Asia at the Crossroads* (Oxford: Oxford University Press, 2005).
20. Other than this ideological tussle, the renewed emphasis on religion merely as an Islamist specificity has led the ongoing interface between three Abrahamic traditions to a crucial phase underwriting the Huntingtonian hypothesis in which September 11 has been seen both as a symptom and a cause for a deepening gulf.
    For a review of this discursive polarity, see Iftikhar H. Malik, *Crescent between Cross and Star: Muslims and the West after 9/11* (Oxford: Oxford University Press, 2006).
21. In his address to a select gathering in London, even Prince Charles went to great lengths in decrying capitalism and consumerism as the two serious most threats to ecological balance with their dire ramifications for the world at large. Robert Verkaik, 'Just 96 Months to Save the World, Says Prince Charles', *Independent*, 9 July 2009. http://www.independent.co.uk/environment/green-living/just-96-months-to-save-world-says-prince-charles-1738049.html.
22. S. R. Vali Nasr, *The Dispensable Nation: American Foreign Policy in Retreat* (New York: Anchor Books, 2015).
23. Cornell West, a prominent African American, has often criticized President Obama for drone attacks causing large-scale 'collateral killings', while in his own country Obama has tried to show solidarity with African American youths who often fall victim to stop-and-frisk processes. West said this following the judicial acquittal of George Zimmerman, who had earlier killed Trayvon Martin in Florida. Jermaine Spadley, 'Cornell West: Obama Is a Global Zimmerman

(a video)', *Huffington Post*, 22 July 2013, http://www.huffingtonpost.com/2013/07/22/cornel-west-barack-obama_n_3635614.html.
24. *Guardian*, 23 April 2015.
25. The military coup against President Mohammad Morsi of Egypt on 3 July 2013 certainly dashed hopes amongst many who had felt that ballot-based politics would eventually consolidate itself over any other form of unilateralism.
26. Ernest Gellner, *Muslim Society* (Cambridge: Cambridge University Press, 1993).
27. While some of these writers have been amply reviewed, the insidious nature of attacks by Gisele Littman (Bat Ye'Or), an Israeli writer, and a few others have often invited only brief media comments, though there is a greater need to expose their single-minded obsession with Islam. Like Pipes, they play on European fears by suggesting the ultimate ideological and demographic conquest of Europe by Muslims through 'Eurabia' and 'Dhimmitude'. See Bat Ye'Or, *Eurabia: The Euro-Arab Axis* (Teaneck: Fairleigh Dickinson, 2005). Geller and Spencer have been undertaking full-time campaigns against Islam at various levels, and their website, other than their works and speeches, offers a whole spectrum of Islamophobia: www.jihadwatch.org; also, Raphael Israeli, *The Islamic Challenge in Europe* (Fredericton, New Brunswick: Transaction Publishers, 2008).
28. Among others, Ayaan Hirsi Ali has reiterated it quite emphatically in her recent work. See her *Heretic: Why Islam Needs a Reformation Now* (New York: Harper, 2015).
29. Tariq Ali, *The Clash of Fundamentalisms* (London: Verso, 2005).
30. See Mahmood Mamdani, *Good Muslim, Bad Muslim: America, the Cold War, and the Roots of Terror* (New York: Three Leaves Publishing, 2005); and Khaled Abou El Fadl, *The Great Theft: Wrestling Islam from the Extremists* (New York: HarperOne, 2007).
31. For example, Farid Esak, *On Being Muslim* (Oxford: Oneworld, 2009).
32. For instance, Ziauddin Sardar, *Desperately Seeking Paradise: Journeys of a Sceptical Muslim* (London: Granta Books, 2005).
33. Despite being called the 'Martin Luther of Islam' euphemistically, Ramadan's understanding of Islam as a universal faith and not a territory- or time-specific ideology helps him posit it as conducive to all the traditional, modernist and plural imperatives. See Tariq Ramadan, *What I Believe* (Oxford: Oxford University Press 2009); also, *Western Muslims and the European Islam* (Oxford: Oxford University Press, 2005).
34. Shabbir Akhtar, *Islam: A Political Religion. The Future of an Imperial Faith* (London: Routledge, 2011). One has to be mindful of the fact that soon after the Rushdie affair, Akhtar warned Muslims of an impending debacle in Europe more in league with anti-Semitism. Quoted in Talal Asad, *Genealogies of Religion: Discipline and Reasons of Powers in Christianity and Islam* (Baltimore: John Hopkins University Press, 1993), 305. Akhtar had taken up issues with Naipaul – more like Edward Said – but has come down more clearly and forcefully on the side of Islamic theology, in which his own knowledge of the three Abrahamic traditions puts him in a rather enviable position for a comparative analysis.
35. Hussein Agha and Robert Malley, 'The Arab World Is Dead, But the Egyptians May Revive It', *Guardian*, 15 February 2011. http://www.theguardian.com/commentisfree/2011/feb/15/arab-world-egypt-revolution.
36. El Hassan bin Talal, 'Don't Fear the Wave', ibid., 16 February 2011.
37. For an early persuasive comment, see W. C. Smith, *Modern Islam in India: A Social Analysis*, (London: V. Gollancz, 1946).
38. Here, I am referring to authors like Fazlur Rahman, whose *Islam and Modernity* certainly merits greater attention at the moment, especially in his native country.
39. India is emerging as a case study in which Muslims happen to be a minority, whereas Turkey is a Muslim majority polity, and thus these two parallel models could allow a strong element of optimism, though in both these case studies there are still some strong roadblocks.
40. For such a comparative study, see Amyn B. Sajoo, ed., *Civil Societies in the Muslim World: Contemporary Perspectives* (London: I. B. Tauris, 2004).

41. Studies on Pakistan have often focused on 'high politics' in which the state, Islam and geopolitics have been the main areas of discussion, whereas societal configurations, demographic changes and class formations have mostly remained marginal.
42. For the identification of civil society organizations working for gender empowerment in places like Karachi, see Anwar Shaheen, 'Contribution of the NGOs to Social Science Research in Pakistan', Inayatullah, Rubina Saigol, Pervez Tahir, Inayatullah eds., *Social Sciences in Pakistan: A Profile* (Islamabad: Council of Social Sciences, 2005).
43. Commentators such as S. M. Naseem, Akbar Zaidi and numerous others have raised these issues quite often. For a detailed perspective, see Iftikhar H. Malik, *Pakistan: Democracy, Terror, and the Building of a Nation* (London: New Holland Publishers, 2010), 113–15.
44. Yoginder Sikand, '"Progressive Islam" in Pakistan', *Himal Magazine*, May–June 2006. For his later critique, see *Beyond the Border: An Indian in Pakistan* (New Delhi: Penguin Books, 2011).
45. Subhas Kapila, 'Pakistan: Do a "Civil Society" and a "Peace Constituency" Exist?' South Asia Analysis Group, Paper No. 917, 18 August 2006.
46. 'Aman Ki Asha', *News*, 1 January 2011. In 2012, the Pew Center undertook an extensive survey of public opinion in the subcontinent and found a popular desire for peaceful and friendlier relations between India and Pakistan. A press report highlighted those findings by noting, 'The Washington-based Pew Global Attitudes Project, which interviewed thousands of people in both countries, notes: "Indians and Pakistanis see their often fractious relationship in a similarly negative light. But both want their bilateral relations to improve"'. To achieve this target, '"majorities in both countries want to see their governments pursue efforts to better cross-border ties", the report adds. The face-to-face survey of more than 4,000 people in India was conducted between March 19 and April 19. A similar survey was done in Pakistan earlier this year. Seven-in-ten Indians and roughly six-in-ten Pakistanis (62 per cent) think it is important to improve relations. Nearly two-thirds of both Indians and Pakistanis say that increased trade between the two countries would be a good thing. But, while supportive, Indians are less-intensely focused than Pakistanis on resolving the Kashmir dispute. About six-in-ten Indians (59 per cent) say it is very important to resolve Indo-Pakistani differences over Kashmir, compared with roughly eight-in-ten Pakistanis (79 per cent) who hold such strong sentiments'. Anwar Iqbal, 'Majorities in India and Pakistan Want Better Ties'. *Dawn*, 9 December 2012.
47. Umer Farooq, 'Pak-India ties: Expect No Drastic Changes for Now', *Dawn*, 6 July 2013.
48. The BBC Urdu report from Swat, 26 July 2013, http://www.bbc.co.uk/urdu/pakistan/2013/07/130726_swat_women_jirga_sa.shtml.
49. Following the assassination of Salman Taseer in 2011 and with some lawyers lionizing Mumtaz Qadiri, the assassin, several commentators initially worried about openly criticizing vigilantism in the name of prophetic honour. Gradually, even some clerics began to challenge one another on taking the law into their own hands, overriding the universal values of a tolerant Islam. However, many women felt strongly enough to defy this kind of obscurantism. See *Dawn*, 19 February 2011.
50. For example, see Salman Ahmad, *Rock & Roll Jihad: A Muslim Rock Star's Revolution* (London: Simon & Schuster, 2010). Arieb Azhar has often contributed pieces on cultural issues to *Dawn*, while others have been touring the country and playing music to bring diverse people together and let them relate with one another through music and folk culture.
51. For instance, during Ramadan these private channels started competing to draw more viewers so as to claim more commercial sponsorship, and one egocentric anchor went beyond a reasonable limit by offering two infant orphans to two childless couples. See Rob Crilly, 'Pakistan's Top TV Cleric Gives Babies Away in Hit Ramadan Show', *Telegraph*, 24 July 2013. http://www.telegraph.co.uk/news/worldnews/asia/pakistan/10199944/Pakistans-top-TV-cleric-gives-babies-away-in-hit-Ramadan-show.html.
52. Declan Walsh, 'Could Revolution Spread from Egypt to Pakistan? The Country Is Ripe for Revolt Though It Would Mean Ousting the Army', *Guardian*, 15 February 2011.

53. He was viewing Pakistan as 'China's problem' and did not notice anything positive in the contemporary denominators, as he observed: 'I just spent several weeks in Pakistan. One thing I discovered was the insecurity in a way I had never seen it, even in military cantonments. The other was that China's influence in Pakistan was much greater and deeper than I had imagined it to be. In a sense that's India's problem, but in the long run, it will be China's problem'. Stephen Cohen, 'Pakistan's Road to Disintegration', an interview with Bernard Gwertzman, Council on Foreign Relations, 6 January 2011, see www.cfr.org/pakistan/pakistans-road-disintegration/p23744, accessed in Oxford on 21 February 2011.
54. In his speeches and television interviews, Imran Khan became the transmitter of Pakistan's growing dismay and critique of corruption and misgovernance. His criticism of drone attacks and preference for talking to the extremists instead of using brutal force sat well with ordinary Pakistanis but not necessarily with the ruling elite and their external backers. For his views, see Imran Khan, *Pakistan: A Personal Journey* (London: Bantam Press, 2011). Following the elections of 2013, his Tehreek-i-Insaaf emerged as the third-largest political force in the country, though his own fall from an elevated rostrum just before the polls impacted both his health and the overall the direction of his party. He still continued to believe in negotiating with the Taliban though, like many other Pakistanis, retrospectively appeared a bit reticent given the mushrooming of more than two dozen groups in the FATA, all claiming to be Pakistani Taliban. Imran Khan's interview with Jon Snow, Channel Four News, 24 July 2013, monitored in Bath.
55. 'For decades, Pakistan has refused to tax its feudal landlords, leading to a 12 percent tax/GDP ratio and a high dependency on foreign donors, with 99 percent of the population reporting attendant corruption. Only 860,000 of the 183 million population pay tax. Amnesty offered in December 2012 to the richest tax evaders to pay a 40,000-rupee penalty on undervalued income and on assets of as much as 5 million rupees has had little response [...] The neglected agricultural sector provides 23 percent of the GDP and 44 percent of the country's labor force, and non-agricultural activity in the rural areas has been lagging. Textiles and apparel provide 16 percent of the country's exports, and 40 percent of its employed labor force, with small and medium enterprises comprising 80 percent of the total non-agricultural employment. The official unemployment rate, as reported by the International Labor Organization is 6 percent, but this does not take into account the large percentage of the underemployed in both agriculture and the large urban informal sector'. Ranis, 'Is Pakistan a Failing State?'

6 The United States and Pakistan: Friends or Foes!

1. Quoted in James Boone, 'Bin Laden Killing: Official Report Criticises Pakistan and US. Leaked Report into Killing of Al-Qaida Chief Criticises Both Pakistan and US, Which It Says "Acted Like A Criminal Thug"', *Guardian*, 9 July 2013. http://www.theguardian.com/world/2013/jul/08/osama-bin-laden-pakistan-criticised.
2. Mark Mazzetti and Mark Landler, 'Despite Administration Promises, Few Signs of Change', *New York Times*, 2 August 2013. For more details on drone warfare and 'collateral damage', and the resultant anger across Pakistan, see Mark Mazzetti, *The Way of the Knife: The C.I.A., a Secret Army, and a War at the Ends of the Earth* (New York: Penguin Books, 2013).
3. Zbigniew Brzezinski, Inaugural Lecture, Conference on 'Lessons & Legacies of the Conflicts in Iraq, Afghanistan & Pakistan', Southern Methodist University, Dallas, 16 November 2009. The author is aware that the Dallas conference has been a unique experience in academic interaction on all sides given that, while discussing the intricacies of the US-South Asian politics, he was the only one from amongst the participants who came from that part of the world in addition to his identity as a European Muslim academic.
4. 'Simon Schama on Obama's America', BBC2, 12 January 2012. The one-hour programme devoted to the first year of Obama's presidency, sought parallels with President Harry Truman

and his entanglement in Korea where, in his determination to confront communism, the US president had to dissuade General Douglas McArthur from turning the costly war into a feared third global conflagration. Truman, more like Obama, faced pressure from a popular and self-righteous general, as General Stanley McChrystal and his Pentagon colleagues urged the sending in of more troops and resources to fight the Taliban.

5. An Israeli analyst, while commenting on US ventures since September 11, reminded his readers of the Vietnam war and Somerset Maugham's novel *The Quiet American*, as he noted, 'If the Quiet American, in his usual mixture of idealism and ignorance, decides to bring democracy and all the other goodies there [Yemen], that will be the end of this happiness. The Americans will sink into another quagmire, tens of thousands of people will be killed, and it will all end in disaster.

   'It may well be that the problem is rooted – inter alia – in the architecture of Washington DC.

   'This city is full of huge buildings populated with the ministries and other offices of the only superpower in the world. The people working there feel the tremendous might of their empire. They look upon the tribal chiefs of Afghanistan and Yemen as a rhinoceros looks down at the ants that rush around between its feet. The Rhino walks over them without noticing. But the ants survive.' Uri Avnery, 'The Quiet American', *Haaretz*, 9 January 2012.

6. 'The Obama administration is increasingly reliant on drone attacks despite stiff opposition in Pakistan, where they are widely seen as an unacceptable breach of sovereignty. Last year there were at least 45 attacks, compared with 27 in 2008'. Declan Walsh, 'CIA Drone Strike Missed Mehsud, Say Pakistani Taliban', *Guardian*, 14 January 2010. Since the death of seven CIA agents in Khost on 30 December 2009 in a suicide bombing, constant surveillance and frequent attacks by predatory aircraft in the FATA have helped the Pakistani Taliban enlist more recruits.

7. For a more recent review, see Yunas Samad, *The Pakistan-US Conundrum: Jihadists, the Military and the People – The Struggle for Control* (London: Hurst, 2011); also, Daniel S. Markey, *No Exit from Pakistan: America's Tortured Relationship with Islamabad* (Cambridge: Cambridge University Press, 2013).

8. In his statement to the House of Commons on 20 January 2010, Prime Minister Gordon Brown characterized these border tracts in a rather alarmist way, and that has been the norm all across NATO and its allies, possibly with the exception of Turkey.

9. The other questions ranged about visits to Pakistan, the location of Oxford and the purpose of my visit to Texas, despite the fact that he had already studied a whole bundle of e-mails with invitations from the university's Tower Center. Getting directions from his contacts on the phone, he seemed to be irreverent towards my profession, nationality, prior visa facilitation and such other facts.

10. More than 38 colleges and some halls underwrite these academic *tribes* in an otherwise immensely decentralized Oxford, and their students and alumni certainly identify themselves in reference to their individual institutions. For outsiders, it is just one university, but it is in fact its constituent colleges which work as autonomous 'mini universities' in their own right.

11. Even from the viewpoints of its own national and global interests, a world power like the United States needs to stay connected with these places through these intermediaries, especially when it has become so difficult for American academia and other citizens to travel to and study the Muslim lands and peoples. Disconnecting with a vast section of Muslim intellectuals, academics, writers and activists may be harmful to these groups, yet this loss at various level for the United States is already apparent to any keen observer.

12. The EU nations, with variations, have contributed funds and troops towards the security operations in Afghanistan and, according to a report, even before 'the surge' under Obama, the EU nations contributed around 43 per cent of the troops in the war-torn country. Daniel Korski, 'Shaping Europe's Afghan Surge', Policy Brief, London: European Council on Foreign Relations, 2009.

13. This was evident even at early stages through peace marches and media comments. Even after ten years, serious questions about the legality and morality of the invasion of Iraq were being investigated, reflecting a major unease with the official policies. On 12 January 2010, a nine-member Dutch inquiry committee openly questioned the Dutch decision to join Washington and London in an illegal invasion, especially when there were serious questions about the evidence on weapons of mass destruction. Headed by a former Supreme Court judge, it found that the invasion had 'no sound mandate in international law'. The Dutch report coincided with a similar though not a comprehensive inquiry being held in Britain under the leadership of Sir John Chilcott. For details on the Dutch report, see *Guardian*, 13 January 2010, and George Monbiot, 'Wanted Tony Blair for War Crimes. Arrest Him and Claim Your Reward', *Guardian*, 26 January 2010.
14. Craig Unger, *The Fall of the House of Bush: The Delusion of the Neoconservatives and American Armageddon* (New York: Simon & Schuster, 2008).
15. Such comments were not just confined to the traditional anti-American elements amongst Europe's Left, but rather were quite wide ranging. For a review, see Iftikhar H. Malik, *Crescent between Cross and Star: Muslims and the West after 9/11* (Oxford: Oxford University Press, 2006); and Ziauddin Sardar, *Why Do People Hate America?* (London: Disinformation, 2002). For an interesting liberal view, see Tariq Ali, *The Clash of Fundamentalisms: Crusades, Jihads and Modernity* (London: Verso, 2002).
16. Paul Krugman, 'Errors and Lies', *New York Times*, 18 May 2015.
17. From amongst several such early works, see Robert J. MacMahon, *The Cold War on the Periphery: The United States, India and Pakistan* (New York: Columbia University Press, 1996).
18. Shirin Tahir-Kheli, *The United States and Pakistan: The Evolution of an Influence Relationship* (New York: Praeger, 1982).
19. For further details in this area, see Iftikhar H. Malik, *Islam, Nationalism and the West: Issues of Identity in Pakistan* (Oxford: Macmillan-St. Antony's Series, 1999), 220–49.
20. For a searchlight on these trajectories, see Iftikhar H. Malik, *State and Civil Society in Pakistan: Politics of Authority, Ideology and Ethnicity* (Oxford: St. Antony's-Macmillan Series, 1997).
21. This has not stopped these American establishments from criticizing Pakistan, especially its security agencies like the ISI, for providing sustenance to militant groups operating in Kashmir and Afghanistan. In addition, Pakistan's nuclear programme has often provided fuel to such damnation, whereas even lobbyists – both expatriate and American – have occasionally been investigated for their connections with Pakistan. Investigations of Ghulam Nabi Fai, a Kashmiri activist, and of Robin Raphel, a long-time American diplomat and State Department official, have been quoted as part of case studies of American official rebukes of pro-Islamabad voices. Kamran Yousaf, 'Pakistan Accuses US of "Slander Campaign"', *Express Tribune*, 22 July 2011. http://tribune.com.pk/story/214916/pakistan-accuses-us-of-slander-campaign/; and for Fai's biographical and professional details, see Kashmir American Council, 'A Case-Study of Dr. Ghulam Nabi Fai', http://www.kashmiri.com/10-homepage/30-a-case-study-on-dr-ghulam-nabi-fai.

    Raphel was being investigated in November 2014 on suspicions of sharing intelligence with some 'foreign' country: Anne Gearan and Adam Goldman, 'U.S. Diplomat and Longtime Pakistan Expert Is under Federal Investigation', *Washington Post*, 6 November 2014.
22. This triumphalism is evident in several works such as George Crile, *My Enemy's Enemy: The Story of the Largest Covert Operation in History: The Arming of Mujahideen by the CIA* (London: Atlantic Books, 2003); and Bruce Riedel, *What We Won. America's Secret War in Afghanistan, 1979–89* (Washington, DC: Brookings Institution Press, 2014).
23. For his self-congratulatory biography, see Pervez Musharraf, *In the Line of Fire: A Memoir* (New York: Simon & Schuster, 2006).
24. For more on the civil society and its recent struggle for full-fledged democratization, an independent judiciary and egalitarian policies, see Iftikhar H. Malik, 'Civil Society in Pakistan: Stake Holders in a Contested State', Pakistan Security Research Unit, No. 50, 2009, http://spaces.brad.ac.uk: 8080/download/attachments/748/Brief+50.pdf.

25. Samuel M. Hersh, 'Defending the Arsenal: In an Unstable Pakistan, Can Nuclear Warheads Be Kept Safe'? *New Yorker*, 9–16 November 2009.
26. Seymour M. Hersh, 'The Killing of Osama bin Laden', *London Review of Books*, 21 May 2015. For a related comment, see Owen Bennett-Jones, 'The Bin Laden Questions', *The News*, 26 May 2015.
27. Based on interviews with ordinary people, politicians and retired army officers in December 2009 across the country.
28. Several studies highlight such and many more contestations within the country. See Farzana Shaikh, *Making Sense of Pakistan* (London: Hurst, 2009).
29. More recent academic and journalistic works on Pakistan have often posited it as a country faced with serious internal and regional 'messy' issues. See Anatol Lieven, 'Pakistan: The Mess We Can't Ignore', *New York Review of Books*, 20 March 2014, http://www.nybooks.com/articles/archives/2014/mar/20/pakistan-mess-we-cant-ignore/.
30. The recent problems are linked with the issues of governance, daredevil foreign policies and uneven economic performance, which have had their roots especially in the overthrow of an elected regime in 1999 by General Musharraf. His Kargil campaign earlier that year had already maligned the country abroad as an irresponsible regional actor, whereas his coup only aggravated the malaise. For further details, see Owen Bennett-Jones, *Pakistan: Eye of the Storm* (London: Yale University Press, 2009).
31. The most serious accusation came from Admiral Mike Mullen, the chairman of the Joint Chiefs of Staff, soon after a Taliban attack on the US Embassy in Kabul in September 2011. He had been working closely with the Pakistani military for a number of years, but in a Congressional hearing, he noted, 'With ISI support, Haqqani operatives planned and conducted that truck bomb attack, as well as the assault on our embassy. We also have credible evidence that they were behind the June 28th attack against the Intercontinental Hotel in Kabul and a host of other smaller but effective operations'. According to him, 'the Haqqani network acts as a veritable arm of Pakistan's Inter-Services Intelligence agency'. Elisabeth Bumiller and Jane Perlez, 'Pakistan's Spy Agency Is Tied to Attack on U.S. Embassy', *New York Times*, 22 September 2011.

    In recent times, various writers have put the onus of responsibility on Pakistan for NATO's failure in Afghanistan. See Carlotta Gall, *The Wrong Enemy: America in Afghanistan, 2001–2014* (New York: HoughtonMifflin, 2014). Some analysts have, instead, urged for a continued American engagement with Pakistan. See, Daniel S. Markey, *No Exit from Pakistan*.
32. For details on the John Kerry-Sartaj Aziz press conference after three days of negotiations in Islamabad, see *Dawn*, 1 August 2013.
33. Two former ambassadors, in fact, highlighted the need for focused stabilization in US–Pakistani relations, especially after the stormy events of 2011: Teresita and Howard Schaffer, 'Resetting the U.S.-Pakistan Relationship,' *Foreign Policy*, March 19, 2012. http://foreignpolicy.com/2012/03/19/resetting-the-u-s-pakistan-relationship/.
34. K. Alan Kronstadt, *Pakistan-U.S. Relations* (Washington, DC: Congressional Research Service, 2012), 2.
35. The National Intelligence Council and the CIA, *Global Trends 2015: A Dialogue about the Future with Nongovernment Experts*, December 2000, 64–6, http://www.fas.org/irp/cia/product/globaltrends2015/. The report had predicted an escalation in Indo–Pakistani relations overshadowing other regional issues.
36. 'Pakistan Will Be a Failed State by 2015, CIA', *Times of India*, 13 February 2005.
37. Frederick Kagan and Michael O'Hanlon, 'Pakistan's Collapse, Our Problem', *New York Times*, 18 November 2007, quoted in Andrew Gavin Marshall, 'Imperial Eye on Pakistan – Pakistan in Pieces', *Global Research*, 28 May 2011. The author acknowledges a few other references from the same paper.
38. Harrison felt that the Pashtuns would join their fellow tribesmen from across the border, and altogether 40 million in number they would form their own state, whereas 23 million Sindhis

might establish their independent Sindhudesh, and Baloch too would opt for secession, leaving only Punjab to work on its own. Selig S. Harrison, 'Drawn and Quartered', *New York Times*, 1 February 2008.
39. The National Intelligence Council and the CIA, *Global Trends 2025: A Transformed World*, November 2008, 45 and 72, http://www.dni.gov/files/documents/Newsroom/Reports%20 and%20Pubs/2025_Global_Trends_Final_Report.pdf.
40. Peter Goodspeed, 'Mexico, Pakistan Face 'Rapid and Sudden' Collapse: Pentagon', *National Post*, 15 January 2009. Such official assessments were picked up by the Indian media to show what appeared to be Pakistan on the way to a quick and volatile end, generating a debate about the nature of its relationship with its neighbour to the west. While some analysts would see such predictions with a greater sense of awe due to their ramifications for India, several others would simply welcome such a scenario. The collapse of Pakistan, to the latter, was in India's interests as it would deny China a major role in South Asia, and routes to Central Asia would open up for India. Bharat Verma, 'Stable Pakistan Not in India's Interest', *Indian Defence Review*, 11 September 2008, quoted in Marshall, 'Imperial Eye on Pakistan'.
41. Farhan Bokhari et al., 'U.S. Special Forces Strike in Pakistan', CBS News, 3 September 2008, www.cbsnews.com/stories/2008/09/03/terror/main4409288.shtml.
42. Declan Walsh, 'US Forces Mounted Secret Pakistan Raids in Hunt for al-Qaida', *Guardian*, 21 December 2009.
43. Ayaz Amir, 'So, Finally a Farewell to Arms', *The News*, 21 June 2013.
44. Benazir Bhutto, in her second book, highlighted the contradictory and immensely dangerous Western policies in the Muslim regions, which often contravened popular and democratic precepts. Benazir Bhutto, *Reconciliation: Islam, Democracy and the West* (London: Simon & Schuster, 2008).

A large number of Pakistanis also believe that their country is a victim, following the rash and ever-escalating warring policy pursued by Washington and Islamabad. Imran Khan has often articulated such thinking, in which he views the war on terror as the bane of Pakistan's volatility. In a seminar in London in mid-January 2010 convened by Intelligence Squared, he spoke quite clearly on these issues, and interestingly several other speakers concurred with him in suggesting a review of military-centric policies. For the proceedings and presentations, see http://www.intelligencesquared.com/iq2-video/2010/pakistan-what-next.
45. For an interesting rebuke by a Muslim royal from Qatar's ruling family, during her inauguration of a new building at St. Antony's College, Oxford, see Sean Coughlan, 'Muslims "Dehumanised" Warns Qatar's Sheikha Moza', BBC online, 26 May 2015.
46. Pakistani officials have often accused India of fomenting trouble in Balochistan and other border areas. Pakistanis have been weary of several Indian consulates all along the Pak–Afghan border and feel that India provides financing and weapons to Baloch insurgents and other such elements that may have their own axes to grind. Pakistan's former interior minister, Rahman Malik, in a statement in the Pakistani Senate claimed to have proof of India's involvement in Balochistan. *News*, 14 January 2010. Reasons for Pakistan fears of India's involvement in Afghanistan were also acknowledged by James Dobbins, the US envoy for Af–Pak. 'Pakistani Fears over India's Afghan Role "Not Groundless"', BBC, 7 August 2013, http://www.bbc.co.uk/news/world-asia-india-23598521.
47. 'Terrorism and Indo-Pakistani Escalation: CPA Contingency Planning Memorandum No. 6', Report by Daniel Markey for the Center for Preventive Action, Council on Foreign Relations, January 2010, http://www.cfr.org/publication/21042.

Robert Gates, the US secretary of defense, on his visit to India, gave a rather blunt warning against any possible attack by the Islamists aimed at provoking a war between the two rivals. Gates's remarks reflected a continuing unhappiness with Islamabad as contrasted with extraordinary softness for Delhi. To him 'the groups also posed an "existential" threat to Pakistan and warned that India's government – which refrained from reprisal attacks on Pakistan after the Mumbai assault – wasn't likely to exercise similar restraint if new attacks occurred on its territory. "I think it's not unreasonable to assume that Indian patience would be limited were there to be further attacks", he said'. Yochi J. Dreazen, 'Gates Says Al Qaeda Seeks to Trigger India Pakistan War', *Wall Street Journal*, 20 January 2010, http://online.wsj.com/article/SB10001424052748704320104575014752587809016.html. During 2013, the British police investigated Altaf Hussain on charges of money laundering, assassinations and incitement for violence in Karachi, where MQM hit men would strike at the orders of the London-based leader. In the process, the British media published some allegations by former MQM strong men now in exile in London that they had been trained by India along with receiving monetary support for such elements. For details, see Owen Bennett-Jones, 'Altaf Hussain, the Notorious MQM Leader Who Swapped Pakistan for London', *Guardian*, 29 July 2013, http://www.guardian.co.uk/world/2013/jul/29/altaf-hussain-mqm-leader-pakistan-london.

48. Ahmed Rashid, 'A Bridge to Build between India and Pakistan', *Washington Post*, 25 November 2009.

7   European Union and Southwest Asia: Perceptions, Policies and Permutations

1. Fariba Nawa, *Opium Nation: Child Brides, Drug Lords and One Woman's Journey through Afghanistan* (New York: Harper Perennial, 2011), 304–5.
2. For a quick survey of the post–World War II evolution of the EU, from a bilateral trading concern to a complex and perhaps the most integrated multistate alliance, see John Pinder and Simon Usherwood, *The European Union: A Very Short Introduction* (Oxford: Oxford University Press, 2013) and Desmond Dinan, *Ever Closer Union: An Introduction to European Integration*, (Basingstoke: Palgrave Macmillan, 2011). For its international relations, see Christopher Hill and Michael Smith, *International Relations and the European Union* (Oxford: Oxford University Press, 2011).
3. Compared to other regions, studies on EU-South Asian relations are fewer as it is an emerging academic field, though there are several papers and reports on the subjects. However, these reports usually deal with bilateral issues. Other than a few specific studies, the following volumes have chapters devoted to individual South Asian states and their relations with the EU, especially after September 11. For instance, Jean-Joseph Boillot, *Europe After Enlargement: Economic Challenges for EU and India* (London: Academic Foundation, 2005); H. S. Chopra and Robert Frank, *National Identity and Regional Cooperation: Experiences of European Integration and South Asian Perceptions* (New Delhi: Manohar, 2004); R. K. Jain, *India and the European Union: Building a Strategic Partnership* (New Delhi: Pee Pee Publishers, 2007); Shazia Aziz Wulbers, *EU-India Relations: A Critique* (New Delhi: Academic Foundation, 2008); Urfan Khaliq, *Ethical Dimensions of the Foreign Policy of the European Union: A Legal Appraisal* (Cambridge: Cambridge University Press, 2008); Stig J. Hansen et al., *The Borders of Islam: Exploring Huntington's Faultlines, from Al-Andalus to the Virtual Ummah* (New York: Columbia University Press, 2010); EU Commission, *New Business Opportunities for EU Companies in Pakistan: An Investor's Guidebook* (Luxembourg: EU Publication Office, 2005), http://bookshop.europa.eu/en/new-business-opportunities-for-eu-companies-in-pakistan-pbKQ5704887/); Richard G. Whitman and Stefan Wolff, eds., *The EU as a Global Conflict Manager* (London: Routledge, 2012). The *Pakistan Journal of European Studies*, a quarterly publication of the University of Karachi, has regular contributions on various aspects of the EU's engagements with South Asian states. By 2013, it had already published 29 volumes: http://www.asce-ku.com.pk/journals.ht,ml.

   Shada Islam, based in Brussels, has periodically published reports and articles dealing with the EU's thematic, regional and global engagements. Other than being part of a think tank, she is a regular columnist for *Dawn*, South Asia's leading newspaper: http://x.dawn.com/author/dawnshadaislam/.

4. For this interface, see Robert McMahon, *The Cold War on the Periphery: The United States, India, and Pakistan* (New York: Columbia University Press, 1996).
5. On this 'China factor', see Neville Maxwell, *India's China War* (Harmondsworth: Penguin Books, 1972); Ma Jiali et al., *China-South Asian Relations* (E-resource), Reading: Paths International, 2010. http://www.lib.sp.edu.sg/availlim/search~S0?/aJia%2C+Xu/ajia+xu/1%2C0%2C0%2CE/frameset&FF=ajiali+ma&1%2C1%2C.
6. Among numerous scholarly works and military histories of the NATO, one may also include studies by and for NATO: http://natolibguides.info/maritimesecurity/books.
7. NATO's rationale and role in a post–Cold War world first came out into the open during the Balkan crisis in which it just managed an unchallenged aerial superiority, though on the ground, it proved ineffective. In Bosnia, the Serb and Croat forces, daring both the UN and NATO, routinely violated the international havens or safe areas for refugees and IDPs. It is true that the UN found itself on the horns of a dilemma and could not even maintain its traditional role as peacekeeper and allowed extreme events like Srebrenica to happen, yet NATO equally displayed fissures among the EU nations and the United States. Kofi Annan, subsequently, following an inquiry, accepted the UN failure in not protecting the Bosnian refugees. 'UN Admits It Appeased Bosnian Serbs in '95', *International Herald Tribune*, 16 November 1999. The UN troops led by the French General Philippe Morillon stepped aside when Serbs led by Ratko Mladic separated more than 10,000 Muslim men and boys from their families before murdering them outside Srebrenica in July 1995. Also: http://srebrenica-genocide.blogspot.co.uk/2011/10/yasushi-akashi-architect-of-disaster-in.html.

Thus, both multilateral institutions were found wanting in establishing peace by rolling back violence in the former Yugoslavia. Douglass Hurd, Boutros Boutros-Ghali, Kofi Annan and Yasushi Akashi all remained on the sidelines, while commanders such as Generals Michael Rose and Morillon failed to undertake any proactive or protective measures in UN-led safe havens. All of them have left copious details in their self-defence, but the fact remains that the two most powerful alliances in human history, dominated by the North Atlantic states, were found wanting on many counts. It is quite true that NATO's subsequent operations in Kosovo showed some resolve to rectify earlier legacies. For some contemporary writings on the Balkans and failure of world multilateral alliances, see David Rieff, *Slaughterhouse: Bosnia and the Failure of the West* (New York:: Simon & Schuster, 1995); David Rhode, *A Safe Area. Srebrenica: Europe's Worst Massacre Since the Second World War* (London: Pocket Books, 1997); Roy Gutman, *A Witness to Genocide* (Shaftesbury: Prentice Hall 1993); Misha Glenny, *The Balkans, 1804–1999: Nationalism, War and the Great Powers* (London: Granta Books, 1999); Douglas Hurd, *Memoirs* (London: Little, Brown, 2003); Boutros Boutros-Ghali, *Unvanquished* (New York: Random House, 1999); Michael Rose, *Fighting for Peace: Lessons from Bosnia 1994* (London: Sphere, 1999); David Owen, *Balkan Odyssey* (London: Phoenix, 1996); Carl Blidt, *Peace Journey: The Struggle for Peace in Bosnia* (London: Weidenfeld & Nicolson, 1998); Richard Holbrooke, *To End a War* (New York: Random House, 1998); and, Kofi Annan, *Interventions: A Life in War and Peace* (Harmondsworth: Allen Lane,, 2012). I have commented on these events while reviewing these and various other works on the Balkans: Iftikhar H. Malik, *Islam, Globalisation and Modernity: The Tragedy of Bosnia* (Lahore: Vanguard Books, 2004).

On NATO, there is a profusion of autobiographies, textbooks, scholarly treatises and specialized reports in addition to its coverage through scholarly journals, dailies and its own public relations domain. For a textbook history and overview of the alliance especially in view of US unilateralism, see Stanley Sloan, *NATO, the European Union, and the Atlantic Community : The Transatlantic Bargain Challenge* (Oxford: Rowman & Littlefield Publishers, 2005); and Gulnur Aybet and Rebecca Moore, eds., *NATO: In Search of a Vision* (Washington, DC: Georgetown University Press, 2010).
8. Almost every EU nation is home to Ultra-Right parties, which combine exclusive nationalism with an assertive blend of Christianity and, despite their contemporary focus on Europe's

Muslim communities, remain very critical of immigration and pluralism. In Britain other than the British National Party, the English Defense League and, to a great extent, the UK Independence Party keep pushing the polity more towards a racialized dispensation. Even the mainstream parties such as the Conservative and Labour often appear to be appeasing such constellations. France's National Front and its counterparts in the Netherlands and Austria have become even ruling factions given their larger share in votes. For an overview, see Pete Simi and Robert Futrel, 'Neo-Nazi Movements in Europe and the United States', *Wiley-Blackwell Encyclopedia of Social and Political Movements*, published online 14 January 2013: doi: 10.1002/9780470674871.wbespm353.

9. These acronyms are of multilateral, international bodies created in different regions to spearhead greater cooperation among member states in a number of areas:
   ASEAN   The Association of Southeast Nations
   GCC   The Gulf Co-operation Council
   NATO   North Atlantic Treaty Organization
   OAU   Organisation of African Unity
   OIC   Organization of Islamic Cooperation
   SAARC   South Asian Association for Regional Cooperation.
10. Lee Yoong, ed., *Asean Matters: Reflecting on the Association of Southeast Asian Nations* (Hackensack, NJ: World Scientific Pub., 2011).
11. During the debates over the possibility of a shared EU constitution, such observations were noted quite often, and in fact, countries like Ireland, Poland and Italy and leaders such as former French president Valerie Giscard d'Estaing vocally articulated this Christian identity of Europe. Despite a periodic reiteration of making the EU more plural at various levels, it is still a long way away from becoming inclusive. Even among the EU's election monitoring teams, which are supposed to work across the world, overwhelmingly consist of white men as these EU jobs, in most cases, are based on nominations from the respective member states. Such facts are quite revealing when comparing the EU's frequent exhortations to the world at large on universal empowerment. Even in otherwise peaceful Scandinavia or countries without any tainted colonial hang-ups, the accent on exclusive and racialized nationalism has been persistently visible. While collective tragedies like the massacres by Anders Breivik in Norway in 2011 may be seen as solitary events, their interconnectedness with actions by similar other neo-Nazi groups in Europe and in North America cannot be underestimated. Even the Boston Marathon bombers, like Breivik, were influenced by racist typologies after internalizing supremacist literature on the Internet.
12. For a critical perspective, see Arun Kundani, *The End of Tolerance: Racism in 21st Century Britain* (London: Pluto, 2007). Mak Chishty, a senior Scotland Yard official of Muslim background, even went to the extent of suggesting the monitoring of the 'private space' of Muslim children to guard them against possible radicalization. *Guardian*, 26 May 2015. http://www.theguardian.com/world/2015/may/24/jihadi-threat-requires-move-into-private-space-of-uk-muslims-says-police-chief.
13. For some of the early and enduring ethno-national movements, see Subrata Mitra and Alison Lewis, eds., *Subnational Movements in South Asia* (Denver, CO: Westview, 1998).
14. Several specialized studies in South Asia focus on interstate issues and think tanks, and in addition the media often end up flagging their own distinct statist stances. India, Pakistan, Bangladesh and Sri Lanka lead the region with such think tanks, often led by retired generals, diplomats and former intelligence officials. These institutes and centres may have their own younger groups of scholars or researchers, but top-down 'grand narratives' predetermine their output.
15. For a compendium of opinions and activism from both sides, see Smitu Kothari and Zia Mian, eds., *Bridging Partition: People's Initiatives for Peace between India and Pakistan* (New Delhi: Orient BlackSwan, 2010). In addition, the Jang Group of Pakistani newspapers and the *Times of India* formed a media-based channel called Aman Ki Asha (Hope for Peace) which, through articles,

mutual visits, the celebration of each other's festivals and achievements and by conducting opinion polls has been trying to create a better understanding of people-to-people relationships, often called second- and third-track diplomacy. See http://amankiasha.com/.

16. Jon Henley, 'Walls: An Illusion of Security from Berlin to the West Bank', *Guardian*, 19 November 2013. http://www.theguardian.com/uk-news/2013/nov/19/walls-barrier-belfast-west-b-ank

17. Some of the early works in these areas are still valid: Robert Osgood, *Ideals and Self-Interest in America's Foreign Relations: The Great Transformation in the Twentieth Century*, (Chicago: University of Chicago Press, 1957) and Robert Jervis, *Perception and Misperception in International Politics* (Princeton: Princeton University Press, 1976).

18. While one finds ample material on political, economic and security factors underpinning Western foreign policies, not enough has been documented on the resources, channels and impact of public diplomacy that the rich nations with international outreach have been pursuing. Even postcolonial studies focus on the element of continuity in newer states through surrogacy, but tend to ignore rather apolitical channels, which play a crucial role in forming supportive opinion at various levels across the developing world. A few works appeared in the 1980s dealing with US public diplomacy, but a critical and in-depth evaluation of its organs such as the Fulbright Program, USAID, USIS, the Ford Foundation, the Peace Corps and several such other agencies and foundations remains to be completed. For an early and a rather uncritical work of the US Information Agency (USIA), see Allen C. Hansen, *USIA: Public Diplomacy in the Computer Age* (New York: Praeger, 1984). Based on extensive data and some challenging fieldwork, I included a chapter in one of my earlier works: Iftikhar H. Malik, *Islam, Nationalism and the West: Issues of Identity in Pakistan* (Oxford/New York: Macmillan-St. Antony's Series, 1999), 220–49.

19. This is how the ancient Greeks like Herodotus defined the 'known' world, which remained divided between civilized and barbarian communities – the ascriptive connotations from North Mediterranean lands. Herodotus, *The Histories*, edited by John M. Marincola and Aubery de Selincourt (Harmondsworth: Penguin, 2003).

20. There are numerous studies and visual presentations on the Crusades. For a recent single-volume work, see Thomas Asbridge, *The Crusades: The Authoritative History of the War for the Holy Land* (London: Ecco Press, 2011).

21. There are several contemporary works by Arab, Berber and Spanish authors on Medieval Sicily and what happened to local Muslims and Jews after the Norman Conquest. For a recent work, see Alex Metcalfe, *The Muslims of Medieval Italy* (Edinburgh: Edinburgh University Press, 2009).

22. To some writers, the suppression of debate and *ijtiha'ad* originated during the late-Abbasid period when Sunni orthodoxy took control in the garb of Asharism. See Robert R. Reilly, *The Closing of the Muslim Mind: How Intellectual Suicide Created the Modern Islamist Crisis* (Wilmington: ISI Books, 2011).

23. John Darwin, *After Tamerlane: The Rise and Fall of Global Empires, 1400–2000* (London: Penguin, 2008), and Christopher Bayly, *The Birth of the Modern World: 1780–1914* (Oxford: Blackwell: 2004).

24. An interesting work locates the salience of Western nations in reference to long-term civilizational achievements called 'social development', which allowed Europe a sustained element of progress and even dominance over the rest. Ian Morris, *Why the West Rules – for Now: The Patterns of History, and What They Reveal about the Future* (London: Profile, 2011) and *The Measure of Civilization: How Social Development Decides the Fate of Nations* (London: Profile, 2013).

25. On 12 December 2013, the EU, through a majority vote awarded Pakistan the Generalised System of Preferences (GSP), which would mean that 20% of Pakistani goods such as textiles could enter the bloc without duties being levied on them, while 70% would be liable to reduced duties. This special award was already available to both Bangladesh and Sri Lanka, and Pakistani allowance was due until 2015. It was felt that Pakistan's trade would benefit to

the volume of $1 to 2 billion annually, and was heralded by the Sharif government as a major economic breakthrough. *Dawn*, 12 December 2013.
26. *Dawn*, 18 June 2013.
27. *Guardian*, 12 August 2010.
28. EU External Action, 'EU and Pakistan Launch Strategic Dialogue', http://eeas.europa.eu/top_stories/2012/050612_pakistan_en.htm.
29. *Dawn*, 5 June 2012.
30. Council of the European Union (Luxembourg), 'Council Conclusions on Pakistan', 24 June 2013, http://consilium.europa.eu/uedocs/cms_data/docs/pressdata/EN/foraff/137582.pdf.
31. Shada Islam, 'EU Can Help Pakistan's New PM Tackle Tough Agenda', Friends of Europe, 13 May 2013, http://www.friendsofeurope.org/.
32. *Dawn*, 12 December 2013.
33. For historical details on the EU mission and objectives along with details on resources and budgetary allocations, see European Commission, *Country Strategy Paper: Islamic Republic of Afghanistan, 2007–13*, http://eeas.europa.eu/afghanistan/csp/07_13_en.pdf. (1,030 million euros were earmarked for this period for various areas of reconstruction and infrastructure).
34. "The EU is one of the major donors of development and humanitarian assistance to Afghanistan. Between 2002 and 2011, it contributed some 2.5 billion to the country, including over 500 million in humanitarian assistance. The EU's assistance has progressed from humanitarian support to its current focus on the country's reconstruction and support for the National Priority Programmes. This is how official reports record the financial injections, which are undoubtedly quite impressive in terms of allocations and volumes. European Commission, 'Development and Cooperation – Europeaid: Afghanistan', EU Assistance Programme, 2007–2013, 6 August 2013, http://ec.europa.eu/europeaid/where/asia/country-cooperation/afghanistan/afghanistan_en.htm.
On the EU network of NGOs and related news stories, see http://www.ennanet.eu/.
35. This is not to suggest that the EU–NATO interface is totally clear, as ambiguities and parallel policies often cause aberrations, and then the growing fatigue on the part of the EU societies in pursuing war while underwriting huge expenses exacerbates such roadblocks. In an era of post-2008 cuts in public services and expenditures across Europe, EU and NATO officials have tried for further clarity in their respective areas. See the Centre for European Studies (CES), *Breaking Down the Walls: Improving EU-NATO Relations*, http://isiseurope.wordpress.com/2013/05/28/breaking-down-the-walls-improving-eu-nato-relations/ and: http://thinkingeurope.eu/events/breaking-down-walls-improving-eu-nato-relations.

Conclusion: Pashtun Troubled Lands, Uncertain Southwest Asia or a New Beginning!

1. Parting comments by President Hamid Karzai as quoted in the *News*, 23 September 2014. Also, Rod Nordland, "In Farewell Speech, Karzai Calls American Mission in Afghanistan a Betrayal', *New York Times*, 23 September 2014: http://www.nytimes.com/2014/09/24/world/asia/hamid-karzai-afghanistan.html?_r=0
2. 'It's like Alcoholics Anonymous. Step one is admitting you have a problem. Well, I have a problem. So do my peers. And thanks to our problem, now all of America has a problem. To wit: two lost campaigns and a war gone awry'. For details of his interview with National Pubic Radio on 9 November 2014, see http://www.npr.org/2014/11/09/361746282/a-3-star-general-explains-why-we-lost-in-iraq-afghanistan; also Daniel P. Bolger, *Why We Lost? A General's Inside Account of the Iraq and Afghanistan Wars* (New York: EamonDolan, 2014).
3. Patrick Cockburn, 'Bowe Bergdahl Release: Email Exchange Reveals Extent of US Failure in Afghan War', *Independent*, 3 June 2014. Bowe Bergdahl, the US sergeant and a Taliban prisoner,

was reportedly unhappy with the way Afghans were, in general, treated by the American forces. '"The US army is the biggest joke the world has to laugh at", wrote Sergeant Bergdahl in an e-mail later published by *Rolling Stone* magazine. "It is the army of liars, backstabbers, fools, and bullies. The few good SGTs [sergeants] are getting out as soon as they can, and they are telling us privates to do the same" [...] Instead, he found that US soldiers regarded Afghans with aggressive contempt: "I am sorry for everything here. These people need help, yet what they get is the most conceited country in the world telling them that they are nothing and that they are stupid, that they have no idea how to live"'.

4. Stuart Tootal, *Danger Close: Commanding 3 Para in Afghanistan* (London: John Murray, 2009), 21.
5. Sherard Cowper-Coles, *Cables from Kabul: The Inside Story of the West's Afghanistan Campaign* (London: HarperPress, 2012), 69.
6. For further details, Malik Siraj Akbar, 'The End of Pakistan's Baloch Insurgency?' *Huffington Post*, 3 November 2014. http://www.huffingtonpost.com/malik-siraj-akbar/the-end-of-pakistans-balo_b_6090920.html.
7. Anand Gopal, *No Good Men Among the Living: America, the Taliban, and the War through Afghan Eyes* (New York: Metropolitan Books, 2014).
8. 'The White House's inability thus far to publicly articulate a commitment of troops for Afghanistan after 2014 is wreaking unnecessary havoc, we're told by current and former administration officials. It's making it difficult for allies to plan ahead for their forces, and for the American military itself to prepare for next year. Meanwhile, informed observers say that the White House's apparent indecision or delay appears to have no political gain at home and only a political cost overseas. At home, the American public is increasingly wary of the war in Afghanistan – only about 28 percent believe the war is worth fighting, according to a recent *Washington Post*-ABC News poll. Those defense and administration officials, speaking privately, say they are scratching their heads over the lack of a decision, whatever it may be, or why the Obama administration would allow officials to float the idea of a "zero option" – no troops after 2014 as an apparent bluff in security negotiations – only to quickly acknowledge that no such option really exists. While the bilateral security agreement with Afghanistan remains a distinct sticking point, most government officials and national security experts quietly believe the White House is undermining its strategic objectives there by remaining mum on the matter'. Mark Lubold, *Foreign Policy Situation Report*, Washington, DC, 14 August 2013.
9. Drone attacks and midnight raids across Afghanistan are not reported in the media. In the same way, reports of fatalities from the FATA get reported, but remain cursory without identifying the victims. There have been more than 100,000 NATO troops in Afghanistan, and of those, 68,000 were from the United States, whose casualties in this war by August 2013 totaled around 2,100. In 2011–12, some Afghan trainees were also involved in green-on-blue attacks, which, following strict segregation gradually fell down in frequency. More dependence on drones, to a great extent, obviated the need for 'boots on the ground'. Still, both warring sides often confronted each other through aerial attacks, which gradually became a more routine answer to Taliban offensives. Still, ISAF soldiers especially in Pashtun regions, like the British in Helmand during 2006–9, kept losing their lives. On 11 August, the Taliban reportedly killed three American soldiers in Paktia province. www.reuters.com.

On presidential and provincial elections, and the ensuing stalemate between Ashraf Ghani and Abdullah Abdullah, see the *Los Angeles Times*, 25 April 2014.
10. *Economist*, October 2014.
11. Despite Sharif's participation in Modi's oath taking in Delhi, both the neighbours were back to the familiar square one, with India cancelling bilateral talks at the foreign ministerial level and their respective border forces engaged in sporadic skirmishes. *Times of India*, 3 September 2015: http://timesofindia.indiatimes.com/world/pakistan/India-Pakistan-tensions-can-become-dangerous-Daily/articleshow/48784607.
12. *Dawn*, 13 August 2013.

13. In the Kashmir Valley, it began with the killing of five Indian soldiers, apparently by militants, some of whom were wearing Pakistani military uniforms, and with some Indian parliamentarians demanding a strong reprimand of Pakistan. Mobs even attacked the Pakistani embassy in Delhi amidst blame and counterblame from both the governments. The ruling Congress, in view of a growing challenge from the BJP in the elections of 2014 did not want to look weak and thus fell in competition with its rivals in denouncing Pakistan for orchestrating violence in Kashmir. However, media reports from outside South Asia suggested a new generation of Muslim Kashmiris taking up arms against India largely because of longer curfews, the lack of developmental policies and growing grievances against the security forces for manhandling Kashmiri Muslim youths and women. India's failure to assuage Kashmiri grievances and its rather strong-arm politics over the past two decades had triggered a new wave of alienation among Kashmiris that foreign journalists were able to detect at various levels. See Jason Burke, 'Kashmir Conflict Ebbs as New Wave of Militant Emerges', *Guardian*, 11 August 2013. http://www.theguardian.com/world/2013/aug/11/kashmir-conflict-new-wave-militants
14. 'Pakistan Jailbreak: Taliban Free 248 in Dera Ismail Khan', BBC (online), 30 July 2013.
    The Pakistani Taliban have been involved in killing pro-Islamabad tribal chieftains along with selective murders of more than 500 politicians belonging to the Awami National Party (ANP). The ANP could not run its election campaign in 2013 despite the fact that it had been in power KP for five years. The TTP did not spare even Pashtun women belonging to the ANP and on 17 August 2013 killed Mrs Najma Hanif in her Peshawar home. Killing women and children has been taboo in Pashtun society for a very long time, and such murders only betrayed the intensity of the TTP-led campaign. Mrs Hanif was a widow, whose husband, Hanif Gul Jadoon, and a son were earlier killed on Eid day in 2011. *Dawn*, 17 August 2013.
15. *News International*, 8 August 2013.
16. For a moving account by a witness to such a daily loss of human lives in his city, see Vaqar Ahmad, 'Thirty Funerals and an Eid', *Dawn*, 9 August 2013. For a pervasive sense of desperation across the country, see Babar Sattar, 'The Emirate of TTP', *Dawn*, 12 August 2013.
17. Pilotless drone technology elicited interest from the CIA and Pentagon since its inception during the 1980s in the California home of Abraham Karem, an Israeli immigrant. By 2003, US drones were logging 1,500 hours a month in Iraq and by 2010, 20 such flights were providing 500 hours of video surveillance in Afghanistan. Moreover, under President Obama they have multiplied at an enormous rate. By 2013 their total flying hours over Southwest Asian skies ran into several millions. See Medea Benjamin, *Drone Warfare: Killing by Remote Control* (London: 2012) and Mirza Shahzad Akbar, 'Obama's Forgotten Victims', *New York Times*, 22 May 2013. A comprehensive report conducted by Stanford–Reprieve researchers, *Living under the Drones* (2012), noted the following: 'The best currently available public aggregate data on drone strikes are provided by The Bureau of Investigative Journalism (TBIJ), an independent journalist organization. TBIJ reported that from June 2004 through mid-September 2012, as per available data, drone strikes killed 2,562–3,325 people in Pakistan, of whom 474–881 were civilians, including 176 children. According to TBIJ, these strikes also injured an additional 1,228–1,362 individuals'. http://www.livingunderdrones.org/, and http://www.reprieve.org.uk/press/2012_09_25_drones_pakistan_reprieve_stanford_nyu/.
18. In early August there were reports of Israeli drone attacks over Egypt's Sinai Peninsula at a time when the largest Arab nation suffered from serious polarization following the overthrow of the Morsi regime on 3 July 2013. J. Khoury and G. Cohen, 'Israeli Drone Strikes Sinai Rocket-Launching Site, Kills Five', *Haaretz*, 11 August 2013, http://www.haaretz.com/news/diplomacy-defense/premium-1.540699.
    The UN Secretary-General, during an interview in Islamabad on 13 August 2013, expressed his reservations against missile attacks by the predatory aircraft, though he seemed to agree to their role for surveillance. BBC Urdu, 13 August, 2013: http://www.bbc.co.uk/urdu/pakistan/2013/08/130813_ban_ki_moon_pak_visit_rk.shtml.

19. Sandy Gall, *War against the Taliban: Why It All Went Wrong in Afghanistan?* (London: Bloomsbury, 2012), 24–60.
20. Peter Bergen, *The Osama bin Laden I Know: An Oral History of al-Qaeda's Leader* (New York: Free Press, 2006) and Gary Berntsen and Ralph Pezzullo, *Jawbreaker. The Attack on bin Laden and al-Qaeda: A Personal Account by the CIA's Key Field Commander* (Los Angeles: Three Rivers Press, 2006).
21. Secretary [Dr.] John Reid's Press Conference in Kabul, June 2006, quoted in Gall, *War against the Taliban*, 85.
22. Matt Waldman, *The Sun in the Sky: The Relationship between Pakistan's ISI and Afghan Insurgents*, Carr Centre for Human Rights Policy at Kennedy School of Government, Harvard, June 2010, quoted in Gall, *War against the Taliban*, 305.
23. Ambassador Karl Eikenberry, a former head of US troops in Afghanistan during 2006–7 and then the envoy, had warned the Obama administration against sending more troops into Afghanistan and thus had taken a stand against Generals David Petraeus and Stanley McChrystal, who wanted a bigger 'surge'. His secret reports of 6 and 9 November 2009 were leaked to the *New York Times*, causing a major embarrassment, but by the time the documents were published on 26 January 2010, the envoy had recanted and claimed to have agreed with the policy. For original leaked messages, see http://documents.nytimes.com/eikenberry-s-memos-on-the-strategy-in-afghanistan.

    For a comment and the press coverage, see http://documents.nytimes.com/eikenberry-s-memos-on-the-strategy-in-afghanistan.
24. Sherard Cowper-Coles, *Cables from Kabul*, xxii and xxiv.
25. Ibid., 14. The rivalries between the Foreign and Commonwealth Office (FCO) and DFID begin to find their entry into the early pages of this diplomatic narrative. The officials from the latter department are remembered, especially by their military counterparts, as 'tree-huggers', 16.
26. Ibid., 32 and 58. Cowper-Coles found this assessment echoed in the report by the House of Commons Foreign Affairs Committee, published in March 2011, http://www.publications.parliament.uk/pa/cm201011/cmselect/cmfaff/c514-ii/c51401.htm.
27. Ibid., 59, 63 and 66.
28. Ibid., 69–73 and 157.
29. Nine days later, in another report, the British newspaper quoted Karzai as saying to journalists in Davos that the British campaign in Helmand had made matters worse, as he observed: 'There was one part of the country where we suffered after the arrival of the British forces. Before that we were fully in charge of Helmand [...] The mistake was that we removed a local arrangement without having a replacement'. Quoted in ibid., 137–8. During this period of ill feeling, Paddy Ashdown's nomination as the 'super envoy' for Afghanistan was also rejected by the regime.
30. Ibid., 284.
31. Nicholas Barrington, *Envoy: A Diplomatic Journey* (London: I. B. Tauris, 2014), 274–5.
32. Campaign for Innocent Victims in Conflict (CIVIC), *Civilians in Armed Conflict: Civilian Harm and Conflict in Northwest Pakistan* (Washington, DC: CIVIC, 2010), 1.
33. It is quite interesting to note that several ventures to help all kinds of Afghans were begun during this period, and it appeared as if the country, other than its own expatriates, would be receptive to senior advisers, private security firms and even individual entrepreneurs. For an interesting work of this genre, claiming to help Afghan women and be a reminder of the high moral ground of the previous centuries, see Deborah Rodrigues, *The Kabul Beauty School: The Art of Friendship and Beauty* (London: Sphere, 2014). The saloon trainer eventually discovered herself as a novelist in her *The Little Coffee Shop of Kabul* (London: Sphere, 2013). This is not to underestimate the commitment to the work or the caliber of people like her or some others, whose self-discovery owed itself to Afghanistan and elicited a wider readership and following. For instance, Rory Stewart, *The Places in Between* (London: Picador, 2014); Khaled Hosseini,

The Kite Runner (London: Bloomsbury, 2003), *A Thousand Splendid Suns* (London: Bloomsbury, 2007), and *And the Mountains Echoed* (London: Bloomsbury, 2013); also, Asne Seiersad, *The Bookseller of Kabul* (London: Virago, 2004) and Nadeem Aslam, *Maps for Lost Lovers* (London: Faber, 2005) and *The Blind Man's Garden* (London: Faber and Faber, 2013). Of course, works by journalists, academics, former diplomats, military officers and security experts could run into several dozens, and that aspect of Afghan war itself is worth a separate research study.

34. By this time, amidst drone attacks and increased militancy, Benazir Bhutto acknowledged Pakistan's deterioration into an epic centre of multiple forms of violence. Her own book appeared two weeks after her murder in Rawalpindi, on 27 December 2007. See Benazir Bhutto, *Reconciliation: Islam, Democracy, and the West* (New York: Simon & Schuster, 2008).

35. Pakistan became the non-trustworthy nation for many Americans, and the media coverage of its 'double face' reverberated in various comments on the Internet. For instance, the *New York Times* belatedly attributed the death of a US soldier in the Teri Mangal border area of Kurram Agency in 2007 to Pakistani troops, in a report on 27 September 2011. Tom Lazarus, one of the commentators of this report, carried by a news website, posted his remarks as follow:

'well, we could at least bomb isi headquarters and then deny responsibility or blame it on "rogue elements". see how they like it.

'the fact remains that pakistan is the worst terrorist state in the world, the worst nuclear proliferator, and the majority of its people are backwards, benighted cretins who applaud the assassination of their own politicians, approve of fathers killing their own daughters for aspiring to be more than sex-slave commodities and haven't the desire or will to change their paranoid, treacherous, kleptocratic leadership. this is a place where rape is a judicial punishment rather than a crime. It's the sewer of the universe and should be walled off to fester in its corrupt, misogynist [sic.], barbaric, seventh-century religious tribal hell'. http://slatest.slate.com/posts/2011/09/27/teri_mangal_attack_pakistan_military_blamed_for_u_s_soldiers_200.html.

36. John Brennan was viewed as the architect of drone-led aerial warfare, and it sounded quite successful as it decreased the need for 'boots on the ground' especially at a time when IED were claiming several fatalities. Panetta led the CIA when the US Navy SEALs mounted the Abbottabad operation on 2 May 2011. They, along with Admiral Mike Mullen, had worked in close collaboration with Generals Pervez Musharraf, Ashfaq Parvez Kayani and Ahmed Shuja Pasha, who had, in fact, permitted the CIA-operated attacks on the FATA as early as 2004. This was affirmed by Pasha, the former Director-General of the ISI, in his statement to the Abbottabad Commission, which has been copiously discussed in various other media reports. See Khaled Ahmed, 'The Ghost of Osama bin Laden', *Newsweek*, 26 July 2013, http://newsweekpakistan.com/the-ghost-of-osama-bin-laden/.

37. 'UK Is Using Drones in Afghanistan, Ministry of Defence Confirms', *Huffington Post* (online), 27 April 2013. Also: http://dronewars.net/.

38. *News International*, 9 November 2014. According to any early report in 2014, China had agreed to undertake several projects in energy sector in Pakistan totalling $42 billion within a span of three to four years. *Daily Mail*, 9 November 2014. This was affirmed in April 2015 during the visit by the Chinese president when several memoranda were signed.

39. For details, see Iftikhar H. Malik, 'Hope and Caution: A New Phase in Pak-China Relations', TurkeyAgenda, online, 23 April 2015, http://www.turkeyagenda.com/hope-and-caution-a-new-phase-in-pak-china-relations-2333.html.

40. James Risen and Matt Apuzzo, 'Getting Close to Terror, But Not to Stop It. Port Authority Officer Kept Sources with Ties to Iran Attacks', *New York Times*, 8 November 2014. See: https://www.balloon-juice.com/2014/11/10/long-read-getting-close-to-terror-but-not-to-stop-it/.

41. Jay Solomon and Carol E. Lee, 'Obama Wrote Secret Letter to Iran's Khamenei about Fighting Islamic State', *Wall Street Journal*, 6 November 2014. (In fact, this was the fourth letter

NOTES

by the US president to Iran's leadership). http://www.wsj.com/articles/obama-wrote-secret-letter-to-irans-khamenei-about-fighting-islamic-state-1415295291.

42. In an interview with a French news agency, Musharraf, while accusing India of helping Baloch dissidents and some Pakistani Taliban in their warfare against his country, warned of a possible Indo–Pakistani polarity in Afghanistan. He viewed it as fallout from the Western withdrawal from Afghanistan. 'Musharraf Warns of Proxy War with India in Afghanistan', *Dawn*, 18 November 2014.

43. Some reports documented New Delhi's efforts to help the ANA by arming it with Russian weapons, which might cause a serious reaction both from Pakistan and China. See Ahmed Rashid, 'India Risks Destabilising Afghanistan', BBC Online, 7 May, 2014, http://www.bbc.co.uk/news/world-asia-27258566.

    Pakistani support for the Taliban, both at the official and public levels, has been widely covered by journalists such as Carlotta Gall, Christina Lamb and Lucy Morgan Edwards. In her latest work, Lamb, not much known for any soft corner for Pakistan, considers the Pakistani ISI as causing the failure of Western military campaigns in Afghanistan, which rather looks far-fetched given the strength and resources of the intelligence agencies, defence establishments and economies of 30 most powerful nations in the world. One wonders how a single intelligence agency of a rather struggling country could undertake such a feat, while its record in Karachi or Balochistan itself has elicited criticism for not gaining an upper hand on militancy. Needless to say, in her earlier works, she had lionized Karzai, though for Western governments he also turned out to be a major disappointment. See Christina Lamb, *Farewell Kabul: From Afghanistan to a More Dangerous World* (London: HarperCollins, 2015).

44. Moeed Yusuf, 'Our Internal Challenge', *Dawn*, 13 May 2014. Some analysts felt dismayed over drift or the lack of vigorous policies to eradicate militancy, but failed to see its complex and multidimensional causes. Other than local issues of power and economy, geopolitics, foreign interventions and an indiscreet usage of military power do not offer any tangible solution to such multifaceted challenges. Nor can one reduce them to an *Islamist* issue in which madrasas might be only producing an unending supply of jihadists and suicide bombers. At various levels, a multipronged initiative led by civilians and fully supported by the media, clerics and military can help Pakistan regain peace.

45. As reported by the Global Terrorism Index, 2013 had already seen a 20 per cent rise in violence, with Iraq, Syria, Afghanistan, Pakistan and Nigeria accounting for 80 per cent of terror-related fatalities, which were totaled at 20,000 altogether. *Guardian*, 18 November 2014.

46. Abubakar Siddique, *The Pashtun Question: Key to the Future of Pakistan and Afghanistan* (London: Hurst, 2014). While Siddique wants Pashtun nationalism to be strengthened, he recommends a soft border between the two countries that, ironically, might make it difficult for their regimes to police it, yet easier for radicals to move across. However, each government will have to stop sheltering militants from the other side operating as proxies, as was noted by a reviewer: 'Mullah Omar is based in Pakistan and the Pakistani Taliban's leader, Mullah Fazlullah, operates from Afghanistan. Distrust between the governments in Kabul and Islamabad is so acute that the intelligence agencies of both sides are happy to host each other's enemies'. Owen Bennett-Jones, 'Across the Durand Line', *London Review of Books*, 18–25 September 2014.

BIBLIOGRAPHY

Reports

Abdul, Basit, and Rathore, Mujtaba. *Pakistan Security Report 2009*. Islamabad: Pakistan Institute of Peace Studies, 2010. http://pakpips.com/downloads/131.pdf.

Afghanistan Analysts Network. *Thematic Dossier IV: Afghanistan's 2014 Presidential and Provincial Council Elections*. http://www.afghanistan-analysts.org.

Ahmad, Mumtaz. *Madrasa Reforms and Perspectives: Islamic Tertiary Education in Pakistan*. Washington, DC: The National Bureau of Asian Research, 2009.

Amnesty International. *Will I Be Next? U.S. Drone Strikes in Pakistan*. London, 2013. http://www.amnestyusa.org/research/reports/will-i-be-next-us-drone-strikes-in-pakistan.

Centre for European Studies (CES). *Breaking Down the Wall: Improving EU–NATO Relations*. May 2013.

Council of the European Union (CEU). *Council Conclusions on Pakistan*. June 2013.

Central Intelligence Agency (CIA), *Global Trends 2025: A Transformed World*, National Intelligence Council Report, November 2008. http://www.aicpa.org/research/cpahorizons2025/globalforces/downloadabledocuments/globaltrends.pdf.

Dalrymple, William. *Deadly Triangle: India, Pakistan and Afghanistan*. Washington, DC: Brookings Institution, 2013.

European Commission. *Country Strategy: Islamic Republic of Afghanistan, 2007–13*. European Commission, July 2013.

Grare, Frederic. *Pakistan: The Myth of an Islamist Peril*. Carnegie Endowment for International Peace, 2006.

Human Rights Commission of Pakistan. *State of Human Rights in Pakistan*. Lahore, 2013.

Johnston, Patrick B., and Anoop K. Sarbahi. *The Impact of US Drone Strikes on Terrorism in Pakistan and Afghanistan*. Rand Corporation, 2013.

Korski, Daniel. *Shaping Europe's Afghan Surge*. European Council on Foreign Relations. 2009.

Kronstadt, Alan K. *Pakistan-U.S. Relations*. Washington, DC: Congressional Research Service, 2012.

———. *Global Trends 2015: A Dialogue about the Future with Nongovernment Experts*. The National Intelligence Council Report, December 2000.

Lubold, Mark. *Foreign Policy Situation Report*. Foreign Policy Group, 14 August 2013.

Malik, Iftikhar H. *Civil Society in Pakistan: Stake Holders in a Contested State*. Pakistan Security Research Unit Report No. 50. Bradford, September 2009. https://www.dur.ac.uk/resources/psru/briefings/archive/Brief50.pdf.

Markey, Daniel. *Terrorism and Indo-Pakistani Escalation: CPA Contingency Planning Memorandum No. 6*. Council on Foreign Relations, January 2010.

Marshall, Andrew Gavin, 'Imperial Eye on Pakistan-Pakistan in Pieces', *Global Research*, 28 May 2011: http://www.globalresearch.ca/imperial-eye-on-pakistan/25009

Page, David, and Shirazuddin Siddiqi. *The Media of Afghanistan: The Challenges of Transition*. BBC Media Action. Policy Briefing No. 5. March 2012.

Pakistan Institute of Peace Studies. *Media Safety in Pakistan: A Study of Threats to Journalists in Pakistan*. Islamabad, 2014.

Roger, Christopher. *Civilians in Armed Conflict: Civilian Harm and Conflict in Northwest Pakistan*. A CIVIC report. 2010.

Books and Articles

Abbas, Hassan. *Pakistan's Drift into Extremism: Allah, the Army and America's War on Terror*. London: Routledge, 2004.

———. *The Taliban Revival: Violence and Extremism on the Pakistan-Afghanistan Frontier*. New Haven: Yale University Press, 2014.

Aftab, Asma. *Gender Politics: Falsifying Reality. Feminism: Another Perspective*. Islamabad: Emel Books, 2011

Ahmad, Aziz. *Studies in Islamic Culture in the Indian Environment*. Delhi, 1999.

Ahmad, Feroz. *Ethnicity and Politics in Pakistan*. Karachi: Oxford University Press, 1998.

Ahmed, Akbar S. *Millennium and Charisma among Pathans: A Critical Essay in Social Anthropology*. London: Routledge and Kegan Paul, 1976.

———. *Resistance and Control in Pakistan*. London: Routledge, 1991.

Ahmed, Ishtiaq. *Pakistan: The Garrison State*. Karachi: Oxford University Press 2013.

———. *Punjab: Bloodied, Partitioned and Cleansed. Unravelling the 1947 Tragedy through Secret British Reports and First-Person Accounts* Karachi: Oxford University Press, 2012.

Ahmed, Khaled. *Sectarian War: Pakistan's Sunni-Shia Violence and Its Links to the Middle East*. Karachi: Oxford University Press, 2012.

Ahsan, Aitzaz. *The Indus Saga and the Making of Pakistan*. Karachi: Oxford University Press 1996.

Akbar, M. J. *Tinderbox: Past and Future of Pakistan*. Delhi: Harper Perennial, 2012.

Akhtar, Shabbir. *Islam: A Political Religion. The Future of an Imperial Faith*. London: Routledge, 2011.

Albinia, Alice. *Empires of the Indus: The Story of a River*. London: John Murray, 2009.

Ali, Ayaan Hirsi. *Why Islam Needs a Reformation Now?* New York: Harper, 2015.

Ali, Tariq. *The Clash of Fundamentalisms: Crusades, Jihad and Modernity*. London: Verso 2003.

Allen, Charles. *God's Terrorists: The Wahhabi Cult and the Hidden Roots of Modern Jihad*. London: Abacus, 2007.

———. *Soldier Sahibs: The Men Who Made the North-West Frontier*. London: John Murray. 2012.

Ansari, Sarah. *Life after Partition. Migration, Community and Strife in Sindh: 1947–1960*. Karachi: Oxford University Press, 2005.

Asad, Talal. *Genealogies of Religion: Discipline and Reasons of Powers in Christianity and Islam*. Baltimore: Johns Hopkins University Press, 1993.

———. *On Suicide Bombing*. New York: Columbia University Press, 2007.

Asbridge, Thomas. *The Crusades: The Authoritative History of the War for the Holy Land* London: Ecco Press, 2011.

Aslam, Nadeem. *The Blind Man's Garden*. London: Faber and Faber 2013.

———. *Maps for Lost Lovers*. London: Faber, 2005.

Atwood, Rodney. *The March to Kandahar: Roberts in Afghanistan*. Barnsley: Pen & Sword Military, 2008.

Aybet, Gulnur, and Rebecca Moore, eds. *NATO: In Search of a Vision*. Washington, DC: Georgetown University Press, 2010.

Ayoob, Mohammed. *The Many Faces of Political Islam: Religion and Politics in the Muslim World*. Ann Arbor: University of Michigan Press, 2008.

Azad, Abul Kalam. *India Wins Freedom: the Complete Version*. New Delhi: Orient Longman, 1988.

Aziz, K. K. *The Murder of History: A Critique of History Textbooks Used in Pakistan*. Lahore: Sang-i-Meel Publications 2010.

Baldwin, Shauna Singh. *The Tiger's Claw*. Toronto: Knopf, 2004.

———. *We Are Not in Pakistan*. Fredericton, New Fredericton: Goose Lane. 2007.

———. *What the Body Remembers?* Toronto: Knopf, 1999.

Banerjee, Mukulika. *The Pathan Unarmed: Opposition and Memory in the North-West Frontier*. Oxford: James Currey, 2000.

Barrington, Nicholas. *Envoy: A Diplomatic Journey*. London: I. B. Tauris, 2014.

———. *Nicholas Meets Barrington: The Personal Journey of a Former Diplomat*. London: I. B. Tauris, 2014.

BIBLIOGRAPHY

Barth, Fredrik. *Features of Person and Society in Swat*. London: Routledge and Kegan Paul 1981.
———. *Political Leadership among the Swat Pathans*. London: Athlone Press 1959.
Barthorp, Michael. *Afghan Wars: And the North-West Frontier 1839–1947*. London: Cassell, 2002.
Barzalai, Yaniv. *102 Days of War: How Osama bin Laden, al Qaeda & the Taliban Survived 2001*. Washington, DC: Potomac Books, 2014.
Basu, Shrabani. *Spy Princess: The Life of Noor Inayat Khan*. Stroud: Sutton, 2006.
Begg, Moazzam. *Enemy Combatant: A British Muslim's Journey to Guantanamo and Back*. London: Free Press, 2006.
Benjamin, Medea. *Drone Warfare: Killing by Remote Control*. London: Verso, 2012.
Bennett-Jones, Owen. *Pakistan: Eye of the Storm*. London: Yale University Press, 2009.
Bergen, Peter. *The Osama bin Laden I Know: An Oral History of al-Qaeda's Leader*. New York: Free Press, 2006.
———, ed. *Talibanistan: Negotiating the Borders between Terror, Politics, and Religion*. New York: Oxford University Press 2013.
Berman, Paul. *Terror and Liberalism*. New York: W. W. Norton, 2001.
Bhatia, Shyam. *Goodbye Shahzadi: A Political Biography of Benazir Bhutto*. New Delhi: Lotus Collection, 2008.
Bhutto, Benazir. *Daughter of the East: An Autobiography*. London: Pocket, 1988.
———. *Reconciliation: Islam, Democracy and the West*. New York: Siomon & Schuster, 2008.
Bhutto, Zulfikar Ali. *The Myth of Independence*. London: Oxford University Press, 1969.
Boillot, Jean-Joseph. *Europe After Enlargement: Economic Challenges for EU and India*. London: Academic Foundation, 2005.
Bolger, Daniel P. *Why We Lost? A General's Inside Account of the Iraq and Afghanistan Wars*. New York: EamonDolan, 2014.
Braithwaite, Rodric. *Afgansty: The Russians in Afghanistan, 1979–89*. London: Profile, 2011.
Burke, Jason. *Al-Qaeda: The True Story of Radical Islam*. London: Penguin, 2007.
———. *On the Road to Kandahar: Travels through Conflict in the Islamic World*. London: Penguin, 2007.
Burki, Shahid Javed. *Changing Perceptions, Altered Reality: Pakistan's Economy under Musharraf, 1969–2006*. Karachi: Oxford University Press 2007.
Burns, Nicholas. 'The Passage to India: What Washington Can Do to Revive Relations with New Delhi'. *Foreign Affairs* 93, no. 5 (2014): 132–41.
Butalia, Urvashi. *The Other Side of Silence: Voices from the Partition of India*. New Delhi Penguin Books, 1998.
Cadogan, E. *The India We Saw*. London: John Murray, 1933.
Campbell, George. *The Afghan Frontier*. London: E. Stanford, 1879.
Caroe, Olaf. *The Pathans: 550 B. C.–A. D. 1957*. Karachi: Oxford University Press, 1983.
Chandrasekaran, Rajiv. *Little America: The War within the War for Afghanistan*. London, Bloomsbury, 2012.
Chesler, Phyllis. *An American Bride in Afghanistan: A Memoir*. Basingstoke: Palgrave Macmillan, 2013.
Churchill, Winston. *The Story of the Malakand Field Force*. London: Longmans, 1898.
Clinton, Hillary R. *Hard Choices*. New York: Simon & Schuster, 2014.
Cloughley, Brian. *A History of the Pakistan Army: Wars and Insurrections*. Karachi: Oxford University Press 2006.
Cohen, Stephen P. *The Idea of Pakistan*. Washington, DC: Brookings Institution Press 2004.
Coll, Steve. *Ghost Wars: The Secret History of the CIA, Afghanistan and Bin Laden*. London: Penguin Books, 2005.
Constable, Pamela. *Playing with Fire: Pakistan at War with Itself*. London: Random House, 2011.
Corera, Gordon. *Shopping for Bombs: Nuclear Proliferation, Global Insecurity, and the Rise and Fall of the A. Q. Khan Network*. London: Oxford University Press, 2006.
Cowper-Coles, Sherard. *Cables from Kabul. The Inside Story of West's Afghanistan Campaign*. London: HarperPress 2012.
Crile, George. *My Enemy's Enemy: The Story of the Largest Covert Operation in History. The Arming of the Mujahideen by the CIA*. London: Atlantic Books, 2003.

Dabashi, Hamid. *Brown Skins, White Masks*. London: Pluto, 2011.
———. *Post-Orientalism: Knowledge and Power in Time of Terror*. Fredericton, New Brunswick: Transaction Publishers, 2009.
Dalrymple, William. *The Last Mughal. The Fall of a Dynasty*. Delhi, 1857; London: Bloomsbury, 2006.
———. 'A New Deal in Pakistan'. *New York Review of Books*, 3 April 2008, http://www.nybooks.com/articles/2008/04/03/a-new-deal-in-pakistan/.
———.'Pakistan in Peril'. *New York Review of Books*, January 2009, http://www.nybooks.com/articles/2009/02/12/pakistan-in-peril/.
———. *Return of the King: The Battle for Afghanistan*. London: Bloomsbury 2013.
Darwin, John. *After Tamerlane: The Rise and Fall of Global Empires, 1400–2000*. London: Penguin, 2008.
Devji, Faisal. *Muslim Zion: Pakistan as a Political Idea*. London: Hurst, 2013.
Dinan, Desmond. *Ever Closer Union: An Introduction to European Integration*. Basingstoke: Palgrave Macmillan, 2011.
Dorronsoro, Gilles. *Revolution Unending: Afghanistan, 1979 to the Present*. New York: Columbia University Press, 2005.
Dupree, Louis. *Afghanistan*. Princeton: Princeton University Press, 1980.
El Fadl, Khaled Abou. *The Great Theft: Wrestling Islam from the Extremists*. New York: HarperOne, 2007.
Erikson, Thomas Hylland. *Fredrik Barth: An Intellectual Biography*. London: Pluto, 2015.
Esak, Farid. *On Being Muslim*. Oxford: Oneworld, 2009.
Fair, C. Christine. *Fighting to the End: The Pakistan Army's Way of War*. New Delhi: Oxford University Press, 2014.
Fergusson, James. *Taliban: The True Story of the World's Most Feared Guerrilla Fighters*. London: Bantam, 2010.
Fuller, Graham. *A World without Islam*. Boston: Little, Brown and Company, 2010.
Gall, Sandy. *War against the Taliban. Why It All Went Wrong in Afghanistan*. London: Bloomsbury, 2012.
Gall, Carlotta. *The Wrong Enemy: America in Afghanistan, 2001–2014*. New York: Houghton Mifflin Harcourt, 2014.
Gandhi, Rajmohan. *Punjab: A History from Aurangzeb to Mountbatten*. Delhi: Aleph, 2013.
Gates, Robert M. *Duty: Memoirs of a Secretary at the War*. London; WH Allen, 2014.
Gellner, Ernest. *Muslim Society*. Cambridge: Cambridge University Press, 1993.
Giustozzi, Antonio, ed. *Decoding the New Taliban: Insight from the Afghan Field*. London: Hurst, 2009.
———. *Koran, Kalashnikov and Laptop: The Neo-Taliban Insurgency in Afghanistan*. London: Hurst, 2007.
Gisutozzi, Antonio, and Tom Farrell. 'The Taliban at War: Inside the Helmand Insurgency, 2004–12'. *International Affairs* 89, no. 2 (2013): 845–71.
Glenny, Misha. *The Balkans, 1804–1999: Nationalism, War and the Great Powers*. London: Granta Books, 1999.
Gopal, Anand. *No Good Men Among the Living: America, the Taliban, and the War through Afghan Eyes*. New York: Metropolitan Books, 2014.
John Gray, *Black Mass: Apocalyptic Religion and the Death of Utopia*. London: Penguin, 2008.
———. *Al-Qaeda and What It Means to Be Modern*. London: Faber, 2003.
Griffiths, John C. *Afghanistan: Land of Conflict and Beauty*. London: Andre Deutsch, 2009.
Haeri, Shahla. *No Shame for the Sun: Lives of Pakistani Professional Women*. Syracuse: Syracuse University Press, 2002.
Haq, Samiul. *Afghan Taliban. War of Ideology, Struggle for Peace*. Islamabad: Emel Books, 2015.
Haqqani, Husain. *Magnificent Delusions: Pakistan, the United States and an Epic History of Misunderstanding*. New York: PublicAffairs, 2013.
———. *Pakistan: Between Mosque and Military*. Lahore: Vanguard Books, 2005.

BIBLIOGRAPHY

Hamid, Mustafa Hamid, and Leah Farrall. *The Arabs at War in Afghanistan*. London: Hurst, 2015.

Haroon, Sana. *Frontier of the Faith: Islam in the Indo-Afghan Borderland*. New York: Columbia University Press, 2007.

Hasan, Mushirul. *Legacy of a Divided Nation: India's Muslims since Independence*. Delhi: Oxford University Press, 2001.

Hazem, Kandil. 'The End of Islamism'. *London Review of Books*, 3 July 2013, http://www.lrb.co.uk/blog/2013/07/04/hazem-kandil/the-end-of-islamism/.

Hersh, Seymour M. 'The Killing of Osama bin Laden', *London Review of Books*, 21 May 2015. http://www.lrb.co.uk/v37/n10/seymour-m-hersh/the-killing-of-osama-bin-laden.

Hill, Christopher, and Michael Smith. *International Relations and the European Union*. Oxford: Oxford University Press, 2011.

Hitchens, Christopher. 'From Abbottabad to Worse', *Vanity Fair*, July 2011.

Hopkirk, Peter. *The Great Game: On Secret Service in High Asia*. London: John Murray, 2006.

Hosseini, Khaled. *The Kite Runner*. London: Bloomsbury, 2004.

Hurd, Douglas. *Memoirs*. London: Little, Brown, 2003.

Hussain, Zahid. *Frontline Pakistan: The Struggle with Militant Islam*. London: I. B. Tauris, 2007.

Iqbal, Muhammad. *The Reconstruction of Religious Thought in Islam*. London: Oxford University Press, 1934.

Ismail, Aquila. *Of Martyrs and Marigolds*. Charleston: CreateSpace, 2012.

Israeli, Raphael. *The Islamic Challenge in Europe*, Fredericton, New Brunswick: Transaction Publishers, 2008.

Jaffrelot, Christophe, ed. *Pakistan: Nationalism without a Nation*. London: Zed Books, 2002.

Jain, R. K. *India and the European Union: Building a Strategic Partnership*. New Delhi: Pee Pee Publishers, 2007.

Jalal, Ayesha. *The State of Martial Rule: The Origins of Political Economy of Pakistan's Defence*. Cambridge: Cambridge University Press, 1990.

Jalalzai, Musa Khan. *Whose Army? Afghanistan's Future and the Blueprint for Civil War*. New York: Algora Publishing, 2014.

Jamie, Kathleen. *Among Muslims: Meeting at the Frontiers of Pakistan*. London: Sort Of Books, 2002.

Johnson, Rob. *The Afghan Way of War. Culture and Pragmatism: A Critical History*. London: Hurst, 2013.

———. 'Afghanistan: Unfriendly Fire'. *History Today*, July 2012.

Jones, Philip E. *The Pakistan People's Party: Rise to Power*. Karachi: Oxford University Press 2003.

Kamran, Tahir. 'Contextualizing Sectarian Militancy in Pakistan: A Case Study of Jhang'. *Journal of Islamic Studies* 20, no. 1 (2009): 55–85.

Kaplan, Robert D. *Soldiers of God: With Islamic Warriors in Afghanistan and Pakistan*. London: Vintage Books, 2001.

Keay, John. *Explorers of the Western Himalayas, 1820–95*. London: John Murray, 1996.

Kennedy, Charles H., ed. *Pakistan at the Millennium*. Karachi: Oxford University Press, 2003.

Khaliq, Urfan. *Ethical Dimensions of the Foreign Policy of the European Union: A Legal Appraisal*. Cambridge: Cambridge University Press, 2008.

Khan, Imran. *Pakistan: A Personal Journey*. London: Bantam, 2012.

———. *Warrior Race: A Journey through the Land of Tribal Pathans*. London: Chatto & Windus, 1993.

Khan, Mahvish. *My Guantanamo Diary: The Detainees and the Stories They Told Me*. New York: PublicAffairs, 2009.

Khan, Muhammad Ayub. *Friends Not Masters: A Political Autobiography*. Oxford: Oxford University Press, 1967.

Khan, Nichola. *Mohajir Militancy in Pakistan: Violence and Transformation in the Karachi Conflict*. London: Routledge, 2012.

Khan, Riaz Mohammad. *Afghanistan and Pakistan: Conflict, Extremism, and Resistance to Modernity*. Baltimore: Johns Hopkins University Press, 2011.

Koofi, Fawzia, with Nadene Ghauri. *The Favored Daughter: One Woman's Fight to Lead Afghanistan into the Future*. Basingstoke: Palgrave Macmillan, 2013.

Kundani, Arun. *The End of Tolerance: Racism in 21st Century Britain*. London: Pluto, 2007.
Lamb, Alastair. *Kashmir: A Disputed Legacy, 1846–1990*. Hertingfordbury: Roxford, 1991.
Lamb, Christina. *Farewell Kabul: From Afghanistan to a More Dangerous World*. London: HarperCollins, 2015.
———. *The Sewing Circles of Heart: My Afghan Years*. London: Flamingo, 2003.
———. *Waiting for Allah: Pakistan's Struggle for Democracy*. London: Hamish Hamilton 1991.
Ledwidge, Frank. *Investment in Blood: The True Cost of Britain's Afghan War*. New Haven, CT: Yale University Press, 2014.
Levy, Bernard-Henri. *Who Killed Daniel Pearl?* Translated by James X. Mitchell. London: Duckworth, 2003.
Lewis, Bernard. *The Crisis of Islam: Holy War and Unholy Terror*. London: Weidenfeld & Nicolson, 2003.
Lewis, Michael. 'Drones and the Boundaries of the Battlefield'. *Texas International Law Journal* 47, no. 2 (2012): 293–314.
Lieven, Anatol. *Pakistan: A Hard Country*. London: Penguin, 2011.
McMahon, Robert J. *The Cold War on the Periphery: The United States, India and Pakistan*. New York: Columbia University Press, 1996.
Mai, Mukhtar. *In the Name of Honour: A Memoir*, with Marie Therese-Cuny and Linda Coverdale. London: Virago, 2007.
Maley, William, ed. *Fundamentalism Reborn? Afghanistan and the Taliban*. London: Hurst, 1998.
Malik, Iftikhar H. *Crescent Between Cross and Star: Islam and the West after 9/11*. Karachi: Oxford University Press, 2006.
———. *Islam, Nationalism and the West: Issues of Identity in Pakistan*. Oxford: St. Antony's-Macmillan Series, 1999.
———. *The History of Pakistan*. Westport, CT: Greenwood Press, 2008.
———. *Jihad, Hindutva and the Taliban: South Asia at a Crossroads*. Karachi: Oxford University Press, 2005.
———. 'Military Coup in Pakistan: Business as Usual or Democracy on Hold!' *Round Table: The Commonwealth Journal of International Affairs* (2001): 360: 357–77: http://www.tandfonline.com/doi/abs/10.1080/00358530120065336.
———. 'Pakistan in 2001: The Afghanistan Crisis and the Rediscovery of the Frontline State', *Asian Survey*, 42, no. 1 (2002): 204–12: http://as.ucpress.edu/content/42/1/204.
———. *State and Civil Society in Pakistan: Politics of Authority, Ideology and Ethnicity*. Oxford: St. Antony's-Macmillan Series 1997.
Malkasian, Carter. *War Comes to Garmser: Thirty Years of Conflict on the Afghan Frontier*. London: Hurst, 2013.
Mamdani, Mahmood. *Good Muslim, Bad Muslim: America, the Cold War and the Roots of Terror*. New York: Three Leaves Publishing, 2005.
Markey, Daniel S. *No Exit from Pakistan: America's Tortured Relationship with Islamabad* Cambridge: Cambridge University Press, 2013.
Marsden, Peter. *The Taliban: War, Religion and the New Order in Afghanistan*. London: Zed Books, 1998.
Marshall, Andrew Gavin. 'Imperial Eye on Pakistan: Pakistan in Pieces'. *Global Research*, 28 May 2011. http://www.globalresearch.ca/imperial-eye-on-pakistan/25009.
Matinuddin, Kamal. *The Taliban Phenomenon: Afghanistan, 1994–1997*. Karachi: Oxford University Press 1998.
Mazzetti, Mark. *The Way of the Knife: The C.I.A., a Secret Army, and a War at the Ends of the Earth*. New York: Penguin Books, 2013.
Metcalf, Barbara and Thomas. *A Concise History of India*, Cambridge: Cambridge University Press, 2006.Metcalf, Barbara. *Islamic Revival in British India: Deoband, 1860–1900*. Princeton: Princeton University Press, 1982.
Mountstuart, Elphinstone. *An Account of the Kingdom of Caubul and Its Dependencies in Persia, Tartary and India*. London: Richard Bentley, 1839.

Mousavi, Sayed Asghar. *The Hazaras of Afghanistan: An Historical, Cultural, Economic and Political Study.* Richmond: Curzon, 1998.

Musharraf, Pervez. *In the Line of Fire: A Memoir.* New York: Simon & Schuster, 2006.

Naipaul, V. S. *Beyond Belief: Islamic Excursions among the Converted.* London: Abacus 1998.

———. *Among the Believers: An Islamic Journey.* London: Picador, 2003.

Nasr, Seyyed Vali Reza. *The Indispensable Nation: American Foreign Policy in Retreat.* New York: Anchor Books, 2014.

———. *The Shia Revival: How Conflicts within Islam Will Shape the Future.* New York: W. W. Norton, 2007.

———. *Mawdudi and the Making of Islamic Revolution.* New York: Columbia University Press, 1996.

Nawa, Fariba. *Opium Nation: Child Brides, Drug Lords, and One Woman's Journey through Afghanistan.* New York: Harper Perennial, 2011.

Nawaz, Shuja. *Crossed Swords: Pakistan, Its Army, and the Wars within.* Karachi: Oxford University Press, 2008.

Nevill, H. L. *North-West Frontier: British and Indian Army Campaigns on the North-West Frontier of India, 1849–1908.* London: John Murray, 1912.

Nichols, Robert, ed. *The Frontier Crimes Regulation: A History in Documents.* Karachi: Oxford University Press, 2013.

———. *Settling the Frontier: Land, Law and Society in the Peshawar Valley, 1500–1900.* Karachi: Oxford University Press, 2001.

O'Balance, Edgar. *Afghan Wars: Battles in a Hostile Land: 1839 to the Present.* Oxford: Brassey's, 2003.

Pandey, Gyanandra. *The Construction of Communalism in Colonial North India.* New Delhi: Oxford University Press, 2006.

———. *Remembering Partition: Violence, Nationalism and History in India.* Cambridge: Cambridge University Press, 2001.

Panetta, Leon. *Worthy Fights: A Memoir of Leadership in War and Peace.* Harmondsworth: Penguin, 2014.

Paracha, Nadeem Farooq. 'In Pakistan, Well-To-Do and Willing to Terrorize', *Deutsche Welle*, 28 May 2015, http://www.dw.de/in-pakistan-well-to-do-and-willing-to-terrorize/a-18481412.

Parshley, Lois. 'The Life and Death of Sabeen Mahmud'. *New Yorker*, 28 April 2015, http://www.newyorker.com/news/news-desk/the-life-and-death-of-sabeen-mahmud.

Pottinger, G. *The Afghan Connection. The Extraordinary Adventures of Major Eldred Pottinger.* Edinburgh: Scottish Academic Press, 1983.

Qadiri, Muhammad Tahir-ul. *Fatwa on Terrorism and Suicide Bombings.* London: Minhaj Ul Quran, 2011.

Rahman, Fazlur. *Islam and Modernity: Transformation of an Intellectual Tradition.* Chicago: University of Chicago Press, 1982.

Rahman, Tariq. *Language and Politics in Pakistan.* Karachi: Oxford University Press, 1996.

Ramadan, Tariq. *What I Believe.* Oxford: Oxford University Press, 2010.

Ranis, Gustav. 'Is Pakistan a Failing State?' *Yale Global*, 25 April 2013, http://yaleglobal.yale.edu/content/pakistan-failing-state.

Rashid, Ahmed. *Descent into Chaos: How the War against Islamic Extremism Is Being Lost in Pakistan, Afghanistan and Central Asia.* London: Allen Lane, 2008.

———. *Pakistan on the Brink: The Future of America, Pakistan, and Afghanistan.* London: Allen Lane, 2012.

———. *Taliban: Islam, Oil and the New Great Game in Central Asia.* London: I. B. Tauris, 2002.

Rhode, David. *A Safe Area. Srebrenica: Europe's Worst Massacre Since the Second World War.* London: Pocket Books, 1997.

Richards, David. *Taking Command.* London: Headline, 2014.

Rieck, Andreas T. *The Shias of Pakistan: An Assertive and Beleaguered Minority.* London: Hurst, 2013.

Riedel, Bruce. *Avoiding Armageddon: America, India, and Pakistan to the Brink and Back.* Washington, DC: Brookings Institution Press, 2013.

———. *The Search for Al Qaeda: Its Leadership, Ideology, and Future.* Washington, DC: Brookings Institution Press, 2010.

———. *What We Won: America's Secret War in Afghanistan, 1979–89*. Washington, DC: Brookings Institution Press, 2014.
Rittenberg, Stephen. *Ethnicity, Nationalism, and the Pakhtuns: the Independence Movement in India's North-West Frontier Province*. Durham: Carolina Academic Press, 1988.
Rizvi, Hasan-Askari. *The Military and Politics in Pakistan, 1947–1997*. Lahore: Sang-e-Meel Publications, 2000.
Roberts, S. R. *Forty-One Years in India*, 2 vols. London: Richard Bentley, 1898.
Robertson, G. S. *The Kafirs of the Hindu-Kush*. London: Lawrence & Bullen, 1900.
Rodrigues, Deborah. *The Kabul Beauty School: The Art of Friendship and Beauty*. London: Sphere, 2014
———. *The Little Coffee Shop of Kabul*. London: Sphere 2013.
Rose, David. *Guantanamo: America's War on Human Rights*. London: Faber, 2004.
Rose, Michael. *Fighting for Peace: Lessons from Bosnia*. London: Warner, 1999.
Roy, Olivier. *Globalised Islam: The Search for a New Umma*. New York: Columbia University Press, 2006.
———. *The Failure of Political Islam*. London: I. B. Tauris, 1994.
———. *Islam and Resistance in Afghanistan*. Cambridge: Cambridge University Press 1990.
Rubin, Barnett. *The Fragmentation of Afghanistan: State Formation and Collapse in the International System*. New Haven, CT: Yale University Press, 2002.
Rushdie, Salman. *Imaginary Homelands: Essays and Criticism, 1981–1991*. Harmondsworth, 1991.
———. *The Midnight's Children*. London: Vintage, 2008.
———. *Joseph Anton*. London, 2013.
Ruthven, Malise. 'Righteous and Wrong'. *New York Review of Books*, 19 August 2010, http://www.nybooks.com/articles/2010/08/19/righteous-wrong/.
Saeed, Ahmad. *Anjuman-i-Islamia Amritsar, 1873–1947* (in Urdu). Lahore: Research Society of Pakistan, 1986.
Sajoo, Amin, ed. *Civil Society in the Muslim World: Contemporary Perspectives*. London: I. B. Tauris, 2004.
Sale, Florentia Wynch. *Journal of Disasters in Affghanistan, 1841–2*. London: John Murray, 1843.
Samad, Yunas. *The Pakistan-US Conundrum. Jihadists, the Military and the People: The Struggle for Control*. London: Hurst, 2011.
Sardar, Ziauddin. *Desperately Seeking Paradise: Journeys of a Sceptical Muslims*. London: Granta, 2005.
———. *Why Do People Hate America?* London: Disinformation, 2002.
———. *Orientalism*. London: Open University Press, 1999.
Schofield, Victoria. *Every Rock, Every Hill*. London: Century, 1984.
———. *Kashmir in Conflict: India, Pakistan and the Unending War*. London: I. B. Tauris, 2010.
Seierstad, Asne. *The Bookseller of Kabul*. London: Little, Brown, 2003.
Shah, Aqil. *The Army and Democracy: Military Politics in Pakistan*. Cambridge, MA: Harvard University Press, 2014.
Shah, Sayyid W. A. *Ethnicity, Islam and Nationalism: Muslim Politics in the North-West Frontier Province, 1937–1947*. Karachi: Oxford University Press, 1999.
Shahzad, Saleem. *Inside Al-Qaeda and the Taliban: Beyond Bin Laden and 9/11*. London: Pluto, 2011.
Shaikh, Farzana. *Making Sense of Pakistan*. London: Hurst, 2009.
Siddiqa, Ayesha. *Military Inc.: Inside Pakistan's Military Economy*. Karachi: Oxford University Press, 2007.
Siddique, Abubakar. *The Pashtun Question: Key to the Future of Pakistan and Afghanistan*. London: Hurst, 2014.
Sikand, Yoginder. *Beyond the Border: An Indian in Pakistan*. New Delhi: Penguin, 2011.
———. '"Progressive Islam" in Pakistan'. *Himal Magazine*, May–June, 2006, http://himalaya.socanth.cam.ac.uk/collections/journals/hsa/pdf/HSA_19_03_2006.pdf.
Singh, Jaswant. *Jinnah: India-Partition-Independence*. New Delhi: Rupa & Co., 2009.
Smith, Clive Stafford. *Bad Men: Guantanamo Bay and the Secret Prisoners*. London: Weidenfeld & Nicolson, 2007.

Smith, W. C. *Modern Islam in India: A Social Analysis.* London: V. Gollancz, 1946.
Spain, James. *The Way of the Pathans.* London: R. Hale, 1962.
———. *The Pathan Borderland.* The Hague: Mouton, 1963.
Stein, Aurel. *On Alexander's Track to the Indus: Personal Narrative of Exploration on the North-West Frontier of India.* London: Macmillan, 1929.
Stewart, Jules. *The Savage Border: The History of the North-West Frontier.* Stroud: Sutton, 2007.
Stewart, Rory. *The Places in Between.* London: Picador, 2014.
Sultan-i-Rome. *Swat State (1915–1969): From Genesis to Merger.* Karachi: Oxford University Press, 2009.
Tawil, Camille. *Brothers in Arms: Al-Qaida and the Arab Jihadists.* London: Saqi, 2010.
Talbot, Ian and Gurharpal Singh, eds. *Region and Partition: Bengal, Punjab and the Partition of the Subcontinent.* Karachi: Oxford University Press, 1999.
Tootal, Stuart. *Danger Close: Commanding 3 Para in Afghanistan.* London: John Murray, 2009.
Unger, Craig. *The Fall of the House of Bush: The Delusion of the Neoconservatives and American Armageddon.* New York: Simon & Schuster, 2008.
Usherwood, Simon. *The European Union: A Very Short Introduction.* Oxford: Oxford University Press, 2013.
Victoria, Brian D. *Zen at War.* New York: Rowman & Littlefield Publishers, 2006.
Wheen, Francis. *How Mumbo-Jumbo Conquered the World? A Short History of Modern Delusions.* London: Harper Perennial, 2004.
Wolpert, Stanley. *Jinnah of Pakistan.* New York: Oxford University Press, 1984.
———. *Shameful Flight: The Last Years of British Empire in India.* New York: Oxford University Press, 2006.
———. *Zulfi Bhutto of Pakistan: His Life and Times.* New York: Oxford University Press, 1993.
Woodward, Bob. *Bush at War.* New York: Simon & Schuster, 2002.
———. *Obama's Wars.* New York: Simon & Schuster, 2011.
———. *Veil: The Secret Wars of the CIA, 1981–1987.* London: Headline, 1988.
Worthington, Andy. *The Guantanamo Files: The Stories of the 774 Detainees in America's Illegal Prison.* London: Pluto, 2007.
Wulbers, Shazia Aziz. *EU-India Relations: A Critique.* New Delhi: Academic Foundation, 2008.
Yousaf, Mohammed, and Mark Adkin. *Afghanistan: The Bear Trap. The Defeat of the Superpower.* Barnsley: L. Cooper, 2001.
Ye'Or, Bat. *Eurabia: The Euro-Arab Axis.* Teaneck: Fairleigh Dickinson, 2005.
Yousafzai, Malala. *I Am Malala.* London: Weidenfeld & Nicolson, 2013.
Zaeef, Mulla Abdus Salam. *My Life with the Taliban.* London: Hurst, 2011.
Zaidi, Akbar. 'Contesting Notions of Pakistan'. *Economic and Political Weekly* 45, 10 November 2012, http://www.epw.in/journal/2012/45/book-reviews/contesting-notions-pakistan.html.
Zaman, Muhammad Qasim. 'Sectarianism in Pakistan: The Radicalization of Shia and Sunni Identities'. *Modern Asian Studies* 32, no. 3 (1998): 689–716.
———. *The Ulama in Contemporary Islam: Custodians of Change.* Karachi: Oxford University Press 2004.
Ziring, Lawrence. *Pakistan: At the Crossroad of History.* Oxford: OneWorld, 2003.
———. *Pakistan: The Enigma of Political Development.* Folkstone: Dawson, 1980.

Newspapers, Magazines, Websites and Television Channels

BBC
Bureau of Investigative Journalism
Critical Muslim
Daily Times
Dawn

Economic and Political Weekly
Economist
Friday Times
Globe and Mail
Granta
Guardian
Haaretz
Herald
http://www.csis.org
http://www.hrw.org
http://www.pkpolitics.com
http://www.williamdalrymple.com
http://www.worldpublicopinion.org
Independent
Nation
News International
New York Times
Times
Wall Street Journal
Washington Post

INDEX

A
Abbas, Hasan 11
Abbottabad 8, 18, 21, 110, 137, 145
    Commission, 77, 103
Abdali, Ahmed Shah 25, 41, 49
Abdullah, Abdullah 24, 36, 135, 147
Afghan 12, 17, 34
    Refugees 48
Afghani Arabs 7
Afghan Army 16
Afghan allies 18
Afghan civil society 96
Afghan Jihad 49
Afghan National Army (ANA) 51, 124, 130, 139, 148
Afghan National Police (ANP) 51
Afghan Taliban 11, 13, 15–17, 21, 23, 31–32, 34, 36, 43
Afghani Pashtuns 35–36, 53–149
Afghanistan 1, 3–4, 10, 13, 16, 18–21, 23, 30, 32–35, 38–39, 40, 42–44, 46–47, 50, 59–149
Afghan Tajiks 140
Afghan Uzbek(s) 37, 59, 141
Afghan Women 35
Africa 5, 7–8, 12, 31, 36, 61, 71–72, 78, 93, 117–18, 121, 141, 147
African National Congress 141
Afridi region 44
Ahmad, Qazi Hussein 50
Ahmadi (s) 54, 70
Ahmed, Akbar 10, 31
Ahmed, Tufail 50
Akhtar, Shabbir 92
Akora Khattak 11, 22, 46, 49, 55
Al-Afghani, Jamal-ud-Din, 75
Albinia, Alice 10
Al-Ghamdi, Javaid 11, 54
Ali, Syed Ameer 75
Ali, Tariq 91–92
Algeria 130
Allen, Charles 11

Al-Qaeda 2, 5, 7–10, 21, 23, 30, 35–36, 46, 53–143
Amin, Hafizullah 44
Amir, Ayaz 53
Anjuman-i-Sipah-i-Sahaba 85–86
Arab 4, 7
Arab Afghans 35
Arab League 117
Arab Spring 48, 93, 101
Army Public School 16, 89, 134, 137
Ashcroft, John 106
Ashna, Israel 26
Ashoka 120–21
Ashton, Baroness Catherine 126–28
Association for South-East Asian Nations (ASEAN) 117, 119
Aurat Foundation 94
Australia 103, 139
Austria 74, 124
Awami National Party (ANP) 14, 19, 134, 144
Ayoob, Mohammed 46

B
Baba, Rahman 26
Babar, Naseerullah 40, 45, 60
Babur 25,
Badakhshan 40
Baghdad 146
Bagram 1, 5, 37, 142
Bahadur Khan University 20
Bajaur 17, 85
Baldwin, Shauna Singh 79–82
Balkans 31, 44,
Baloch 3, 4, 9, 39
Baloch Liberation Army (BLA) 20, 134
Balochistan 7, 9, 19–20, 22, 39, 42, 44–46, 49, 50, 134, 148
Bamiyan 40
    Buddhas 37, 61
    massacres 37
    Shias 49
Bangladesh 91, 96

English Defence League 74
Europe, Islam 73–74, 103–4, 108,
European Commissioner for Humanitarian
    Affairs 41
European Enlightenment 73
European Union {EU} 44, 105
    Afghanistan, 123–30
    Pakistan, 115–31, 142
    Southwest Asia, 139–40, 142

F
Fahim, Muhammad 22, 36
Faiz, Faiz Ahmed 79
Farrell, Theo 51
Faqir of Ippi 14, 28
Fazlullah, Maulvi 14, 17, 18, 86, 127, 144
Fazl-ur-Rahman, Maulana 49
Federally Administered Tribal Areas (FATA) 3,
    5–6, 9, 13, 15, 17–18, 19–21, 23, 32, 35,
    53–148
Fergusson, James 33, 38
First Gulf War 45
First World War 28
France 90, 123, 146
Frontier Constabulary 16
Frontier Crimes Regulation (FCR)
    Background 3, 148
Fundamentalism Reborn 44

G
Gall, Sandy 137–38
Gandhara 13
Gandhi, Mahatma 71, 78, 122
Gangetic Delta/Valley, 67
Gaza 105
Geller, Pamela 73
Gellner, Ernest 91
Germany 72, 74, 80, 123
Ghani, Ashraf 16, 24, 31, 65, 133, 135,
    146–47
Ghaus, Mullah 43
Ghazni 2
Ghilzai 41
Gilani, Yousaf Raza 14
Giustozzi, Antonio 11, 50
Gopal, Anand 135
Grand Trunk Road 49
Great Game 10, 44
Guantanamo 1, 5, 23, 37–38, 57, 62–64, 142
Guardian 83–4
Gujarat 21, 68, 105
Gul, Hamid 138

Gulf Cooperation Council (GCC) 117
Gwadar 146

H
Hadda, Mullah 28
Hamas 4, 33, 46, 91
Hanafi, Jamil 31
Hangu 16, 20
Hasan, Mullah Mohammed 40, 43
Haq, Maulana Samiul 11, 22, 35, 49
Haqqani, Husain 11
Haqqani, Jalalud Din 36, 65, 141
Haqqani, Sirajud Din 109, 138, 145
Hazaras 20, 22, 35–36, 40–41, 43, 56, 59, 136,
    141
Hekmatyar, Gulbuddin 36, 40, 43–44, 49, 64,
    109
Heller, Rick 33
Helmand 2, 51, 137–40, 145–46
Herat 3, 40, 45, 49, 59
Hersh, Seymour 108
Hezbollah 33, 46, 91
Himalayas 9
Hindko 27
Hinduism 4
Hindustan 27
Hindutva 72, 77, 118, 123
Hindu-Kush 1, 10, 104
Hizbul Mujahideen 33
Hizb-i-Islami 36, 43–44
Holbrooke, Richard 8, 106, 139–40
Hopkirk, Peter 10
Hotakis 25
Human Rights Commission of Pakistan
    (HRCP) 98, 130
Hussain, Altaf 86
Hussain, Saddam 32, 137, 143
Hussain, Zahid 11
Hyderabad 70
Hyman, Anthony 45

I
Ijtihaadi 11
Ikhwan 42
India 4, 7, 9–10, 15, 18, 20–21, 24–25, 36, 47,
    67–68, 75–78, 88–90, 107–8, 114
Indian National Congress 4, 75–78, 97
Indo-Aryan 25
Indo-Pakistani relations 6, 8–9, 16, 21, 25,
    86–90, 95–8, 101–2, 109, 111–12, 125,
    136, 142, 148
Indonesia 91

Indus 1, 3, 104
Indus Valley {civilization} 1, 6, 10, 12–13, 16, 67, 78, 84–85, 101, 114, 120–22
Institute of Strategic Studies (ISS) 46
International Security Assistance Force (ISAF) 7–8, 15, 43, 51, 54, 62, 133–35
Iqbal, Muhammad 11, 75, 122
Iran 3, 7, 10, 20, 22, 24, 37, 39, 45, 111, 147–48
Iranian revolution 20
Iraq 5, 8, 20, 32, 55, 64, 72, 104, 113, 139, 146
Islam 10, 33, 35, 39, 48, 73–75, 90–92, 130
Islamabad 6, 14–20, 23, 36, 46–47, 98, 109, 144
Islamabad Red Mosque 14, 93
Islamic Fundamentalism 48
Islamic Jihad 16, 33
Islamic State of Iraq and Syria (ISIS) 17–18, 91, 124, 146
Islamism 2, 42, 45–46
Islamization 15, 50
Islamofascism 2
Islamophobia 32, 61, 118, 122
Ismaili Shias 16, 89
Israel 73–74, 76, 90, 104, 108, 147
Israeli, Raphael 91

J

Jahangir, Asma 98
Jalal, Ayesha 11
Jalalabad 3, 59, 147
Jamaat-i-Islami (JI) 11, 22, 42, 46, 50, 75, 107
Jamiat-i-Ulama-i-Islam (JUI) 11, 22, 42, 49, 50
Jamiat-Ulama-i-Islam (JUI-F) 19, 49
Jammu 3, 33
Japan 103, 123, 139
Jews 33
Jhang 70
Jihad 10, 44, 85
Jihadists 1, 3, 11, 15–16, 35
Jinnah, M. A., 6, 19, 67, 75–8,
Jowzjan Province 41
Jandullah/Jundullah 9, 16, 89, 134, 147

K

Kabul (regime) 3, 6, 15–17, 22–25, 34, 38, 40, 43, 45, 47, 49, 51, 59, 97, 106, 133–38, 143–49
Kalashas 27
Kandahar 2, 3, 25, 38–39, 45, 47, 56, 58, 62–63, 97, 145

Kaplan, Robert 10
Karachi 3, 6, 9, 16–17, 20, 22, 25, 36, 46, 55, 85, 89, 97, 106, 134, 148
Kargil Heights 4
Karzai, Hamid (regime) 11, 32, 36, 51, 60–144, 148–49
Kashmir 3, 4, 10, 47, 72, 104–9, 117–31, 136, 138
Kashmir, Azad 22, 126
Kashmir Liberation Front 33
Kashmir Valley 4, 21, 96, 136
Kashmiri, Ilyas 55, 86
Kathmandu 47
Kayani, Pervez 17, 134
Kazakhstan 60
Keay, John 10
Kenya 61, 130
Kerry, John 89, 103, 111, 135
Khalili, Karim 22, 36–37, 41, 141
Khalilzad, Zalmay 5, 60–63, 106, 144
Khalistan 118
Khamenei, Ayatollah Ali 50, 147
Khan, Abdul Ghani 26
Khan, Abdul Ghaffar Khan 19, 71
Khan, Amanullah 28
Khan, Asfandyar Wali 19, 86
Khan, Ayub 85, 99
Khan, Daud 28, 39, 129
Khan, Genghis 25, 26
Khan, Imran 8, 19, 69, 86, 94, 101, 109, 135–36
 on drone attacks 111
Khan, Ismael 22, 36, 59
Khan, Noor Inayat {Nora Baker} 80
Khan, Sir Syed Ahmed 67–68, 71, 78
Khans 5, 10, 15
Khattak, Ajmal 26
Khattak, Khushal Khan 26
Khomeini, Imam Ruhollah 39
Khost 2, 5,
Khyber Pakhtunkhwa (KP) 3, 9, 15, 17–19, 22, 49, 50, 104, 109, 136, 144
Khyber Pass 19, 85, 124
Kipling, Rudyard 10, 27
Kohat 3, 98
Kunduz 3, 5, 40–41, 63
Kunhar 2, 14, 17
Kurds 32
Kurram (Agency} 16, 20, 44, 70, 85

L

Lahore 4, 16, 39, 87, 93, 98
Lamb, Christina 34

Lashkar-e-Jhangvi (LeJ) 7, 11, 16, 19, 20, 85, 86
Lashkar-e-Tayyaba (LeT) 7, 95
Lebanon 71, 91, 105, 147
Lewis, Bernard 73–74, 91
Libya 8, 90, 92, 113, 122, 139
Lieven, Anatol 77
Likud 4
Lindisfarne, Nancy 31–32
Line of Control (LOC) 3–4, 136
Lobo, Debra 89
Lord Roberts 10

M
Madrasas 2,
Mackenzie, Richard 45
Madrid bombing 56
Madrasa-i-Haqqania 55
Mahasabha 78
Mahmud, Sabeen 89
Mai, Mukhtaran 98
Malakand 3, 14–15, 44
Malaysia 91
Maley, William 44–45, 48, 56
Mamdani, Mahmood 92
Mardan 3
Marsden, Peter 10, 48
Masson, Charles 27
Masud, Khalid 11
Masud, Ahmad Shah 22, 36, 40–41, 43, 46
Matinuddin, Kamal 10, 46–48
Mawdudi, Syed 49
Mazar-i-Sharif 40, 47, 63
Mazari, Abdul Ali 22, 41, 43
Mehran Naval Base (Karachi) 134
Mehsud, Baitullah 17, 28, 86, 97, 98, 144
Mehsud, Hakimullah 7, 17, 19, 86, 111
Menon, V. P. 78
Middle East 8, 12, 123, 137
  Baathists and Kurdish groups, 146–47
Miliband, David 139
Mingora 3, 14, 99
Miran Shah 19
Modi, Narendra 4, 97, 136
Mohmand 17, 85, 145
Mohmand Agency 18
Mohammedi, Nabi 43
Mojjeddedi, Sibghatullah 43, 45, 49
Mongol invasion 73, 92, 121
Moro Liberation Army 33
Moscow 34, 43, 103
Mossad 109

Mountbatten, Louis 78
Mountstuart, Elphinstone 27
Mousavi, Askar 31
Mufti Mahmud, Maulana 49
Muhammad, Nek 7
Muhammad, Maulana Soofi 14
Mujahideen 3, 33, 36, 39, 43–46, 50, 58
Mullen, {Admiral} Michael 69, 110, 145
Mumbai 8, 21, 87, 97
Musharraf, Pervez {regime} 4, 5, 6, 14, 16–17, 37, 42, 50, 56–143
Muslim Brotherhood 33, 46, 75, 91
Muslim League, All-India 50, 67, 75–78, 91, 97
Muslim West Asians 8
Muslims 4, 21–22, 35, 42, 75
  in Sicily and Spain, 121
Muttahidda Majlis-i-Ammal (MMA) 7, 50
Muttahida Qaumi Movement (MQM) 19, 68
Muttawakil, Mullah 43
Myanmar 27, 72, 76, 105

N
Nahdlatul Ulama, Indonesia 91
Najibullah, Mohammad 34, 43
Nangarhar 2
Naipaul, V. S. 73, 91–92
Nasr, Vali Reza 8
Nawa, Fariba 53
Nazarbayev, Noor Sultan 60
Nehru, Jawaharlal 76–78
New Delhi 47
New York Times 74
Nichols, Robert 10
North Africa 8, 12, 93, 121, 147
North Atlantic 6, 22
North Atlantic Treaty Organization (NATO) 1, 6–8, 10, 13, 15–16, 18–19, 21, 23, 38, 43, 54–145
North Korea 21
Northern Alliance 7, 12, 24, 36–37, 45, 59, 64, 65, 130, 133, 136, 141, 143, 147
North-West Frontier Province (NWFP) 3, 42, 45
North Waziristan 3, 16–19, 69, 83, 89, 142
Nuristan-Chitral 3

O
Obama Administration 16, 23, 24, 90, 103–14, 135–47
Obama, Barack 7, 8, 18, 23, 57, 65, 69, 89
Omar, Mullah Muhammad 11, 17–18, 22, 28, 35–40, 43, 49, 56, 58–60, 136, 138, 141, 144

Orakzai 44
Organization of African Unity (OAU) 117
Organization of Islamic Cooperation (OIC) 117
Orientalism 21, 29
Orientalist writings 10
Ottoman(s) 73, 146–47

P

Pahlawan, Malik 41
Pakhtuns 2, 7, 24
Pakistan 3, 10–13, 17–21, 24, 30, 34, 38–39, 42, 45, 47, 68
  Army 6, 17, 40, 45, 99–100, 107, 127–28, 142, 144–45
  Balochistan 56, 68–9, 83, 118
  Bengalis, East Pakistan 70, 83
  Citizens 17
  Civil society 83–102
  Consulate 45
  Expatriate scholars 76–7
  EU relations 115–31
  Geo-politics 67–149
  Islamic revolution 49
  Khyber-Pakhtunkhwa 56, 84, 126
  Literature 79–81, 100–101
  Music 100
  Northern Areas 126
  Nuclear 112, 126
  Partition 75–78, 88, 95
  Punjabi 83
  Sindh 70, 83
  Sovereignty 18, 19
  Taliban 50, 134–36
  Violence 67–148
  Women 81, 84–102
Pakistanis 15, 19, 32, 80–81, 128
Pakistani ISI 35–37, 40, 46, 62, 69, 100, 107–8, 127, 138
Pakistani Intelligence Agencies 4, 18, 36, 98, 100
Pakistani Jihadi groups 17
Pakistan People's Party (PPP) 6, 14, 19, 50, 68, 97, 128, 134, 145
Pakistani Military establishment 7,
Pakistan Muslims League (PML) 6, 97, 128
Pakistan-Saudi relations 108
Pakistan-U.S. relations 103–14
Pakistani
  Civilians 20
  Defence Establishment 40, 45
  Islamists 36
  Soldiers 20
Pakistani Taliban (TTP) 7, 9, 15–18, 20, 23, 36, 45, 53–149
Paktia 2
Palestine/Palestinian(s) 55, 72, 74, 104
Panetta, Leon 18–19, 145, 146
Panjshir Valley 43
Pasha, Shuja 103
Pashtun 14–15, 17–21, 35, 43
  Cleric-politicians 49
  Movement 43, 118
Pashtun(s) 2–3, 7, 9, 11–13, 15, 20, 22, 27, 29, 30–33, 35–41, 44, 47, 57, 70, 84, 97, 104, 112, 133–34, 139, 142–43, 147–49
  Ethnicity 21
  Inhabitants 21
  Language 24
  Literary traditions 26
  Militancy 21
  Nationalist Party 15
  Origins 25
  Peasants 51
  Population 25
  Revolt 28
  Societies 10
  Urban diaspora 25
  Women 98–99
Pashtunwali 28, 30, 49
Pearl, Daniel 55
Pegida 74
Pentagon 8,
Peoples Republic of China 9
Perle, Richard 106
Persian 141
Peshawar 3, 14, 16, 25, 45–46, 49, 89, 97, 129, 134
Petraeus, David 146
Pipes, Daniel 73–74, 91
Poland 74
Political Islam 9, 21, 23, 33, 42, 46, 92–93
Pothowari 27
Provincially Administered Tribal Areas (PATA) 3
Pull-i-Charkhi 37, 142
  PunjabMilitants 4, 17, 20, 22, 45
Punjabi Taliban 17, 22, 27, 40, 54
  Pushto{Pashto} 26
Pushtuns {also see Pashtuns/Pakhtuns} 2, 6, 45

Q

Qadri, Muhammad Tahir-ul, 54, 135–36
Qatar 112–13, 136, 145
Quetta 3, 16, 19, 20, 36, 45, 70, 85–86, 98, 109, 136, 145

R

Rabbani, Burhanuddin 36, 43, 45, 47, 49
Rahman, Fazlur 11, 49
Rahman, Waliur 19
Raj 10, 44, 68, 70, 85
Ramadan, Tariq 92
Ranis, Gustav 83
Rashid, Ahmed 10, 34, 40–42, 45, 48, 56
   Background 39
   Far Eastern Review 39
   Political Islam 42
   Taliban: Islam, Oil and the New Great Game in Central Asia 38
Rawalpindi 4, 20, 98
Reagan, Ronald 90
Red Mosque 7, 16
Rehman, Waliur 7
Reid, John 137
Research and Analysis Wing (RAW) 36
Rigi, Abdul Malik 147
Roberts, Lord 10
Roy, Oliver 45, 46
Rubin, Barnett 10
Rubinstein, Alvin Z., 106
Rumsfeld, Donald, 64, 106, 137–38
Rushdie, Salman 79, 83
Russia 19, 45, 65, 73, 80, 92, 129

S

Sadiq, Naeem 67
Safawid Empire 121
Saikal, Amin 11
Salafi(s) 5, 42, 53, 113
Salala 18, 110, 145
Samjhota train 21
Saraiki 27
Saudi Arabia 44–45, 61, 138, 145
Saudi-Iranian conflict 21
Sayyaf, Abdur Rasul 43, 45
Semple, Michael 140
Senegal 91
September 11 1, 9, 11, 21–22, 30, 32–34, 36–37, 42, 50, 80–81, 89, 104–14, 142–43
Schofield, Victoria 10
Shaikh, Farzana 76–77
Shaikh, Omar Saeed 55
Sharani, Nazif 31
Sharia 14
Sharif, Nawaz {regime) 4–6, 14, 16, 19–20, 69, 86, 107, 135–48
Sharif, Raheel 17, 134
Sharif, Saidu 14
Shaukat Khanam Cancer Hospital 94
Shebarghan 41
Shia(s) 16, 19–21, 32, 44, 54–56, 89
Shikarpur 16, 89
Shomali Plains 40, 63
Siachen Glacier 4, 21, 96
Sibi 20
Siddiqui, Afia 110
Sidhwa, Bapsi 79
Sikand, Yoginder 95
Simla 36
Sindhis 4
Singh, Jaswant 77–78
Singh, Manmohan 86
Sinjiang 9–10, 105
Slessor, Captain 10
Snowden, Edward 105
Sohrab Goth 17
Somalia 21, 23, 81
South Asian Association for Regional Cooperation (SAARC), 115–31, 134–35
South Asian states 10, 12, 67, 68, 79, 85, 95–8, 111–31, 147–49
South Asian writers 78–82
Southwest Asia 9–11, 14, 18, 20–21, 50, 103, 118–19, 133–49
Soviet Invasion 1, 22, 25, 39, 45, 103
Soviet Union 4, 28, 86
   War 34, 106, 124
   Withdrawal 44
Southeast Asia 92–93
South Waziristan 17, 19, 97
Spain 92
Spain, James 10
Spencer, Robert 73, 91
Spin Boldak 40
Sri Lanka 55, 71, 118
Stranger, The 8
Sufis 42
Suleiman Mountains 10
Sunni 6, 9, 20–21, 32, 49
   Afghans 41
   Caliphate 17
   Iraqis 146
   Islam 20
   Majoritarianism 20

Sunni – *continued*
 Tajiks 49
 Taliban 32, 43, 133–49
 Uzbeks 49
Swat 3, 13, 14, 30, 32, 44, 76–77, 99, 134, 142, 144
Sweden 72
Syria 8, 23, 90, 113, 139, 146–47

T
Tajik 22, 25, 35–36, 41, 44
Taliban 2–3, 5, 9, 10, 14–15, 21, 22, 30, 32–34, 37, 38, 39, 40–41, 43–148
Tamerlane 25, 122
Tamils 4, 55
Tanzania 61
Tarrar {Colonel/Imam} Sultan Amir 40, 45, 138
Taseer, Aatish 67
Taseer, Salman 98
Tashkent 43
Tehreek-i-Insaaf (PTI) 19,
Tehreek-i-Nifaz-i-Shariat-i-Muhammadi (TNSM) 14,
Tehreek-i-Taliban, Pakistan (TTP) 7, 14–21, 23, 32, 42, 133–49
Tehran 44
Times of India 111–12
Tirah Military Campaign 28, 44
Tirah Valley 18
Tootal, Stuart 133, 137
Tora Bora 5
Tufail Muhammad, Maulana 49
Tunisia 91–92
Turangzai, Haji 28
Turis 20
Turkey 43–44, 48, 76, 90–91

U
Ulama 9
Uloom, Darul 46
Umma 2
United Kingdom 5, 75–77, 80, 90, 107–8, 123–29, 137–48
 British Foreign and Commonwealth Office, 140–41
 DFID, 138
 East India Company 80
 ISIS 146
 policies 133–49
Unocal 60
US Central Intelligence Agency (CIA) 17, 103–14
US Defence Secretary 18, 106

US embassies 36
US Navy SEALs 18, 69, 110, 145
Unical 40
United Arab Emirates 61
United Baloch Army 134
United Provinces (UP) 20, 78
United States 3, 5–8, 16–18, 23, 31, 32, 36–38, 44, 50, 55, 57, 60, 62–65, 70–71, 75, 80–81, 88–90, 97, 102–14, 116, 117, 120, 123, 133–36, 140, 147
Urdu 9, 17, 22, 93–94
Uzbek(s) 22, 25, 35, 40–41, 43

V
Vajpayee, Atal Behari 4
Vietnam 72, 103, 124, 140

W
Wahhabis 87, 113, 144
Wahdat-i-Islami 43
Wagah 89
Waldman, Matt 138
Washington 7, 16, 18–19
Washington Post 74
Waziristan 2, 7, 28, 44
Western special forces 17
White House 23, 36,
Wirsing, Robert 11
Wolfowitz, Paul 106
Women's Action Forum 94
Woodward, Bob 11

Y
Yemen 8, 23, 104, 113
Ye'or, Bat (Gisele Littman); Christian-Zionists 73, 91
Yugoslavia 86
Yousafzai, Malala 14, 98
Yusufzai(s) 29

Z
Zaeef, Mullah Abdus Salam 11, 35, 37–38, 55–63, 97
 his companions in Taliban, 58,
Zarb-e-Azb 17, 19
Zardari, Asif Ali 14, 69, 86, 98, 104, 125–27, 144–45
Zia-ul-Haq 39, 49–50, 86, 98, 106–7, 112–13, 125
Ziarat 19
Zikris 70
Zionists 73, 76, 109

www.ingramcontent.com/pod-product-compliance
Lightning Source LLC
Chambersburg PA
CBHW021826300426
44114CB00009BA/336